OXFORD PHILOSOPHICAL TEXTS

G. W. Leibniz

Philosophical Texts

CU00956952

OXFORD PHILOSOPHICAL TEXTS

Series Editor: John Cottingham

The Oxford Philosophical Texts series consists of authoritative teaching editions of canonical texts in the history of philosophy from the ancient world down to modern times. Each volume provides a clear, well laid out text together with a comprehensive introduction by a leading specialist, giving the student detailed critical guidance on the intellectual context of the work and the structure and philosophical importance of the main arguments. Endnotes are supplied which provide further commentary on the arguments and explain unfamiliar references and terminology, and a full bibliography and index are also included.

The series aims to build up a definitive corpus of key texts in the Western philosophical tradition, which will form a reliable and enduring resource for students and teachers alike.

PUBLISHED IN THIS SERIES:

Berkeley *A Treatise Concerning the Principles of Human Knowledge* (edited by Jonathan Dancy)
Berkeley *Three Dialogues between Hylas and Philonous* (edited by Jonathan Dancy)
Hume *An Enquiry concerning the Principles of Morals* (edited by Tom L. Beauchamp)
Leibniz *Philosophical Texts* (edited by R. S. Woolhouse and Richard Francks)
Mill *Utilitarianism* (edited by Roger Crisp)

FORTHCOMING TITLES INCLUDE:

Frege *Philosophical Writings* (edited by Anthony Kenny)
Hume *A Treatise of Human Nature* (edited by David Fate Norton and Mary J. Norton)
Kant *Groundwork for the Metaphysics of Morals* (edited by Thomas E. Hill and Arnulf Zweig)
Kant *Prolegomena to Any Future Metaphysics* (edited by Günter Zöller)
Spinoza *Ethics* (edited by G. H. R. Parkinson)

G. W. LEIBNIZ

Philosophical Texts

TRANSLATED BY

RICHARD FRANCKS and R. S. WOOLHOUSE

WITH INTRODUCTION AND NOTES BY

R. S. WOOLHOUSE

OXFORD
UNIVERSITY PRESS

OXFORD

UNIVERSITY PRESS

Great Clarendon Street, Oxford OX2 6DP

Oxford University Press is a department of the University of Oxford.
It furthers the University's objective of excellence in research, scholarship,
and education by publishing worldwide in

Oxford New York

Auckland Bangkok Buenos Aires Cape Town Chennai
Dar es Salaam Delhi Hong Kong Istanbul Karachi Kolkata
Kuala Lumpur Madrid Melbourne Mexico City Mumbai Nairobi
São Paulo Shanghai Taipei Tokyo Toronto

Published in the United States
by Oxford University Press Inc., New York

British Library Cataloguing in Publication Data
Data available

Library of Congress Cataloging in Publication Data

Leibniz, Gottfried Wilhelm, Freiherr von, 1646-1716.
Philosophical texts / G. W. Leibniz; translated by Richard Francks
and R. S. Woolhouse: with introduction and notes by R. S. Woolhouse.
(Oxford philosophical texts)
Includes bibliographical references and index.
1. Philosophy. I. Woolhouse, R. S. II. Francks, Richard. III. Title. IV. Series.
B2558.F73 1998 193—dc21 97-28372
ISBN 0-19-875152-4
ISBN 0-19-875153-2 (Pbk.)

7 9 10 8

Typeset by Best-set Typesetter Ltd., Hong Kong
Printed in Great Britain
on acid free paper by
Biddles Ltd. King's Lynn

Contents

Contents

PART 1

Introductory Material

How to Use this Book

This book contains nineteen *Texts*. Most of these are important writings (originally composed in French and Latin, and dating from 1685 to 1714) of Gottfried Leibniz. But some of the replies and comments made by various of Leibniz's contemporaries (such as Antoine Arnauld, Pierre Bayle, and Simon Foucher) are included too. The texts are typically divided into numbered paragraphs or sections; thus the editorial reference 'T1. 2' would be to the second section of the first text, 'T2. 3 §1' would be to the first section of the third subtext of T2.

The book also contains editorial matter of various kinds. So, to begin with, there is a lengthy *Editor's Introduction*, which, besides saying something about Leibniz's life, writings, and influence, also aims to expound and explain Leibniz's main philosophical ideas as they occur in the texts which follow.

The asterisks (*) at various points throughout the book signal the *Notes*, collected at the end of the volume. These notes act as a glossary for various unusual but frequently recurring terms, or as explanations of references to various people, doctrines, or ideas. In addition, there are editorial footnotes to each text which are signalled by superscript numerals. There are also some longer, explanatory notes which appear as appendices at the end of the text to which they refer.

As well as such notes, each text is prefaced by a *Summary*, which provides an outline of the structure of what is about to follow.

In the Editor's Introduction, and elsewhere, pains have often been taken to direct the student towards relatively recent articles and books which provide further explanation or discussion of various central topics. Full details of these, and any other references to the secondary literature, are given in the *Bibliography and Further Reading* section.

Unless the book is being used simply as a means of access to one or other of the texts it contains, a good way to use it in connection with a systematic study of Leibniz would be to begin by reading Section 1 of the Editor's Introduction and then to turn to each text, along with its introductory summary (reading the notes as interest or inclination suggests). Someone who wishes for more direction than this as to what it might be of interest to look for in the texts, or about possible avenues of approach to them, should read the whole of the Editor's Introduction first.

Abbreviations

CSMK	*The Philosophical Writings of Descartes*, trans. J. Cottingham, R. Stoothoff, D. Murdoch, and A. Kenny, 3 vols. (Cambridge, 1984–91).
GM	*Leibnizens mathematische Schriften*, ed. C. I. Gerhardt, 7 vols. (Berlin, 1849–60).
GP	*Die philosophischen Schriften von Gottfried Wilhelm Leibniz*, ed. C. I. Gerhardt, 7 vols. (Berlin, 1875–90; Hildesheim, 1978).
Grua	*G. W. Leibniz: Textes inédits*, ed. Gaston Grua (Paris, 1948).
L	*Gottfried Wilhelm Leibniz: Philosophical Papers and Letters* ed. and trans. L. E. Loemker, 2nd edn. (Dordrecht, 1969).
La	*New Essays concerning Human Understanding, by G. W. Leibniz; together with . . . some of his shorter pieces*, ed. and trans. A. G. Langley, 3rd edn. (La Salle, Ill., 1949).
LF	Louis de La Forge, *Traité de l'esprit de l'homme . . . suivant les principes de René Descartes* (1664).
Lt	*Leibniz: The Monadology and Other Philosophical Writings*, ed. and trans. Robert Latta (London, 1898).
M	*The Leibniz–Arnauld Correspondence*, ed. and trans. H. T. Mason (Manchester, 1967).
Mal. 1674–5	Nicolas Malebranche, *The Search after Truth* (1674–5), trans. T. M. Lennon and P. J. Olscamp (Columbus, Ohio, 1980).
Mal. 1688	Nicolas Malebranche, *Dialogues on Metaphysics* (1688), trans. W. Doney (New York, 1980).
MP	*Leibniz: Philosophical Writings*, ed. and trans. M. Morris and G. H. R. Parkinson (London, 1973).
Princs. Phil.	René Descartes, *Principles of Philosophy*, as in CSMK.
RB	*G. W. Leibniz: New Essays on Human Understanding*, ed. and trans. P. Remnant and J. Bennett (Cambridge, 1981).
UL	*Correspondance de Bossuet*, ed. C. Urbain and E. Levesque, 15 vols., new edn. (Paris, 1912).
WF	*Leibniz's 'New System' and Associated Contemporary Texts*, ed. and trans. R. S. Woolhouse and R. Francks (Oxford, 1997).

Editor's Introduction

1. Introduction

Gottfried Wilhelm Leibniz (1646–1716) wrote no central *magnum opus* that encapsulates the whole of his rich and wide-ranging philosophical thinking. Moreover, his ideas underwent important and interesting changes over time. Consequently, this volume contains, not one definitive work, but a series of shortish texts from different dates.

It is generally agreed that the mid-1680s mark the beginning of maturity in Leibniz's ideas, and the most important item from this period, written when Leibniz was 40, is the 'Discourse on Metaphysics' of 1686 (T1). Though Leibniz did not publish the 'Discourse' it was sufficiently important to him for him to refer back to it when in 1695 he published in a French learned journal, the *Journal des savants*, a short but wide-ranging account of his metaphysical ideas, the 'New System of the Nature of Substances and their Communication, and of the Union which Exists between the Soul and the Body' (T4).

The one work of any length which Leibniz ever published was the *Theodicy* in 1706 (he was then 60). Yet lengthy as it was (far far more so than the 'Discourse' or the 'New System') it has a rather narrower focus and deals primarily with the problem of evil—the problem of how a good God can have created an apparently imperfect world. Despite its more limited scope, however, it often alludes to other elements of Leibniz's thought; and this led to requests for him to publish a collection of some of his earlier and shorter pieces, or to produce, at any rate in outline, a systematically organized account of his overall philosophy.

In response, in 1714 and towards the end of his life Leibniz wrote (though did not publish) the 'Monadology' (T19), a work which very effectively compresses into about 100 short sections all the main ideas, as he then saw them, of his philosophy as a whole.

The three classic Leibnizian works, the 'Discourse' of 1686, the 'New System' of 1695, and the 'Monadology' of 1714, stand out as landmarks by reference to which much else of importance in the very large corpus of his philosophical writing can be located. So, for example, there is the lengthy correspondence with Antoine *Arnauld (T2) in which Leibniz explained, expounded, and defended some aspects of his 'Discourse on Metaphysics'.

For example, too, some of the ideas in the 'New System' were sketched out the year before it was published in a short piece entitled 'The Advancement of True Metaphysics' (T3). Further, the 'New System' itself aroused much interest and comment, both public and private, and, again, Leibniz was led to explain, defend, and develop his ideas. Two of the more important and illuminating exchanges were with Simon Foucher (TT6, 7), and Pierre Bayle (TT10–12, 14–17). Finally, 'Principles of Nature and Grace' (T18) is a short piece which Leibniz wrote at the same time as, and as a companion to, the 'Monadology'.

Our aim here has been to facilitate an understanding of what Leibniz wrote to Arnauld, Foucher, and Bayle by giving not only some of his side of the correspondences, but also some of theirs. The remaining items in this collection of texts ('*Specimen Dynamicum*' (T5), a reply to some of Bayle's difficulties with the 'New System' (T12), 'Nature Itself' (T13)) are pieces which, again, throw light on the ideas of the three 'landmark' texts—the 'Discourse', the 'New System', and the 'Monadology'.

Leibniz was great not only as a philosopher. A recent biographer writes of him that 'Even if he had only contributed to one field, such as law, history, politics, linguistics, theology, logic, technology, mathematics, science, or philosophy his achievement would have earned him a place in history. Yet he contributed to all these fields, not as a dilettante but as an innovator able to lead the specialists' (Aiton 1985, p. ix). So it is hardly surprising that his philosophical interests are themselves wide. He makes interesting and important contributions to the philosophies of mathematics, of mind, of religion, of science, to epistemology, to ethics, to logic, to metaphysics, and to political philosophy.

The student of Leibniz is faced with the facts that he never wrote an account of his philosophy that was lengthy, finished, and definitive; that his philosophy is typically found in short and often unpublished articles, and in letters; and that he varied his presentation and language (and, some would say, his position) to suit the occasion. Nevertheless, he is above all a *systematic* philosopher. This does not mean that it is possible to do what Bertrand Russell (1900/1937, pp. xi–xii) proposed to do—to uncover and construct from Leibniz's writings an atemporal 'system'; for his ideas shifted and changed, and underwent development with time. It does mean that Leibniz always had an awareness of the consequences of whatever idea he happened to be writing about, of its connections with and bearings on others of his ideas. Moreover, at the bottom of all that he says is what might generally be called his *metaphysics*. That is to say, what he says about, for examples, philosophy of mind, epistemology, and philosophy of science most usually has metaphysical underpinnings. The very title of the first text in this collection, the crucially important 'Discourse on Metaphysics', bears witness to this—as do the contents of the essentially or largely metaphysical works, the 'New System', and the 'Monadology'.

The term 'metaphysics' originated as the title given by an early editor to one of the works of the classical Greek philosopher *Aristotle, a work which deals with what he called 'first philosophy'. One of the main concerns of 'metaphysics', or 'first philosophy', is the question what 'being' is. As Aristotle (when translated from Greek, via Latin, into English) put it, this question is the question 'What is substance?'

In the light of Aristotle's own answer to this question about 'substance' or 'being', one way to understand it is as a request for an account of what basic or ultimate reality consists in, and of how other less basic things depend on it. This is certainly how we can understand the approach of Leibniz and others of his time to the question 'What is substance?'

It is abundantly clear that in Leibniz's view the question is of crucial and central philosophical importance. Answers to many other questions and problems depend on the answer to it. Referring to metaphysics as 'this first and architectonic science' (T3. 1), Leibniz identifies 'substance' as one of its foremost concerns. Some of the philosophical difficulties which beset *Spinoza and *Locke would, he says, be solved by a good knowledge of substance, 'the key to philosophy'.[1] Some of *Descartes's mistakes are attributable to his inadequate understanding of it, whereas, says Leibniz, *his own* conception of it is 'so rich, that there follow from it most of the most important truths about God, the soul, and the nature of body, which are generally either unknown or unproved' (T3. 4).

This proud boast is not to be taken lightly, for we will see that what Leibniz says about substance (which comes in this collection of texts as early as T1. 8) underpins what he said in all of the many areas of philosophy to which he contributed. It connects with his views about the relationship between God and the created world, about the nature of matter and the sciences of physics and dynamics, about human freedom, about the relationship between body and mind, and about the nature of the mind.

Later sections of this Introduction will outline some of these views: (2) 'Substance and Matter', (3) 'Physics and Natural Science', (4) 'The Metaphysics of Causation', (5) 'The Union of Body and Mind', (6) 'Humans, Animals, and their Minds', (7) 'God . . . Creation, Freedom, and the Community of Rational Minds'.

---

[1] Letter to Bourguet, 22 Mar. 1714 (GP iii. 567).

In his short piece 'Reflections on the Advancement of True Metaphysics' (T3), Leibniz refers to the classical Greek philosophers *Plato and Aristotle, to the *'later Platonists', to the *'Scholastic philosophers', and, finally, to a philosopher who was still alive when Leibniz was born, Descartes. We will see in what follows in this Introduction that much of what Leibniz says is to be understood in terms of agreements and disagreements with, or reactions to, these philosophers.

2. Substance and Matter

Leibniz's interest in the question of 'substance'—a question about 'being' and the nature of basic reality—was continuous throughout his life and is marked in the three corner-stone texts in this volume, the 'Discourse on Metaphysics' (T1), the 'New System' (T4), and the 'Monadology' (T19).

Even when they did not agree with it, seventeenth-century accounts of 'substance' were often shaped and coloured by what *Aristotle and *'Scholastic philosophers', such as *Aquinas, had said on the topic. Though this influence was particularly strong on Leibniz, it was not the only one, for the scene for his discussion is very noticeably set by the writings of *Descartes too. Leibniz's account of substance has two poles—positively, a revival of a recently rejected aspect of the *Aristotelian tradition, and, negatively, a disagreement with what Descartes had said about, specifically, material substance.

To the fore in his account is the idea of an *individual* substance; reality, in his view, must consist ultimately of discrete individual things rather than of some continuous basic stuff. He wrote to *Arnauld that 'if we cannot discover what is truly a complete being, or a substance, we will have no stopping-point' (T2. 9 §10).

There is here a continuity with Aristotle, in whose metaphysics there is a focus on 'primary' or 'first substances'—individual beings such as Socrates or Bucephalus, which belong to various 'secondary' kinds or species such as 'man' or 'horse'. What constituted their substantiality for Aristotle, what made them 'beings' or basic realities, is that they are things which have qualities or properties which can be predicated of them (e.g. Socrates is learned; Bucephalus is spirited), but which cannot themselves be predicated of anything else. Their properties depend on them, but not they on their properties, for substances can undergo change (as when Socrates becomes learned) whilst still retaining their identity. Remarks of this sort, which Aristotle makes in characterization of his 'individual primary substances', are repeated and echoed in the seventeenth century. For example, the idea that substances are individual things, *with* properties and not themselves the properties *of* anything else, is the starting-point of the important discussion of substance at T1. 8. (For more on this, see T1, App. A.)

Now Leibniz's basically Aristotelian belief that reality must consist of individual substances, and not of some basic stuff or stuffs, is something which sets him against the metaphysical scheme which Descartes, a philosopher of the previous generation, had put forward in his very influential *Principles of Philosophy* (1644). According to Descartes, there are two categories of reality or being: material or corporeal reality, and immaterial, incorporeal, or spiritual reality. Anything that exists or has some degree of reality exists either as *body* (or as a body-dependent modification or property, or, as the common term often had it, 'accident') or exists as a *mind* (or as a mind-dependent mental modification or property).

For each of these two substantial kinds there is, Descartes held, a 'principal property'—a property 'which constitutes . . . [its] nature, and essence, and to which all its other properties are referred' (*Princs. Phil.* 1. 53). The principal property of corporeal substance is 'extension in length, breadth, and depth' (and '[e]verything else which can be attributed to body presupposes extension and is merely a mode of an extended thing . . . For example, shape is unintelligible except in an extended thing; and motion is unintelligible except as motion in an extended space') (*Princs. Phil.* 1. 53). The principal property of mind is 'thought': whatever we find in the mind 'is simply one of the various modes of thinking'. So, imagination, sensation, and will are 'intelligible only in a thinking thing' (*Princs. Phil.* 1. 53).

The second of these categories contains an infinite, all-powerful, uncreated substance (God), and a large number of finite created substances (human minds). The first contains the material world which God created. Though there are many different incorporeal substances (our minds and God), there is not a number of different corporeal substances. Descartes does often talk, in the plural, of bodies, but these (such as a human body, a cat, or a tree) are not different corporeal substances. Aside from the minds of human beings (and higher beings such as angels), God's creation is simply a continuous, homogeneous mass of material stuff, which happens to be divided into various chunks. So in the *Cartesian scheme there are no *individual* material substances, there is only material substance. Minds are individually separate centres of consciousness, but bodies (human bodies, cats, trees) are just different chunks of extended material substance. Standing in opposition to this is Leibniz's view, that individuality is an *essential* feature of the notion of substantiality or being. Though, therefore, Descartes's mental substances are, at least on the face of it, quite acceptable to Leibniz, there is something objectionable about his material substance.

For Leibniz, then, substantiality requires individuality and a certain unity and integrity. Individual substances are 'complete beings' (T2. 9 §10), 'unities' (TT2. 7 §4; 2. 11 §3), 'truly single beings' (T2. 11 §3), they are indivisible (TT1. 32; 2. 7 §4; 2. 11 §1).

In the correspondence with Arnauld 'substantial unity' (TT2. 7 §4), the particular unity and integrity which Leibniz says that substances have, is often referred to, using Scholastic terminology, as unity *per se* (a unity in itself, **unum per se*) rather than unity *per accidens* (an accidental unity, **unum per accidens*). A heap of stones is one single heap, but it is 'a being unified by accident or aggregation' (T2. 4 §16). A human being, however, is an integrated entity, it is a *per se* unity.

Now though nothing could be clearer than that for Leibniz substantiality means unity (of a *per se* and non-accidental kind), it is nothing like so clear exactly what he counts as examples of such unities. The situation is a complex one. There is no unanimity amongst his commentators about how to read him; and at different times (at least according to one way of reading him) he seems to think different things. However, there are two constants in all of this. One is the crucial role in substantial unity of some such thing as an individual mind or soul, or what Leibniz calls a 'substantial form' (or, later, a 'monad'); the other is, relatedly, the rejection of matter as something which is substantial by itself. In different ways these can be seen to figure in two general theories that might be proposed concerning what Leibniz would allow as substantial unities: (*a*) the corporeal substance theory; (*b*) the mental substance theory. The first of these is a theory about substances as material substances; the second is a theory about substances as immaterial substances. On the face of it there is no incompatibility between the two. At any rate, Descartes held that there are both material and immaterial substances, and (according to one reading) there were times at which Leibniz held there are both.

Given these two theories, one possible reading of Leibniz (call it Reading 1) is to see his thought as exhibiting a development from an acceptance of and concentration on material substances (as in theory (*a*)) to a concentration on immaterial substances (as in theory (*b*)), together with a rejection of material substances altogether.

Now in the 'Discourse on Metaphysics' (T1) and his correspondence with Arnauld (T2) it is quite clear that for Leibniz, in opposition to

Descartes, extended matter as such is not in itself a substance. But, according to Reading 1, this does not mean that for Leibniz at this time (1680s) there are no material substances: throughout the Arnauld correspondence he holds that a flesh-and-blood human being has *per se* unity and counts as an individual substance. What it does mean, though, is that, as a material substance, an individual human being must derive its substantiality, its *per se* unity, from a mind, or a mindlike entity which Leibniz calls a 'substantial form'. More precisely, a living human being is conceived as a unified composite in which a mind or form 'animates' (from the Latin *anima*, for soul) or 'informs' a material flesh-and-blood structure which 'embodies' it. This notion of a unified form–matter composite (which Leibniz derives from the Aristotelian tradition) will be discussed more fully later on.

By 1714 and the 'Monadology' (T19), however (according to Reading 1), the material substances of theory (*a*) have dropped out of the picture, and purely immaterial, mindlike entities (now called 'monads'), as in theory (*b*), remain as the only substances. What, then, at this later stage, has become of the earlier corporeal substances such as living human beings? Their minds (or forms) have themselves now become the sole substantial unities, and the matter of their bodies has become something 'ideal', an 'appearance' or 'phenomenon' which 'results', in some way to be discussed, out of purely immaterial minds.

So, on Reading 1, Leibniz moves from treating minds or mindlike entities as the unifying factors in the form–matter composites which are material substances to treating them, and them alone, as substantial unities. Such a move would have been an entirely natural one for Leibniz to make. For, even at the earlier stage when minds or mindlike entities were elements of material substances, Leibniz *also* (as indeed Reading 1 allows) tends to treat them as (immaterial) substantial unities in their own right (TT1. 10–12, 22, 23, 33, 34; 2. 7 §4; 2. 11 §8). That is to say, Leibniz tended to hold, at this earlier stage, that where there is a living human being there are two substances—*not* a mind and a body (as in the Cartesian tradition), but rather a mind and a mind–body composite; and at the later stage he held that there is just one, the mind—the body having become in some sense a mere unreal appearance. Reading 1, as described here, leaves it open how far Leibniz had gone towards rejecting corporeal substances by the time of the 'New System' (T4) of 1695.

It should be noted here that theory (*b*) above, the mental substance theory, is something of an idealization. It runs together the distinctions Leibniz draws (as in Section 6 of this Introduction) between *minds* (*esprits* in French) such as ours, which are rational and self-conscious, and the non-rational *souls* (*âmes*) of non-human animals. There is a further distinction between the souls of familiar animals which have sense-organs and heightened perception, and those of the simpler 'animals' or 'animated machines' which are so important to Leibniz (TT2. 7 §5; 2. 9 §7; 4. 11; 18. 4; 19. 64). The 'substantial forms' (or 'something like what is called a substantial form' (T2. 4 §16)) of the Arnauld correspondence are said 'in some way [to] correspond to the soul' (T2. 4 §16). 'Monads', which are not spoken of as such in print until 1690 (see T13 n. 4), 'could be called souls' (T19. 19) too, except that perhaps that term should be reserved for 'those which have perceptions which are more distinct' (T19. 19)—perhaps familiar animals which have sense-organs.

Something like Reading 1 is acceptable to some Leibnizian commentators, but it is not acceptable to all. Thus, according to what we might call Reading 2, the so-called 'later' view around the time of the 'Monadology' (i.e. that there are no substantial unities other than minds or somesuch), was Leibniz's view all along. According to this reading, the form–matter 'corporeal substances' spoken of so much in the correspondence with Arnauld are 'corporeal *substances*' only in name. They are *not* substantial unities, and the matter of a flesh-and-blood human being is really what even Reading 1 says it is later: something unreal in itself, an ideality which is some kind of 'result' of immaterial minds.[2]

One of the most basic differences between Readings 1 and 2 concerns what Leibniz thought of corporeal matter, such as the bodies of human beings. On neither reading does Leibniz ever hold that matter in and of itself is substantial and an ultimate constituent of reality. But on Reading 2 it is merely ideal and derives what reality it has in some way from minds, while on Reading 1 it features as a real element of unified form–matter corporeal substances. But if it is not substantial, in what way is it actually real? To answer this we must look further at the material form–matter

---

[2] Reading 1 is roughly acceptable to Garber (1985, Sect. 1) and Broad (1975: 87–90). It is sympathetically presented by Sleigh (1990a), whose 'corporeal substance theory' (98) and 'modified substance theory' (99) are related—at least when 'realistically construed', as he says—to Leibniz's theory (*a*), of corporeal substances; and whose 'spiritual theory' (98) and 'monadological theory' (100) are more specific versions of Leibniz's theory (*b*), of immaterial substances. But in the end he turns away from it to something like Reading 2. Both Garber and Sleigh (see also C. Wilson 1989, Sect. 19) hold that the 'Discourse on Metaphysics' (e.g. T1. 9, 14, 15) (and, in Sleigh's case, also the first part of the Arnauld correspondence) more clearly leans towards theory (*b*) alone (though, as Garber in effect explicitly stresses, theory (*a*) and theory (*b*) can be held together). Rutherford expresses scepticism about Reading 1 and inclines towards Reading 2 (1995a: 154–5; 1995b, ch. 10), a reading which is more firmly adopted by Adams (1994, chs. 9–11), and decisively so by Baxter (1995).

theory of corporeal substances which Reading 1 finds in Leibniz's correspondence with Arnauld.

The idea of a 'substantial form' as something which produces 'substantial unity' is, as Leibniz says (TT1. 11; 4. 3), something which he finds in the tradition of philosophy which began with Aristotle and eventually ran through medieval Scholastic thinkers such as Aquinas. In this tradition individual substances, such as Socrates or Bucephalus, were conceived 'hylomorphically', as composites of matter (Greek: *hulē*) and form (Greek: *morphē*). So, to draw an analogy, a house might be understood as *matter*, such as bricks and timber, disposed or arranged in or according to a certain *form*; a bowl or statue is matter, such as bronze, *formed* in a certain way. We might think of the bronze itself as a composite of more basic matter, perhaps Aquinas's ultimate or 'prime' matter, and the form of bronze.

Given what we have seen about Leibniz's reasons for introducing them, it is not surprising that an individual substance, conceived as a composite of 'form' and 'matter', was said to be *unum per se*—an individual in itself and by its nature. This distinguished it from anything that is not absolutely one, but one only *per accidens*, or accidentally. A product of nature, which has a substantial form, such as an individual human, or an animal, was a typical *unum per se*, an individual substance. On the other hand, artefacts, such as ships or clocks, lacked substantial forms. They were not substances, but *entia per accidens* ('accidental beings'), like heaps of pebbles.

Yet 'form'—or 'entelechy', as another term has it (see, for examples, TT4. 3; 19. 18)—is not simply shape (as with the bronze statue). The form of an oak tree encompasses its whole organization and functioning: its various parts and their purposes, such as its leaves and bark and their functions; its characteristic activities, such as its growth by the synthesizing of water and other nutrients, and its production of fruit; its life-cycle from fruit to fruit-bearer. Its being organized and active in this way means that the matter which constitutes an oak tree 'embodies' or is 'informed' by the substantial form 'oak', and it is only by virtue of this that it is an oak tree at all. Its properties and activities 'flow' or 'emanate' from, are 'formally caused' by, its nature: 'a thing's characteristic operations derive from its substantial form'.[3] So, to understand and explain why an individual substance is as it is, and does as it does, is (except when it is on the passive receiving end of the activities of *other* substances) to understand how its properties and changing states 'flow' from the form of the kind of thing it is.

---

[3] Aquinas, *Summa Theologiae*, 3a. 75, 76.

For Leibniz it was an important feature of substantial forms that they produced unified individuals; but it was important too that they produced *active* individuals. Indeed, the centrality of activity in Leibniz's account of substance can hardly be overstressed. He insisted on it from the start. Writing in 1668, he repeated the traditional definition that '*substance* is being which subsists in itself', and then immediately added that '*being which subsists in itself* is that which has a principle of action within itself' (L 115). Then, still ten years earlier than the 'Discourse on Metaphysics', he says that 'the essence of substances consists in the primitive force of action' (L 155). It was, moreover, a view which he never abandoned. Nearly fifteen years on from the 'Discourse' he still insists that 'actions belong to substances. And hence I hold it also to be true that this is a reciprocal proposition, so that not only is everything that acts an individual substance but also every individual substance acts continuously' (T13. 9; also T3. 4; T13. 8).

Leibniz increasingly comes to think of a substance's 'form' or 'soul' in terms of *active force*. He speaks of 'active force, which is in all corporeal substances as such . . . which corresponds to *soul* or *substantial form*' (T5. 6), and says that there 'must be recognized in corporeal substance . . . a primitive motive force. . . . [I]t is this substantial principle which is called the *soul* in living things, and a *substantial form* in others' (T13. 11).

Now according to Leibniz's theory (*a*), of corporeal substances, a person's body considered by itself has no substantial unity and is not a being *per se*. What then is it? It is, he says, an aggregate of things that *are* substantial unities (T2. 13 §1). But what substances are these? They cannot be the corporeal substances of which human bodies are only elements, and they cannot be the immaterial substances, the souls, which are the other element of those corporeal substances.

At first sight it would seem that the aggregated parts of some material body (whether a human or animal body, a watch, or a marble tile) could only be smaller portions of matter, and so must be mere aggregates themselves. But, says Leibniz, since 'beings made up by aggregation have only as much reality as exists in their constituent parts' (M 88; also T2. 11 §3), it would then follow that a material body, so far from being substantial, is not even 'a real entity' (M 88). To be that it would need to be aggregated from things which *are* substances. So, Leibniz concludes, the corporeal element of a corporeal substance is a physical aggregate (like a heap of stones) of smaller corporeal substances (smaller animals, animated beings, or what Leibniz sometimes calls 'animated machines' (T2. 7 §5; see also TT2. 9 §7;

4. 11; 18. 4; 19. 4)). (The matter of *these* substances will itself be aggregated from still smaller animals, and so on *ad infinitum*.)[4]

One of the most basic differences between Readings 1 and 2 of Leibniz's thinking about substances concerns (it was noted above) what he thought of corporeal matter, such as the flesh and blood of human beings, or stones in a heap. According to Reading 1, it features as a real element of genuine corporeal substances, and so the question arose: if it is not substance itself, in what way is it actually real? As we have just been seeing, its reality consists in its being physically composed out of other, smaller, corporeal substances. According to Reading 2, however (and Reading 1 agrees so far as the later Leibniz of the time of the 'Monadology' is concerned), rather than being *physically* aggregated out of corporeal substances, it in some non-physical way 'results' from immaterial, mindlike, non-corporeal substances. But in what way?

Again the situation is a complex one, and it can easily look as though Leibniz has different views about this. One view which is often attributed to him is what in modern discussions of the reality of the material world is known as phenomenalism. According to one form of this, the material world consists only of immaterial minds and their dependent modifications such as ideas, sensations, or perceptions, and the 'reality' of so-called material bodies is no more than the fact that there is agreement or harmony among these perceptions.

This at least seems to be Leibniz's view when he writes, at about the time of the 'Monadology':

I consider the explanation of all phenomena solely through the perceptions of monads functioning in harmony with each other, with corporeal substances rejected . . . It is true that things which happen in the soul must agree with those which happen outside of it. But for this it is enough for the things taking place in our soul to correspond with each other as well as with those happening in any other soul, and it is not necessary to assume anything outside of all souls or monads. According to this hypothesis, we mean nothing else when we say that Socrates is sitting down than that what we understand by 'Socrates' and being 'sitting down' is appearing to us or to others who are concerned'.[5]

It would not be too difficult to read this view into other texts (TT1. 9, 14, 15; 19. 56, 57).

But Leibniz does not always talk as though extended matter is a

---

[4] For further explanation of this line of thought see T2 n. 1 and summary.
[5] Letter to Bartholomew des Bosses, 16 June 1712 (GP ii. 452/L 605).

systematic appearance which consists in there being agreement or harmony amongst the perceptions of immaterial monads. He sometimes talks as though it is in some way a collection or aggregate of monads themselves. In the 'Principles of Nature and Grace' he says that 'bodies' or 'composite substances' are 'collections of simple substances, or *monads*' (T18. 1; see also T19. 2). At least on the face of it there is some continuity here with the 'earlier' view of matter, proposed in Reading 1 for the correspondence with Arnauld. On that view extended bodies are composed or aggregated out of smaller corporeal substances; and on this view they are 'not simply the way things appear to monads' (as on the straightforward phenomenalist version of Reading 2) 'but are in reality pluralities of monads' (Rutherford 1995a: 147). Of course there are discontinuities too; for on this version of Reading 2 bodies cannot be *physical* aggregates of substances or monads, or composed of them as parts, for monads, unlike the smaller corporeal substances of Reading 1, are clearly non-extended.

The exact manner in which non-extended monads do function as elements in the extended aggregates which are corporeal bodies is a further matter of disagreement and divergence of interpretation. Recognizing clearly that 'monads are not *parts* of bodies', Broad, for example, says that 'what we must say is that certain aggregates of these unextended substances present to us the delusive appearance of being extended . . . bodies' (1975: 92). Rutherford, on the other hand, rejects this. He insists that Leibniz's claim is not so much one about how there *appear* to be bodies, but one about what bodies *are*: 'his intention [is] to identify bodies ontologically with pluralities of monads' (1995a: 146).[6]

So, given that, at any rate in the later periods of Leibniz's thought, extended material body is not (as on Reading 1) a physical aspect of corporeal substances, there is still considerable disagreement on how extended corporeal bodies relate to, or 'result' from, non-corporeal substances. Are they, as on the phenomenalist interpretation, a function of the perceptions of non-corporeal monads? Or do 'aggregates' of these non-extended monads present the delusive appearance of being extended bodies (as for Broad)? Or is it that such aggregates are what bodies actually are (Rutherford)? These questions are frequently pursued in the secondary literature (Rutherford 1995a: 146).

---

[6] For the whole question of phenomenalism in Leibniz and the relation between monads and bodies see Adams (1983; 1994, ch. 9), Baxter (1995), Broad (1975, ch. 4), G. Brown (1987b), S. Brown (1984, ch. 10), Furth (1967), Hartz (1992), Jolley (1986), MacDonald Ross (1984a), McGuire (1976), B. Russell (1900, chs. 7, 8), Rutherford (1990a,b; 1994; 1995a; 1995b, chs. 8, 9), Sleigh (1990a, chs. 4, 5), C. Wilson (1989, Sect. 19), M. Wilson (1987).

3. Physics and Natural Science

3.1. The 'Mechanical Philosophy'

As we saw in Section 2, the material world, according to philosophers in the *Aristotelian tradition, was composed of substances, each with its *substantial form. A substance's characteristic properties and behaviour arose from its form and were to be explained by reference to it. This picture of how the material world was to be understood came under increasing pressure in the seventeenth century from the 'mechanical philosophy' of the so-called 'new philosophers'.

According to the mechanical philosophy, the properties of material things are to be explained not in terms of some 'substantial form' which they were supposed to embody, but by reference to the mechanical properties (size, shape, motion) of the matter from which they are composed. This world picture was not as 'new' as its proponents sometimes claimed. 'Corpuscularianism' (the specific form the seventeenth-century mechanical philosophy typically took) was derived from the atomic theory of the early Greek philosophers *Democritus and *Epicurus, who saw the world as basically consisting of no more than material atoms. The collisions between these, as they moved through the void of space, were what underlay all the familiar phenomena of the world.[7]

Leibniz is a 'new philosopher' in his advocacy of the 'matter in motion' world picture of the 'mechanical philosophy' and his rejection of any appeal to substantial forms in physical explanation.[8] '[R]eference to these forms serves no purpose in a detailed explanation in physics, and should not be used in the explanation of particular phenomena' (T1. 10); on the contrary, 'all particular natural phenomena can be explained mathematically or mechanically' (T1. 18; see also TT2. 4 §16; 4. 6).

But how can Leibniz be an advocate of the 'mechanical philosophy', something which rejects the very substantial forms of which (as in Section 2) he makes so much use in his account of substance? The answer is that he denies that substantial forms have any place in *physics* in detailed explanations of natural phenomena, but insists on their place in a *metaphysical* account of the world. Moreover, his view is that without an adequate

---

[7] For further accounts of corpuscularianism and its contrast with what it displaced, see Alexander (1985, ch. 2), Boas (1952), Dijksterhuis (1961, ch. 3F, G), Hall (1960), Pyle (1995).

[8] Though, in common with *Descartes, he does not see matter as composed of ultimate parts and rejects the *'atoms and void' *Epicureanism of many of his contemporaries (see TT 2. 7 §7; 4. 3). (For Leibniz and atomism, see C. Wilson (1982).)

metaphysics, physics will lack proper foundation and invevitably be unsat-isfactory (TT1. 18; 2. 7 §6; 4. 2).

Section 3.3 will explain this last point. It is one which connects with Leibniz's views about motion—one of the two basic elements in the 'matter in motion' world of the new mechanical philosophy. Something more must be said now about the other: matter.

3.2. Passive Properties of Matter

As explained in Section 2, Leibniz disagreed with *Descartes about the metaphysical status of corporeal body or matter—as to its being substan-tial, even as to its being real. But, metaphysical questions about its substan-tiality and reality aside, matter is something with which physics deals. Leibniz diverged from Descartes here too, disagreeing with him about the fundamental properties which physics should recognize in matter. Though he agreed with Descartes that extension is *an* essential feature of matter, he argued that the central *Cartesian doctrine that it is *the* principal property is a serious mistake (TT1. 12; 3. 2; 4. 2; 5. 2). For one thing, he held, extension is not as basic as Descartes thought (T3. 4). For another, if matter were, essentially, nothing but extension, then the physical world would not behave in the way it is observed to behave (T13. 11).

As to the first of these objections Leibniz is firmly of the view that extension is not an ultimate property but that there must be something prior to it and which it presupposes. There must be some other property *in virtue of which* an extended thing is extended and by which its length, breadth, and depth fills space (T5. 36). The 'extension or diffusion' of qual-ities such as whiteness through some milk or of hardness through a diamond provides Leibniz with illustrations of this thought that there must be some property diffused through an extended thing in virtue of which it is extended and which makes it material or, as it were, 'gives it body' (L. 621).

Leibniz uses many different terms for this property. 'Impenetrability', or 'solidity', are perhaps the most illuminating;[9] for the property he has in mind is that in virtue of which two bodies cannot simultaneously occupy the same place. Leibniz believed that Descartes eliminated solidity as part of the nature or essence of material body because he failed to distinguish it from hardness. Hardness (in virtue of which a body's shape will not change under pressure) is, Leibniz agrees, not an essential property; not

---

[9] Other terms are 'antitypy', 'materiality', and 'resistance' (T5. 8).

all, but only some, bodies have it. Solidity, or impenetrability, on the other hand, is what makes it impossible for two bodies (hard or soft) to be together in the same place. It is an essential property which all material things have. Unless they were solid, and therefore mutually impenetrable, bodies would not displace each other in the collisions which, according to the mechanical philosophy, lie at the basis of natural phenomena.

Now it was a natural supposition of the mechanical philosophy that what happens in these collisions—how bodies actually displace and rebound from each other—is not arbitrary, but must be law-governed and regular. And it is a feature of Leibniz's thinking that these regularities must arise out of the nature of matter itself. Matter must be of a nature which suits it to, or gives rise to, the regularities to which we in fact discover it to be subject. However, if matter were merely solid extension (and, going further than Descartes, Leibniz argued that it must at least be this), then the laws of motion would be other than we observe them to be (T13. 11). So, Leibniz concluded, matter is not only extended and solid. There is a further property which it has, a property which he called 'inertia'.

Solidity means that one body cannot come into the place of another unless that other body moves or is moved out of the way; but it gives no reason why a moving body of small extension which collides with a stationary body of large extension might not carry it along with it, with undiminished speed. Yet things manifestly do not happen in this way, and the motion of bodies is therefore not restricted only by their impenetrability. The world is not chaotic as it would be if it were 'no more difficult to move a large body than a small one' (T5. 19; see also T5. 7, 18–20). We have to realize, therefore, not only that a stationary body is impenetrable by another, but also that 'matter resists being moved by a certain *natural inertia*' (T13. 11), an inertia which needs to be overcome by, and at some cost to, another body which gets it to move. Matter 'is not indifferent to motion and rest (as is commonly thought), but requires for its motion an active force proportional to its size' (T13. 11; see also T5. 18–20).

Leibniz refers collectively to the two properties of 'impenetrability' and 'inertia' as 'passive force' or 'passive power' (T5. 7), and describes matter in so far as it has 'passive force' as 'primary matter' (TT5. 7; 13. 11).

3.3. Active Properties of Matter: Motion and Force

Even though it already consists of more than matter as *Descartes analysed it, Leibniz's 'primary matter' as described so far is still merely an incomplete schematic abstraction. There is still more to actual material body (what Leibniz calls 'secondary' matter) than 'passive force'. What more this relates back to Leibniz's disagreement with Descartes (as in Section 2) about the metaphysical status of material body. It relates back to the thought that matter would be a mere phenonenon were it not an aggregate of substances, each of which embodies a substantial form and has, or is, 'active force'.[10] According to Leibniz, matter, such as a piece of wood or of marble, possesses not only the 'passive force' of impenetrability and inertia, but also an 'active force' or 'active power', a force which is *derived from* or has its metaphysical basis in the primitive 'active force' of the forms of the substances out of which it is aggregated (see TT5. 4, 6; 13. 7–8).[11]

'Active force' or, sometimes, 'motive force' (T13. 11), *vis viva*, or 'living force' (T5. 12) is a force associated with motion—which, along with matter, is one of the two basic elements of the 'matter in motion' worldview of the mechanical philosophy of the seventeenth century. Moreover, Leibniz's idea that a moving body has a force associated with it is one which he shares with his immediate predecessor Descartes. But it has a far longer history than that, and something must be said about this in order properly to understand the idea.

*Aristotle taught that everything that is moving must be being moved by something: there must be a 'motor'. So a moving thing is being continuously 'carried along' either by an 'internal' source of motion (as in what Aristotle called 'natural' motion) or by an 'external' source (as in 'unnatural' or 'violent' motion). Thus the motion of a javelin which has been thrown is 'unnatural', for if it had been 'left to itself', and simply dropped, its natural movement would have been downwards. So in its lateral movement through the air, the javelin must have a continuous 'external' source of motion.

According to the theory of 'antiperistasis', the javelin is continuously pushed along by air which comes round from its front end to its rear. Another idea, also discussed by Aristotle, is that the air gets from the hand the ability to act as a 'motor', an ability which is then communicated from one parcel of air to another. So, as though moving by being passed from hand to hand, the javelin moves by being successively passed to different parcels of air. A third idea, suggested in the sixth century by *Philoponus,

---

[10] See above, Sect. 2.

[11] Exactly how derived active force arises from, or relates to, the primitive active force which characterizes substantial form is not clear. Leibniz says little more than that it 'is as it were the limitation of primitive force brought about by the collision of bodies with each other' (T5. 6; see also T13. 11). (For some discussion, see Phemister (1996).)

is that the javelin itself (rather than the air through which it passes) gets from the hand a force which, until it is expended, continuously sustains the motion.

Something like this last idea became popular as part of the so-called *impetus* theory. According to *Buridan, one of its prime proponents in the fourteenth century, in a projectile 'there is impressed something which is the motive force of that projectile . . . the motor in moving a moving body impresses in it a certain impetus or a certain moving force . . . It is by that impetus that the stone is moved after the projector ceases to move.'[12]

The basic conception of the impetus theory of motion, that there is a sustaining force associated with a body's motion, can be found in Descartes. He speaks of a moving body's having a 'force of motion' or 'a power of persisting in motion'. He held, moreover, that this 'force', which moving bodies have by virtue of their moving, is redistributed in collisions between bodies. When, after being hit by another ball, a stationary ball begins to move, it must have acquired an amount of 'moving force' which, correspondingly, has been lost by the other, now less quickly moving, ball. So, a transfer of force from one body to another accelerates the latter and slows down the former. A final and most important point is that, according to Descartes, besides being transferred in collisions from one body to another, the sum total of the force of motion in the universe is a constant. If one part of the material world slows down, then, we must suppose, another part speeds up.[13]

Leibniz too thinks of moving force in these ways—as something which can cause, increase, and sustain motion. It is, for him, 'the force by which bodies actually act and are acted upon by each other . . . [it is] that [force] which is associated with motion . . . and which in turn tends to produce further . . . motion' (T5. 9). Finally and, again, most importantly, he firmly agrees with Descartes's view that the amount of moving force in the world must be a constant (TT1. 17; 3. 4; 5. 17).

It needs to be appreciated that the notion of force which is there in Descartes's and Leibniz's thought is quite different from that which derives from Newton's *Mathematical Principles of Natural Philosophy* (1697). Classical Newtonian dynamics has no force which explains why bodies *keep on* moving. Its 'force' is one which explains acceleration or change of motion and not its continuation. Its force brings about an increase of motion, or a change of direction of motion; and once such

---

[12] Trans. Marshall Clagett, in Clagett (ed.), *The Science of Mechanics in the Middle Ages* (Madison, Wis., 1959), 523.

[13] See *Princs. Phil.* 2. 36–45.

changes have come about, and a body is set on its new way, there is, in Newton's scheme, no 'force' involved in sustaining it. Leibniz, however, insists (rather more than does Descartes) on a 'motive force' which underlies uniform non-accelerated motion.

One place where it makes an appearance is in an argument to the effect that motion must be something more than the kinematic phenomenon of a body's occupying a series of different places, and must be considered dynamically as being caused by an underlying force. One reason why motion must be something more than spatial transfer is that we otherwise could not say which of two reciprocally moving bodies is *really* moving (TT1. 18; 4. 18). A second reason why there must be a dynamical force underlying motion is that, considered purely kinematically, motion consists simply in a body's being in different places at different times, having occupied the intermediate places at intermediate times. So, as far as appearances go, there is no difference *at a moment* between a stationary body and a moving one. Movement, understood kinematically as change of place, essentially happens *over a period*. Yet there must, Leibniz argues, be something true of a moving body *at an instant*, and this is that at each instant it possesses a moving force (TT5. 3; 9. 37; 12. 13; 13. 13).

3.4. *Physical Force and its Measurement*

According to the mechanical conception of it, a conception which in its generalities Leibniz shares with *Descartes, the physical world ultimately consists of no more than collisions between chunks of moving matter, chunks which then move off with changed speed in different directions. As we have seen, this motion is associated, by both Descartes and Leibniz, with a force which gets redistributed among bodies as they collide but which remains a constant in the universe as a whole.

But how is all this motion and its associated force to be quantified and measured? The thought with which Descartes clearly began, and one which is still plausible now to the scientifically untrained mind, is that the amount of motion possessed by a single piece of matter (such as a billiard-ball) is at least partly a simple matter of the speed at which it is moving: at double the speed there is twice as much motion. But motion cannot just be speed, for where there are two balls moving at the same speed there must be more motion than where there is one. Indeed, there is more motion in a larger ball moving at a given speed than in a smaller ball. Reflections like this lead us to the important conclusion, which Descartes promulgated to his followers in the seventeenth century, that 'motion' (or its associated force) is to be measured by size multiplied by speed:[14] 'if one part of matter moves twice as fast as another which is twice as large, we must consider that there is the same quantity of motion in each part' (*Princs. Phil.* 2. 36).

Intuitively reasonable though it may be to measure the 'quantity of motion' or 'force of motion' of a body in this way, one of the more prominent things in Leibniz's writings is the repeated insistence that Descartes has gone completely astray (TT1. 17; 3. 4; 5. 14–16, 25–6, 31; 13. 4).

As explained in detail elsewhere (see T1 n. 17) he argued that a body's force of motion is to be measured not (as Descartes measured it) by its speed, but by the height to which that speed could take it (for example, by rolling up a slope). This height is in fact proportional to the *square* of the speed, and Leibniz came to prefer to express motive force (or *vis viva*, or 'living force' as he then called it) as the product of a body's size and the square of its speed. This contrasts it neatly with Descartes's 'quantity of motion', which is the product of size and speed. Leibniz's argument against Descartes, that force of motion is proportional not to speed but to its square, precipitated the '*vis viva* controversy', which lasted until well on into the next century.[15]

3.5. Physical Force and its Conservation

Though Leibniz disagreed with *Descartes about how force of motion should be measured, he agreed with him that it is not lost in collisions but simply redistributed, and that its total amount in the universe is a constant. But, even though it took them some years to acknowledge it, those who adhered to the Cartesian measure were faced with having to abandon this second element of Cartesian doctrine. For, as Leibniz had learnt from a paper published by *Huygens in 1669, 'Cartesian motion' actually is *not* conserved in collisions, and is therefore not a universal constant quantity.

Using the imaginative device of considering how the same collision would appear to differently moving observers,[16] Huygens showed that, though Descartes was right that the amount of 'motion' of one body in a collision could change only if there was some change in the other, he was

---

[14] The 'size' of a body is obviously the 'quantity of matter' it contains. Newton called this the body's 'mass', and measured it as the product of volume and density. Descartes's view of matter as extension has no obvious room for the notion of density, and, at least 'officially', the size of a body is its volume.

[15] See Iltis (1971, 1973*a*,*b*), Papineau (1977).

[16] This device lies behind Leibniz's remarks about the equivalence of hypotheses at T5. 38.

wrong that these changes must be equal. For example, a perfectly elastic hard body *A*, of one-unit size, moving with three units of speed, which hits a stationary body *B*, twice its size, will rebound from it with one unit of speed and move it with two units. It therefore loses two units of the Cartesian 'quantity of motion', while the other gains four.

This does not mean that the results of collisions are arbitrary and cannot be predicted. For, as Huygens made clear, there are a number of other conservations and regularities in collisions between perfectly elastic hard bodies. For example, the speed of mutual approach of colliding bodies is always the same as the speed of their mutual separation (in the above example: three); the sum total of 'force', according to the Leibnizian measure of it, is the same after a collision as before (in the above example: $(1 \times 3^2) + (2 \times 0^2)$ before the collision; $(1 \times 1^2) + (2 \times 2^2)$ after). There is also conserved a quantity which in some respects is like 'Cartesian motion', a quantity which at the time was called 'direction' or 'quantity of progress' but which now is called 'momentum' (TT8. 7; 19. 80).

The significance of the notion of momentum and of its conservation in collisions has its classical expression in a corollary of the third law of motion of *Newton's *Mathematical Principles of Natural Philosophy*. Newton's measure of the quantity of 'motion' (i.e. momentum) of a moving body differs from Descartes's in that, besides relating to size, it relates not simply to the speed at which the body is moving, but rather also to the *direction* of that speed (i.e. not simply to speed, but to what is technically known as 'velocity'). So, when body *A* rebounds from *B* with undiminished speed there has, despite that unchanged speed, been a change of velocity. If *A* is taken to be moving with a velocity of two units before the collision, then after the collision it is moving with one of minus two units, a change of momentum of four—for it is now going backwards at the same speed as it was before going forwards. So while the collision described two paragraphs earlier does not conserve 'Cartesian motion' it does conserve 'directed motion' or momentum. (With speeds measured in the direction of *A*'s initial motion, the sum of 'directed motion' is (1×3) (for *A*) + (2×0) (for *B*) before the collision, and (-1×1) (for *A*) + (2×2) (for *B*) after.)

*Malebranche was one of those who were reluctant to accept criticism of Descartes's teaching about conservation of quantity of motion. However, in his *Laws concerning the Communication of Motion* of 1692 he finally did recognize that the principle of conservation of Cartesian motion was false when motion was taken 'absolutely' (i.e. with no account of direction). But he merely pointed out, in clarification of what he saw as

24

an ambiguity, that it was nevertheless true when motion was taken 'relatively' (i.e. with direction taken into account). He certainly did not go over to the Leibnizian measure of force. And, indeed, since 'directed motion' or momentum *is* conserved in collisions, why could Leibniz too not have accepted it as a measure of force? The fact that Malebranche called it 'relative motion' is a pointer to why.

The total 'progress' or 'momentum' of a system of bodies is not an absolute in the sense that it is not necessarily changed by a change in the size or speed of those bodies. What is required is a change in the size or speed of the bodies *relative to each other*. So, the total momentum in a system of two bodies of equal size and equal and opposite speed is *unchanged* from zero by a change in the bodies' size and speed *when they are changed equally*. Similarly, even a *decrease* in size or speed of *one* of the bodies could produce an *increase* from zero, in the total momentum of the system.

Earlier we considered a line of thought which led to the Cartesian measure of 'force of motion', and in terms of it these results are intuitively quite unacceptable; and, of course, in this sense in which momentum is a relative quantity, Cartesian motion is an absolute. For its total amount in a system of two bodies of equal size and equal and opposite speed is not zero, and it would be doubled by a doubling in size or speed in each body. Similarly, a decrease in size or speed in *one* of the equal bodies would produce a decrease in the total quantity of Cartesian motion.

As for Leibnizian 'living force', it too is an absolute quantity as Cartesian motion is—not a relative one as is momentum. The 'living force' of a system of bodies is increased or decreased by *any* increase or decrease in the bodies' sizes or speeds. It depends on their sizes and speeds as such, not on their relative sizes and speeds. The 'living force' of a system of two bodies of equal size and equal and opposite speed is not zero and would be doubled by a doubling in size of each body (quadrupled by a doubling in speed of each). Similarly, a decrease in size or speed of one of the equal bodies would produce a decrease in the total amount of 'living force'. As he said, when he 'corrected and rectified' the Cartesian doctrine of the conservation of the quantity of motion, Leibniz took care to put in its place 'the conservation of some other absolute thing'.[17]

---

[17] 'Essay on Dynamics', La 658. For further discussion of various of the ideas broached in this section, see Allen (1984), Bernstein (1981, 1984), Broad (1975: 54–6, 61–7), Buchdahl (1969, ch. 7.3), Gabbey (1971), Gale (1970, 1984, 1988, 1989), Garber (1985, 1994), McGuire (1976), Nason (1946), Okruhlik (1985), Papineau (1977), L. J. Russell (1976), Spector (1975), Westfall (1971, ch. 6), C. Wilson (1987), M. Wilson (1976), Woolhouse (1993, ch. 6.3).

4. The Metaphysics of Causation

From the point of view of the 'mechanical philosophy' of the seventeenth century the most basic case of causation is that of collisions between variously moving chunks of the material world. In collisions, motion, or its force, gets transferred from one body to another (as when, for example, a stationary body is made to move). This raised questions about the metaphysical status of motion and its force and their transfer from one body to another. As John *Toland said just after the end of the century, people are 'extremely puzzled about the *moving force* itself, what sort of being it is; where it resides, in matter or without it; by what means it can move matter; how it passes from one body to another; or is divided between many bodies while others are at rest, and a thousand more such riddles'.[18]

Discussion of these questions took place against the background of a commonly received idea which dates back to *Aristotle: immaterial minds are active, while material bodies are passive. Minds have a power of self-movement and are able to initiate change and motion, both in themselves and in bodies; but bodies lack self-movement and can merely receive motion (either from a mind or another body) which they then retain, or communicate to another body.

On the whole, *Descartes seems not to have been much puzzled about whether the force of motion 'resides in matter or without it', about 'how it passes from one body to another'. He usually seems content to think that it 'resides in matter', and he is able quite unself-consciously to speak of it as being 'mutually transferred when collisions occur' (*Princs. Phil.* 2. 42). But his writings do sometimes suggest a less than full commitment to the idea that the movement of bodies is sustained by their own moving force. Perhaps, he sometimes suggests, the cause of motion lies in God. The force or power which impels bodies and causes their motion 'may be the power of God himself conserving the same amount of transfer [i.e. movement from place to place] in matter as he put in it in the first moment of creation' (CSMK iii. 381).

The possibility raised here, that bodies are sustained in their motion by God, was maintained as a certainty by Descartes's follower *Malebranche. Just as the persistence in existence of a body has to be understood as its constant re-creation by God, so its motion is its re-creation in a series of different places. Accordingly, the force or power of motion is the power of

---

[18] John Toland, *Letters to Serena* (London, 1704; repr. Stuttgart, 1964), 156–7.

God: 'the moving force of a body [is] . . . simply the efficacy of the volition of God who conserves it differently in different places' (Mal. 1688: 159).

The theory of causation involved here is usually known as occasionalism, though Leibniz often refers to it as the 'Cartesian' doctrine. According to it, there is no real or 'primary' causation in the created world. God is the only real and efficacious cause. Its being hit by a moving body is only a 'secondary' cause of the motion of a previously stationary body—merely the 'occasion' for *God* to produce motion in it.

Occasionalism, therefore, holds that material bodies are, in themselves, completely inactive. Moreover (as we shall see in the next section), it denies activity on the part of human minds too. Human minds cannot, despite what was usually thought, initiate motion in bodies, or even change their own states. *All* power and activity, according to occasionalism, is located in a single mind, the infinite mind of God. Thus, so Malebranche argues, the idea that there is 'a certain force . . . in the body moved and that is the cause of its motion' (Mal. 1674–5: 37) is quite wrong, besides being impious and pagan in attributing activity and power to things other than God. Though Malebranche was preceded in his occasionalism by other *Cartesians, such as Louis de *La Forge and Gerauld de *Cordemoy, it was he, so Leibniz says, who 'with his characteristic acumen, presented it very persuasively' (T13. 10).

If material things have no power to keep themselves moving or to move anything else, it follows, Malebranche argued, that they must be moved by mind. But while we can see no connection between the will of finite minds and the movements of bodies, we can see one between them and God's will. So, he concluded, 'the motor force of bodies is therefore not in the bodies that are moved, for this motor force is nothing other than the will of God . . . Nevertheless, a ball is the natural cause of the motion it communicates. A natural cause is therefore not a real and true but only an occasional cause, which determines the Author of nature to act in such and such a manner in such and such a situation' (Mal. 1674–5: 448).

In a letter dating from his early twenties Leibniz agreed with most of these occasionalist ideas: 'Matter in itself is devoid of motion'; 'mind is the principle of all motion'; 'there is no motion, strictly speaking, as a real entity in bodies. . . . [W]hatever moves is continuously recreated'(L 99, 102). But in later years he held very strongly that (as in Section 3.3) moving bodies do have an internal force. The process of this change of view, which did not involve a total break with occasionalism, was as follows.

Malebranche's argument was, first, that moving bodies are not causally active and can neither keep themselves in motion nor move others;

second, that there is no real causal interaction between finite minds and bodies; and, finally, that God alone has force and is active. Writing to Malebranche in 1679, Leibniz agreed with the second of these stages: 'I am entirely of your opinion concerning the impossibility of conceiving that a substance which has nothing but extension, without thought, can act upon a substance which has nothing but thought, without extension.' But while agreeing that mind cannot be acted on by body, Leibniz disagreed about Malebranche's final conclusion that God alone possesses activity and force. Malebranche had not traced things back to first principles, said Leibniz. In his denial of causal interaction between mind and body Malebranche had 'gone only halfway' (L 209).

'*Specimen Dynamicum*' (T5) spells out what Leibniz must have had in mind here about Malebranche's failure to go all the way in his reasoning: Malebranche denied that body has any force or activity because, as he quite correctly saw, this follows from the view, which he had learnt from Descartes, that body is merely extension. But he should have argued the other way and seen that this consequence really 'indicated "a mistaken notion of body"' (T5. 35). Material substance is improperly understood as involving no more than extension; when properly understood it can be seen to involve (as in Section 3.3) forces and activity.

In Malebranche's view we fail to acknowledge God's supreme divinity when we think that anything else could be a real cause with power to act. In Leibniz's view, on quite the other hand, God would *lack* all dignity were he the sole cause of events in the created world. It is far more worthy of God to have created things which themselves are active, and productive of their changes. As Bayle agreed, Leibniz's view squares far better than does the occasionalists' with our ideas of God's power and intelligence (T14. 1).

Connected with this is an objection which Leibniz makes to the effect that occasionalism involves miracles (TT4. 13; 9. 5; 10. 7; 12. 7). Bayle disagreed with this, pointing out that it is a part of occasionalism that God acts 'only according to general laws' (T10. 7; also T14. 2). Occasionalism does not hold that God decides anew on each occasion how bodies should move after a collision or what sensation should be felt when an arm is pricked with a pin. It holds that God makes a general decision that bodies hit thus will always move off so, and that pain is always the sensation felt when arms are pricked. This means that miracles are *not* involved. A miracle, says Bayle, is something produced by God 'as an exception to general laws' (T14. 2).

Leibniz quite clearly took a different view. Even if God's actions were quite regular and in accordance with perfectly general decisions, their results would still be miracles. For Leibniz, a miracle is not something that is unusual—frequency or regularity is of no relevance. A miracle is rather, quite simply, something that results from God rather than from the natures of the things involved. 'It isn't sufficient to say that God has made a general law, for in addition to the decree there has also to be a natural way of carrying it out. It is necessary, that is, that what happens should be explicable in terms of the God-given nature of things' (T12. 7).

But, even given that occasionalism holds that God acts according to antecedently made general decisions and does not decide on each new occasion *how* to act, how does it stand on the question whether God needs to *act* on each new occasion? Even though God has decided *once for all*, and as *a perfectly general* matter, which things will follow which, does he nevertheless need to *act* on each particular occasion?

According to Arnauld, in a part of his correspondence which is not included in this volume, the occasionalists hold that God makes things happen in a certain regular way simply by having decided that they would so happen. They 'do not claim that God causes my arm to move by a new act of will which he has on each occasion that I want to raise my arm'. They claim that God makes things happen 'by that unique act of his eternal will' (GP ii. 84).

Leibniz found this view of things unintelligible. This is beautifully clear in the important article 'Nature Itself' (T13) in which he discusses the occasionalism of Christian Sturm. It is hardly sufficient, he argues, simply that God make general decisions: *the mere making of a decision does not of itself ensure its being carried out.* Not even divine decisions are self-fulfilling; even they need to be put into effect. As Leibniz describes it, Sturm held that 'motions which take place now come about as the result of an *eternal law* which God has set up, a law which he [Sturm] then calls a volition and a *command*'; and, further, that 'no new command or volition is then necessary, far less a new effort' (T13. 5). So, in Sturm's view, events happening *now* are happening simply because of this *prior* decision.

This made no sense at all to Leibniz. Since an 'earlier command does not now exist, it cannot now do anything unless it left behind some continuing effect which still endures and operates'. It is necessary that 'things have been formed by the command in such a way that they are capable of fulfilling the meaning of the command. . . . [T]hings [must] have been given a certain ability, a form or force . . . from which the series of phenomena follows in accordance with the dictates of the original command' (T13. 6).

The upshot of all of this is that, according to Leibniz, Malebranche was right that one created thing does not act on another, but wrong to maintain that all activity resides in God and that all change in the world is due to him. Created things, Leibniz holds, bring about *each their own* changes. It is important to see, however, that just as for the occasionalists God not only brings about the changes in one created thing but brings them about *on the occasion* of changes in other created things, so, for Leibniz, the self-generated changes in one created thing in effect occur *on the occasion* of the *self-generated* changes in another. For Leibniz, that is to say, there is a concomitance or harmony between the changes in one created thing and the changes in another. This important aspect of his theory of causation will be brought out further in Section 5, which concerns the 'causation' between body and mind.

Before moving on to that it should be recalled, however, that the discussion in this section began with the question of the activity involved when chunks of matter participate in the collisions which form a part of the mechanical world picture. Now, in all strictness, Leibniz's view of the non-interactive yet self-active nature of created things applies to individual substances, and—as was abundantly clear from Section 1—chunks of matter do not qualify as such.[19] Despite this, however, Leibniz does sometimes speak as though any change to a mere material body took place as though it were an individual substance—through an autonomous self-activity. After being involved in a collision a stationary body 'is put into motion by *its own force*', he says (T13. 14; see also TT4. 18; 5. 49).

5. The Union of Body and Mind

Discussion of the metaphysics of causation (as in Section 4) took place (it was noted) against the background of the idea that minds have an active power both to change their own states and to move bodies, while material bodies are passive, at any rate to the extent of being unable to *initiate* movement. Quite naturally, therefore, one specific application of the occasionalist view of causation was to the relation between body and mind of human beings. Leibniz's views on this matter are best understood by locating them by reference to those of *Descartes and of the *occasionalists.

---

[19] For a discussion of the question of interaction between non-substantial Leibnizian bodies, see G. Brown (1992), Garber (1985: 89), Miller (1988). For discussion of Leibniz's, the *'occasionalists'', and the *Scholastics' theories of causality, see Ishiguro (1977), O'Neill (1993), Rutherford (1993), Sleigh (1990*b*), Woolhouse (1985).

Descartes seems to have thought of this quite straightforwardly as a matter of real causation. The causes of many changes in our material bodies are located in the body or in the wider material world; but the causes of some of them are mental, as, for example, when I decide to move my arm. Similarly, and in the other direction, the causes of many mental changes are located in the mind; but the causes of some of them lie in the material world, as, for example, when a pin stuck in my arm causes me pain.

Many of Descartes's contemporaries did not see how such causal inter-action between the body and the mind was consistent with his other view that body and mind are substances of two radically different kinds. *Gassendi, for example, spoke of the 'general difficulty . . . of how the cor-poreal can communicate with the incorporeal, and of what relationship may be established between the two' (CSMK ii. 239). But Descartes himself appeared not to see any problem here, and suggested that it is just false to suppose that substances of different natures cannot act on each other.

To an extent, the occasionalists agreed with Descartes in rejecting Gassendi's puzzle. To Louis de *La Forge it was an 'unhappy prejudice' (LF 236) to suppose that the mind could move the body only if it were itself material and so able to be in literal contact with it. He found it far easier to accept that mind could move body than that colliding bodies could move each other. In the end, however (as we saw in the last section), occasional-ism held not only that causation in the material world is only 'secondary', and not true or real causation, but also that this was so of causation between immaterial mind and material world too.

*Malebranche's claim was that 'there is absolutely no mind created that can move a body as a true or principal cause, just as it has been said that no body could move itself'. He argued that 'when we examine our idea of all finite minds, we do not see any necessary connection between their will and the motion of any body whatsoever'. By contrast, when we think of God, 'infinitely perfect and consequently all-powerful', we know that 'there is such a connection between His will and the motion of all bodies, that it is impossible to conceive that He wills a body to be moved and that this body not be moved' (Mal. 1674–5: 448).

Speaking of the 'great mystery of the union of body and soul', Leibniz agreed with Malebranche's conclusion that 'in no way is it conceivable that the one has an influence over the other' (T1. 33). One reason he had for saying this is that, as he wrote at about the same time, there is an incommensurability, or lack of ratio, between the mind and the body: 'there is nothing which could determine what degree of speed a mind should impart to the body'.[20] His point is clear. The idea that collisions *between bodies* should affect their speed and direction is quite straightforward. But the idea that the mind could affect the speed and direction of bodies seems wrong in principle. How could we begin to work out the details of how the speed and direction of a material body would be changed by a mental desire or volition?

Leibniz's '[First] Explanation of the New System' (T8. 7), spells this point out in more detail, in terms of some of the ideas discussed in Section 3. According to Descartes, the total 'quantity of motion' (measured as size multiplied by speed) in the material world remained a constant throughout all other changes. So, when something collides with my stationary arm and causes it to move, the 'quantity of motion' my arm acquires is counterbalanced by a corresponding loss in the colliding object. But the idea that my mind, in voluntary action, gives some 'quantity of motion' to my arm is inconsistent with this doctrine. If my deciding to move my arm were to cause it to move, there would be an increase in the arm's 'quantity of motion' which could not be counterbalanced by a loss in my mind; for my mind has no extended size nor speed, and so no quantity of Cartesian motion. Descartes's belief that in voluntary action the mind acts causally on the body is, it would seem, inconsistent with his own 'law' of the conservation of total quantity of motion.

Now, according to Leibniz, Descartes not only saw this problem, he also thought he had found a solution (T8. 7; see also T19. 80). It is not clear that this is historically accurate.[21] What is clear is that Leibniz is right to reject the solution which he attributes to Descartes: that in voluntary action what happens is not that the action of the mind changes the 'quantity of motion' of the body, but that it *changes the direction* of that motion. As Leibniz concedes, this 'is certainly ingenious' (T8. 7), for (as in Section 3) the 'law' of conservation of quantity of Cartesian motion takes no account of the *direction* of that motion. This 'solution' therefore both saves that law and allows for the mind to cause changes in the body.

As Leibniz makes plain, however, this will not do. His point is not that Descartes's 'law' is actually false (as in Section 3) and so not worth saving. He focuses, rather, on the reason why it is false—namely, precisely because it takes no account of the direction of motion. While Cartesian motion is *not* conserved, 'directed motion' or momentum *is*. And, this being so,

---

[20] Letter from Leibniz to Arnauld, 30 Apr. 1687 (GP ii. 93).
[21] See Garber (1983, Sect. 2, esp. nn. 21 and 35), McLaughlin (1993), Remnant (1979).

there is no room left for the mind to have any causal effect on the speed or direction of motion in the body.

It should be noted that this argument against Descartes's interactionism *applies equally against occasionalism.* It involves an inconsistency with the law of conservation of directed motion not merely for the mind to cause motion in the body but *even for God on the 'occasion'* of some volition in a mind to cause motion in the body. If the cause of a change in the motion of body were ever a mental volition, then, whether it be a 'real' or an 'occasional' cause, the law of conservation of directed motion would be broken. Though Descartes's occasionalist followers disagree with him about the metaphysics of causation, they effectively agree that, whether it is 'real' and 'primary', or 'occasional' and 'secondary', there is causation between mind and body. For Descartes and his occasionalist followers alike, the material world is not closed off from mental causation; but this involves a rejection of the true law of conservation of directed motion. The conclusion to draw is that the mind and body are causally isolated from each other, and that bodily changes always have bodily causes, mental changes always mental causes.

This conclusion is a feature of Leibniz's own account of the relation between body and mind—an account which at first he called the 'hypothesis of concomitance' or of 'agreements', and eventually and most famously 'the system of pre-established harmony'. This, he says, is something which follows from his account of substance (T1. 33). As we saw in Section 4, Leibniz agreed with Malebranche that *if* there were no more to material substance than extension, then there could be no activity and no real causation in the material world. He suggested, however, that Malebranche had faced the wrong way, and should have seen that material substances therefore are more than extension and involve activity and substantial forms. The resulting conception of an individual substance, which emerges in the 'Discourse on Metaphysics' (T1) and the correspondence with Arnauld (T2), is one according to which 'all its actions come from its own depths' (T2. 13 §1).

Now this account of substance, Leibniz says, provides us with an explanation 'of the great mystery of the union of the soul and the body': '[W]e have said that everything which happens to the soul and to each substance is a consequence of its notion. Therefore, the mere idea or essence of the soul specifies that all its appearances or perceptions must arise spontaneously from its own nature, and in just such a way that they correspond of themselves . . . to what happens in the body' (T1. 33; see also T5. 35).

There is no causal interaction between mind and body; each is responsible for its own changes. But the two series of changes nevertheless 'correspond'.

When Leibniz explained all of this to him, Arnauld could at first see no difference between occasionalism and this hypothesis of concomitance. According to Leibniz, the reason my arm rises when I wish to raise it is not because my wish is the cause of the movement. It is because God, having taken advance consideration of my wish, arranged things so that the rising of my arm coincided with my wish. But how does this differ, wondered Arnauld, from saying that my will is the occasional cause of the arm's movement and God the real cause? What Arnauld had failed to grasp is that, though neither view holds that my will is the real cause of the arm's movement, the occasionalist holds that God is, whereas Leibniz holds that the body is. For Leibniz, there is no causal interaction between mind and body; each is responsible for its own changes, and has no causal dependence on the other. '[E]verything happens in the soul as if there were no body, just as . . . everything happens in the body as if there were no soul' (T16. 8).

Leibniz's explanation of the 'union of body and mind' in his 'New System' (T4) was what caught Pierre Bayle's attention (TT10, 14). Leibniz's replies to Bayle's scepticism about that explanation spell things out in more detail (TT11, 12, 15–17). As against the apparent unlikeliness that *everything* in the material world should be a result of purely mechanical material causes, Leibniz makes much of the unlimited possibilities of mechanism. Just as we 'could make a machine which was capable of walking around a town for a time, and of turning precisely at the corners of certain streets' (T16. 3), so there is nothing impossible in principle for all material bodies, created by the infinite wisdom and power of God, to be 'natural mechanisms' (T16. 5). Bayle also had problems with the idea that the soul brought about all of its own changes: why should minds give themselves feelings of pain (T14. 9)?

Now from Descartes's and Malebranche's points of view the 'union' between mind and body consists in there being causal connections ('real' or 'occasional') between them. From that position it would seem that Leibniz, who denies all causal connection between them, is effectively *dis*-uniting the mind and the body. Moreover, if the two *are* disunited, as Leibniz seems to be saying, then why, Bayle wondered, should a contented dog ever feel pain (T10. 6)?

But though he denies that they are *causally* connected, Leibniz does not say that they are completely *unconnected*. They *are* united, but by a non-causal 'concomitance', 'agreement', or 'harmony'. God has arranged things so that the dog's feeling pain coincides with its having just been hit, and also (what Bayle fails clearly to realize) that it would not have felt pain had it not been hit:

> God . . . created the machine of the world from the first in such a way that . . . it should turn out that the springs of bodies should of themselves be ready, exactly as required at just the moment when the soul has an appropriate wish or thought—which in turn it has had only in conformity with the preceding state of bodies. In this way the union of the soul with the machine of the body . . . consists only in that concomitance which displays the wonderful wisdom of the Creator far better than any other theory.[22]

Of course, 'agreement' or 'concomitance' must involve something more than things taking place in both the mind and the body merely at the same time. Corresponding is more than merely coinciding (T12. 5); and, accordingly, Leibniz specifies the non-causal relation between body and mind as being that of 'expressing' or 'representing'. He speaks of 'the representational nature of the soul which must express what happens . . . in its body' (T12. 12; also TT1. 33; 12. 3, 4; 19. 62) and, rather less frequently, he refers to the mind's having its representations in the body (T16. 7).

The 'representational concomitance' which Leibniz envisages between the mind and the body differs from the causal interaction envisaged by Descartes and (in terms of 'secondary' causation) by Malebranche, in that it is *complete*. For Descartes the union between body and mind is a matter of the causes of changes in the one sometimes being located in the other. But he does not of course hold that this union is completely thoroughgoing. Sometimes, that is to say, things happen in the mind (or the body) as a result of other things in the mind (or the body) and completely independently of anything in the body (or the mind). But besides a *complete* causal *dis*unity of body and mind, Leibniz maintains a complete 'agreement' between them. In his view, *everything* that happens in the mind has a correspondence with something in the body. Leibniz spelt this out to Bayle: '[C]ertain movements, which are rightly called involuntary, have been attributed to the body to such an extent that they have been believed to have nothing corresponding to them in the soul: and conversely it has been thought that certain abstract thoughts were not represented in the body. But both of these are mistaken' (T16. 14).

Descartes's distinction between events in the mind in respect of which it is active and those in respect of which it is passive and 'have the body as

---

[22] Letter from Leibniz to Arnauld, 30 Apr. 1687 (GP ii.94–5); see also TT11. D, E; 12. 2.

their cause' is captured and reinterpreted in terms of a distinction between the distinct representation which is thought, and the confused representation which is sense-perception (TT1. 13; 16. 15–18). '[T]hat whose expression is the more distinct is judged to act, and that whose expression is the more confused is judged to be passive' (MP 79).

What Leibniz says must be taken at face value. He says elsewhere that even the movements of our lymph, of the viscera, or the circulation of the blood have their 'representations' in the mind. The fact that these are often indistinct and confused is an important feature of the discussion with Bayle (TT12. 12; 16. 15, 18–19). Moreover, besides holding that everything that happens in the body is represented, even if confusedly, in the mind, Leibniz maintains that everything that happens *in the rest of the world* is represented there too. This is clearly so of some things in the wider world—the sound of a distant bell, for example. But Leibniz holds that this is so of all. The 'body expresses the whole universe through the interconnection of all matter in the plenum, [and so] the soul also represents the entire universe' (T19. 62; see also T12. 2, 3).

Connected with this last point is an idea which Leibniz first expresses in the 'Discourse on Metaphysics', but which forms an essential part of the 'Monadology'. In the 'Discourse' he claims that it is the nature of an individual substance to have 'a notion so complete that it is sufficient to include, and to allow the deduction of' all its predicates (T1. 8).[23] But, 'if we consider carefully the interconnectedness of things', this means that in an individual's substantial soul 'there are for all time remnants of everything that has happened to him, and marks of everything that will happen to him—and even traces of everything that happens in the universe' (T1. 8). So the whole world 'is multiplied as many times as there are substances, and in the same way the glory of God is redoubled by so many quite different representations of his work' (T1. 9; see also TT1. 14; 2. 11 §9; 12. 3; 19. 62).[24]

6. Humans, Animals, and their Minds

In the Scholastic tradition on which Leibniz drew (as we saw in Section 2), human beings are not alone in having *substantial forms. Moreover, forms

---

[23] For more on this, see T1 n. 1.

[24] For discussion of Leibniz's and the occasionalists' theories of the relation between body and mind, see Broad (1975: 118–24), S. Brown (1984 ch. 11; 1990), Sleigh (1990a, ch. 7), Woolhouse (1988).

of other living things, such as oak trees or horses, were called, with a meaning rather wider than ours today, their 'souls'. But the 'souls' of oak trees, of horses, and of human beings formed a hierarchy. All living things, both plants and animals, nourish themselves and reproduce; but only animals (both human and non-human) have sensation; and only human animals are capable of rational thought and choice. So three kinds of soul were recognized: 'vegetative' or 'nutritive', 'sensitive', and 'rational' or 'intellective'.

In his own way Leibniz continued to recognize something like these traditional distinctions between different kinds of 'souls' or 'substantial forms'. He distinguished humans from other animals by their possession of a *rational soul*, or *mind* (French: *esprit*) (TT4. 5–11; 18. 5; 19. 29). Because of this, humans have *thought* and *understanding*, things which Leibniz connects with the ability to derive 'eternal truths' such as the truths of geometry (TT18. 5, 14; 19. 29, 30). He connects it also with self-consciousness and memory, things which allow of the moral and personal identity necessary for divine reward and punishment (TT1. 34; 2. 7 §3; 19. 29, 30), and for them to enter into community with God (TT18. 15; 19. 84). But the human soul is not only 'rational', it is 'sensitive' (T19. 82) too: for what characterizes animals as such, whether human or non-human, is the activity of *sensation*. Thus, animal bodies have sense-organs which focus, or make distinct, and heighten the impressions made on them by sound waves, light-rays, and so on (TT18. 4; 19. 25).

*Aristotle distinguished living things in general from inanimate matter, by reference to the vegetative soul of self-nutrition. For Leibniz, however, the principle of life is perception. Perceiving is what *any* corporeal substance (including the minute animated substances out of which matter is aggregated) does; and perception is defined as the expression or representation of the many in the one, or of the composite in the simple (T2. 11 §5).[25]

The difference between *perception*, which all living things have, and animal *sensation*, is that the latter is 'heightened perception', the focused perception made possible by the possession of sense-organs. Just as animal sensation is explained in terms of the perception which is common to all substances, so human understanding is explained in its terms too. While sensation is heightened or focused perception, thought and understanding

---

[25] For a discussion of the notion of perception as expression, see Brandom (1981), Kulstad (1977, 1982), McRae (1976, ch. 3).

is 'apperception', or 'consciousness' or 'reflective knowledge' of perception (T18. 4).[26]

Leibniz's distinction between different kinds of minds, with their different levels of mental activity, is something else which sets him against Descartes and his followers. Recognizing (as does Leibniz too) that animals do not have the kind of mental life that humans do, they concluded (as Leibniz does not) that they have no mental life at all and that 'there are no souls in animals' (T18. 4; see also T19. 14).

Indeed, when Leibniz was taking up and making his own use of the Scholastic tradition of recognizing different kinds of souls, and of understanding plants, animals, and humans in terms of them, Descartes was famous for having rejected it. He construed all 'living' things, other than humans (and higher beings such as angels), in purely material terms. He held that all the functions which previously were referred to 'sensitive' or 'vegetative' souls were to be understood solely in terms of physical mechanisms. Everything from the digestion of food through to the reception of stimuli by the eyes and ears and the movements of limbs in appropriate reaction were, for him, all nothing more than movements of matter. Speaking of a 'living' animal as a machine, he says that its 'functions follow from the mere arrangement of the machine's organs every bit as naturally as the movements of a clock or other automaton follow from the arrangement of its counter-weights and wheels' (CSMK i. 108).

Now in respect of most of the functions which were formerly attributed to 'vegetative' or 'sensitive' souls, humans are no different from other animals for Descartes. He understood many of their activities purely mechanically too. But humans had been supposed to have 'intellective' souls also, to be capable of understanding and rational thought; and Descartes did not seek to absorb the functions of this 'soul' into the mechanical workings of matter. He assigned these functions to an immaterial mind, the unique possession of human beings. Moreover, though reaction to sensory stimuli could be a purely bodily mechanical affair (as with non-human animals), with humans it involved the mind too. For Descartes, 'thought', the essential property of mind, extended beyond pure ratiocination to 'imagination, sensation and will' (*Princs. Phil.* 1. 53).

In his own way, then, and while rejecting all other souls, Descartes retained the intellectual soul. In doing this he did not go as far as ancient materialists such as *Epicurus, or more recent ones such as *Hobbes.

---

[26] For Leibniz on different kinds of minds, see Alles (1933), Broad (1975, ch. 4, sects. 4, 6, 8, ch. 5), S. Brown (1984, ch. 11, sect. 6.1), Furth (1967), Kulstad (1983, 1991), McRae (1976, ch. 5), Miles (1994), Parkinson (1982), B. Russell (1900, chs. 11, 13).

According to them, even specifically human activities such as thought and feeling were to be understood purely mechanically, as no more than motions in matter. Leibniz, of course, does not go as far as Descartes. He firmly rejects what he sees as Descartes's treatment of animals as 'soulless' or 'inanimate' machines. It should be noted, however, that when his doctrine of pre-established harmony between body and mind (as discussed in the last section) is brought into the picture, there are respects in which, in Leibniz's view, Descartes did not go far enough in his mechanization; perhaps paradoxically at first sight, there are respects in which Leibniz is on the side of the materialists as against the Cartesians.[27]

What Leibniz's doctrine of pre-established harmony says about the bodies of non-human animals is in entire agreement with, and indeed reinforces, all that Descartes held. According to Descartes, non-human animals are simply machines; like clocks, all that they do can be explained in terms of the motions of matter. Yet, unlike Leibniz, he does not hold the same of the bodies of human animals. For him they are not just machines, for (as indeed we saw in the last section) some of what their body does is caused by their mind. So, according to that half of Leibniz's doctrine of pre-established harmony which concerns bodies, the complete materialism of Hobbes or Epicurus is right (in no case for them are there immaterial minds to affect the body, and human beings are purely mechanical too), and Descartes's semi-materialism, just because it does not apply to humans, is wrong.

This at first sight surprising affinity with the materialists comes out explicitly in Leibniz's replies to Bayle. Discussing his doctrine of pre-established harmony he says that 'everything happens in the body . . . as if the wicked doctrine of . . . Epicurus and Hobbes . . . were true; or as if man himself were only body, or an automaton. Thus they extended to man what the Cartesians maintain with regard to all other animals' (T16. 8).

As for the other half of the doctrine of pre-established harmony, according to which the mind is, as Leibniz says, a 'spiritual automaton', Descartes again is partially *right*, but only *partially* right. But this time the materialists, instead of being completely right, are completely wrong. He is right and they are wrong about *our* having immaterial substantial souls. But he is wrong in holding that we alone have them, and wrong in holding that our body sometimes acts on them: 'internal experience—the consciousness we have of the "I" which perceives what passes in the body—refutes

---

[27] For discussion of Leibniz's relation to materialism, see Jolley (1978), Seager (1991), M. Wilson (1974).

the Epicurean doctrine. And perception, since it cannot be explained by shapes and motion, establishes the other part of my theory: we are obliged to admit an *indivisible substance* in ourselves, which must itself be the source of its phenomena' (T16. 8).

We saw in Section 2 that there are times when Leibniz treats substantial forms or souls (for example, a rational human mind) not only as elements of a material substance (a human being) which accounts for their substantial unity, but also as things which themselves are substantial unities. Considered apart from the human body, the mind is a substance in its own right (TT1. 10–12, 22, 23, 33, 34; 2. 7 §4; 2. 11 §8). Despite this, however, Leibniz clearly holds, quite to the contrary of what Arnauld expected (T2. 8 §7), that there never are any forms that are not embodied in matter and are not elements of corporeal substances (T19. 14; see also TT2. 11 §7; 4. 7; 19. 72). This being so, there is never 'death in the strict sense, which consists in the detaching of the soul' but only bodily 'enfolding and diminution' (T19. 73). At death the soul does not leave the body—just as, according to Leibniz's *preformationism, at birth it does not join it. Rather it remains embodied in at least some part of the corpse. When a living insect is torn up and destroyed its 'soul' will 'remain in a certain part which is still alive' (T2. 9 §8). Furthermore, though God could destroy souls, they are, in themselves, 'indestructible by natural means' (T2. 7 §4) and 'must always continue to exist' (T4. 4).

Leibniz reports that what partly motivated the Cartesians to maintain that animals are different from humans, completely 'soulless' machines, was the desire to escape the dilemma that either all animals have immortal souls or humans do not (T2. 11 §1). But he himself is not shy of asserting the first of these alternatives—even though he thinks 'that there is a world of creatures—of living things and animals, entelechies, and souls—in the smallest part of matter' (T19. 66).

As we have seen, however, human beings, unlike other living creatures, have rational souls; they are self-conscious and possess a moral identity which suits them for divine reward and punishment. Accordingly, Leibniz treats their 'birth' and 'death' somewhat differently from those of other animals. Animal souls have all existed from the beginning of the world (TT2. 7 §3; 4. 7): the birth of a non-human animal does not require the creation of a new soul; it is only a matter of 'the transformation of another animal which is already alive, but which is often imperceptible' (T2. 7 §3). But human beings *do* merit a new creation and 'the rational soul is created only at the time of the formation of its body' (T2. 7 §3) out of its biological beginnings. In an initial draft of one of his letters (T2. 6) to Arnauld,

Leibniz is unsure of the exact details: perhaps the rational mind displaces an animal soul which was embodied in the semen before it developed into a human body; or perhaps God adds rationality to that previously non-rational soul (see also T19. 82).[28]

As for their 'death', though he often says nothing to the contrary, Leibniz sometimes speaks as though human beings are not subject to bodily transformations of the same kind as those of other animals. At one point he says to Arnauld that God not only 'creates minds when it is time' (T2. 9 §7) but also 'separates them from bodies (at least from their grosser bodies) through death' (T2. 9 §7). The reason Leibniz gives for this detachment from a gross body is that they must retain their distinctly human properties of memory and self-consciousness. Presumably the idea is that they could not do this if they were associated with some small, quite inappropriately organized, part of a corrupting corpse.

7. From God to the Best Possible World: Creation, Freedom, and the Community of Rational Minds

God in Leibniz's philosophy is as he is in the lives of the faithful—an abiding presence. According to Bertrand Russell, however, the 'weakest part in Leibniz's philosophy, the part most full of inconsistencies' is the use it makes of the 'lazy device of reference to an Omnipotent Creator' (B. Russell 1900/1937: 172). Russell does not detail what he has in mind here, though perhaps an equally unsympathetic reader could suggest places where Leibniz does seem to use God as a 'lazy device'.

But the 'Discourse on Metaphysics', for example, does not just *refer to* God. Mostly it is *about* him and our relationship to him, not only as a matter of abstract metaphysics, but also from the more practical point of view of piety and religion. The same is true of many other parts of Leibniz's writing where God appears. Moreover, even in the conceptual complexities of Leibniz's metaphysical analyses, God does not figure as a merely added-on extra. He fills certain crucial roles and is there for good reasons. Doing away with God would require showing that, to the contrary, the roles he plays are actually dispensable, or else would require finding some other way of filling them.

Though, in the main, his writings simply take God as a given, Leibniz does present rational arguments for his existence. Following Russell, it has

[28] For some discussion, see Fouke (1991).

41

been usual to distinguish four of these: the ontological (see T1. 23), the cosmological (see T19. 36–7, 45), the argument from eternal truths (see T19. 43–6), and the argument from pre-established harmony (see T4. 16).[29]

A noteworthy feature of Leibniz's discussion is his frequent criticism of the ontological argument as used by Descartes. All Descartes has really shown, Leibniz says, by the appeal he makes to the concept of God, is not that God exists but that God exists *if he is possible*. The proof, Leibniz says, needs augmenting by a demonstration (which he provides—see T19. 45) that our concept of God is coherent.

The cosmological argument argues from the existence of the world to that of a creator; and the creation of this world by God is governed by two principles, which are of some importance in Leibniz's philosophy. One is the principle of sufficient reason, according to which 'no fact could ever be true or existent . . . unless there were a sufficient reason why it was thus and not otherwise' (T19. 32; see also TT1. 3; 18. 7).[30] So, Leibniz argues,

[29] For all the proofs, see Broad (1975, ch. 7.2), Gotterbarn (1976), Parkinson (1965, ch. 4), Rescher (1979, ch. 14), B. Russell (1900, 1937, ch. 15). For the ontological argument in particular, see Adams (1994, chs. 5–6), Blumenfeld (1972, 1995a), Lomansky (1970); for the argument from eternal truths, see Adams (1994, ch. 8), Broad (1972, ch. 7.2), B. Russell (1900, 1937, Sects. 111–13); and for the cosmological argument, see Blumenfeld (1995a).

Figuring in the second argument is a disagreement with Descartes about whether 'eternal' truths such as the necessary truths of geometry are dependent on God's will as well as on his understanding (see TT1. 2, 2. 4 §3, 19. 46). His own view is that they are objectively true, independently of God's decision. For this Cartesian background, see Frankfurt (1977), Kemp Smith (1952: 177–88), M. Wilson (1978, ch. 3.3).

[30] For discussions of the principle of sufficient reason, see Broad (1946), Brody (1977, Sect. 3), Couturat (1972), Frankel (1986), Hanfling (1981), Parkinson (1969), Rescher (1952), Rutherford (1992), Sleigh (1982, 1983), Wrenn (1972, Sect. 1).

The principle of sufficient reason is, Leibniz says, one of 'two great principles' on which 'our reasonings are founded' (T19. 31). The other is the 'principle of contradiction', 'in virtue of which we judge to be false anything that involves contradiction, and as true whatever is opposed or contradictory to what is false' (T19. 31). (See also TT1. 13; 19. 33–4.) In the early years of this century both Russell and Couturat placed great importance on these, the latter claiming (as in Woolhouse 1994: i. 2) that 'the entire *Monadology*' is derived from it.

The situation is complex in a number of ways, and these complexities involve important features of Leibniz's philosophy. To begin with there is terminological unclarity. At times the 'principle of sufficient reason' is applied by Leibniz to all truths, both necessary and contingent, and it dictates of them all that there must be a reason for their truth. Then, in the case of necessary truths, this reason is the principle of non-contradiction, and in the case of contingent truths it is 'the principle of the best'.

At other times, however, the 'principle of sufficient reason' is not so much something which stands above the principles of non-contradiction and of the best, but rather is identical with the latter. (For a discussion of the relation between these principles, see Couturat (1972), Rescher (1952), B. Russell (1900, chs. 2, 3).)

A further complexity concerning the 'two great principles' on which our reasonings are based stems from their being connected with the distinction between necessary and contingent

though any particular fact in the world is explicable by reference to some other particular, this could be 'continued endlessly' (T19. 36). Hence, there must, outside the series of contingencies which constitutes this world, be a 'sufficient or final reason' (T19. 37; also T18. 8); and this we call God.

But there must be a sufficient reason too, not only for God's creating a world at all, but also for his creating *this* world rather than some other (T19. 53–8; also T18. 8). Leibniz locates this in the principle of the best.[31] 'It follows from the supreme perfection of God that in producing the universe he chose the best possible' (T18. 10; see also TT1. 1; 18. 9; 19. 53–8).

Often Leibniz's idea seems to be that God considers the various possibilities as to how the actual world could be, possibilities which 'put forward their claims to existence in proportion to their perfections' (T18. 10; also T19. 54); that then, from these, God, in his wisdom and goodness, chooses the best; and, finally, that then through his power, he actualizes it. But sometimes Leibniz speaks as though various possibles not merely 'put forward' a claim to existence, but of themselves have 'a certain urgency towards existence . . . a pre-tension to exist'[32]—as though the best possible world brings itself into existence.

Leibniz is quite positive that the ideas of goodness and beauty are not human fictions, and also that it would be quite wrong to claim that God just arbitrarily decides by his will (rather than judges by his understanding) what is good (T1. 2). But, being good, could God have failed to create anything other than the best possible world? Despite what Leibniz says (T1. 13), some of his readers have wondered what freedom and choice God really has, and whether any worlds other than this one really are possible (Blumenfeld 1975; O. A. Johnson 1954; Nason 1942, as in Woolhouse 1981: 25–6; Resnik 1973).

---

truth. This results in their involvement in the question (as in T1, Appendix A) of Leibniz's theory of truth and his apparent claim that all truths are analytic. This involvement is so close that Couturat identifies the theory of truth and the principle of sufficient reason (as in Woolhouse 1994: i. 1–2; see also Rescher 1979: 23).

At one time (see Parkinson 1995: 203) Leibniz tried to distinguish necessary from contingent truths by means of a distinction between finite and infinite analysis. Thus at T19. 33 (and T1. 13), during a discussion of the principle of contradiction, necessary truths or 'truths of reason' are said to be provable via a finite analysis, while at T19. 36 (though not at T1. 13) there is some hint (made more explicit in other places (see Parkinson 1995: 203)) that contingent truths involve infinite analysis. (See Blumenfeld 1984–5, Carriero 1993, 1995, Maher 1980, Rescher 1981d, Sleigh 1982.)

[31] See n. 30 above.

[32] 'On the Ultimate Origination of Things' (L 487). For discussion, see Blumenfeld (1973), Hostler (1973), Shields (1986), Wrenn (1972).

What, however, are the objective criteria according to which this world is the best possible? The 'Discourse on Metaphysics' indicates that it is the best not only in 'a metaphysical sense', but also 'morally speaking' (T1. 1). The 'metaphysical' goodness of the world consists in God's having designed it in such a way that 'the simplicity of means is balanced against the richness of ends' (T1. 5; see also TT1. 21; 18. 10). Comparing God to an expert geometer, a good architect, or a prudent householder, Leibniz explains that he has in mind that God has so structured the world that a 'variety, richness, and abundance' (T1. 5) of natural effects is produced by the laws of nature 'always in the easiest and the most determinate ways' (T1. 21).[33] As for the 'moral' goodness of the world, it consists in God's having created it with the happiness of human minds as his principal aim (see also TT1. 4; 4. 15; 18. 15; 19. 84–5). Of course there is, or appears to be, evil in this best possible world. How this can be is something discussed both by Leibniz and by his interpreters (Blumenfeld 1995b; Howe 1971; Latzer 1994; C. Wilson 1983, 1989, ch. 8).

Associated with the fact that God's creation is both 'metaphysically' and 'morally' the best are two distinct ways in which God is related to different parts or aspects of it. He is related to it as an expert architect or designer (TT1. 35; 18. 10, 15; 19. 87), and he is also, and somewhat differently, related to it as a monarch and moral legislator (TT18. 15; 19. 84–6).

In so far as God stands to the world as 'an inventor . . . to his machine' (T19. 84), Leibniz describes it as the 'Kingdom of Nature'. This is the world as the 'mechanical philosophy' sees it, the physical world as governed by efficient causality and by the laws of motion. But within this natural world there is a moral world (T19. 86), an order of things which constitutes the 'Kingdom of Grace' (see also T5. 24).

It is a function of all created substances to be 'living mirrors or images' of God's creation understood as the Kingdom of Nature (T19. 83; see also TT1. 35; 18. 12, 13). This follows from the fact (as in Section 5) that their bodies, with which their souls are in pre-established harmony, react to all physical changes in the universe. But, as we saw in Section 6, there is a hierarchy of souls—at the top of which are human souls, rational minds with a moral identity and the ability to reason. These, therefore, express not only God's Kingdom of Nature, but also God himself; they are not only 'mirror[s] of . . . created things', but also 'image[s] of the deity' (T18. 14;

[33] For a discussion of what is meant by God's having acted for the best, see Blumenfeld (1995b), G. Brown (1987a, 1988), Gale (1974, 1976), Hintikka (1972), Hirschmann (1988), Lovejoy (1972), Rescher (1969, sect. 5; 1979, ch. 4; 1981c), Rutherford (1995b, pt. 1), Seager (1981), C. Wilson (1983).

see also TT1. 35; 19. 83). As such they are members of the Kingdom of Grace and of the City of God where God is as 'a prince is to his subjects, and indeed what a father is to his children' (TT19. 84; see also TT1. 35; 18. 15).

Being images of God consists partly in being able to know and admire his greatness and goodness, and to love him (TT1. 35, 18. 14, 19. 86). It also, Leibniz says, consists in being able to produce something which resembles his creation (T18. 14). One thing Leibniz has in mind here is that human beings are able to make discoveries about the laws which govern the Kingdom of Nature, and to know the 'eternal' truths which reside in his understanding (TT1. 35; 18. 14; 19. 83). Another is that they are able, like God himself, but unlike things subject to the purely mechanical causality of the Kingdom of Nature, to act voluntarily (T19. 79). Because of this and because, as rational souls, human beings have self-consciousness and memory, they are susceptible to divine reward and punishment (TT1. 34; 2. 7 §3).

Indeed, in the Kingdom of Grace, Leibniz tells us, there is 'no crime without punishment, no good act without its appropriate reward' (TT18. 15; 19. 88, 90). God has achieved this by establishing a harmony between the two Kingdoms, of Nature and of Grace—a harmony effectively built into the pre-established harmony between body and mind (as in Section 5). Sins and good actions will bring along with them their own punishments and rewards through the natural order of bodies (T19. 89). Just as Leibniz's account of the relation between body and mind rules out the need for any intervention by God, so the moral ends of the Kingdom of Grace are achieved by the natural world's working purely according to its own laws (G. Brown 1988; Hirschmann 1988; Rutherford 1995b, chs. 1–3).

As members of the Kingdom of Grace, we, as rational creatures, act voluntarily, according to final causes—according to our perception of what is right and good (T19. 79). A constant complaint about Leibniz, however, is that, within his philosophy as a whole, he cannot accommodate freedom. Indeed, it was precisely this issue that immediately caught Antoine Arnauld's eye when Leibniz sent him the summary of the 'Discourse on Metaphysics'. In this Leibniz claims that the 'individual notion of each person involves once and for all everything that will ever happen to him' (T1. 13), and Arnauld drew from this the conclusion that everything that happened to Adam did so through a 'fatal necessity'. Leibniz appears to have satisfied Arnauld in the end (T2. 5 §1). But the question of the compatibility of his metaphysics with human freedom in particular, and contingency in general, is one which Leibniz was again made to face,[34] and one which has occupied his readers ever since.[35]

8. Leibniz: Life and Influences

Leibniz was born in 1646 in Leipzig, where his father was a professor of philosophy. At university there he specialized in law, having laid a general foundation in classical languages and subjects such as philosophy and mathematics. In 1667, under the patronage of Baron von Boineburg and having already declined an offer of a post as professor of law at the University of Altdorf, he got employment with the Elector of Mainz in connection with a project of recodifying and systematizing German law. Having also an interest in political questions, he was sent to Paris in 1672 to encourage Louis XIV to invade Egypt—a devious attempt to divert the King's intentions away from Leibniz's native Germany. During the four years he spent in Paris he studied mathematics with Christian *Huygens, met philosophers such as Antoine *Arnauld and Nicolas *Malebranche, and made a close acquaintanceship with the writings of *Descartes. He cherished a deep desire to get a research post with the Paris Academy of Sciences but, continually failing in this, he returned to Germany in 1676 as Court Councillor and Librarian to the Duke of Brunswick in Hanover. Though often sent away on diplomatic missions, Leibniz's home was Hanover until the end of his life in 1714.[36]

A systematization of Leibniz's philosophy by Johann Christian Wolff (1679–1754) was dominant in German universities in the first part of the eighteenth century. This was one important source of Leibniz's great influence on Immanuel Kant (1724–1804); another was the posthumously published *New Essays* (1765), which was influential on German thought as a whole too.

It was, similarly, partly through Wolff's presentation of him, partly

---

[34] By François Lamy and Isaac Jaquelot, for example (see WF, chs. 6, 7).

[35] For free will in particular, see Blumenfeld (1982, 1988–9), Borst (1992), Frankel (1984), O. A. Johnson (1954), Murray (1995), Parkinson (1970), Phemister (1991), Seidler (1985). For contingency (and its distinction from necessity), see the references at the end of n. 30 above and at T1, App. A.

[36] Aiton (1985) provides the most detailed and recent biography of Leibniz; MacDonald Ross (1984*b*) provides a far shorter but very informative account of Leibniz's life as well as a very accessible outline of his philosophical, mathematical, and scientific ideas; and Ariew (1995) provides a very useful record of Leibniz's life and works. Relatively comprehensive accounts of Leibniz's philosophy as a whole may be found in Broad (1975), S. Brown (1984), Jolley (1995), Rescher (1979), and in the more advanced, but classic, B. Russell (1900, 1937).

through his own works, that Leibniz figured in eighteenth-century French thought. For some time he had supporters, such as Bernard de Fontenelle (1657–1757), Gabrielle du Châtelet (1706–49), Pierre de Maupertuis (1698–1759), and Denis Diderot (1713–84). But opinion shifted and he was criticized by Étienne Condillac (1715–80), in his *Treatise of Systems* (1749), and by François Voltaire (1694–1778), whose *Candide* (1759) famously satirized Leibniz's dealings in the *Theodicy* with the problem of evil and his 'optimistic' notion that this is the best of all possible worlds.[37]

But since then Leibniz has always found European partisans, being seriously studied by and having marked influence on continental philosophers such as Maine de Biran (1766–1824), Edmund Husserl (1859–1938), Martin Heidegger (1889–1976), and, most recently, Gilles Deleuze (1925–95).

In contrast, one of Leibniz's editors was able to write at the end of the nineteenth century, that 'in . . . [Britain] Leibniz has received less attention that any other of the great philosophers' (Lt, p. v). On this side of the Channel Leibniz's reputation had certainly suffered from the start by the fact that the supporters of Isaac Newton (1642–1727) accused him of plagiarism in the matter of the invention of the differential calculus. Perhaps also there is something in Voltaire's view that European and British philosophers have temperamentally different styles.

But in the twentieth century, prefaced as it was by the publication of Bertrand Russell's very influential and stimulating *Critical Exposition of the Philosophy of Leibniz* (1900), Leibniz's stock has been high. Russell's ideas, and the closely related ones of the Frenchman Louis Couturat,[38] about the dependency of Leibniz's metaphysics on his logic 'lifted Leibniz studies out of the doldrums' (Sleigh 1990*a*: 8).[39] Since then, Leibniz has never wanted in the English-speaking world for those who have found his rich and complex ideas absorbing in their own right—even though their study has often been distorted by the preconception, encouraged by idealizing nineteenth-century histories of philosophy, that Leibniz should be approached as a member of a 'school' of Continental Rationalism, a

---

[37] For more detail on Leibniz's early reception, see C. Wilson (1995), and Barber (1955).

[38] See Couturat (1901, 1972) and, besides B. Russell (1900, 1937), B. Russell (1903).

[39] It is interesting to note that, at first, Russell knew of Leibniz only through the 'Monadology' (the last text in this volume), which he saw as 'a kind of fantastic fairy tale, coherent perhaps, but wholly arbitrary'. It was his later reading of the 'Discourse on Metaphysics' and the letters to Arnauld (TT1, 2) that 'threw a flood of light . . . on all the inmost recesses of Leibniz's philosophical edifice' (B. Russell 1900/1937, p. xiii).

'school' whose opposition with its rival, British Empiricism, was supposed to have reached some sort of resolution in the philosophy of Kant.

There is, of course, a vast but implicit influence whenever use is made of the differential calculus, not least because of the survival of the symbolism he introduced. But he is often explicitly called as a witness by those who find he shares their vision of the world as a radically harmonious, interconnected whole, penetrated through and through by life. Similarly, his view that richness and variety of phenomena count towards one possible world's being better than another has sometimes been drawn on by recent 'green', environmental movements.

Though Leibniz was a philosopher with synoptic vision his thought moved just as easily at the level of detail, and it is at this level that he most usually figures in more purely academic Anglo-American philosophy.

His name is perhaps most often invoked in connection with the semantics which, in recent decades, logicians have developed for so-called modal notions, such as that of necessity. Leibniz does of course talk of possible worlds (e.g. T19. 53), and, as a logician himself, he is also interested in such modal notions. But it is far from clear that there is a real link here. As one scholar has argued, it is misleading to try to make the connection, for there is a poor fit between the use Leibniz made of the concept of possible worlds and his own exploration of modal notions (Adams 1994).

Discussions of language acquisition and concept formation often refer to his remarks in the Preface to his *New Essays* about innate ideas; and what he has to say on the topic frequently undergoes some exploration by those who are interested in the subject of relations, either for its own sake, or for its relevance to other topics, such as the possible 'supervenience' of mental on physical properties. Indeed, Bertrand Russell reports that he 'first realised the importance of the question of relations when . . . working on Leibniz' (B. Russell 1959: 48).[40]

Leibniz's name is never absent from discussions of the principle of identity of indiscernibles according to which two things with all their properties in common are in reality one and the same thing (see T15, note 1); and this principle's converse, often appealed to in the philosophy of mind to show that states of mind cannot be identical with brain states because they have different properties, is often called 'Leibniz's law'.

Some of this is perhaps little more than lip-service to a famous name.

[40] Further testimony to the importance of Russell's early study of Leibniz is offered elsewhere in this book, as also in his *Autobiography*, where he writes that 'I often have imaginary conversations with Leibniz, in which I tell him how fruitful his ideas have proved' (B. Russell 1967: i. 280).

But there are places where Leibniz's influence across 300 years is still a vital and living one. Even leaving aside Continental philosophers such as Deleuze, he gets more than merely nominal credit for his development of a relational account of space and time (see T16, Summary). Similarly, two central and associated doctrines of his philosophy of mind are, often wittingly, leant on and reworked in recent discussions. One is his rejection of a materialist theory of the mind, so nicely summed up in his image of the mill (T19. 17). The other is his unequivocal rejection, applauded by many recent philosophers, of Cartesian interactionism and Malebranchian occasionalism, on the grounds that they require psychophysical laws and an abandonment of the idea that the material world must be causally closed (see Section 5). This denial, both of a reduction of the mental to the material, and of causal interaction between mind and body, leaves the question of the relation between the two crying out for an answer. Leibniz's answer, in terms of a pre-established harmony, is usually scoffed at as a historical oddity. But perhaps his stress that the harmony is a matter of 'representation' and 'expression' will yet be noticed, taken seriously, and reappraised.

Texts Printed in this Edition

While some of the translations included here are new (TT1, 2, 5, 13, 18, 19), others (TT3, 4, 6–12, 14–17) are taken, sometimes with small changes, from our *Leibniz's 'New System' and Associated Contemporary Texts* (Oxford, 1997). Consequently, this volume has inherited many of the debts listed in that earlier one. It has, however, incurred debts of its own, and thanks are due also to John Bradshaw, Joseph Melia, Liz Naylor, Marie-Christine Wright, and an anonymous reader for Oxford University Press.

PART 2

The Texts

1

DISCOURSE ON METAPHYSICS (1686)

Summary of the Text

The 'Discourse on Metaphysics' is the earliest expression of Leibniz's philosophi-cal thought in anything like a systematic form. Quite possibly it was written as the metaphysical underpinning for ambitions Leibniz had concerning reconciliation of the Catholic and Protestant churches.

Its thirty-seven sections fall naturally into five groups: (i) on the nature of God and of his actions (Sects. 1–7), and (ii) on the nature of created substances (Sects. 8–16); (iii) on natural philosophy and the nature of corporeal bodies (Sects. 17–22); (iv) on human understanding, the human will, and their relation to God (Sects. 23–31); and (v) on the consequences of all of this for piety and religion (Sects. 32–7).

The second of these groups of sections is a locus classicus *for Leibniz's theory of individual substances, and of their mirroring of the whole universe each from its own point of view. The introduction, at Section 17, of scientific considerations might (even given their importance—as in Introduction, Sect. 3—in Leibniz's thought) appear almost as an aside—certainly it comes as something of a sur-prise. But, as Leibniz says at T3. 2, such things follow from his account of sub-stance. There also follows from this what is said in the fourth group of sections (Sects. 23–31), where Leibniz gives us elements of his theory of knowledge, his philosophy of mind, his ethics and philosophy of religion, and—to mention one thing in particular—the beginnings of his account of the relationship between body and mind. C. Wilson (1989, ch. 3), provides an excellent discussion of many of the themes of the 'Discourse'.*

———

From the French at GP iv. 427–63 (and, for the section headings, GP ii. 12–14). This work, to which Leibniz himself gave no title and which he referred to merely as 'a short discourse on Metaphysics', was unpublished in his lifetime and was first printed in 1846. Bertrand Russell (1900/1937, xiii–xiv) drew attention to its importance when, discovering it at the turn of the century, he spoke of the 'flood of light' it threw 'on all the inmost recesses of Leibniz's philo-sophical edifice'.

Material in angle brackets is based on various of Leibniz's manuscript corrections and varia-tions (as in *Discours de métaphysique*, ed. H. Lestienne (Paris, 1907; 2nd edn. 1952)).

THE TEXT

1. *The divine perfection, and that God does everything in the most desirable way.* The most widely accepted and the most meaningful notion of God which we have is fairly well expressed in these terms, that God is an absolutely perfect being; but the consequences of this have not been sufficiently well thought out. In order to go into them a little further it should be noted that there are several completely different perfections in nature, that God possesses them all together, and that each one belongs to him in the highest degree. It is also necessary to understand what a perfection is. Here is a very reliable indicator: a form or nature which cannot be taken to the highest degree is not a perfection—for example, the nature of number or shape. For the largest of all numbers (or, better, the total number of all numbers), as well as the largest of all shapes, implies a contradiction, whereas the greatest knowledge, and omnipotence, do not involve any impossibility. Therefore power and knowledge are perfections, and in so far as they belong to God, they are unbounded. It follows from this that God, who possesses supreme and infinite wisdom, acts in the most perfect manner, not only in a metaphysical sense, but also morally speaking. And it follows that as far as we are concerned we can say that the more we are enlightened and informed about the works of God, the more we are inclined to find them excellent, and exactly in accordance with what we could have wished for.

2. *Against those who maintain that there is no goodness in God's works, and that the rules of goodness and beauty are arbitrary.* So I am far from the opinion of those who hold that there are no rules of goodness and perfection in the nature of things, or in the ideas that God has of them; and that God's works are good only for the merely formal reason that God did them. For if that were so, God, knowing that he is their originator, would have had no need to consider them afterwards to find that they were good, as Holy Scripture testifies he did. But Scripture seems to have used this anthropomorphism only to teach us that their excellence can be recognized when they are considered in themselves, even when we do not think about this completely bare denomination which relates them to their cause. This is all the more so since it is by the consideration of his works that we discover the workman. Therefore those works themselves must carry his imprint. I confess that to me the contrary opinion seems very dangerous and gets

54

close to that of recent innovators,[1] whose view is that the beauty of the universe, and the goodness that we attribute to God's works, are only fancies thought up by people who think of God as being like themselves. And what is more, it seems to me that in saying that things are good not by some rule of goodness but only by God's will, without realizing it we destroy all God's love and all his glory. For why should we praise what he has done, if he would be equally praiseworthy for doing quite the opposite? Where would his justice and his wisdom be, if there were only a kind of despotic power, if will took the place of reason, and if, in accordance with the tyrant's definition, what the most powerful wanted was on that account just? Besides which, it seems that any will implies some reason for willing, and that this reason is naturally prior to the will. This is why I also find the claim by some other philosophers[2] completely strange when they say that the eternal truths of metaphysics and of geometry, and therefore also the rules of goodness, justice, and perfection, are only the effects of God's will. In contrast to this it seems to me that they are the consequences of his understanding, and do not depend at all on his will, any more than does his essence.

3. Against those who think that God could have done things better. Nor could I ever endorse the view of some moderns who rashly maintain that what God does is not of the utmost perfection, and that he could have done things much better. For it seems to me that the consequences of this opinion are completely contrary to the glory of God. Just as a lesser evil is relatively good, so a lesser good is relatively evil. To act with fewer perfections than one could is to act imperfectly; to point out to an architect that he could have done his work better is to find fault with it. Again it goes against Holy Scripture, which assures us of the goodness of God's works. Since imperfections go on down to infinity, whatever God's work were like it would always have been good in comparison with some less perfect, if that were enough. But a thing is hardly praiseworthy if it is good only in this way. I believe that one could find an infinity of passages in the Holy Scriptures and the writings of the Holy Fathers which would be in favour of my opinion, whereas hardly any could be found for that of these moderns. In my view theirs is completely unknown in antiquity, and is only founded on the inadequate knowledge we have of the general

---

[1] An early draft of the 'Discourse' makes clear he has *Spinoza in mind (see *Ethics*, pt. 1, app.).

[2] e.g. *Descartes (CSMK ii. 291).

harmony of the universe and of the hidden reasons for God's conduct, which makes us recklessly judge that many things could have been done better. Furthermore, these moderns rely on some clever arguments which are far from sound. They believe that nothing is so perfect that there is nothing more perfect; but this is an error. They also think that in that way they can allow for God's liberty, as if it were not the highest liberty to act perfectly, in accordance with sovereign reason. For to believe that God sometimes acts without any reason for his choice, besides seeming to maintain something that could never happen, is an opinion which is hardly compatible with his glory. For example, let us suppose that God chooses between *A* and *B*, and that he opts for *A* without having any reason for preferring it to *B*. I say that that action of God would at the least not be at all praiseworthy. Because all praise must be grounded in some reason, which, *ex hypothesi*, is absent here. By contrast, I hold that God does nothing for which he doesn't deserve to be glorified.

4. *How the love of God requires complete contentment and acceptance with regard to what he has done.* In my view the general understanding of the great truth that God always acts in the most perfect and the most desirable way possible is the basis for the love that we owe to God above all things. For whoever loves finds contentment in the happiness or perfection of the loved one, and of his actions. To will the same and to dislike the same is true friendship. And I believe that it is difficult to love God properly if one is not disposed to want what he wants, when one has the ability to change it. In fact those who are not satisfied with what God does seem to me to be like malcontent subjects whose intentions are not very different from those of rebels. So in accordance with these principles I maintain that in order to act in conformity with the love of God it is not enough to force oneself to be patient, but we must be truly satisfied with everything that happens to us as a consequence of his will. I mean this acceptance with respect to the past; for we should not be *quietists*[3] about the future, and stupidly wait with folded arms for what God will do, as in the fallacy of what the ancients called *logon aergon* or the argument for idleness. So far as we can judge it, we should act according to the **presumptive will of God*, striving with all our power to contribute to the general good, and in particular to the ornament and perfection of what concerns us, or of what is close to us and is, so to speak, within reach. For if perhaps the way events

---

[3] Those who surrender their desires to God's will.

turn out shows that God did not on this occasion want our good will to have its effect, it does not follow that he did not want us to do what we did. On the contrary, as he is the best of masters, he never asks more than the right intention, and it is for him to know the right time and place for those good intentions to be realized.

5. *What the rules of perfection of divine conduct consist in, and that the simplicity of means is balanced against the richness of ends.* So it is enough to have confidence in God, to believe that he does everything for the best, and that nothing can harm those who love him. But to have particular knowledge of the reasons which led him to choose this arrangement of the universe, to allow sin, to dispense his saving grace in a certain way, is beyond the power of a finite mind, especially when it has not yet attained the delight of seeing God. Some general remarks can nevertheless be made about the workings of providence in the governing of things. We can say that someone who behaves perfectly is like an expert geometer who knows how to find the best construction for a problem; or like a good architect who utilizes the location and the ground for his building in the most advantageous way, leaving nothing discordant, or which doesn't have the beauty of which it is capable; or like a good head of a household, who manages his property in such a way that there is no ground left uncultivated or barren; or like a clever stage-manager who produces his effect by the least awkward means that could be found; or like a learned author, who gets the most reality into the least space he can. Now, the most perfect of all beings, and which occupy the least space, that is to say which obstruct each other the least, are minds, whose perfections are virtues. That is why there is no doubt that the happiness of minds is the main aim of God, which he carries out as far as the general harmony will permit. We will say more about this later. As to the simplicity of God's ways, it properly relates to means, whereas on the other hand, their variety, richness, or abundance relate to ends or effects. The one should be balanced against the other, as the expenses allowed for a building are balanced against its desired size and beauty. It is true that things cost God nothing, less indeed than it costs a philosopher to invent theories as he constructs his imaginary world, since God has only to make a decree for a real world to be produced; but in regard to wisdom, decrees or theories function as costs in proportion to their independence from each other—for reason requires that multiplicity of hypotheses or principles be avoided, rather as the most simple system is always preferred in astronomy.

6. *That God does nothing disorderly, and that it is not even possible to imagine events which are not regular.* God's wishes or actions are usually divided into the ordinary and the extraordinary. But we should remember that God does nothing that is not orderly. Therefore what counts as extraordinary is only so with respect to some particular order established among created things. For as regards the universal order, everything conforms to it. So much is this true that not only does nothing happen in the world which is absolutely irregular, but also we can't even imagine such a thing. Suppose, for example, that someone puts a number of completely haphazard points on paper, as do people who practise the ridiculous art of geomancy.[4] I say that it is possible to find a geometrical line whose notion is constant and uniform according to a certain rule, such that the line passes through all the points, and in the same order as they were drawn. And if someone drew a continuous line which is sometimes straight, sometimes follows a circle, and sometimes of some other kind, it would be possible to find a notion or rule or equation common to all the points on this line in virtue of which these same changes would occur. And, for example, there is no face whose contours are not part of a geometrical line, and which could not be drawn in a single line by some rule-governed movement. But when a rule is very complex, what is conformable to it is seen as irregular. So one can say that in whatever way God had created the world, it would always have been regular and in some general order. But God chose the way that is most perfect, that is to say that which is simultaneously simplest in theories and the richest in phenomena—as would be a geometrical line whose construction was easy yet whose properties and effects are very admirable and very far-reaching. I make use of these comparisons in order to sketch some imperfect picture of the divine wisdom, and to say something which might at least raise our minds to some sort of conception of what cannot be adequately expressed. But I do not at all claim that they explain the great mystery on which the whole universe depends.

7. *That miracles are in conformity with the general order, although they are contrary to subordinate rules. What God wants and what he allows; general and particular will.* Now since nothing can happen which is not orderly, it can be said that miracles are as orderly as natural operations, which are so-called because they conform to certain subordinate rules which we call the nature of things. For we can say that this nature is only a habit of God's, which he can dispense with for a reason stronger than the one which

---

[4] Foretelling the future by means of lines and figures.

moved him to make use of those rules. As for general or particular wills, depending how we want to take it, we can say that God does everything according to his most general will, which is conformable to the most perfect order that he has chosen; or we could also say that he has particular wills, which are exceptions to those subordinate maxims already mentioned. Because the most general of God's laws, which regulates the whole order of the universe, is exceptionless. We can also say that God wants everything which is an object of his particular will; but as for the objects of his general will (such as are actions of other created things, particularly of those which are rational) with which God chooses to concur, we must make a distinction: if the action is good in itself, we can say that God wants it, and sometimes commands it, even if it doesn't happen. But if it is bad in itself, and good only by accident (because what happens afterwards, and especially punishment and reparations, corrects its wickedness, and repays the evil with interest, so that in the end there is more perfection in the whole sequence than if all this evil had not happened), then it must be said that God allows it but not that he wants it, even though he concurs in it because of the laws of nature that he has established and because he sees how to derive a greater good from it.

8. *In order to distinguish between God's actions and those of created things, it is explained what the notion of an individual substance consists in.*[5] It is fairly difficult to distinguish God's actions from those of created things. Some believe that God does everything, and others think that he only conserves the force he has given to created things. We shall see in what follows to what extent either of these things can be said. Now since actions and passions properly belong to individual substances (actions belong to subjects) [see also T13. 9], it is necessary to explain what such a substance is. It is certainly true that when several predicates are attributed to the same subject, and this subject is not attributed to any other, it is called an individual substance. But that is not enough, and such an explanation is only nominal. It is necessary, therefore, to consider what it is to be truly attributed to a certain subject. Now it is obvious that all true predication has some foundation in the nature of things, and when a proposition is not identical, that is to say when the predicate is not expressly included in the subject, it must be virtually included in it. This is what philosophers call *in-esse*, and they say that the predicate *is in* the subject. So the subject term must always involve that of the predicate, in such a way that anyone who understood

---

[5] See App. A for some discussion of Sects. 8 to 11.

the subject notion perfectly would also see that the predicate belongs to it. This being so, we can say that the nature of an individual substance or of a complete being is to have a notion so complete that it is sufficient to include, and to allow the deduction of, all the predicates of the subject to which that notion is attributed. In contrast with this, an accident is a being whose notion does not involve everything which can be attributed to the subject to which that notion is attributed. ⟨Thus the circular shape of Gyges' ring does not contain everything that the notion of that individual ring contains, whereas God sees the individual notion of the ring—such as that it will be swallowed by a fish and nevertheless returned to its master.⟩ Thus, the quality of being a king, which belongs to Alexander the Great, is an abstraction from the subject, and so is not sufficiently determinate to the individual, and does not involve the other qualities of the same subject, nor everything which the notion of that prince includes; whereas God, who sees the individual notion or haecceity [see also T6 n. 2] of Alexander, sees in it at the same time the foundation and the reason for all the predicates which can truly be said to belong to it, such as, for example, that he would conquer Darius and Porus, even to the extent of knowing a priori (and not by experience) whether he died a natural death or by poison, something which we can know only from history. And, moreover, if we consider carefully the interconnectedness of things, we can say that in the soul of Alexander there are for all time remnants of everything that has happened to him, and marks of everything that will happen to him—and even traces of everything that happens in the universe, although it is only God who can recognize them all.

9. *That each singular substance expresses the whole universe in its own way, and that everything that happens to it is included in its notion, with all the circumstances and the whole series of external things.* Several considerable paradoxes follow from this, amongst others that no two substances are entirely alike, and differ only in number.[6] ⟨Another is that if bodies are substances their nature cannot possibly consist only in size, shape, and motion; there must be something else.⟩ What St *Thomas affirms on this point about angels or intelligences ('that here every individual is a lowest species') is true of all substances, provided one takes the specific difference in the way that geometers take it with regard to their figures. Another is that a substance cannot begin except by creation, nor come to an end except by annihilation; that one substance cannot be divided into two, nor one made from

---

[6] For discussion of Leibniz's principle of the identity of indiscernibles, see T15 n. 1.

two, so that there is no natural increase or decrease in the number of substances, although they are often transformed. Moreover, each substance is like a whole world, and like a mirror of God, or indeed of the whole universe, which each one expresses in its own fashion—rather as the same town is differently represented according to the different situations of the person who looks at it. In a way, then, the universe is multiplied as many times as there are substances, and in the same way the glory of God is redoubled by so many quite different representations of his work. In fact we can say that each substance in some way carries the imprint of the infinite wisdom and omnipotence of God, and imitates them in so far as it is capable of it. For it expresses, albeit confusedly, everything which happens in the universe, past, present, and future, and this has some resemblance to an infinite perception or understanding. And as in their turn all other substances express this one and adapt themselves to it, we can say that it extends its power over all the others, in imitation of the Creator's omnipotence.

10. *That the doctrine of substantial forms has some value, but such forms make no difference to phenomena, and should not be used to explain particular effects.* It seems that the ancients, as well as many able men accustomed to deep thought who taught theology and philosophy several centuries ago, and some of whom were also admirable in their holiness, had some understanding of what we have said. That is what led them to introduce and to defend *substantial forms, which are so decried today. But they were not so far from the truth, nor so ridiculous as the common run of our new philosophers suppose. I agree that reference to these forms serves no purpose in a detailed explanation in physics, and should not be used in the explanation of particular phenomena. That is where our *Scholastics went wrong, and the doctors of the past in following their example: they believed they could explain the properties of bodies by referring to forms and qualities, without taking the trouble to find out how they worked: as if we were happy to say that a clock has a time-indicative quality deriving from its form, without considering what all that amounted to. (That might in fact be enough for someone who bought it, provided he left its maintenance to someone else.) But this weakness and misuse of forms should not make us reject something an understanding of which is so vital in metaphysics, to the extent that I maintain that without it we would not properly understand the first principles, and could not raise the mind to the knowledge of incorporeal natures and the wonders of God. However, a geometer does not have to worry about the famous labyrinth of the composition

of the continuum [see T7 n. 2], and a moral philosopher, or even less a jurist or politician, need not trouble himself with the huge difficulties to be found in trying to reconcile free will with God's providence; for the geometer can do all his demonstrations, and the politician can conclude all his deliberations, without going in for these discussions, which are nevertheless necessary and important in philosophy and theology. In the same way a physicist can explain his observations, sometimes using simpler observations he has already made, sometimes geometrical and mechanical demonstrations, without any need for general considerations which belong to another sphere; and if he appeals to the concourse of God, or to some soul, *archée* [*archeus], or other thing of that kind, he is talking nonsense, just as much as someone who in an important practical deliberation went into large-scale reflections about the nature of destiny and our freedom. Indeed men often enough unthinkingly make this mistake, when they bother their heads by thinking fatalistically, and sometimes are even deterred by it from some good resolution, or some important action.

11. *That the reflections of the so-called Scholastic theologians and philosophers should not be completely despised.* I know I am putting forward a considerable paradox in claiming to rehabilitate to some extent the ancient philosophy, and to recall substantial forms when they have been all but banished. ⟨But I do this only hypothetically, in so far as we can say that bodies are substances.⟩ But perhaps I will not be quickly criticized when it is known that I have meditated at length on modern philosophy, that I have devoted a lot of time to physical observations and geometrical demonstrations, and that I was long persuaded of the pointlessness of these entities. But in the end I was obliged to take them up again despite myself, as if by force. This was after researches of my own which made me see that our moderns do not do justice to St Thomas and to other great men of that time, and that in the views of Scholastic philosophers and theologians there is much more of value than people suppose, provided they are used correctly and in their proper place. In fact I am convinced that if some exact and thoughtful mind took the trouble to clarify and digest their thoughts, in the way the analytic geometers do, he would find a considerable treasure of many very important and completely demonstrable truths.

12. *That the notions which make up extension involve something imaginary, and cannot constitute the substance of body.* But, to return to the thread of our

reflections, I believe that anyone who thinks about the nature of sub-stance, as I have explained it above, will find ⟨either that in metaphysical strictness bodies are not substances (as indeed was the view of the *Platonists), or⟩ that the whole nature of body does not consist solely in extension, that is to say in size, shape, and motion [see TT5. 2; 6. 18, 19]. We must also accept that there is something which has some resemblance to a soul, and which is commonly called a substantial form—even though it has no effect on phenomena, any more than does the soul of an animal, if it has one. It can in fact be proved that the notions of size, of shape, and of motion are not as distinct as we imagine, and that they involve some-thing imaginary and relative to our perceptions, as also (but much more so) do colour, heat, and other similar qualities, which we can doubt are really there in the nature of external things. This is why qualities of this kind could never constitute a substance. Moreover, if there is no principle of identity in bodies other than those we have just mentioned, then a body can never persist for more than a moment. However, the souls and sub-stantial forms of other bodies are quite different from intelligent souls, the only ones which know their own actions, and which not only do not natu-rally come to an end, but in fact always retain the foundation of the knowl-edge of what they are. This is what makes them alone liable to punishment and reward, and what makes them citizens of the republic of the universe, of which God is the monarch. It also follows that all other creatures must serve them, of which we will speak more fully later.

13. *That since the individual notion of each person involves once and for all everything that will ever happen to him, we can see in that notion the a priori proofs or reasons for the truth of every event, or why one thing happens rather than another. But although certain, these truths are nevertheless contingent, for they are based on the free will of God and of created things. It is true that there are always reasons for their choices, but those reasons incline without necessitating.*[7]

---

[7] For the notion of inclination without necessitation, see also Sect. 30. Elsewhere Leibniz says, 'I am of the opinion that the will is always more inclined towards the direction it takes, but that it is never under any necessity to take it. It is certain that it will go in that direction, but it is not necessary that it will. This is on the model of the famous saying "the stars incline but do not necessitate", although here the case is not exactly the same. For the event towards which the stars tend (to speak as ordinary people do, as if there were some basis to astrology) does not always come about, whereas the direction towards which the will is more inclined never fails to be taken' (*Theodicy*: GP vi. 126–7).

But before going any further, we must try to resolve a great difficulty which can arise from the foundations we have laid down. We have said that the notion of an individual substance involves, once and for all, everything that will ever happen to it; and that in considering that notion one can see in it everything that can ever be truly said of it, just as we can see in the nature of a circle all the properties that can be deduced from it. But it seems that this means that the difference between contingent and necessary truths will be destroyed, and that there will no longer be any room for human freedom, and an absolute fate will reign over all our actions as well as over all the rest of the events in the world. To this I reply that we have to make a distinction between what is certain and what is necessary. Everyone agrees that future contingents are definite, since God can foresee them; but this is not to say that they are necessary. But (it will be said) if some conclusion can be infallibly deduced from a definition or notion, it will be necessary. And here we are maintaining that everything which happens to a person is already included implicitly in that person's nature or notion, just as its properties are in the definition of a circle; so the difficulty still remains. In order to settle it decisively, I say that connection or sequencing is of two kinds. One is absolutely necessary, and its contrary implies a contradiction; such deduction pertains to eternal truths, such as those of geometry. The other is necessary only *ex hypothesi*, and, so to speak, accidentally; this is contingent in itself, and the contrary does not imply a contradiction. This kind of connection is founded not on completely pure ideas and on God's understanding alone, but also on his free decrees, and on the history of the universe. Let us take an example. Since Julius Caesar will become lifelong dictator and master of the Republic, and will overthrow the freedom of the Romans, these actions are comprised in his notion; because we are assuming that it is the nature of this kind of perfect notion of a subject to include everything, so that the predicate will be involved in it, *ut possit inesse subjecto* [so that it can be in the subject]. We could say that it is not because of that notion or idea that he will perform the action, since that notion applies to him only because God knows everything. But, it will be insisted, his nature or form corresponds to that notion, and since God has imposed this character on him, it is thereafter necessary for him to comply with it. I could reply to that by instancing the case of future contingents—they have as yet no reality except in God's understanding and will, yet since God has therein given them that form in advance, they will nevertheless have to correspond to it. But I prefer to resolve difficulties rather than excuse them by the example of other similar difficulties, and what I am going to say will serve to clarify the one case as well as the other. So it is here that we have to apply the distinction between different kinds of connnection. I say that what happens in accordance with its antecedents is definite, but is not necessary; if anyone did the contrary, he would not be doing anything impossible in itself, although it is (*ex hypothesi*) impossible that it should happen. For if some person were capable of completing the whole demonstration by means of which he could prove this connection of the subject (which is Caesar) with the predicate (which is his successful enterprise), he would then show that the future dictatorship of Caesar had its foundation in his notion or nature, that a reason can be found there why he resolved to cross the Rubicon rather than stop, and why he won rather than lost the day at Pharsalus: that it was rational and therefore definite that this would happen, but not that it is necessary in itself, or that the contrary implies a contradiction. In a similar way it is rational and definite that God will always do the best, although what is less perfect implies no contradiction. For we would find that the demonstration of this predicate of Caesar's is not as absolute as those of numbers or of geometry—it presupposes the sequence of things that God has freely chosen and which is founded on God's primary free decision, which is always to do what is most perfect, and on the decision God made (as a consequence of that primary one) with regard to human nature, which is that man will always (though freely) do what seems the best. Now, any truth which is founded on this sort of decision is contingent, even though it is certain, because decisions in no way alter the possibility of things. And, as I have already said, although God certainly always chooses the best, that does not stop something less perfect from being and remaining possible in itself, even though it will not happen—for it is not its impossibility but its imperfection which makes him reject it. But nothing is necessary if its opposite is possible. We will, therefore, be in a position to resolve these kinds of difficulty, however great they may seem (and in fact they are no less serious for every one else who has ever dealt with this matter), so long as we keep fully in mind that all these contingent propositions have reasons why they are so rather than otherwise—or alternatively (and this is the same thing), that they have a priori proofs of their truth which make them certain, and which show that the connection of the subject with the predicate in these propositions has its foundation in the nature of each. But they do not have necessary demonstrations, because those reasons are only based on the principle of contingency or of the existence of things, that is, on what is or what appears the best among a number of equally possible things. By contrast, necessary truths are founded on the principle of contradiction, and on the possibility or impossibility of essences themselves, without any regard to the free will of God or of created things.[8]

(14.) *God produces a variety of substances according to the different views he has of the universe, and by God's intervention the particular nature of each substance results in a correspondence between what happens to one and what happens to all the others, without their directly acting on one another.* Having come to know something of what the nature of substances consists in, we must try to explain their dependence on one another, and their actions and passions. Now, firstly, it is quite clear that created substances depend on God, who conserves them and indeed who produces them continuously by a kind of emanation, just as we produce our thoughts. For God, so to speak, turns on all sides and considers in all ways the general system of phenomena which he has found it good to produce in order to manifest his glory. And as he considers all the faces of the world in all possible ways—for there is no aspect which escapes his omniscience—the result of each view of the universe, as looked at from a certain position, is, if God finds it good to actualize his thoughts and to produce it, a substance which expresses the universe in conformity with that view. And as God's view is always correct, so too are our perceptions; it is our judgements which are our own and in which we go wrong. We said above, and it follows from what we have said here, that each substance is like a separate world, independent of every other thing except God. So all our phenomena, that is to say everything which can ever happen to us, can only be consequences of our being. These phenomena maintain a certain order in conformity with our nature, or with the world which is in us, so to speak, and we are therefore able to make observations which are useful for guiding our conduct, and which are justified by the favourable outcome of future phenomena, so that often we can judge the future by the past without falling into error. We could therefore say that these phenomena are true, without concerning ourselves with whether they are external to us, or whether others perceive them too. Nevertheless, it is certainly true that the perceptions or expressions of all substances correspond with one another in such a way that each one, by carefully following certain principles or laws that it has observed, finds itself in agreement with others which do the same—just as when several people have agreed to meet together in some place on a certain pre-arranged day, they can in fact do so if they choose. Now

---

[8] For the 'principle of contingency' and the 'principle of contradiction', see Introduction, Sect. 7 n. 30.

although they all express the same phenomena, their expressions do not therefore have to be perfectly alike; it is enough that they are correlated— just as a number of spectators believe they are seeing the same thing, and do in fact understand each other, even though each one sees and speaks according to his point of view. Now it is God alone (from whom all individuals continuously emanate, and who sees the universe not only as they see it, but also completely differently from them all) who is the cause of this correspondence in their phenomena, and brings it about that what is particular to one is public to all. Otherwise there would be no connection between them. It can therefore be said, in a way, and in a good sense, although one far from common usage, that one particular substance never acts on another particular substance any more than it is acted on by it. For consider: what happens to each one is only a consequence of its idea or complete notion and nothing else, because that idea already involves all predicates or events, and expresses the whole universe. In reality nothing can happen to us other than thoughts and perceptions, and all our future thoughts and perceptions are only the consequences (albeit contingent) of our preceding thoughts and perceptions. So if I were capable of considering distinctly everything which is happening or appearing to me now, I would be able to see in it everything which will ever happen or appear to me for all time. And it would not be prevented, and would still happen to me, even if everything outside me were destroyed, so long as there remained only God and me. But since we attribute what we perceive in a certain manner to other things, as though they were causes acting on us, we must consider the basis of this judgement, and what truth there is in it.

15. *The action of one finite substance on another consists only in an increase in the degree of its expression combined with a decrease in that of the other, God having formed them in advance in such a way that they fit together.* But without entering into a lengthy discussion it is enough for now to reconcile metaphysical language with practice by saying that we rightly attribute more to ourselves those phenomena which we express more perfectly, and we attribute to other substances what each of them expresses best. So a substance which is infinitely extended, in so far as it expresses everything, comes to be limited by its more or less perfect manner of expression. In this way, therefore, we can understand how substances obstruct or limit one another, and consequently we can say that in this sense they act on one another, and are obliged to fit in, so to speak, with each other. For it can happen that a change which enhances the expression of one diminishes

that of another. Now, the virtue of a particular substance is to express the glory of God well, and it is to the extent that it does so that it is less limited. And each thing, when it exercises its virtue or power, that is to say when it is active, changes for the better, and extends itself to the extent that it is active. So when a change occurs which affects several substances (and actually all changes touch them all) I believe we can say that one which thereby immediately passes to a higher degree of perfection or to a more perfect expression exercises its power and *acts*; and one which passes to a lesser degree shows its weakness and *is acted on*. I hold also that every action of a substance which has perception signifies some *pleasure*, and every passivity some *sadness*, and vice versa. It can easily happen, nevertheless, that a present advantage is destroyed by a greater evil which follows. And that is why we can sin when we are active or exerting our power and finding pleasure in it.

16. *God's extraordinary concourse*[9] *is included in what our essence expresses, for this expression extends to everything. But it goes beyond the forces of our nature or of our distinct expression, which are finite and follow certain subordinate rules.* It now remains for us only to explain how it is possible that God sometimes has influence on men or on other substances by an extraordinary or miraculous concourse, given that as everything that happens to them is merely a consequence of their nature, it would seem as if nothing extraordinary or miraculous can ever happen to them. But we must remember what we said above about the place of miracles in the universe: that they always conform to the universal law of the general order, even though they are above subordinate rules. And since every person and every substance is like a little world which expresses the larger world, we can also say that such an extraordinary action by God on a substance is none the less miraculous, even though it is comprised in the general order of the universe in so far as it is expressed by the essence or individual notion of that substance. This is why if we include in our nature everything that it expresses, nothing is supernatural to it, because it extends to everything; an effect always expresses its cause, and God is the true cause of substances. But what our nature expresses more perfectly belongs to it more particularly,

[9] The notion of God's concourse with the world is derived from Scholastic theology. His ordinary concourse is, as in Sect. 14, simply his bringing into existence and conserving created things, each with their own natures which they express. His extraordinary or miraculous concourse results in 'supernatural' occurrences which go beyond those natures. For some reading on 'miracles', see T10 n. 1.

since, as I have just explained, it is in that that its power consists, and that it is limited. Therefore there are many things which are beyond the powers of our nature, and even beyond those of all limited natures. Consequently, in order to speak more clearly I say that miracles and the extraordinary concourse of God have the peculiarity that they cannot be foreseen by the reasoning of any created mind, however enlightened, because the distinct comprehension of the general order is beyond them all. By contrast, everything which is called natural depends on less general rules that created things can understand. So in order that our words should be as blameless as their meaning, it will be as well to link certain ways of speech with certain thoughts: that which includes all that we express can be called our essence, and in so far as it expresses our union with God himself, it has no limits, and there is nothing beyond it. But what is limited in us can be called our nature or our power, and in this respect what is beyond the nature of any created substance is supernatural.

17. *An example of a subordinate rule of natural law, which shows that God always systematically conserves the same force, but not, contrary to the *Cartesians and many others, the same quantity of motion.*[10] I have already often mentioned the subordinate rules, or laws of nature, and I think it would be good to give an example. Our new philosophers standardly make use of the famous rule that God always conserves the same quantity of motion in the world. In fact it is very plausible, and in days gone by I used to think it was indubitable. But I have since realized where the mistake lies. It is that M. *Descartes and many other able mathematicians have believed that the quantity of motion, that is to say the speed times the size of the moving thing, is exactly the same as the moving force; or, geometrically speaking, that forces are directly proportional to speeds and bodies. Now it is rational that the same force should always be conserved in the universe. And when we look carefully at the phenomena we can clearly see that there is no place for perpetual mechanical motion, because otherwise the force of a machine, which is always slightly diminished by friction and so soon has to come to an end, would be restored, and consequently would increase of itself without any new impulse from outside. We also observe that a body's force is diminished only to the extent that it gives some of it to adjacent bodies, or to its own parts in so far as they have their own independent motion. Therefore, they thought that what can be said of force can also be said of quantity of motion. But in order to show the difference, I make an *assumption*: that a

[10] See App. B.

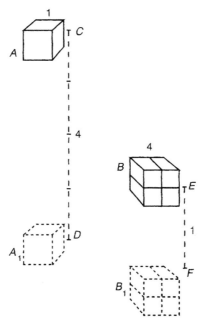

Fig. 1.1.

body falling from a certain height acquires enough force to rise back up again, if its direction carries it that way, unless it is prevented. For example, a pendulum would raise itself back to exactly the height from which it had fallen, if the resistance of the air and various other little obstacles did not slightly diminish the force it had acquired. I shall also make this *assumption*: that as much force is necessary to raise a one-pound body A to the height of four fathoms (CD), as to raise a four-pound body B to the height of one fathom (EF) (see Fig. 1.1). All this is accepted by our new philosophers. It is clear, then, that body A, having fallen from the height CD, has acquired exactly as much force as has body B which has fallen from the height EF. For body B, when it has reached F, has the force to climb back up to E (by the first assumption), and so has the force to carry a four-pound body (its own body, that is) to the height of one fathom (EF); and, similarly, the body A, when it has reached D, has the force to climb back to C, and so has the force to carry a one-pound body (its own body, that is) to the height of four fathoms (CD). Therefore (by the second assumption) the forces of these two bodies are equal. Let us now see whether the quantities of motion are the same on the one side as on the other. But here one will be surprised to find that there is a very great difference. For it has been demonstrated by *Galileo that the speed acquired in the fall CD is double the speed acquired in the fall EF, although the height is quadruple. So let us multiply body A, which is equal to 1, by its speed, which is 2, and the product, or the quantity of motion, will be 2; on the other hand, multiply the body B, which is equal to 4, by its speed, which is 1, and the product or the quantity of motion will be 4. Therefore the quantity of motion of body A at the point D is half the quantity of motion of body B at the point F, and yet their forces are equal. There is a clear difference, therefore, between quantity of motion and force—which is what we were trying to show. We can see from this that *force* should be estimated by the size of the effect it can produce—for example, by the height to which a heavy body of a particular size and type can be raised, which is very different from the speed that can be given to it. In order to give it twice the speed, more than double the force is required. Nothing could be simpler than this proof, and M. Descartes only fell into error here because he put too much trust in his thinking, even when it was insufficiently mature. But I am astonished that his followers have not recognized this mistake since. And I am afraid they are beginning gradually to resemble some of the *Peripatetics whom they deride, and that they are getting into the habit, like them, of consulting the books of their master rather than reason and nature.

18. *The distinction between force and quantity of motion is important. Amongst other things it shows that in order to explain corporeal phenomena we must appeal to metaphysical considerations apart from extension.* This consideration of force as distinct from quantity of motion is of some importance, not only in physics and in mechanics for discovering the true laws of nature and rules of motion—and indeed for correcting several practical errors which have crept into the writings of some able mathematicians—but also in metaphysics for understanding its principles better. For motion, if one considers only what it precisely and formally comprises (that is to say, change of place), is not an entirely real thing, and when several bodies change their relative positions, it is not possible by consideration of those changes alone to determine to which of them motion or rest should be attributed—as I could show geometrically, if I wanted to break off to do it. But the force or immediate cause behind those changes is something which is more real, and there is enough of a basis for attributing it to one body rather than to another; and it is, moreover, only by this that we can know to which one the motion better belongs. Now, this force is something different from size, shape, and motion, and from that we can see that not everything that we can conceive in bodies is a matter of extension and its modifications, as our moderns persuade themselves. So we are again

obliged to reintroduce certain beings or forms which the moderns have banished. And it becomes more and more apparent that although all particular natural phenomena can be explained mathematically or mechanically by those who understand them, the general principles of corporeal nature and even of mechanics are nevertheless metaphysical rather than geometrical, and relate to certain indivisible forms or natures, as the causes of appearances, rather than to corporeal or extended mass. And this is a reflection which is able to reconcile the mechanical philosophy of the moderns with the circumspection of some intelligent, well-intentioned people who fear, with some reason, that we might be endangering piety by moving too far away from immaterial beings.

19. *The usefulness of final causes in physical science.* As I do not like to think badly of people, I am not criticizing our new philosophers for attempting to expel final causes from physics, but I have nevertheless to confess that the consequences of this view seem to me dangerous—particularly when it is combined with the one I refuted at the beginning of this discourse, which seems to go as far as to reject them altogether, as if God in acting did not intend any end or good, or as if the good were not the object of his will. I hold that, on the contrary, that is just where we should look for the principle of all existent things and of the laws of nature, because God always aims at the best and the most perfect. I am quite willing to admit that we are liable to go wrong when we try to determine God's ends or counsels, but that is only when we want to tie them down to some particular design, thinking he had only some single thing in view, whereas he has regard for everything simultaneously. So, for example, it is a great mistake to think that God made the world only for us, although it is true that he made it all for us, and that there is nothing in the universe which does not concern us and which is not also adjusted in view of the concern he has for us, in accordance with the principles stated above. So when we see some good effect or some perfection which happens or which follows from the works of God, we can certainly say that it was God's aim, because he does nothing by accident. He is not like us, who sometimes fail to do what is good. This is why, so far from being mistaken in this—like over-enthusiastic political observers who attribute too much subtlety to the designs of princes, or like commentators who see too much learning in their author—one could never attribute too much consideration to this infinite wisdom. There is no subject in which there is less fear of error, so long as we only make affirmations, and provided we avoid negative propositions which limit the designs of God. Everyone who sees the admirable structure of animals is led to rec-

ognize the wisdom of the Creator of things, and I advise those who have some feeling of piety, and indeed of true philosophy, to avoid the expressions of certain so-called free-thinkers who say that we see because we happen to have eyes, but not that the eyes were made for seeing. If one seriously maintains these views which attribute everything to the necessity of matter or to some kind of chance (although either of these will seem ridiculous to those who have understood what I have explained above), one will find it difficult to be able to recognize an intelligent author of nature. For effects must correspond to their causes, and indeed are known best by the knowledge of their causes; so it is irrational to introduce a sovereign intelligence which organizes things, and then, instead of its wisdom, to use only the properties of matter to explain phenomena. It would be as though, in explaining a great prince's victory in taking some important place, a historian were to say it was because small particles of gunpowder, released by the touch of a spark, went off with a speed capable of impelling a hard, heavy body against the walls of the place, while the branches of the particles of copper in the cannon were so well interlaced as not to be pulled apart by that speed—instead of showing how the conqueror's foresight made him choose the appropriate time and means, and how his power overcame all obstacles.

20. *A memorable passage by Socrates in Plato's 'Phaedo', against over-materialist philosophers.* This reminds me of a beautiful passage by Socrates in Plato's *Phaedo*, which agrees wonderfully well with my views on this point, and seems to have been expressly written against our over-materialist philosophers. This agreement made me want to translate it, although it is a little long. Perhaps this sample will stimulate someone to make available to us many other beautiful and solid thoughts to be found in the writings of this famous author.[11]

21. *If mechanical rules depended only on geometry and not on metaphysics, the phenomena would be quite different.* Now since the wisdom of God has always been recognized in the detail of the mechanical structure of particular bodies, it must clearly also be shown in the general economy of the world and in the constitution of the laws of nature. And that is clearly so, because the counsels of this wisdom are discernible in the general laws of motion. For if bodies were only extended masses, and motion were only change of place, and if everything should and could be deduced by a geometrical necessity from these definitions alone, it would follow, as I have

[11] In a marginal note Leibniz wrote, 'To be inserted here is the passage from Plato's *Phaedo* [97B–99C] in which Socrates mocks Anaxagoras, who introduces mind but makes no use of it.'

shown elsewhere, that the smallest body, meeting the largest body at rest, would give it the same speed as it itself had, without losing any of its own. And a number of other such rules would have to be admitted, completely contrary to the formation of a system. But the decision by the divine wisdom to conserve always the same total force and direction has provided one. In fact I find that many natural effects can be demonstrated twice over, firstly by reference to efficient causes, and again by reference to final causes—for example, by appealing to God's decision to produce his effect always in the easiest and the most determinate ways (as I have shown elsewhere in explaining the rules of reflection and refraction, and about which I shall say more presently).

22. *Reconciliation of two methods, one of which works through final causes, the other through efficient causes, in order to satisfy both those who explain nature mechanically and those who appeal to incorporeal natures.* It is good to point this out, in order to reconcile those who hope to give a mechanical explanation of the formation of the basic tissue of an animal, and the whole mechanism of its parts, with those who explain that same structure through final causes. Both are good, both can be useful, not only for admiring the ingenuity of the great workman, but also for discovering something useful in physics and in medicine. Authors who follow these different routes should not abuse each other. For I see that those who believe in explaining the beauty of divine anatomy laugh at the others, who think that an apparently fortuitous motion of particular fluids could have produced such a beautiful variety of limbs, and they call such people rash and profane. They, on the other hand, call the others simple and superstitious, and say they are like the ancients who took physical scientists to be impious when they held that it was not Jupiter who produced thunder but some kind of matter in the clouds. It would be best to combine the two approaches, because—if a mundane comparison may be permitted—I recognize and praise a workman's skill not only by showing what designs he had in making the parts of his machine, but also by explaining the tools he used to make each part, especially when those tools are simple and ingeniously contrived. God is such a skilful worker that he could produce a machine a thousand times more ingenious than those of our bodies, using only various quite simple fluids that were expressly produced, so that ordinary laws of nature were all it took to organize them in the appropriate way to produce such an admirable effect. But it is also true that this would not be so if God were not the designer of nature. However, I find that the way of efficient causes, while in fact being deeper and in some way more

immediate and a priori, is correspondingly rather difficult when it comes to detail; and I believe that our philosophers are for the most part still far removed from it. By contrast, the way of final causes is easier, but is nevertheless frequently of use in discovering important and useful truths, truths which one would take a long time to find by the other, more physical route. Anatomy provides important examples of this; and *Snell, the first formulator of the rules of refraction, would have been a long time finding them, if he had tried first to find out how light is formed. But evidently he followed the method which the ancients used for catoptrics,[12] which is in fact that of final causes. For, by looking for the easiest way to get a ray from one given point to another by reflection in a given plane (on the assumption that this is the way nature was designed), they discovered the equality of the angles of incidence and of reflection—as we can see in a little treatise by *Heliodorus of Larissa and elsewhere. M. Snell, as I believe, and after him (although without knowing about him) M. *Fermat, have more ingeniously applied this to refraction. Since rays in the same media observe the same ratio of sines as that between the resistances of the media, this turns out to be the easiest, or at least the most determinate route to get from a given point in one medium to a given point in another. The demonstration of this same theorem which M. *Descartes tried to give by the way of efficient causes is far from being as good. There is at least room to suspect that he would never have found it by his method if he had not been told in Holland of Snell's discovery [see also T5. 24].[13]

23. *Returning to immaterial substances, it is explained how God acts on the mind's understanding, and whether we always have an idea of what we are thinking about.* I have thought it appropriate to stress to some extent these considerations about final causes, incorporeal natures, and an intelligent cause in relation to bodies, in order to show their usefulness even in physical science and mathematics. On the one hand I hope this will clear the mechanical philosophy of the profanity it has been charged with, and on the other I hope it will raise the minds of our philosophers from purely material considerations to more noble contemplation. It is now time to return from bodies to immaterial natures, and in particular to minds, and to say something about the way in which God chooses to enlighten and to act on them. There is no doubt that here too there are certain laws

---

[12] The part of optics which deals with reflection as by a mirror.

[13] For a discussion of Leibniz's thinking about the appeal to final causes in optics see Buchdahl (1969: 425–34), Hirschmann (1988). For Descartes, Snell, and Fermat in this connection Buchdahl (1969: 136–47), Dugas (1955: 254–9), Sabra (1967: 4–5), and CSMK i. 156–64.

of nature, of which I will be able to speak more fully elsewhere. For the moment it will be enough to say a little about ideas—as to whether we see all things in God, and how God is our light. Now it is appropriate to point out that misusing ideas gives rise to many errors. For, when we reason about something, we imagine we have an idea of it, and on this basis some ancient and modern philosophers have grounded a very imperfect proof of God. Thus, they say, it is certain that I have an idea of God or of a perfect being, because I can think about him, and one cannot think without an idea. Now the idea of this being involves all perfections, and existence is one of them—consequently, it exists. But we often think of impossible chimeras—for example, of the greatest speed, or the largest number, or the meeting of a conchoid with its base or rule—so this reasoning will not do. In this sense, therefore, we can say that there are true and false ideas, according to whether the thing in question is possible or not. And we can boast of having an idea of the thing only when we are assured of its possibility. So the above argument only proves that God necessarily exists if he is possible. It is indeed an excellent privilege of the divine nature to need only its possibility or essence in order actually to exist—exactly what is called an *ens a se* [*ens per se*].[14]

24. *What clear and obscure, distinct and confused, adequate and inadequate, intuitive and suppositive knowledge are; nominal, real, causal, and essential definition.* To understand the nature of ideas better we must say something about the different kinds of knowledge. When I can recognize one thing among others without being able to say what its differences or properties consist in, my knowledge is *confused*. In this way we sometimes know *clearly*, without being in any way in doubt, whether a poem or a painting is good or bad, because there is a certain *je ne sais quoi* which pleases or offends us. But when I can explain the evidence I am using, the knowledge is *distinct*. An assayer's knowledge is like this; he can distinguish true from false gold by means of certain tests or marks which make up the definition of gold. But distinct knowledge has different levels, because the notions which enter into the definition usually require definition themselves, and are known only confusedly. But when everything which enters into a definition or an item of distinct knowledge is known distinctly, right down to the primary notions, I call the knowledge *adequate*. And when my mind simultaneously and distinctly understands all the primary ingredients of a notion, it has *intuitive* knowledge of it. This is very rare; most human

[14] Leibniz has Descartes's ontological proof of the existence of God in mind here (see Introduction, Sect. 7).

knowledge is only confused, or *suppositive*. It is also important to distinguish *nominal* and *real* definitions: I call it a *nominal definition* when it can still be doubted whether the notion defined is possible; for example, if I say that an endless spiral is a solid line whose parts are congruent or could be placed one on top of another, anyone who does not already know from elsewhere what an endless spiral is can doubt whether such a line is possible—even though this is in fact a reciprocal property of an endless spiral, because other lines whose parts are congruent (and the circumference of a circle and a straight line are the only ones) are planar, that is to say they can be described in a plane. This shows that any reciprocal property can serve as a nominal definition; but when the property shows the thing's possibility, it makes a *real definition*. Now in so far as we have only a nominal definition, we cannot be sure of the consequences that we draw from it, because if it conceals some contradiction or impossibility, inconsistent conclusions could be drawn from it. This is why truths certainly do not depend on names, and are certainly not arbitrary, as some new philosophers have believed.[15] Finally, there is also a considerable difference between different kinds of real definition; for when possibility is proved only by experience, the definition is merely real and nothing more: as in the definition of quicksilver, whose possibility we know because we know that there is in fact a body which is an extremely heavy, yet quite volatile, fluid. But when the proof of the possibility is a priori, the definition is both *real* and *causal*, as when it contains the possible generation of the thing. And when it takes the analysis to its limits or as far as primary notions, without assuming anything which itself requires an a priori proof of its possibility, the definition is perfect, or *essential*.

25. *In what cases our knowledge is combined with the contemplation of an idea.* Now it is obvious that we have no idea of a notion which is impossible. And when our knowledge is merely *suppositive*, we do not contemplate the idea even if we have it. For such a notion is known only in the same way as notions which involve a concealed impossibility, and if it is in fact possible, we cannot learn that it is through that way of knowing. For example, when I think of a thousand, or of a chiliagon, I often do so without contemplating the idea—as when I say that a thousand is ten times a hundred, without bothering to think what ten and a hundred are, because I *suppose* I know, and do not see any need at the moment to stop to think about it. So it can easily happen, and indeed quite often does, that I am mistaken about a notion which I suppose or believe I understand, when in fact it is

[15] Hobbes, *De Corpore* (1655), 1. 3. 7–9.

impossible, or at least incompatible with the others to which I join it; and whether I am mistaken or not, this suppositive manner of conceiving is the same. It is therefore only when our knowledge of confused notions is *clear*, or when our knowledge of distinct notions is *intuitive*, that we see their complete ideas. ⟨However, we actually have in our mind all possible ideas, and indeed in a confused way we think of them all the time.⟩

26. *That we have within us all ideas; Plato's doctrine of reminiscence.* In order properly to understand what an idea is, we must avoid an equivocation. Many people take an idea to be the form or differentia of our thoughts. On this view we have the idea in our mind only when we are thinking of it, and whenever we think of it again we have different but similar ideas of the same thing. But it seems that others take ideas to be immediate objects of our thought, or permanent forms which remain even when we are not contemplating them. In fact our soul does always have in it the ability to represent to itself any nature or form when the occasion for thinking of it arises. And I believe that that ability of our soul, in so far as it expresses some nature, form, or essence, is properly called an idea of the thing, and it is in us, and is always in us, whether we are thinking of the thing or not. For our soul expresses God and the universe, and all essences as well as all existences. This fits in with my principles, for nothing naturally enters our mind from outside, and it is a bad habit of ours to think of our soul as receiving messenger species, or as if it had doors and windows. We have all these forms in our mind and indeed always have had; because the mind always expresses all its future thoughts, and is already thinking confusedly of everything it will ever think clearly. And there is nothing we could ever learn of which we do not already have in our mind the idea, which is like the matter out of which the thought is formed. This is what *Plato understood so well, when he put forward his doctrine of *reminiscence*, which is very sound, provided we take it in the right way and remove the mistake about pre-existence, and do not imagine that the soul must already at some other time have distinctly known and thought about what it learns and thinks about now. He also confirmed his opinion by a beautiful experiment.[16] He introduces a small boy whom he gradually leads to very difficult geometrical truths about incommensurables, without telling him anything, only asking him a sequence of appropriate questions. This shows us that our souls have virtual knowledge of all these things, and that to grasp these truths they need only to have their *attention* drawn to them. Consequently, they have at least the ideas on which those truths depend,

[16] As at *Meno*, 82B ff.

and we can even say that they already possess these truths, if we consider them as relations between ideas.

27. *How our soul can be compared with a blank tablet, and in what way our notions come from the senses.* *Aristotle preferred to compare our souls to as yet blank tablets which could be written on, and he held that there is nothing in our understanding which does not come from the senses.[17] This squares better with popular notions, as is usually the case with Aristotle; whereas Plato goes deeper. However, these traditional or practical forms of speech are acceptable in ordinary usage—just as we see that people who follow *Copernicus still say that the sun rises and sets. In fact I often find that we can give them a good meaning, according to which there is nothing false in them. As I have already remarked, there is a way in which it can truly be said that particular substances act on each other, and, in this same sense (because some external things contain or express more particularly the reasons which determine our soul to certain thoughts), we can also say that we receive knowledge from outside by the agency of the senses. But when we are concerned with the exactness of metaphysical truths, it is important to recognize that the extent and independence of our soul go infinitely further than ordinary people imagine, although in the ordinary practice of life we only attribute to it what is most obviously perceived, and what belongs to us in a particular manner, because there is no point in going any further. It would nevertheless be good to choose specific terms for each sense so as to avoid equivocation. So those expressions which are in our soul, whether conceived or not, can be called *ideas*; but those that are conceived or formed can be called *notions*, or *concepts*. But in whatever way we take it, it is always false to say that all our notions come from the senses that are called external. For the notion I have of myself and of my thoughts, and therefore of being, substance, action, identity, and many others, all come from an internal experience.

28. *God is the only immediate object of our perceptions which exists outside us, and he alone is our light.* Now in strict metaphysical truth there is no external cause which acts on us, except God alone, and he alone communicates himself to us directly in virtue of our continual dependence. It follows that there is no other external object which touches our soul and which directly excites our perceptions. Furthermore, in our soul we have ideas of all things

---

[17] See *De Anima*, 430ª1. At least in this verbal form the doctrine that 'there is nothing in our understanding which does not come from the senses' does not occur in Aristotle and derives from the Scholastics.

only because of the continual action of God upon us: in other words, because all effects express their causes, and so the essence of our soul is a particular expression, imitation, or image of God's essence, thought, and will, and of all the ideas which are comprised in it. So we can say that God alone is our immediate external object, and that we see all things through him. For example, when we see the sun and the stars, it is God who gave us and who conserves in us their ideas, and who by his ordinary concurrence determines us actually to think of them when our senses are suitably disposed in accordance with the laws he has established. God is the sun and the light of souls, the light enlightening every man that comes into this world;[18] and this is not a new opinion. I remember having remarked on other occasions that in addition to Holy Scripture and the Holy Fathers, who have always been more for Plato than for Aristotle, in the time of the Scholastics, many people held that God is the light of the soul, or, as they used to say, 'the active intellect of the rational soul'. The *Averroists took this in the wrong way, but others (among whom I think are *William of St Amour, and several mystical theologians) have taken it in a manner worthy of God and capable of raising the soul to knowledge of its true good.

29. *However, we think directly through our own ideas and not through God's.* However, I do not share the opinion of some able philosophers who seem to maintain that our ideas themselves are not in any way in us, but are in God.[19] In my view this comes from not yet having sufficiently thought about what we have explained here about substances, and about the total extent and independence of our soul, which mean that it contains everything that happens to it, and expresses God, and with him all possible and actual beings, as an effect expresses its cause. And it is in fact inconceivable that I should think with someone else's ideas. And what is more, the soul must actually be affected in a certain way when it thinks of something, and it must have in it in advance not only the passive power of being affected in this way (which is already completely determinate), but also an active power in virtue of which its nature has always contained evidence of the future production of this thought, and dispositions to produce it at the right time. And all this already incorporates the idea comprised in the thought.

30. *How God inclines our soul without necessitating it; that we have no right to complain; that we should not ask why Judas sinned, since that free act is included in his notion; we should only ask why Judas the sinner was admitted into existence*

---

[18] John 1: 9.   [19] Mal. 1674–5, 3. 2. 6.

in preference to some other possible people. Original imperfection or limitation, prior to sin; the different levels of grace. As regards God's action on the human will, there are a number of quite difficult points which it would be tedious to pursue here. Nevertheless, this in outline is what we can say. In his ordinary concourse with our actions, God only follows the laws which he has established; that is to say, he continually conserves and continually produces our being in such a way that our thoughts occur spontaneously and freely in the order laid down by the notion of our individual substance, in which they could be foreseen from all eternity. Furthermore, he determines our will to choose what appears the best, yet without necessitating it. This is in virtue of his decision that our will should always tend to the apparent good, thus expressing or imitating the will of God in certain particular areas, with respect to which this apparent good always has some truth in it. For speaking absolutely, our will is in a state of indifference, in so far as indifference is opposed to necessity, and it has the power to do otherwise, or to suspend its action altogether, both alternatives being and remaining possible. It is therefore up to the soul to take precautions against being surprised by what appears to it by a firm resolution to reflect, and in certain situations not to act or judge without mature and thorough deliberation. It is true, however, and indeed it is certain from all eternity, that a particular soul will not make use of this power on such and such an occasion. But whose fault is that? Does it have anyone to blame but itself? For all such complaints after the fact are unjust if they would have been unjust before it. But would it have been fair for this soul, just before sinning, to complain of God, as if he were determining it to sin? Since God's determinations in these matters are things that cannot be foreseen, how could the soul know that it was determined to sin unless it was already actually sinning? It is simply a matter of choosing not to; and God could not have set an easier or fairer condition than that. Moreover, judges do not look for the reasons which have led a person to have an evil intent, but concern themselves only with how evil it is. But perhaps it is certain from all eternity that I shall sin? Answer that yourself: perhaps not. And instead of wondering about what you cannot know and what can tell you nothing, act according to your duty, which you do know. But someone else will say, how does it happen that this man will certainly sin? The reply is easy: it is that otherwise he would not be this man. For God sees from all time that there will be a certain Judas whose notion or idea, which God has, contains that future free action. The only remaining question therefore is why such a Judas, the traitor, who in God's idea is merely possible, actually exists. But to that question there is no reply to be expected on this earth, except that in general we should say that since God found it good that he should exist, despite the sin which he foresaw, it must be that this evil is repaid with interest somewhere in the universe, that God will derive some greater good from it, and all in all that it will turn out that the sequence of things which includes the existence of this sinner is the most perfect out of all the other possible ways. But while we are travellers in this world we cannot always explain the admirable economy of that choice. It is enough to know what it is without understanding it. And at this point it is time to acknowledge *altitudinem divitiarum* [the extent of the riches], the unfathomable depth,[20] of the divine wisdom, and not to try to find one detail which incorporates infinite considerations. It is, however, clear that God is not the cause of evil. For not only since the loss of man's innocence has his soul been possessed by original sin, but even before that, there was a fundamental limitation or imperfection intrinsic to all created things which makes them capable of sin and of error. Thus there is no more difficulty from the point of view of the supralapsarians[21] than there is for anyone else. And it is this, in my view, that the opinion of St *Augustine and other authors that the root of evil is in nothingness comes down to—that is to say, it is in the privation or limitation of created things, which God by his grace remedies by the degree of perfection that he is pleased to give. This grace of God, whether ordinary or extraordinary, has its levels and its proportions. It is always sufficient in itself to produce an appropriate effect, and, moreover, it is always sufficient, not only to save us from sin, but also to provide salvation, providing that man also contributes to it what he has in himself. But it is not always sufficient to overcome a man's inclinations—otherwise he would no longer be responsible for anything; that is true only in the case of absolutely effective grace, which is always victorious, whether through itself or through the combination of circumstances.

31. *The reasons for election, foreseen faith, middle knowledge,*[22] *absolute decrees, and that everything comes down to the reason why God chose and decided to admit*

---

[20] Rom. 11: 33.

[21] Calvinists who held that God's decrees of predestination were antecedent to the fall.

[22] The notion of 'middle knowledge' was introduced by the Spanish Jesuit Molina (1535–1600) as a way of maintaining the doctrine of the efficacy of divine grace whilst preserving human free will. It is God's knowledge of so-called 'conditionals of freedom'—his knowledge of what a certain individual would freely do in certain circumstances if offered grace. It is a 'middle' between the two kinds of divine knowledge recognized by *Aquinas—'knowledge of vision', God's knowledge of what was, is, or will be actual, and 'simple knowledge', his knowledge of possibles.

into existence a certain possible person, whose notion contains a certain series of graces and free actions. Which removes the difficulties at a stroke. Finally, God's graces are totally pure, and creatures have no right to them. However, although it is insufficient in explaining the choices God makes in dispensing these graces to appeal to either his absolute or his conditional foreknowledge of men's future actions, at the same time we must not imagine that there are absolute decrees, which have no rational grounds. As regards God's foreknowledge of our faith or good works, it is quite true that God has chosen only those whose faith and charity he foresaw, whom he foresaw he would endow with faith. But the same question recurs: why will God give the grace of faith or of good works to some rather than to others? And as regards that knowledge of God which is his foresight, not of faith and of good deeds, but of the material or predisposition for them, or of what man himself contributes towards them (since it is true that there is variation on man's side corresponding to that on the side of grace, and since in fact man, although he needs to be stimulated to the good and converted to it, must also then perform it), it seems to many that it could be said that since God sees what man would do without grace or extraordinary assistance, or at least what there would be from his side if grace were discounted, he could resolve to give grace to those whose natural dispositions were the best, or at least were less imperfect or less sinful. But if that were so, it could be said that those natural dispositions, to the extent that they are good, are also the effect of grace, although in this case ordinary grace, because God has favoured some more than others. Moreover, since according to this doctrine he knows perfectly well that the natural advantages he gives will be the ground for his grace or extraordinary help, is it not true that in the end everything in fact reduces entirely to his mercy? I believe then (since we do not know to what extent or in what way God takes account of natural dispositions in the dispensing of grace) that the most precise and the safest thing to say (in accordance with our principles and as I have already remarked) is that among possible beings there must be the person of Peter or of John whose notion or idea contains this whole sequence of ordinary and extraordinary graces, and all the rest of these events and their circumstances, and that from amongst an infinity of other equally possible people it pleased God to choose that person for actual existence. After that it seems that there is nothing more to ask, and that all the difficulties disappear. For as to this single great question why it pleased God to choose him from among all other possible persons, it would be very unreasonable not to be satisfied with the general reasons that we have given, the details of which are beyond us. So, instead of having recourse to an absolute decree which is unreasonable because there are no reasons for it, or to reasons which do not succeed in resolving the difficulty and themselves stand in need of other reasons, it would be best to say in agreement with St Paul[23] that there are certain great reasons for it, reasons of wisdom or of appropriateness which God has observed and which are unknown to mortals and are founded on the general order, whose aim is the greatest perfection of the universe. The motives of the glory of God and the manifestation of his justice, as well as of his mercy and his perfections generally, and all in all the immense profundity of riches which enraptured the soul of that same St Paul, come down in the end to that.

32. *The usefulness of these principles in matters of piety and religion.* Moreover, the thoughts we have now explained, and in particular the great principle of the perfection of God's operations and that of the notion of a substance which contains all its events together with all their circumstances, so far from harming religion, serve to reinforce it. Far better than the theories we have seen before, they serve to dissipate some very serious difficulties, to inspire souls with love of God and to elevate minds to the understanding of incorporeal substances. For it is clear that all other substances depend on God, in the way that thoughts emanate from our substance; that God is all in all, and that he is intimately united to all created things, though to an extent proportional to their perfection; that it is he alone who by his influence determines them from outside, and therefore, if to act is immediately to determine, it can be said in this sense and in the language of metaphysics that God alone operates on me, and he alone can do me good or harm. Other substances only contribute to the reason for those changes, because God, who has regard to them all, shares out his blessings and makes them adjust to one another. So God alone produces the connection or communication between substances: it is through him that the phenomena of one coincide or agree with those of another, and as a result that there is reality in our perceptions. But it is not always necessary to mention the universal cause in particular cases, and so in practice activity is attributed to particular reasons in the sense that I explained above. We can also see that every substance has a perfect spontaneity (which in intelligent substances becomes freedom), that everything which happens to them is a consequence of their idea or of their being, and that nothing determines them except God alone. This is why a certain person [*Teresa] of very lofty mind and revered holiness used to say that the soul

---

[23] Rom. 8: 28–30; 9: 14–29; 11: 33–5.

should often think in terms of there being only God and it in the world. Nothing can make us understand immortality better than this independence and extent of the soul, which means it is completely protected from everything external, since it alone constitutes its whole world, and together with God is sufficient for itself. It is therefore as impossible that it should come to an end without annihilation as it is that the world of which it is a perpetual living expression should destroy itself. And it is not possible that changes in the extended mass we call our body should do anything to the soul, or that the dissolution of that body could destroy what is indivisible.

33. *Explanation of the communication between the soul and the body, which has beeen taken to be inexplicable or miraculous, and the origin of confused perceptions.* We also get an explanation of the great mystery of *the union of the soul and the body*, that is to say, how it comes about that the passive and active states of the one are accompanied by active and passive states, or by suitable phenomena, in the other. For in no way is it conceivable that the one has an influence over the other, and it is not rational just to fall back on the extraordinary operation of the universal cause in something which is ordinary and particular. Here, then, is the true explanation of it: we have said that everything which happens to the soul and to each substance is a consequence of its notion. Therefore, the mere idea or essence of the soul specifies that all its appearances or perceptions must arise spontaneously from its own nature, and in just such a way that they correspond of themselves to what happens in the whole universe, but also more particularly and more perfectly to what happens in the body which is assigned to it. Because in a way, and for a time, it is because of the relation of other bodies to its own that the soul expresses the state of the universe. This also explains how our body belongs to us despite not being attached to our essence. And I believe that people who think deeply will think well of our principles for that very reason: that they can easily see what the connection between the soul and the body consists in, a connection which seems inexplicable in any other way. We can also see that the perceptions of our senses, even when clear, must necessarily contain some confused feeling. For since all bodies in the universe are in sympathy, ours receives the impressions of all the others, and although our senses bear relations to everything, it is not possible for our soul to attend to everything in all of its particulars. Thus our confused feelings are the result of a variety of perceptions which is indeed infinite—very like the confused murmur a person hears when approaching the sea-shore, which comes from the

putting together of the reverberations of innumerable waves. For if several perceptions do not come together to make one, and there is no one which stands out above all the others, and if they all make impressions which are more or less equally strong and equally capable of catching its attention, the soul can only perceive them confusedly.

34. *The difference between minds and other substances, souls, or substantial forms; and that the immortality we require implies memory.* ⟨Something I don't attempt to decide is whether, in metaphysical strictness, bodies are substances, or whether, like the rainbow, they are only *true* phenomena, and consequently whether there are substances, souls, or substantial forms which are not intelligent. However,⟩ [i]f we suppose that bodies which compose a *unum per se*, such as man, are substances and have substantial forms, and that animals have souls, we have to admit that these souls and substantial forms cannot completely come to an end any more than, in the view of other philosophers, atoms or the ultimate parts of matter can. For no substance ever comes to an end, although it may become very different. They too express the whole universe, although more imperfectly than minds. But the principal difference is that they do not know what they are, nor what they do, and so they cannot reflect, and therefore can never discover necessary and universal truths. It is also for the lack of such self-reflection that they have no moral quality, which means that since they pass through perhaps a thousand transformations (as when a caterpillar changes into a butterfly), it makes no moral or practical difference to speak as if they did cease to exist. The same can be said at the level of physical science, as when we say that bodies perish through dissolution. But the intelligent soul, which knows what it is, and can say that word 'I', which says so much, not only metaphysically remains and subsists more than the others, but also morally remains the same and constitutes the same person. For it is memory, or the knowledge of this 'I', which renders it capable of punishment and reward. Furthermore, the immortality required by morality and religion does not just consist in this perpetual subsistence which goes with all substances, for without the memory of what one has been, it would not be anything desirable. Suppose that someone could suddenly become the King of China, but only on condition of forgetting what he had been, as if he had just been born all over again. Would it not in practice, or in terms of perceivable effects, be the same as if he had been annihilated, and a King of China had been created at the same instant in his place? And that is something which that individual could have no reason to want.

35. *The excellence of minds; that God considers them in preference to other crea-*
tures; that minds express God rather than the world, and that other simple sub-
stances express the world rather than God. But to show by natural reasons that
God will always conserve not only our substance, but also our person (that
is, the memory and the knowledge of what we are—although distinct
knowledge of it is sometimes suspended in sleep or in faints), we must
connect morality to metaphysics. In other words, we must consider God
not only as the principle and the cause of all substances and of all beings,
but also as the leader of all persons or intelligent substances, or as the
absolute monarch of the most perfect city or republic, such as is the universe composed of all minds. For God himself is the most accomplished of
all minds, as well as the greatest of all beings. For minds certainly are the
most perfect of beings, and express the Divinity best. ⟨For minds are either
the only substances there are in the world—if bodies are only true phenomena—or else at least they are the most perfect.⟩ And since the whole
nature, end, virtue, or function of substances is only to express God and
the universe (as I have sufficiently explained), there is no room to doubt
that substances which express it with knowledge of what they do, and
which are capable of understanding great truths about God and the universe, express it incomparably better than those natures which are either
animal and incapable of knowing any truths, or which are completely
lacking in feeling and knowledge. The difference between intelligent substances and those which are not is as great as that between a mirror and a
person who sees. For since God himself is the greatest and wisest of
minds, it is easy to see that beings with whom he can enter into conversation, so to speak, and indeed into society (by communicating to them his
opinions and his will in a particular manner, and in such a way that they
can know and love their benefactor), must concern him infinitely more
than all other things, which can serve only as the tools of minds. In the
same way we see that wise people always value a man infinitely more than
any other thing, however precious it may be. And it seems that the greatest
satisfaction that a soul which otherwise is content can have is to see itself
loved by others; although with regard to God there is the difference that
his glorification and our worship can add nothing to his satisfaction,
because the knowledge of created things, far from contributing to it or
being its partial cause, is only a consequence of his sovereign and perfect
happiness. However, what is good and rational in finite spirits is eminently[24] in him, and just as we would praise a king who preferred to save a

---

[24] God possesses any perfections he has given to his creatures eminently, that is in a higher or
more perfect form.

man's life rather than that of the rarest and most precious of his animals, so we should not doubt that the most enlightened and the most just of all monarchs would think the same.

36. *God is the monarch of the most perfect republic, composed of all minds, and the happiness of this City of God is his main aim.* Minds are actually the most perfectible of substances, and their perfections have the special feature that they obstruct one another the least, or rather that they help one another—for only the most virtuous can be the most perfect friends. It manifestly follows from this that God, who always aims at the greatest perfection in general, will have the most care for minds, and will give them (not only in general, but also to each one in particular) the highest level of perfection that the universal harmony will allow. Indeed we can say that it is in so far as he is a mind that God is the origin of existences—otherwise, if he did not have a will with which to choose the best, there would be no reason for one possible to exist in preference to others. So this quality which God has, of himself being a mind, takes precedence over all other considerations that he can have with regard to created things. Only minds are made in his image, and are of his race, as it were, or as children of his house, for only they can serve him freely, and act with knowledge in imitation of the divine nature. A single mind is worth a whole world, since it not only expresses the world, but also knows it, and governs itself there after the fashion of God, so that it seems that although all substances express all the universe, nevertheless substances other than spirits express the world rather than God, whereas spirits express God rather than the world. This great nobility of nature, which brings minds as near to the Divinity as is possible for mere created things, means that God derives infinitely more glory from minds than from all other beings, or rather that other beings only provide the material for minds to glorify him. This is why this moral quality of God's, which makes him the lord or monarch of minds, involves him, so to speak, personally, in a quite special manner. It is in this that he makes himself human, that he is willing to suffer anthropomorphisms, and that he enters into society with us, as a prince with his subjects. This concern is so dear to him that the happy and flourishing state of his empire, which consists in the greatest possible happiness of the inhabitants, becomes the most supreme of his laws. For happiness is to people what perfection is to beings. And if the first principle of the existence of the physical world is the decision to give it the greatest possible perfection, then the first aim for the moral world or the city of God, which is the noblest part of the universe, must be to spread in it the greatest possible

happiness. So we must not doubt that, in order that his city should never lose anyone, as the world has never lost a single substance, God has ordained everything so that minds not only can live for ever, which is unquestionable, but also that they should always retain their moral quality. Consequently, they will always know what they are, otherwise they would not be susceptible of reward or punishment, which, however, is essential to any republic, and especially to the most perfect, where nothing could ever be neglected. In fact since God is simultaneously the most just and the most good-natured of monarchs, and since he demands only a good will, provided that it is sincere and serious, his subjects could not ask for any better condition. To make them perfectly happy, all that God asks is that they should love him.

37. *Jesus Christ revealed to men the wonderful mystery and laws of the Kingdom of Heaven, and the splendour of the supreme happiness that God prepares for those who love him.* Ancient philosophers had very little knowledge of these important truths. Only Jesus Christ has expressed them divinely well, and in a manner so clear and so accessible that even the dullest minds could understand them. And his gospel has entirely changed the face of all things human. He has told us about the Kingdom of Heaven, that perfect republic of minds which deserves the title of the City of God, and whose admirable laws he has revealed to us. He alone has shown how much God loves us, and how exactly he has provided for everything which concerns us: that since he cares for sparrows, he will not neglect the rational creatures who are infinitely dearer to him; that all the hairs of our heads are counted; that the sky and the earth will perish before the word of God and what relates to the provision of our salvation is changed; that God has more concern for the least of intelligent souls than for the whole machine of the world; that we should have no fear of those who can destroy the body but cannot harm the soul, since God alone can make us happy or unhappy; that the souls of the just are safe in his hands from all the revolutions of the universe, since nothing is capable of acting on them except God alone; that none of our actions is forgotten, and that everything is taken into account, even our idle words, or even a spoonful of water well used; and, finally, that all must result in the greatest good, that the just shall be as suns, and that neither our senses nor our minds have ever tasted anything approaching the happiness which God prepares for those who love him.

APPENDICES

A

Sections 8–11 contain Leibniz's much discussed 'complete notion' account of individual substances.

The traditional *Aristotelian doctrine according to which an individual substance is that to which predicates are attributed but which is not the attribute of anything else is all right as far as it goes, Leibniz says. But it does not go far enough. It does not explain what it is for a substance to have a predicate 'truly attributed' to it.

It is hardly obvious just what it is that Leibniz thinks needs explaining here. It remains unclear even when, towards the end of Sect. 8, we have his explanation—that substances do not just have predicates; they have 'complete notions', notions from which all their predicates can be deduced.

One of Leibniz's steps on the way to this metaphysical conclusion that substances have 'complete notions' is a logical doctrine about truth: all true propositions (e.g. 'Newton was a mathematician') are such that the 'subject term must always involve that of the predicate'.

This logical doctrine that all true propositions are such that the predicate is contained in the subject appears to involve the idea that all propositions are of the subject–predicate form ('Newton was a mathematician'), and that none are of a relational form ('Newton was annoyed with Leibniz'). There has been much discussion whether Leibniz denied relations (both at the level of logic, as here, and the level of metaphysics, as at Sect. 14, according to which 'each substance is like a separate world'): see Cover (1989), D'Agostino (1976), Earman (1977), Hintikka (1972), Ishiguro (1972a, chs. 5, 6; 1972b), Kulstad (1980), Mates (1968, Sect. 6), Mugnai (1981, 1988), Rescher (1981b), Wong (1980).

Bertrand Russell (1900, 1937, ch. 1) and Louis Couturat (1972), in their highly influential work on Leibniz at the beginning of this century, both held this 'notion inclusion' account of truth to be of the utmost importance in Leibniz's thought—the latter saying that the whole of Leibniz's philosophy can be derived from it. It amounts to saying, they held, that all truths are analytic (to describe them in a Kantian, post-Leibnizian way) and hence to saying that all truths are necessary truths. But does Leibniz want to deny that there are contingent truths?

This is a complex and much discussed question—see Abraham (1969), Adams (1977; 1994, sect. 1), Blumenfeld (1988–9), Curley (1972), Dicker (1982), Fitch (1979), Fried (1978), Grimm (1970), Hacking (1982), Hart (1987), Ishiguro (1972a, ch. 7; 1979a), Jarrett (1978), Meijering (1978), Nason (1942), Rescher (1952), B. Russell (1900, 1937, chs. 2, 3), Sleigh (1990a, ch. 5), Vailati (1986), M. Wilson (1969, 1979); and also the reading at the end of Introduction, Sect. 7 n. 30. But it should be borne in mind here that at T2. 4 §13 the 'inclusion' account of truth is explicitly said to apply not just to 'every true proposition' but to 'all true affirmative propositions, necessary or contingent' (T2. 4 §13; see also T1. 13). Leibniz therefore does *not* mean to say that all truths are necessary truths. A further indication of this is his seeming to think that what he is saying is uncontroversial: if this is not truth, he says, then 'I do not know what truth is' (T2. 4 §13) and 'all philosophers should agree' (T2. 4 §14).

Indeed, some commentators suggest that to say that Leibniz has a 'notion inclusion' doctrine of truth, with the implication that all truths are analytic, is misleading. When Leibniz speaks of the predicate's being included in the subject he means, they say, not that there is a necessary connection between them, but only that the predicate holds of the thing that instantiates the subject concept. (See Brody (1977), Ishiguro (1979*a*,*b*), Jarrett (1978), Wiggins (1987).)

Besides this question of how to understand Leibniz's doctrine of truth, there is the further question of how he gets from it to his clearly metaphysical doctrine that individual substances have complete notions. The nature of the relationship between Leibniz's logic and his metaphysics has been much discussed since Russell and Couturat claimed that the latter followed quite directly from the former as its foundation. (See Brody (1977), Couturat (1972), Fleming (1987), A. H. Johnson (1960), MacDonald Ross (1981), Parkinson (1995), B. Russell (1930), ch. 1.)

Finally, there is the question of how to understand the metaphysical doctrine that individual substances have complete notions. It is a doctrine from which Leibniz draws some rather startling consequences (see Broad (1972)); for example, that a substance's notion includes not only everything about it, but also everything about the past, present, and future of the whole universe (Sect. 9). Despite this, Russell took Leibniz's 'complete notion' doctrine to be rather less than exciting. That substances have complete notions amounts, he held, to 'the obvious fact that every proposition about the future is already determined either as true or as false, though we may be unable to decide the alternative' (B. Russell (1930/1937) 46).

According to this, Leibniz is putting forward the 'obvious' idea that if something is true at a certain time, then it always was and always will be true that it is true at that time. In other words, just as at the end of a person's life there are determinate truths about his past (e.g. he broke his leg on his fiftieth birthday), so at the start of his life there already were determinate truths about his future (e.g. that he would break his leg on his fiftieth birthday).

Whether or not the determinacy of the future and the timelessness of truth are as 'obvious' as Russell claims, it is not very plausible to suppose that this is what Leibniz's account of substances as having complete notions amounts to. It hardly does justice to Leibniz's rather exciting formulations of it to the effect that 'every substance contains within its present state all its past states and all those to come' (T2. 11 §9), and that 'the present is big with the future' (T19. 22). (For a development of this point see Woolhouse (1982).) It also leaves unexplained and quite mysterious the connection Leibniz makes between complete notions and substantial forms. Besides what follows here, there is discussion of the connection, or lack of connection, between the two at Adams (1994: 315–16), Bartha (1993), Rutherford (1995b: 138–9), C. Wilson (1989, Sects. 17, 18), Woolhouse (1993: 54–73).

Substantial forms (see Introduction, Sect. 2) are first introduced in an apparent aside at Sects. 10–11. Then, at Sect. 12, it appears that since substances have complete notions it follows not only that body must be more than extension (see Introduction, Sects. 2, 3), but also that we must 'accept that there is something which has some resemblance to a soul, and which is commonly called a substantial form' (Sect. 12).

The substantial forms of the Aristotelian tradition are (as in Introduction, Sect. 2) active, organizing natures of substances as they develop and change through time. So when Leibniz says it is in the nature of an individual substance to have a complete notion he presumably has in mind this idea that what becomes true of a substance does so by virtue of its substantial form. The future states of an individual substance are contained in its present state in the way that a future as a mature oak is contained in an acorn. As Leibniz says, 'in the soul of Alexander there are for all time . . . marks of everything that will happen to him' (Sect. 8).

When Leibniz says that he wants to know what it is for a substance to have a predicate 'truly attributed' to it, it is helpful to read him as being interested in the question how it comes about that substances have the properties that they do. What he wants to know is what it is for some property to be attributable to a substance, not in the straightfoward sense of its being an attribute or property of it, but rather in the stronger sense of the substance itself being *responsible for* its having that property—the sense in which the property is attributable to the substance when it has, as it were, brought that property upon itself. Given that this *is* Leibniz's interest, then his position on the matter is: once God has created them, substances are themselves responsible for *all* their properties; all their properties are 'truly attributable' to them for they all follow from their substantial forms.

One respect in which Leibniz goes beyond the traditional doctrine of substantial forms should be noted. It was part of the tradition that while many of the features and characteristics of an individual substance relate to its embodied form, not all of them do. Many things were supposed to be 'accidental' to an individual substance (and therefore not '*truly* attributable' to it). Many things were supposed to be true of it as a result of its being passively affected by some outside cause. But, as Sect. 8 makes clear, the notion of a Leibnizian substance is 'so complete' as to include 'all the predicates' (Sect. 8); 'everything that happens to [substances] is merely a consequence of their nature' (Sect. 16; see also T2. 13 §1).

The subject of how 'complete' complete concepts are is discussed in Ishiguro (1977, 1979b), Kulstad (1993), Manns (1987). The consequences of the completeness of complete concepts for the identity of individuals and the possibility of their having non-essential properties is discussed in Cover and Hawthorne (1992), Hunter (1981), Mondadori (1973, 1975, 1985), M. Wilson (1979).

1. *Discourse on Metaphysics*

B

The significance of the argument in this paragraph was explained in Introduction, Sect. 3. 4. The argument (which appears again in T5. 25–9) aims to show that the *Cartesians were wrong to use as a measure of the 'motive force' of a moving body the 'quantity of its (Cartesian) motion', i.e. its size times its speed. It will be granted, Leibniz says, that a falling body acquires exactly the amount of 'force' as would be required to raise it (if it were a pendulum, for example) back to its original height; and that the 'force' required to raise a one-pound body to a height of four fathoms is the same as would be required to raise a four-pound body by one fathom. It follows from these two propositions that in falling four fathoms a one-pound body acquires the same amount of 'force' as a four-pound body acquires in falling one fathom. The question now is: do two such bodies, which after their respective falls have the same amount of 'force' as each other, have the same quantity of Cartesian motion?

Leibniz's answer is that they do not. He appeals to some results already obtained by *Galileo according to which the speed acquired by a body in a four-fathom fall will be only twice (not four times) that which is acquired by a body in a one-fathom fall. So at the end of its fall, the one-pound body is moving at only twice the speed of the four-times-larger four-pound body and so has only *half* the 'Cartesian motion' of the larger. Therefore, since the 'motive forces' of the two bodies have already been agreed to be the same, it follows that 'motive force' cannot, contrary to *Descartes, be the same as 'motion'. The force of a moving body is therefore, Leibniz argues, not to be measured by its speed but rather by the effect that speed can produce—for example, the height to which its speed could raise it.

Now though Leibniz says nothing about this here, this height is in fact proportional to the *square* of the speed; for, supposing the four-pound body has one unit of speed after its fall of one fathom, the speed of the one-pound body after its fall of four fathoms is two units. By 1695 Leibniz's preference was to express 'motive force' or 'living force' (*vis viva*) as he came to call it, in this way (T5. 30).

Leibniz's idea of measuring 'motive force' by the effect it can produce is, in itself, uncontentious. But was he right to take the 'effect' which a body's force of motion can produce to be *the height* to which the body can raise itself? It was argued against him that the relevant effect is really *the time* which the body takes to raise itself (or to fall). Thus, since all bodies, whatever their size, fall at the same rate and take twice as long to fall four fathoms as to fall one, it is only to be expected that the four-pound body should have twice as much Cartesian motion as the one-pound body. (For further reading, see Introduction, Sect. 3 nn. 15, 17.)

2

CORRESPONDENCE WITH ARNAULD
(1686–1690)

Summary of the Text

In February 1686 Leibniz sent a section-by-section summary of the 'Discourse on Metaphysics' (T1) to Antoine *Arnauld. (They were sent via Ernst von Hessen-Rheinfels, an acquaintance of both Leibniz and Arnauld and someone who earlier had unsuccessfully tried to convert Leibniz from Protestantism to Roman Catholicism.) The lengthy correspondence which ensued was something which, from time to time, Leibniz thought of publishing together with the 'Discourse'. In reading it one should bear in mind that Arnauld had seen, not the 'Discourse' as a whole but merely the summary headings of its thirty-seven sections. Sleigh (1990a) provides an extensive discussion of the correspondence.

The correspondence falls into three movements. At the outset, freedom and Leibniz's doctrine that substances have complete notions are under discussion. Arnauld then asks Leibniz about his hypothesis of *concomitance between body and mind, and about *substantial forms. As the first of these is the main topic of TT9–12, 14–17, the discussion of it here has been omitted.

What first and very forcibly caught Arnauld's attention was the summary of T1. 13. This amounted, he said, to a denial of human freedom. It meant that once God had created Adam then 'everything which has since happened to the human race, and which will ever happen to it, was and is bound to happen by a more than fatal necessity' (T2. 1).

Pointing out (T2. 2 §1) that the summary of T1. 13 expressly says that this does not follow, Leibniz replied (T2. 2 §2) that Arnauld was confusing hypothetical and absolute necessity—two things which, unknown to Arnauld, Leibniz had distinguished in the main text of T1. 13. Given that God decides to create Adam, then it is absolutely *necessary that he create a creature capable of thought. There is a contradiction in supposing that God could create a human being that was not capable of thought. But it is only* hypothetically *necessary that in creating Adam*

From the French at GP ii. 11–138. Writing from France, Arnauld dates his letters according to the 'new style' Gregorian calendar. Germany did not abandon the Julian calendar until 1701, and Leibniz uses 'old style' dating (or, old style / new style).

God created a being that had such and such posterity. In his creation of Adam the necessity God was under of creating someone with such and such posterity was only the necessity of doing what he had already decided to do. When God decided to create Adam he had in mind not some vague idea but a very specific idea about the whole of his posterity and the whole course of the world (T2. 2 §3). In choosing Adam God had already decided to choose his posterity.

Arnauld rejected the charge of confusing absolute and hypothetical necessity. He replied that he had *been speaking about hypothetical necessity* (T2. 3 §§3–11): indeed, just as it is not absolutely necessary that God create Adam (along with his posterity) so, surely, it is not absolutely necessary that he create any person (along with the capacity for thought). The question, as Arnauld saw it, is, rather: isn't the connection between Adam and what will happen to him going to have to be as 'intrinsic and necessary' as that between a human and the capacity for thought? Unless it is, Arnauld thought, then it can't be true (as Leibniz seems to think it is—see T1, Appendix A) that the notion of Adam includes all that is true of him and his posterity. Yet this can hardly be true since, surely, Adam's descendants came into existence through God's free decision.

Arnauld also finds difficulty with Leibniz's talk of possible Adams, and of ideas of them (T2. 3 §§13–14). If it is not necessary that Adam had three children then having three children can't be contained in any idea of a possible Adam, for such ideas must contain all that is essential to Adam.

Moreover, though he can understand talk about possibilities relative to the Adam which God created, Arnauld says that he cannot understand what purely possible Adams are.

In his reply in July of the same year (T2. 4) Leibniz first addresses Arnauld's question concerning the nature of the connection between the notion of Adam, on the one hand, and all that is true of him and his posterity, on the other. It is, he says, intrinsic, but not necessary independently of God's free decisions. What is true of Adam is included in his notion—not, however, in the way that the properties of a triangle necessarily are included in its notion, but rather included by virtue of God's choice. They are included because of God's will and not as something which God by his understanding could find already to be there.

In making this point Leibniz refers (as a proof that there must be complete notions) to the predicate-in-subject principle of T1. 8 (T2. 4 §8). This figures again at the end of the letter (Sects. 13–15), when Leibniz refers to various other things which follow from it, things which, unknown to Arnauld, were outlined in T1. 9, 14–16. One of these is the hypothesis of concomitance, and this leads Leibniz to introduce, as a final point, the notion of 'substantial form'.

Arnauld's reply (T2. 5) signals a shift in his intitially hostile attitude to the 'shocking' summary of T1. 13, and marks a change in the focus of his interest.

2. Correspondence with Arnauld

The shift was brought about by what Leibniz had said about the predicate-in-subject principle, and the new focus of Arnauld's attention was on two of the things to which it had led—the hypothesis of concomitance and the notion of substantial form.

As mentioned earlier, the subsequent discussion between Leibniz and Arnauld of the first of these has been omitted here. The present extracts from their correspondence deal with the discussion which was provoked by Leibniz's remark that '[I]f the body is a substance, and not . . . a being unified by accident . . . we have to conceive of it as having something like what is called a substantial form' (T2. 4 §16).

The main line of thought which underlies all that Leibniz says in explanation of this is: extended matter, considered as extended, is divisible; and anything that is divisible is a being by aggregation, something without substantial unity. Therefore, a flesh-and-blood human being, on pain of being a mere aggregate and not a substantial unity, must be more than extended matter—and this will require substantial forms (T2. 4 §16). Moreover, any aggregated being, such as a piece of matter, if it is to be real and not a mere phenomenon like a rainbow, must be composed of things which are not also aggregates themselves but which have true substantial unity (T2. 9 §1).

On the face of it (see T2. 9 §1) there are four ways in which the requirement that real, non-phenomenal matter must be made up of real unities might be fulfilled. Other than (1) simply denying that matter is real and made up of real unities, one might (2) hold that extension is made up of mathematical points as real unities, or (3) hold that it is made up from physical atoms as real unities (see T2, note 2). The fourth way and, as is plain from Introduction, Section 2, the way favoured by Leibniz, is (4) to hold that it is made up from true substantial unities, of the kind that involve substantial forms. (When this argument occurs later, in T4, substantial unities are also called 'formal atoms', 'animated points', 'atoms of substance' (Sects. 3, 11).)

Now as to Leibniz's initial remark that if the human body is a substance it must have something like substantial form or soul, Arnauld assumes (along Cartesian lines) that the body indeed is substantial, and is so quite independently of any soul that might be associated with it. He therefore asks what the connection is between any substantial form our body might have and our actual soul (T2. 5 §3). Leibniz's reply (T2. 7 §2) makes clear that he simply does not accept the second part of Arnauld's assumption: independently of, and apart from, soul the body is not a substance; the connection between our soul and the substantial form which Leibniz understands as being in a substantial human body is that they are one and the same.

2. Correspondence with Arnauld

Arnauld also asks whether or not substantial forms themselves are divisible (T2. 5 §3). Even though he clearly recognizes that part of Leibniz's point in introducing them is to have indivisible, substantial unities out of which extended divisible material things are aggregated, it looks to Arnauld as if forms too are going to be divisible. Certainly a marble tile, for example, is divisible, and therefore, presumably, its substantial form is also.

Leibniz makes clear in reply that forms are indivisible, as are all genuine substances (T2. 7 §4). A marble tile, however, is not a real substantial unity any more than a collection of fish in a frozen pond is. It is not a complete non-aggregated being. In terms of physical cohesion or closeness of physical contact, a tile, or the frozen fish, are different from a heap of stones, but all three are merely accidental unities, beings by aggregation. Leibniz is certain about what a substantial unity is: an 'animated machine, the substantial form of which creates substantial unity which is independent of the external union of contact' (T2. 7 §5). He is also certain that without there being corporeal substances for it to be aggregated out of, matter would be an illusion. But as to exactly which things are substantial unities—what about the sun? the moon? trees? horses?—Leibniz is consistently certain only that human being are (TT2. 5 §3; 2. 7 §§5, 9; 2. 9 §§1–2, 9).

The introduction of substantial forms gives rise to other questions which run through the correspondence. One is whether Leibniz is right to insist on a connection between substantiality and unity (TT2. 8 §5; 2. 9 §§1–2). Another, and connectedly, is whether he is right to think, as he does, of substances as being indivisible (T2. 7 §§3, 4).

So far as souls or immaterial or incorporeal *substances are concerned, this is a doctrine Leibniz shares with Descartes (T2. 11 §1), and Arnauld is perfectly happy with the idea that immaterial human souls are indivisible and, consequently, indestructible (T2. 8 §8); but he is far less happy with extending this to the souls of other animals (TT2. 8 §7; 2. 9 §7; 2. 10 §7; 2. 11 §6).*

As for material or corporeal *substances, Arnauld will accept indivisibility in the one case of the 'whole, made up of soul and body, which is called man', for 'it is indivisible in the sense that no one can conceive of half a man' (T2. 8 §8). But he will not accept other cases: 'what will you say about worms which have been cut in two, and each part continues to move as before?' (T2. 8 §7).*

His point is that whereas the division of the substantial unity which is a man does not produce two other substantial unities, the division of a worm does produce other worms. There is a sense in which men are indivisble and worms are not. Leibniz's reply follows simply enough (T2. 9 §8). Even if they both move, the two halves of the original 'animated', 'ensouled', living substantial worm are not both 'animated', 'ensouled', living worms. Only one will be a living, substantial worm, the other will be simply matter. Though Leibniz does not put the point like this, one of the halves is analogous to an amputated limb, which is merely a chunk of matter; the other is analogous to the still substantial human being from which that matter is now severed.

THE TEXT

2.1. *Arnauld to von Hessen-Rheinfels, 13 March 1686*
I have received what your lordship has sent me of M. Leibniz's metaphysical thoughts . . . I find many things in these thoughts which alarm me, and which nearly all men, unless I am mistaken, will find so shocking that I do not see what can be the use of a document which it seems will be rejected by the whole world. I shall give as an example only what it says in article 13: 'the individual notion of each person involves once and for all everything that will ever happen to him, etc.'. If that is so, then God was free to create or not create Adam; but given that he wanted to create him, then everything which has since happened to the human race, and which will ever happen to it, was and is bound to happen by a more than fatal necessity. For the individual notion of Adam involved that he would have so many children, and the individual notion of each of these children involved everything that they would do, and all the children that they would have, and so on. So there is no more freedom in God with regard to all that, given that he wanted to create Adam, than in claiming that God was free, given that he wanted to create me, not to create a nature capable of thought. . . .

2.2. *Leibniz to von Hessen-Rheinfels, 12 April 1686*
. . . [1] He [Arnauld] chooses one of my theses to show that it is dangerous. . . . I shall try to get him to give up this strange opinion which he has formed rather too readily. I said in the thirteenth article of my synopsis that the individual notion of each person involves once and for all everything that will ever happen to him. He concludes from this that everything that happens to a person, and even to the whole human race, is bound to happen by a more than fatal necessity. As if notions or predictions made things necessary, and as if a free action could not be included in the notion or perfect view that God has of the person to which it pertains. . . . However, I expressly stated in the same article that I do not accept any such consequence. . . .

[2] I come to the proof of his inference [namely, 'If that is so . . . [as in T2. 1 . . .] a nature capable of thought']. . . . These last words ought really to contain the proof of the conclusion, but it is very clear that they confuse *hypothetical necessity* with *absolute necessity*. A distinction has always been drawn between what God is absolutely free to do and what he has obliged himself to do as a consequence of certain decisions which he has already taken, almost all of which have already taken account of everything. It is hardly worthy of God to conceive of him (under the pretext of maintaining his liberty) in the way that some *Socinian thinkers do, as like a man who makes decisions according to the circumstances, and who would now not be free to create what he thought good if his first decisions about Adam or others already involved reference to things about their posterity. By contrast, everyone agrees that God has regulated from all eternity the whole course of the universe, without that's diminishing his liberty in any way. It is also clear that this objection separates God's decisions one from another when really they are all related together. For we shouldn't consider God's decision to create a certain Adam in isolation from all the others he has made with regard to Adam's children and the whole human race—as if God first decided to create Adam with no thought about his posterity, even though by doing so, according to me, he took away his freedom to create Adam's posterity as seemed good to him. This is very strange reasoning. [3] Instead we must consider that God does not choose a vague Adam, but a specific Adam whose perfect representation can be found amongst the possible beings in the ideas of God, accompanied by certain individual circumstances and who, among other predicates, also has that of eventually having a certain posterity. God, I say, in choosing him, already considers his posterity, and chooses both at the same time. I do not understand how there is anything wrong with this; if he acted differently, he would not act like God. Let me use a comparison. A wise prince who chooses a general whose connections he knows, in effect simultaneously chooses various colonels and captains whom he perfectly well knows that the general will recommend, and whom he would not want to refuse to him, for certain reasons of prudence which do not in any way destroy his absolute power, or his freedom. There is all the more reason why the same is true in the case of God. So in order to proceed correctly, we must take account of a certain more general and more comprehensive decision which God has made with regard to the whole order of the universe—for the universe is like a whole which God grasps in a single view. This decision in effect comprehends his other decisions with regard to the contents of this universe, including among others that to create

such and such an Adam who is related to the whole of his posterity, which God has also chosen to be as it is. . . . [4] In fact the wiser one is, the less one has *independent decisions*, and the more one's views and decisions are comprehensive and *connected*. Each particular decision involves a relation to all the others, so that they harmonize as much as possible. Far from finding anything shocking in that, I should think that the opposite destroys God's perfection. . . .

[5] If one thinks only a little about what I have said, one will find that it is also obvious from the terms themselves. For by Adam's individual notion I most certainly mean a perfect representation of a particular Adam who has certain individual conditions which distinguish him from an infinity of other possible people, who closely resemble him but who are nevertheless different from him (just as all ellipses differ from a circle, however much they may approximate to it), and to whom God has preferred this Adam, because it pleased him more to choose exactly this order of the universe. Everything that follows from his resolution is necessary only by a hypothetical necessity, and in no way destroys God's freedom, or that of created minds. There is a possible Adam with a certain posterity, and an infinity of others whose posterity would be different. Isn't it true that these possible Adams (if one may so call them) are different from each other, and that God chose from them just one, which is precisely ours? There are so many reasons which prove the impossibility, not to say the absurdity, and indeed the impiety, of the opposite, that I believe all men are fundamentally of the same opinion, when they think a little about what they are saying. . . .

(2.3.) *Arnauld to Leibniz, 13 May 1686*
[1] I shall, then, simply tell you what the difficulties are which I still have with the proposition: 'The individual notion of each person involves once and for all everything that will ever happen to him'.

[2] It seemed to me that it follows that the individual notion of Adam involved that he would have so many children, that the individual notion of each of these children involved everything that they would do, and all the children that they would have, and so on. I believed that it could be inferred from that that God was free to create or not create Adam, but given that he wanted to create him, then everything which has since happened to the human race was and is bound to happen by a fatal necessity— or, at least, that there is no more freedom for God with regard to all that, given that he wanted to create Adam, than not to create a nature capable of thought, given that he wanted to create me.

[3] It doesn't seem to me, sir, that in speaking like this I have confused hypothetical necessity with absolute necessity. For, on the contrary, I never speak there about anything but hypothetical necessity. It is only that I find it strange that all human events should be as necessary (by hypothetical necessity) from the mere supposition that God wanted to create Adam, as it is necessary (by hypothetical necessity) that there should be in the world a nature capable of thought just because he wished to create me.

[4] On this point you say various things about God which do not seem to me sufficient to resolve my difficulty.

1. That '[a] distinction has always been drawn between what God is absolutely free to do and what he has obliged himself to do as a consequence of certain decisions which he has already taken' [T2. 2 §2]. That is certainly true.

2. That '[i]t is hardly worthy of God to conceive of him (under the pretext of maintaining his liberty) in the way that some Socinian thinkers do, as like a man who makes decisions according to the circumstances' [T2. 2 §2]. That thought is very foolish: I agree.

3. That we must not 'separate God's decisions when really they are all related together'. And so 'we shouldn't consider God's decision to create a certain Adam in isolation from all the others he has made with regard to Adam's children and the whole human race' [T2. 2 §2]. This too is something I agree with. But I do not yet see that it can help to resolve my difficulty.

[5] For 1. I confess in good faith that I did not understand that by the individual notion of each person (Adam, for example), which you say involves once and for all everything that will ever happen to him, you meant that person as he is in the divine understanding, rather than as he is in himself. For it seems to me that we do not normally consider the specific notion of a sphere in relation to its being represented in the divine understanding, but in relation to what it is in itself. And I thought that it would be the same with the individual notion of each person, or of each thing.

[6] 2. However, it is enough for me to know that that is the way you are thinking for me to go along with it, while trying to see whether it resolves all the difficulty I am having with it. I do not yet see that it does.

[7] For I agree that the knowledge God had of Adam when he decided to create him involved that of everything that happened to him, and everything which has happened and is to happen to his posterity. So taking the individual notion of Adam in this sense, what you have said about it is quite certain.

[8] I similarly admit that the decision he made to create Adam was not separate from the one he made about what would happen to him, and about all his posterity.

[9] But it seems to me that after that we still have to ask (and this is what causes my difficulty) whether the relation between these objects (I mean Adam on the one hand, and on the other everything which was to happen to him and to his posterity) is what it is in itself, independently of all God's free decisions, or whether it was dependent on them. That is to say, whether it is only as a consequence of the free decisions by which God ordained everything which would happen to Adam and to his posterity that God knew everything which would happen to Adam and to his posterity: or whether there is, independently of those decisions, an intrinsic and necessary connection between Adam on the one hand, and what has happened and will happen to him and to his posterity on the other. Unless it is the latter I do not see that what you say can be true, namely, 'that the individual notion of each person involves once and for all all that will ever happen to him'; even taking that notion in relation to God.

[10] And it seems that it is this latter that you stick with. For I think you suppose that as we understand things, possible things are possible before all God's free decisions. From which it follows that what is involved in the notion of a possible thing is involved in it independently of all God's free decisions. Now you hold that God found among possible things a possible Adam 'accompanied by certain individual circumstances and who, among other predicates, also has that of eventually having a certain posterity'. So there is, according to you, an intrinsic relation so to speak, one independent of *all* God's free decisions, between this possible Adam and all the individual persons of all his posterity, and not only the persons, but in general everything that was to happen to them. Now it is this, sir—I will not pretend otherwise—that I find incomprehensible. For it seems to me that you maintain that this possible Adam (which God chose in preference to all other possible Adams) was related to all the same posterity as the created Adam: since according to you he is, as far as I can judge of it, just the same Adam, considered first as possible, and then as created. Now if that is so, here is my difficulty.

[11] How many men are there who came into the world only by God's completely free decisions, such as Isaac, Samson, Samuel, and so many others? When therefore God knew them conjointly with Adam, it was not because they were involved in the individual notion of possible Adam, independently of God's decisions. So it is not true that all the individual persons in Adam's posterity were involved in the individual notion of pos-

sible Adam, because they would have had to be involved in it independently of the divine decisions.

[12] The same can be said about an infinity of human events which have happened by God's very particular orders, such as, among others, the Judaeo-Christian religion, and above all the incarnation of the divine word. I do not know how anyone can say that all of that was involved in the individual notion of possible Adam. For what is considered as possible must have everything we conceive it as having under that notion, independently of God's decisions.

[13] Furthermore, sir, I do not know how, when taking Adam as an example of a particular nature, you can conceive of several possible Adams. It is as if I were to conceive several possible 'me's, which certainly is inconceivable. For I cannot think of myself without considering myself as a singular nature, so distinct from every other existent or possible nature that I can no more conceive of various 'me's than I can conceive a circle that does not have all its diameters equal. The reason is, that these various 'me's would be different from each other, otherwise they would not be several 'me's; so there would have to be one of these 'me's which is not me—which is a manifest contradiction.

Now, sir, allow me to transfer to this what you say about Adam, and see for yourself whether it is tenable. Amongst possible beings God has found in his ideas several 'me's, of which one has for its predicates having several children and being a doctor, and another has living in celibacy and being a theologian. Since he has decided to create the latter, the me which now exists contains in its individual notion living in celibacy and being a theologian, whereas the first would have involved in its individual notion being married and being a doctor. Isn't it clear that there would be no sense in talking like this? For my 'me' is necessarily such and such an individual nature, which is the same thing as having such and such an individual notion; so it is as impossible to conceive contradictory predicates in the individual notion of me as to conceive a 'me' different from me. From which we have to conclude, it seems to me, that since it is impossible that I should not have always remained me, whether I had been married or had lived in celibacy, the individual notion of me involves neither the one nor the other of these two states. Just as we should conclude that this square of marble is the same, whether it is at rest or in motion; so neither rest or motion is involved in its individual notion. This is why, sir, it seems to me, I should regard as involved in the individual notion of myself only that which is such that I would no longer be me, if it were not in me. Everything which, on the other hand, is such that it could be in me or not

[margin handwritten notes: but small changes e.g. hair]

103

be in me, without my ceasing to be myself, cannot be considered as being involved in my individual notion, even though because of the order of God's providence—which does not change the nature of things—it cannot happen that it would not be in me. That is my view, which I think conforms with everything which has always been believed by all the philosophers of the world. . . .

[14] I also find many uncertainties in the way we normally represent God as acting. We imagine that before he willed to create the world he envisaged an infinity of possible things from which he chose some and rejected others: several possible Adams, each one with a large succession of people and events, with which he has an intrinsic relation. And we suppose that the relation of all these other things with one of these possible Adams is exactly like that which we know the created Adam had with all his posterity. This makes us think that it is that one, out of all possible Adams, which God chose, and that he did not want any of the others. . . . I confess in good faith that I have no idea of these purely possible substances, which, that is to say, God will never create. And I am strongly inclined to think that they are chimeras that we make up for ourselves, and that what we call possible, purely possible, substances can only be God's omnipotence, which since it is pure activity, does not allow any possibility in God. But we can conceive of possibility in the natures that he has created, for as they are not by their essences actual beings, they are necessarily composed of potential and actual. This allows me to conceive of them as possible, as I can also do with an infinity of modifications which are in the power of these created natures, such as the thoughts of intelligent natures, and the shapes of extended substance. But I am much mistaken if there is anyone who dares say he has an idea of a possible, purely possible, substance. For my part I am convinced that, although we speak so much of these purely possible substances, we nevertheless never conceive of any of them except through the idea of one of those which God has created. . . .

[15] [W]e should look for true notions, of things that we know, whether species or individuals, not in God, who from our point of view lives in a light which is inaccessible, but in the ideas of them that we find in ourselves. Now I find in myself the notion of an individual nature, for I find the notion of *me*. I have therefore only to consult it in order to know what is involved in that individual notion, just as I have only to consult the specific notion of a sphere in order to know what is involved in it. Now I have no other method for doing that than to ask what there is that is such that a sphere would not be a sphere if it didn't have it (such as having all

the points on its circumference equally distant from the centre), and what would not make a sphere cease to be a sphere (such as having a diameter of one foot when another sphere might have one of ten feet, or a hundred). In this way I judge that the former is involved in the specific notion of a sphere, and that the latter, having a greater or a smaller diameter, is not. I apply the same method to the individual notion of *me*. I am certain that in so far as I think, I am me. For I cannot think if I do not exist, nor exist if I am not me. But I can think that I will take such and such a journey, or that I will not take it, whilst remaining quite certain that neither the one nor the other prevents me from being me. So I remain quite certain that neither of them is involved in the individual notion of *me*. But God has foreseen, you will say, that you will take this journey. Indeed. So it is indubitable that you will take it? Again, indeed. That changes nothing in the certainty I have that whether I take it, or do not take it, I will still be me. I must therefore conclude that neither the one nor the other enters into my 'me', into my individual notion, that is to say. That, it seems to me, is what we should hold on to, without bringing in God's knowledge, in order to find out what is involved in the individual notion of each thing. . . .

2.4. *Leibniz to Arnauld, 4/14 July 1686*

[1] As I have great regard for your judgement I was delighted to see that you have moderated your criticism after seeing my explanation of the proposition which I think is important and which had seemed strange to you: 'that the individual notion of each person involves once and for all everything that will ever happen to him'. At first you concluded from it that, given only the assumption that God decided to create Adam, all other human events which happened to Adam and to his posterity followed from it by a fatal necessity: God would no longer have the freedom to decide on them, any more than after having taken the decision to create me he is able not to create a creature capable of thought.

[2] I had replied to this that since God's plans concerning this whole universe are interconnected in accordance with his sovereign wisdom, he took no decision concerning Adam without thereby taking a decision about everything which had any connection with him. So it is not because of the resolution taken with regard to Adam, but because of the resolution taken at the same time with regard to all the rest (to which that which was taken with regard to Adam involves a perfect relation), that God decided upon all human events. In this it seemed to me that there is no fatal necessity, nor anything contrary to God's freedom, any more than there is in the

generally accepted hypothetical necessity that exists even in the case of God himself, for him to carry out what he has decided.

[3] You agree, sir, in your reply, about the interconnectedness of divine decisions that I had advanced before, and you are even good enough to admit that you took my proposition quite differently at first, because 'we do not normally', for example, (these are your words) 'consider the specific notion of a sphere in relation to its being represented in the divine understanding, but in relation to what it is in itself' [T2. 3 §5]; and you had thought (not without reason, I admit) that it would be the same with the individual notion of each person. For my part, I thought that full and comprehensive notions were represented in the divine understanding as they are in themselves.[1] However, now that you know that that is the way I am thinking, that is enough for you to go along with it, while trying to see whether it resolves the difficulty. It seems then that you accept, sir, that when it is explained in this way my position with regard to full and comprehensive notions, as they are in God's understanding, is not only harmless, but is in fact certain; for here are your words: 'I agree . . . [as at T2. 3 §7] is quite certain'. We shall see shortly what the difficulty you still find in it consists in. However, I must say a word in explanation of the difference there is in all this between the notions of species and those of individual substances, in connection with the divine will rather than in connection with simple understanding. The most abstract specific notions contain only necessary or eternal truths, which do not depend on God's decisions (whatever the *Cartesians say)—and it seems that you too take no account of them on this point. But the notions of individual substances, which are complete and capable of entirely distinguishing their subject, and which consequently contain contingent truths or truths of fact, and individual circumstances of time, of place, and so on, must also contain in their notion (considered as possible) God's free decisions (also considered as possible), because those free decisions are the principal source of existences or facts; whereas essences are in the divine understanding before consideration by the will.

[4] That should help us to understand everything else better and to resolve the difficulties which you still seem to have with my explanation; for this is how you continue, sir: 'But it seems to me that after that we still have to ask . . . [as at T2. 3 §9] posterity on the other'. It seems to you that I will choose the latter option, because I said that 'God found among the

[1] In his copy of the letter Leibniz deleted this sentence; also he wrote in the margin, '*Full* concepts contain all the predicates of a thing, e.g. heat; *complete concepts* contain all the predicates of a subject, e.g. this hot thing. In individual substances they coincide.'

possibles an Adam accompanied by certain individual circumstances and who, among other predicates, also has that of eventually having a certain posterity.' Now you think I will agree that possibles are possible before any of God's free decisions. So assuming this explanation of my view according to the second alternative, you think, sir, that it has insurmountable difficulties, for there are, as you quite rightly say, 'an infinity of human events . . . [as at T2. 3 §12] God's decisions'.

[5] I have tried to report your difficulty correctly, sir, and here is how I hope to resolve it as completely as you could wish. For it must be resolvable, since it cannot be denied that there truly is this kind of full notion of Adam, accompanied by all his predicates and conceived as possible, which God knows before deciding to create him—as you have just agreed. I think, then, that the dilemma of the two alternative explanations that you present has a middle path: the relation I see between Adam and human events is intrinsic, but not necessary independently of God's free decisions: because God's free decisions, considered as possible, enter into the notion of the possible Adam, and the actualizing of these same decisions is the cause of the actual Adam. I agree with you against the Cartesians, that possibles are possible before any of God's actual decisions, but not without sometimes presupposing those same decisions considered as possible. For the possibilities of individuals or of contingent truths involve in their notion the possibility of their causes, namely God's free decisions. In this they are different from the possibilities of species or eternal truths, which depend only on God's understanding, without assuming his will, as I have already explained above.

[6] That may be enough, but in order to make myself better understood, I shall add that I think that there was an infinity of possible ways of creating the world according to the different plans that God could form, and that each possible world depends on certain principal plans or aims on the part of God, which are peculiar to it; that is to say, it depends on certain basic free decisions (conceived of as possible) or laws of the *general order* of that possible universe, to which they are suited and whose notion they determine, as well as the notions of all the individual substances which must enter into that particular universe. For everything is in *order*, even miracles, although they are contrary to some subordinate maxims or laws of nature. So no human event could fail to happen as it actually has happened, once the choice of Adam is made; but not so much because of the individual notion of Adam, although that notion involves it, but because of God's plans, which also enter into that individual notion of Adam, and which determine that of the whole of this universe, and consequently

both that of Adam and that of the other individual substances of this universe. For each individual substance expresses the whole universe of which it is a part according to a certain relation, through the interconnectedness which exists between all things because of the links between God's decisions or plans.

[7] I note that you make another objection, sir, which is not based on consequences that seem to be contrary to liberty, like the objection I have just answered, but which is based on the thing itself, and on the idea we have of an individual substance. For since I have the idea of an individual substance, that is to say, of *me*, it seems to you that it is there we should look for what should be said about individual notions, and not in the way God conceives of individuals. And just as I only have to consult the specific notion of a sphere in order to see that the number of feet in the diameter is not determined by that notion, so in the same way (you say) I clearly find, in the individual notion that I have of myself, that I will be myself whether I make or do not make the journey that I have planned.

[8] To give a clear reply, I agree that the connection between events, although certain, is not necessary, and that I am free to make or not make this journey, for although it may be involved in my notion that I will make it, it is also involved that I will make it freely. And there is nothing in all that is in me that can be conceived in general terms (that is, in terms of essence, or of a specific or incomplete notion) from which one can deduce that I will necessarily make it, whereas from the fact that I am a man one can conclude that I am capable of thought. Consequently, if I do not make the journey, that will not conflict with any eternal or necessary truth. However, since it is certain that I will make it, there must obviously be some connection between me, who am the subject, and the making of the journey, which is the predicate, for in a true proposition the notion of the predicate is always present in the subject. So there would be a falsity if I did not make it which would destroy my individual or complete notion, or what God conceives or conceived of with regard to me even before resolving to create me; for that notion involves, as possibilities, existences or truths of fact, or God's decisions, on which facts depend.

[9] I also agree that in order to decide about the notion of an individual substance it is useful to consult that which I have of myself, just as we have to consult the specific notion of the sphere in order to decide on its properties. Although there is quite a difference. For the notion of me in particular, and that of every other individual substance, is infinitely more extensive and more difficult to comprehend than a specific notion like that of a sphere, which is incomplete and does not involve all the circumstances

which are necessary in practice for arriving at a particular sphere. In order to understand what *myself* is, it is not enough that I can feel myself to be a substance which thinks; we would have to conceive distinctly of what distinguishes me from all other possible minds, of which I have only confused experience. That means that although it is easy to see that the number of feet in the diameter is not involved in the notion of the sphere in general, it is not so easy to see for certain (although one can see it quite probably) whether the journey that I plan to make is involved in my notion— otherwise it would be as easy to be a prophet as to be a geometer. However, just as experience is insufficient for me to be aware of an infinity of insensible things in the body, but of which general consideration of the nature of body and of motion can convince me, so although experience does not make me feel everything which is involved in my notion, I can know in general that everything which pertains to me is involved in it, by the general consideration of the individual notion.

[10] There is no doubt that since God can and in fact does form this complete notion which involves what is sufficient to explain all the phenomena which will happen to me, it is therefore possible, and it is the true complete notion of what I call me, in virtue of which all my predicates pertain to me as their subject. We could therefore prove it just the same without mentioning God, except so far as is necessary to indicate my dependence; but we show this truth more forcibly by deducing the notion in question from the divine understanding as its source. I admit that there are many things in the knowledge of God that we can never comprehend; but it seems to me that there is no need to get involved in them in order to answer our question. Moreover, if in the life of some person, or even in all of this universe, something went differently than it does, nothing would stop us from saying that it would be another person, or another possible universe, which God had chosen. So it truly would be another individual; and there must be an a priori reason (independent of my experience) which makes it true to say that it is I who was in Paris and that it is still I, and not another, who am now in Germany. Consequently, that notion of myself must connect or comprehend the two different states. Otherwise it could be said that it is not the same individual, even though it appears to be. And in fact some philosophers who have not sufficiently understood the nature of substance and of individual beings, or beings *per se*, have thought that nothing remains truly the same.[2] And that, amongst other

---

[2] Perhaps a reference to *Plato, for Leibniz elsewhere says of him that he believed that 'material things were in perpetual flux' ('A letter . . . to M. Desmaizeaux', WF 240).

reasons, is why I think that bodies would not be substances if there were nothing in them but extension.

[11] I believe, sir, that I have now resolved the difficulties concerning the principal proposition; but as you also make some important remarks about some incidental expressions which I have used, I shall try to explain those as well. I said that the assumption from which all human events can be deduced is not that of the creation of a vague Adam, but that of the creation of such and such an Adam, with all these circumstances determined, chosen from amongst an infinity of possible Adams. You make two significant remarks about this: one against the plurality of Adams, and the other against the reality of merely possible substances. As for the first point, you quite rightly say that it is no more possible to conceive several possible Adams, taking Adam to be a singular nature, than to conceive several 'me's. I agree with that, but in speaking of several Adams, I was not taking Adam as a determinate individual, but as a person conceived of in general terms—that is, under circumstances which seem to us to determine Adam as an individual, but which in truth do not sufficiently determine him as one, such as when we mean by Adam the first man, whom God puts in a garden of pleasure and which he leaves because of sin, and from whose side God draws a woman. But all that does not determine him sufficiently well, and so there would be several disjunctively possible Adams, or several individuals whom all of that would fit. That is true whatever finite number of predicates which are incapable of determining all the rest we may take; but what determines a particular Adam must involve absolutely all his predicates, and it is that complete notion which determines generality so that the individual is reached. In fact, I am so far from the plurality of the same individual, that I am quite convinced of what St *Thomas had already taught regarding intelligences, and which I take to be generally true, namely that it is not possible that there should be two individuals who are exactly similar, or who differ only numerically.[3]

[12] As for the reality of 'purely possible substances, which, that is to say, God will never create', you say, sir, that you are 'strongly inclined to think that they are chimeras'. I do not disagree with that, if you mean (as I think you do) that they have no other reality than what they have in the divine understanding, and in God's active power. However, you see from that, sir, that we have to fall back on God's knowledge and power in order to explain them properly. I also find what you say next to be very sound— that we never conceive of any purely possible substance 'except through

---

[3] For discussion of Leibniz's principle of the 'identity of indiscernibles', see T15 n. 1.

the idea of one' (or through the ideas comprised in one) 'of those which God has created'. You also say: 'we imagine that . . . [as at T2. 3 §14] any of the others'. Here you seem to acknowledge, sir, that these ideas, which I accept are mine (provided the plurality of Adams and their possibility is understood according to the explanation that I have given, and provided that all of this is taken as being according to the way in which we conceive of some order in the thoughts or operations that we attribute to God), enter quite naturally into the mind, when we think about this matter a little, and indeed cannot be avoided. They perhaps displeased you only because you thought that the intrinsic relation here could not be reconciled with God's free decisions. Everything that is actual can be conceived as possible, and if the actual Adam will in the course of time have such and such a posterity, the same predicate cannot be denied to that Adam when conceived as possible—especially as you admit that God envisages all these predicates in him when he decides to create him. So they do belong to him; and I do not see that what you say about the reality of possibles contradicts it. For something to be called possible, it is sufficient that a notion can be formed of it, even though it is only in the divine understanding, which is, so to speak, the land of possible realities. So in speaking of possibles I require only that true propositions can be formed about them, just as we can, for example, see that a perfect square implies no contradiction, even though there is no perfect square in the world. If we tried to reject pure possibilities absolutely, we would destroy contingency and freedom; for if there were nothing possible other than what God actually creates, then what God creates would be necessary, and if God wanted to create something he would not be able to create anything else, and would have no freedom of choice.

[13] All of this makes me hope . . . that at the end of the day your thoughts will turn out to be not so far from mine as they appeared at first. You agree, sir, with the connectedness of God's decisions; you accept that my principal proposition is certain, in the sense I gave it in my reply. You only doubted whether I make that connectedness independent of God's free decisions, and that quite rightly worried you. But I have shown that according to me it depends on those decrees, and it is not necessary, even though it is intrinsic. You stressed the difficulty there would be in saying that if I do not make the journey that I am due to make, I would not be me, and I have explained how one can say it, and how not. Finally I gave a decisive argument, which in my view amounts to a proof. This is that in all true affirmative propositions, necessary or contingent, universal or singular, the notion of the predicate is always in some way included in that of the

subject—the predicate is present in the subject—or I do not know what truth is.

[14] Now, I want nothing more in the way of connectedness here than what is found objectively between the terms of a true proposition, and it is only in this sense that I say that the notion of an individual substance involves all its events and all its denominations, even those that are commonly called *extrinsic* (that is to say, which belong to it only in virtue of the general interconnectedness of things, and of the fact that it expresses the whole universe in its way) because *there must always be some foundation for the connection between the terms of a proposition, and it must be found in their notions.* That is my great principle, with which I believe all philosophers should agree, and of which one of the corollaries is the common axiom that nothing happens without a reason, and that one can always explain why things have gone as they have rather than otherwise, even though that reason often inclines without necessitating, since perfect indifference is a chimerical and incomplete supposition. It can be seen that from the above principle I draw consequences which are surprising; but that is only because people have not got used to pursuing far enough the things we know most clearly.

[15] I will add, that the proposition which occasioned all this discussion is very important, and deserves to be firmly established, for it follows from it that each individual substance expresses the whole universe entirely in its way and according to a certain relation, or, so to speak, in accordance with the point of view from which it regards it; and that its subsequent state is a consequence (although free, or contingent) of its preceding state, as if there were only it and God in the world. So every individual substance or complete being is like a world apart, independent of everything else except God. Nothing so powerfully demonstrates not only that our soul is indestructible, but also that it always retains in its nature traces of all its preceding states, with a potential memory which can always be excited since it has consciousness, or knows in itself what each of us calls 'I'. This makes it susceptible of moral qualities and of punishment and reward—even after this life, because immortality without memory would not be enough. But this independence does not rule out intercourse between substances; for since all created substances are continually produced by the same sovereign being in accordance with the same plans, and express the same universe or the same phenomena, they fit in with one another precisely. And that leads us to say that one acts on the other, because one expresses more distinctly than the other the cause or reason for the changes, rather in the way that we attribute motion to a boat rather

than to the whole sea. And we are right in that, even though abstractly speaking we could maintain another description of their motion, since motion, abstracted from its cause, is always a relative thing. It is in this way that, in my view, we must understand the mutual intercourse between created substances, and not by some influence or real physical dependence which can never be distinctly conceived. This is why, when it is a question of the union of the soul and the body, or of the activity or passivity of a mind with respect to another created thing, many people have had to agree that their direct intercourse is inconceivable. However, the theory of occasional causes is unsatisfactory, it seems to me, to a philosopher. For it introduces a kind of continual miracle—as if at every moment God were changing the laws of bodies on the occasion of the thoughts of minds, or changing the regular course of the soul's thoughts by exciting other thoughts in it, on the occasion of the movements of the body; in general, as if God involved himself in the ordinary course of events otherwise than merely in keeping each substance on its course and following the laws established for it. There is therefore only the *theory of concomitance, or of the mutual agreement of substances*, which explains everything in a manner which is comprehensible and worthy of God, and which indeed is demonstrable and inevitable in my view given the proposition that we have just established. It seems to me that it also fits in with the freedom of rational creatures much better than does the *theory of impressions, or that of occasional causes*. God created the soul from the outset in such a way that standardly there is no need for any such alterations; and what happens to the soul comes to it from its own depths, without its needing thereafter to accommodate itself to the body, any more than the body does to the soul. Each one following its own laws (the one acting freely, the other without choice), they correspond, the one with the other, in the same phenomena. Yet the soul is nevertheless the form of its body, because it expresses the phenomena of all other bodies according to their relation to its own.

[16] It is perhaps more surprising that I deny what nevertheless seems so clear—the action of one corporeal substance on another. But others have already denied it, and we should consider it more a play of the imagination than a distinct conception. If the body is a substance, and not a mere phenomenon, like the rainbow, or a being unified by accident or by aggregation, like a heap of stones, it cannot consist in extension, and we have to conceive of it as having something like what is called a substantial form, which in some way corresponds to the soul. Almost despite myself I have finally been convinced of this, after having earlier been very far from it. Nevertheless, however much I agree with the Scholastics in this general

113

and so to speak metaphysical explanation of the principles of bodies, I am as corpuscularian as could be in the explanation of particular phenomena, and there it means nothing to bring in forms and qualities. Nature must always be explained mathematically and mechanically, provided we know that the principles or laws of mechanics or of force themselves do not depend only on mathematical extension, but on various metaphysical explanations.

2.5. *Arnauld to Leibniz, 28 September 1686*

... [1] I am satisfied with the way you explain what had shocked me at first, with regard to the notion of an individual nature. . . . I have particularly been struck by the thought that in all true affirmative propositions, necessary or contingent, universal or singular, the notion of the attribute is in some way included in that of the subject: the predicate is present in the subject [*praedicatum inest subjecto*]. . . .

[2] I prefer to ask you to clarify for me two things I found in your last letter . . . The first is what you mean by 'the theory of concomitance and of the mutual agreement of substances', by which you claim that we should explain what happens in the union of the soul and the body, and the activity or passivity of a mind in regard to another created thing. . . .

[3] The second thing about which I would like clarification is when you say, 'If the body . . . [as at T2. 4 §16] corresponds to the soul'. There are many things to ask about that.

1. Our body and our soul are two substances which are really distinct. Now if we put into the body a substantial form over and above extension, we cannot imagine that they would make two distinct substances. I cannot therefore see how this substantial form could have any connection with what we call our soul.

2. This substantial form of the body would have to be either extended and divisible or non-extended and indivisible. If we say the first [*sic*, the second?], it seems it must be *indestructible* along with our soul. And if we say the latter [*sic*, the former?], it seems that nothing is gained towards making the body *unum per se, as opposed to its consisting only in extension. For it is the divisibility of extension into an infinity of parts which makes it difficult to conceive it as a unity; this substantial form cannot help with that, if it is as divisible as extension itself.

3. Is it the substantial form of a slab of marble which makes it one? If it is, what becomes of this substantial form when it ceases to be one because it gets broken in two? Is it annihilated, or has it become two? The first is

inconceivable if the substantial form is not a manner of being but a substance. And it cannot be said that it is a manner of being or a modality, since the substance of which this form would be the modality would have to be extension—which apparently is not your thought. And if the substantial form becomes two from the one that it was, why not just say that of extension itself, without the substantial form? . . .

5. To what do you attribute the unity we give to the earth, to the sun, to the moon, when we say that there is only one earth that we live on, only one sun which shines on us, only one moon which revolves in so many days round the earth? Do you think that this requires that the earth, for example, composed of so many heterogeneous parts, has a substantial form which is proper to it which gives it that unity? There is no indication that you think that. I shall say the same of a tree, or a horse. And then I shall move on to all the compound things. Milk, for example, is composed of serum, of cream, and of the clotting matter. Does it have three substantial forms, or only one?

6. In the end it will be said that it is not worthy of a philosopher to admit entities of which we have no clear and distinct idea, and that we have no such idea of these substantial forms; and, furthermore, according to you they cannot be proved by their effects, since you admit that all the particular phenomena of nature should be explained by the corpuscular philosophy, and that it is saying nothing to adduce such forms.

7. There are *Cartesians, who in order to find a unity in bodies have denied that matter is infinitely divisible, and have asserted that we have to admit indivisible atoms. But I do not think that you are of their opinion.[4] . . .

2.6. *Draft of Leibniz to Arnauld, 28 November / 8 December 1686 (T2. 7)*

. . . [1] The other difficulty is incomparably greater, concerning *substantial forms and the souls of bodies, and I must confess that I am not at all satisfied on this. First we would have to be sure that bodies are substances and not just true phenomena, like the rainbow. But assuming that they are, I think we can show that a corporeal substance does not consist in extension or in divisibility. For you will grant me that two bodies which are at a distance—for example, two triangles—are not really one substance. But now let us suppose that they come together to form a square: can merely being in contact make them into a substance? I don't think so. But every extended mass can be considered as made up of two, or a thousand,

---

[4] See App.

others. Extension comes only from contact. Thus you will never find a body of which we can say that it is truly a substance: it will always be an aggregation of many substances. Or rather, it will never be a real being, since the parts which make it up face just the same difficulty, and so we never arrive at real being, because beings by aggregation can have only as much reality as there is in their ingredients. From this it follows that the substance of a body—if they have them—must be indivisible, and it doesn't matter whether we call that a soul or a form. And what is more, the general notion of an individual substance—which seems, sir, to be quite to your taste—proves the same thing. Extension is an attribute which could never make up a complete being; and we could never get from it any action or change: it only expresses a present state, and never the future or the past, as the notion of a substance must do. When two triangles are joined together, we could never deduce how they came to have been joined, for it could have happened in various ways. But anything which can have several causes can never be a complete being. I admit, though, that it is very difficult to resolve some of the questions you mention. I think we have to say that if bodies have substantial forms—for example, if animals have souls—then those souls are indivisible. That is also the opinion of St *Thomas. Are such souls then indestructible? I admit that they are—and just as it could be that, in accordance with the views of M. *Leeuwenhoek, all generation of animals is only the transformation of an already living animal, so there are also grounds to believe that death is nothing but a further transformation. But the soul of a man is something more divine: it is not only indestructible, but it always knows itself, and remains *conscia sui* [conscious of itself]. With regard to its origin, we can say that God produced it only when the animated body which exists in the seed proceeds to take on human form. The animal soul which animated that body before the transformation is annihilated when the rational soul takes its place; or perhaps God changes the one into the other by giving the former a new perfection through his extraordinary influence—that is a detail about which I am unclear.

[2] I don't know whether the body, considered in isolation from the soul or substantial form, can be called a substance. It could well be a machine, an aggregation of several substances. So if you ask me what I would say about the form of a corpse or about a slab of marble, I would say that they are perhaps united *per aggregationem* [*ens per aggregationem*] like a heap of stones, and are not substances. We could say the same thing of the sun, the earth, or machines, and with the exception of man there is no body of which I can say for certain that it is a substance rather than an aggregation

of several substances, or perhaps a phenomenon. However, it seems to me certain that if there are corporeal substances, man is not the only one, and it seems probable that animals have souls, although they lack consciousness. . . .

[3] It would be unworthy of a philosopher to admit forms with no reason, but without them it is incomprehensible that bodies could be substances.

2.7. *Leibniz to Arnauld, 28 November/8 December 1686*

. . . [1] As regards the two difficulties which you find in my letter . . . I think you yourself have explained sufficiently well what you had found obscure in my thoughts about the theory of concomitance. . . .

[2] [W]ith regard to the other question, which concerns substantial forms: the first difficulty that you suggest, sir, is that our soul and our body are two substances which are really distinct, and it seems therefore that the one cannot be the substantial form of the other. I answer that in my opinion our body in itself, or the *corpse*, considered in isolation from the soul, can only improperly be called *a substance*, like a machine, or a heap of stones, which are only beings by aggregation (for the regularity or irregularity of the arrangement of a thing makes no difference to its substantial unity). . . .

[3] As regards the second problem, I agree that the substantial form of the body is indivisible, and it seems to me that that is also the opinion of St *Thomas. I also agree that all substantial forms and all substances are indestructible and indeed ingenerable . . . They could therefore never come into existence except by an act of creation. And I am strongly inclined to believe that the generation of all animals which are deprived of reason, which do not require a new act of creation, is only the transformation of another animal which is already alive, but which is often imperceptible— on the lines of the changes which occur to a silkworm and other similar creatures. . . . Thus animal souls will all have been created from the beginning of the world . . . but the rational soul is created only at the time of the formation of its body, since it is entirely different from the other souls that we know of, because it is capable of reflection, and imitates the divine nature on a small scale.

[4] In the third place, I think that a slab of marble is perhaps only like a heap of stones, and so could never pass for a single substance, but only for an assemblage of many substances. For imagine there were two stones, for example the diamond of the Grand Duke and that of the Great Mogul. We can use a single collective noun to do service for both of them, and say that

they are a pair of diamonds, although they are a long way apart from one another; but we would not say that they constitute a substance. Now, matters of degree play no part here. If we gradually bring them closer together, therefore, and even bring them into contact, they will not be any more substantially united. And if when they were in contact we joined them to some other body which prevented them from separating—for example, if we mounted them in a single ring—the whole thing would make up only what is called *unum per accidens. Because it is as if by accident that they are forced to move in unison. I therefore hold that a slab of marble is not a single complete substance, any more than the water in a pond together with all its fish would be, even if all the water and all the fish were frozen together . . . There is as much difference between a substance and a being of that kind as there is between a man and a group such as a nation, an army, a society, or a college; these are moral beings, in which there is something imaginary, or something which depends on the inventions of our minds. Substantial unity requires a complete indivisible being, which is indestructible by natural means, because its notion contains within itself everything that is ever going to happen to it. Such a thing could never be found in either shape or motion, each of which indeed contains within itself something imaginary, as I have just shown, but only in a soul or substantial form, something like what I call myself. . . . Now, the myself that I have just mentioned, or what corresponds to that in every individual substance, could never be made or unmade by the bringing together or the taking apart of pieces, which has nothing to do with making up a substance. I could not say exactly whether there are true corporeal substances other than those which are animated, but at least souls serve to give us some knowledge of others by analogy.

[5] . . . [F]ifthly, if you ask me in particular what I say about the sun, the globe of the earth, the moon, trees and similar bodies, and even animals, I could not say with absolute certainty whether they are animated—or at least whether they are substances—or whether they are simply machines or aggregations of several substances. But I can at least say that if there are no corporeal substances of the kind that I have in mind, then bodies will only be true phenomena, like the rainbow. Because not only is a continuum divisible to infinity, but every part of matter is actually divided into other parts which are as different from each other as the two diamonds mentioned above. And since that goes on and on in the same way, you will never arrive at something of which you can say it is a true being until you find animated machines, the substantial form of which produces a substantial unity which is independent of the external union of contact. And if

there are none, it follows that except for man there is nothing substantial in the visible world.

[6] Sixthly, as the notion of an individual substance in general that I have given is as clear as that of truth, the notion of a corporeal substance must be so too, and therefore also that of a substantial form. But even if it were not, we have to accept many things the knowledge of which is not sufficiently clear and distinct. I hold that the notion of extension is even less clear and distinct, as witness the strange difficulties over the composition of the continuum. In fact we can say that there is no precise, fixed shape of a body, because of the actual subdivision of its parts. And therefore bodies would without doubt be imaginary things, or only apparent, if there were nothing but matter and its modifications. However, it is useless to mention the unity, notion, or substantial form of bodies when we are trying to explain particular phenomena of nature, just as it is useless for geometers to consider the problems about the composition of the continuum when they are trying to work out some particular problem. But these things are nevertheless important and worthy of consideration in their correct place. All the phenomena of bodies can be explained mechanically, or by the corpuscular philosophy, in accordance with certain principles of mechanics which are taken for granted without worrying about whether or not there are souls. But in the final analysis of the principles of physics, and of mechanics itself, it turns out that those principles cannot be explained solely by the modifications of extension, and the nature of force itself requires something else.

[7] Finally, in seventh place, I remember that in order to preserve substantial unity in bodies M. *Cordemoy, in his treatise on distinguishing the soul from the body, thought himself obliged to accept atoms, or indivisible extended bodies, so as to be able to find something fixed to constitute a simple being. But you were right to think, sir, that I would not be of that opinion. It seems that M. Cordemoy had recognized something true; but he had not yet seen what the true notion of a substance consists in, or that it is there that the key to the most important knowledge lies. The atom which contains only a shaped mass of infinite hardness (which I hold would not be compatible with divine wisdom, any more than would a vacuum) could never contain within itself all its past and future states, and even less those of the entire universe.

2.8. *Arnauld to Leibniz, 4 March 1687*

. . . [1] As to the second problem, I now understand your view quite differently from before. I thought you were reasoning as follows: bodies must be true substances; they cannot be true substances if they have no true unity, and they cannot have true unity if they don't have a substantial form. Therefore the essence of body cannot be extension, but every body, in addition to extension, must have a substantial form. I replied then that a divisible substantial form—as they nearly all are, according to the opinion of the supporters of substantial forms—could never give a body a unity which it would not have had without that substantial form.

[2] You agree with that, but you claim that all substantial forms are indivisible, indestructible, and ingenerable, and cannot be produced except by a true act of creation.

[3] From this it follows . . . that any body which can be divided into parts each of which remains of the same nature as the whole, such as metals, stones, wood, air, water and other liquid bodies, has no substantial form. . . . There will therefore be only animals which have substantial forms. According to you, therefore, it will be only animals that are true substances. . . . And yet you are not so sure of that, since you say that if the lower animals have no soul or substantial form, it follows that apart from man there will be nothing substantial in the visible world, because you claim that substantial unity requires a complete indivisible being—and one which is indestructible by natural means—which could only be found in a soul or substantial form of the kind which we call myself.

[4] All that comes down to saying that all bodies of which the parts are only mechanically united are not substances, but only machines or aggregations of several substances.

[5] I shall start with this last point, and I tell you frankly that it is nothing but a dispute about a word. St *Augustine sees no difficulty in recognizing that bodies have no true unity, because unity must be indivisible, and no body is indivisible. There is therefore no true unity except in minds, any more than there is a true myself. But what conclusion do you draw from that? That there is nothing substantial in bodies which have no soul or substantial form. In order for this conclusion to be sound you would need first to have defined 'substance' and 'substantial' in these terms: 'I call "a substance" or "substantial" that which has true unity.' But since that definition has not yet been accepted, any philosopher has as much right to say 'I call "a substance" whatever is not a modality or a way of being', and can therefore maintain that it is a paradox to say that there is nothing substantial in a block of marble, for that block of marble is certainly not the way of being of some other substance. And all you could say is that it is not a single substance, but several substances mechanically joined together. Now it seems to me a paradox, that philosopher would say, that there should be nothing

substantial in what is made up of several substances. And he might add that he understands even less when you say that 'bodies would without doubt be imaginary things, or only apparent, if there were nothing but matter and its modifications' [T2. 6 §6]. Because you regard matter and its modifications as the only thing that has no soul or indivisible, indestructible, and ingenerable, substantial form; and it is only in animals that you think there are such forms. You would therefore have to say that all the rest of nature is 'only imaginary, or apparent', and you would have to say the same thing all the more about all the works of man.

[6] I could not agree with those latter propositions. But I can see no obstacle to believing that in the whole of corporeal nature there are only 'machines' and 'aggregations' of substances, because none of these parts can be said strictly speaking to be a single substance. That shows only something which it is very important to notice (as St Augustine did): that thinking or spiritual substance is much more excellent than extended or corporeal substance, in that only spiritual substance has true unity, a true myself, which corporeal substance does not have. From that it follows that we cannot use that fact to prove that extension is not the essence of body since it would not be a true unity if it had extension for its essence, because perhaps it is of the essence of body to have no true unity, as you say it is of all bodies which are not joined to a soul or a substantial form.

[7] But I do not understand, sir, what it is that leads you to think that animals have these souls or substantial forms which you claim must be 'indivisible, indestructible, and ingenerable'. It is not that you think it necessary in order to explain what they do, because you say explicitly that 'all the phenomena of bodies can be explained mechanically, or by the corpuscular philosophy, in accordance with certain principles of mechanics which are taken for granted without worrying about whether or not there are souls' [T2. 7 §6]. It is also not because it is necessary that the bodies of animals should have true unity and should not be merely machines or aggregations of substances, because if plants can be nothing more than that, what necessity could there be for animals to be anything different? And, moreover, I cannot see how this idea could easily be sustained if you are going to make these souls indivisible and indestructible, because what will you say about worms which have been cut in two, and each part continues to move as before? If fire took hold of one of those houses where they keep a hundred thousand silkworms, what would become of those hundred thousand indestructible souls? Would they subsist while separated from all matter, like our souls? In the same way, what became of the souls of those millions of frogs which Moses killed when he put an end

to the plague? And of the uncountable number of quails which the Israelites killed in the desert, and of all the animals which died in the Flood? And there are other difficulties about the way in which these souls get into each animal as soon as they are conceived: were they there in the seed? . . .

[8] It remains only to talk of the unity which the rational soul provides. I agree that it possesses a true and perfect unity, and a true myself, and also that in some way it communicates this unity and this myself to that whole, made up of the soul and the body, which is called man. Although that whole is not indestructible—because it comes to an end when the soul is separated from the body—it is indivisible in the sense that no one can conceive of half a man. But if we consider the body separately, then just as our soul does not communicate its 'indestructibility', so I do not see that properly speaking it communicates its true unity, either–or its indivisibility. Although it is united to our soul, it remains true that its parts are only united together mechanically, and that it is therefore not a single corporeal substance but an aggregation of several corporeal substances. It remains just as divisible as all the other bodies in nature. But divisibility is contrary to true unity; it therefore does not have true unity. But it does, you say, through the soul. That is to say that it belongs to a soul which is truly one; but that is not a unity which is intrinsic to the body, but something comparable to the unity of different provinces which make up one kingdom because they are governed by a single king.

[9] However, even if it is true that there is no true unity except in intelligent natures which can say myself, there are nevertheless various degrees of what is loosely called unity and which is appropriate to bodies. For even if there is no body which considered by itself is not several substances, it is none the less reasonable to attribute more unity to bodies whose parts fit together into a single design, such as a house or a watch, than to those whose parts are merely close to each other, such as a heap of stones, or a sack of coins. And strictly speaking it is only these latter that we should call 'accidental aggregations' [*aggregatum per accidens*]. Almost all the bodies in nature which we call 'one'—such as a piece of gold, a star, a planet—are of the first kind; but there are none in which we see it more clearly than in animals and plants, without there being any need for that reason to start giving them souls. (And indeed it seems you do not give souls to plants.) For why shouldn't a horse or an orange tree be regarded as a complete and finished product, just as much as a church or a watch? What difference does it make from the point of view of being called 'one' (with the kind of unity that is appropriate to bodies, and so has to be different from that

which is appropriate to spiritual nature) that their parts are only mechanically united, and they are therefore machines? Is it not the greatest perfection they could have to be such wonderful machines that only an all-powerful God could have made them? Our body considered on its own is therefore of that type. And the relation it has to an intelligent nature which is united to it and which governs it is capable of adding some further unity to it, but that is not a unity of the kind which belongs to spiritual natures.

2.9. *Leibniz to Arnauld, 30 April 1687*

... [1] If the view I have—that substance requires a true unity—were based only on a definition which I had made up contrary to standard usage, it would be only a 'dispute about a word' [T2. 7 §5]. But quite apart from the fact that ordinary philosophers have taken the word in more or less the same way, distinguishing between *unum per se* and *unum per accidens*, substantial form and accidental form, imperfect and perfect mixtures, natural and artificial things, I take things at a higher level, and, leaving aside language, I believe that where there are only beings by aggregation, there will not in fact be any real beings. Any being by aggregation presupposes beings endowed with true unity, because it derives its reality only from that of the things which make it up. It will therefore have no reality at all if every being of which it is composed is itself a being by aggregation, for whose reality we have to find some further basis, which in the same way, if we have to go on searching for it, we will never find. I agree, sir, that 'in the whole of corporeal nature there are only machines' (often animated ones), but I do not agree that there could be 'only aggregations of substances' [T2. 8 §6]: if there are aggregations of substances, then necessarily there must also be true substances from which all those aggregations result. So we must necessarily end up either with mathematical points, which some authors hold extension to be made up of; or with atoms, like *Epicurus and M. *Cordemoy—which you, like me, have already rejected; or we will have to say that there is no reality in bodies; or, finally, we will have to accept that there are in bodies substances which possess a genuine unity. I have already said in another letter that the composite which is made up of the diamond of the Grand Duke and that of the Great Mogul can be called a pair of diamonds, but that is only a being of reason; if they were brought together, that would be a being of imagination or of perception, a phenomenon that is, because contact, shared motion, co-operating in a single design do not change anything in substantial unity. ...

[2] It would seem, moreover, that what makes the essence of a being by aggregation is only the way of being of the things that make it up; for example, what makes the essence of an army is just the way of being of the men who make it up. That way of being therefore presupposes a substance, whose essence is not itself the way of being of a substance. So every machine also presupposes some substance in the parts of which it is made, and there is no multitude without true unities. To cut the point short, I hold as an axiom the following proposition which is a statement of identity which varies only in the placing of the emphasis: nothing is truly *one* being if it is not truly one *being*. It has always been held that *one* and *being* are reciprocal things. It is one thing to be a being, quite another to be a number of beings; but the plural presupposes the singular, and where there is no being, still less is there a number of beings. . . .

[3] I do not say that there is nothing substantial or nothing but what is apparent in things which have no true unity, because I allow them always as much reality or substantiality as there is true unity in what enters into their composition.

[4] You object, sir, that it could be of the essence of body to have no true unity [T2. 8 §6]; but then it would be of the essence of body to be a phenomenon, bereft of all reality, like a well-ordered dream. For phenomena themselves—such as the rainbow, or a heap of stones—would be completely imaginary if they were not composed of beings which have true unity.

[5] You say you do not understand what it is that leads me [T2. 8 §7] to believe in these substantial forms, or rather these corporeal substances endowed with true unity. But it is because I cannot conceive of any reality without a true unity. And according to me the notion of a singular substance contains consequences which are incompatible with a being by aggregation. I believe there are properties in substance which could never be explained by extension, shape, and motion. And what is more a body has no exact, fixed shape, because of the actual subdivision of the continuum to infinity; and motion, in so far as it is only a modification of extension, or a change in surroundings, contains something imaginary, in that we cannot specify to which subject, out of all those which are changing, a motion belongs, without going back to force, which is the cause of motion, and which is found in a corporeal substance. I accept that we have no need to mention these substances and qualities in order to explain particular phenomena . . . We can explain the particularities of nature mechanically, I agree; but only after having accepted, or taken for granted, the principles of mechanism itself, which can only ever be established a

priori by metaphysical reasoning. And the difficulties of the composition of the continuum will never be resolved as long as we consider extension as making up the substance of bodies, and we confuse ourselves with chimeras of our own devising.

[6] I also think that to want to try to restrict true unity or substance almost to man alone is to be as limited in metaphysics as were in physics those who had the world enclosed in a ball.[5] And since true substances are both expressions of the whole universe regarded from a certain direction, and also replications of God's work, this view is in keeping with the greatness and the beauty of God's works, because such substances can never prevent one another from performing those works in this universe as far as is possible, and as far as higher reasons allow. The assumption of pure, naked extension destroys all this wonderful variety. Mere mass (if it were possible to conceive such a thing) is as far below a substance which can perceive, and which represents the whole universe according to its point of view and in accordance with the impressions—or rather relations—which its body is given either mediately or immediately of all others, as a corpse is below an animal, or rather as a machine is below a man. That is how the outlines of the future are formed in advance, and how the traces of the past are conserved for ever in every thing, and how cause and effect express one another perfectly, down to the slightest circumstance, even though the effect depends on an infinity of causes, and even though every cause has an infinity of effects. This would not be possible if the essence of body consisted in a certain shape, motion, or modification of extension, which was determined. . . .

[7] The multitude of souls (to which I do not thereby always attribute desire or pain) should not cause us any difficulty, any more than the *Gassendists' multiplicity of atoms, which are just as indestructible as these souls. On the contrary, it is a perfection in nature to have many of them, since a soul, and indeed an animated substance, is infinitely more perfect than an atom, which has no variation or subdivision, whereas every animated thing contains a world of diversities in a true unity. And experience supports this multitude of animated things. We find that there are a prodigious number of animals in a drop of water infused with pepper, and you can kill millions of them at once, so many that neither the frogs of the Egyptians that you mention, sir, nor the quails of the Israelites, can come near it. If those animals have souls, we will have to say of their souls what we can probably say of the animals themselves, namely,

---

[5] Perhaps a reference to Parmenides (5th century BC), according to whom reality is, or is like, an indivisible, homogeneous sphere.

that they have been living since the creation of the world, and will continue to do so until its end, and that just as their generation seems to be nothing but a change which takes the form of growing, so their death will be nothing but a change which takes the form of a diminution, which makes the animal sink down again into a world of little creatures among which its perceptions are more limited, until such time as it might perhaps receive the order to take the stage again. . . . But minds are not subject to these cycles; or rather these cycles of bodies must play a part in the divine economy through their relation to minds. God creates minds when it is time, and separates them from bodies (at least from their grosser bodies) through death, because they must always retain their moral qualities and their memory in order to be perpetual citizens of the all-perfect universal republic of which God is the ruler. That republic can never lose any of its members, and its laws are superior to those of bodies. I accept that a body on its own, without a soul, has only a unity of aggregation; but the reality which it still possesses derives from the parts which make it up, and which retain their substantial unity because of the countless living bodies which are contained within them.

[8] However, although it could be that a soul has a body which is composed of parts animated by separate souls, the soul or form of the whole thing is not for that reason made up of the souls or forms of the parts. And as for insects[6] that are cut up: it isn't necessary for the two halves still to be animated in order for them still to possess some movement. At least, the soul of the complete insect will remain in just one of the parts, and just as in the formation and growth of the insect the soul was present from the beginning in a certain part which was already alive, so it will stay after the destruction of the insect in a certain part which is still alive . . .

[9] I quite agree that there are degrees of accidental unity. An orderly society has more unity than a confused mob, and an organized body, or a machine, has more unity than a society; that is to say, it is more appropriate to think of them as one thing, because there are more relations between the ingredients. But in the end all these unities derive their completeness only from thoughts and appearances, like colours and other phenomena which we nevertheless continue to call real. The tangibility of a heap of stones or of a block of marble no more proves its substantial reality than its visibility does that of a rainbow; and since nothing is so solid that it does not possess some degree of fluidity, perhaps that block of marble is only a heap made up of an infinity of living bodies, or something like a lake full of

---

[6] i.e. the worms of T2. 8 §7.

fish—even though such animals are normally distinguishable to the eye only in a body which is half rotten. We can therefore say of these composites and similar things what *Democritus rightly said, namely 'they exist by opinion, by convention'. And *Plato is of the same opinion with regard to everything that is purely material. Our minds observe or understand certain true substances which possess certain modes. Those modes contain within them certain relations to other substances, as a result of which the mind has occasion to join them together in thought, and to let a word stand for all of them together. This is very convenient for reasoning; but we should not let ourselves be misled into thinking they are so many substances or truly real beings. . . .

[10] We will never find anything systematic which can make a true substance out of beings by aggregation. For example, if parts which work together to the same end are more suited to making up a true substance than those which are in contact, then all the officers of the Dutch East Indies Company will make up a substance, much more than a heap of stones. But what is a common end other than a resemblance, or a sequence of actions and passions which our mind notices in different things? And if you prefer unity by contact, you will find other difficulties. Hard bodies may have their parts united only by the pressure of bodies around them and of themselves, and in their substance they may have no more union than a heap of sand without lime. Why should several rings interlinked to form a chain compose more of a true substance than if they each had openings in them so that you could take them apart? It could be that none of the parts of the chain was in contact with the next, and didn't even enclose it, and yet that they were so interwoven that unless you took hold of them in a certain way you could never take them apart, as in Figure 2.1.

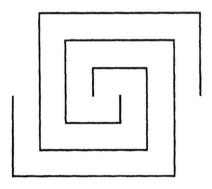

FIG. 2.1.

Should we say in that case that the substance which these things make up is as it were in suspense, and depends on the future skill of a person who might want to take them apart? Fictions of the mind, everywhere; and if we cannot discover what is truly a complete being, or a substance, we will have no stopping-point. . . .

2.10. *Arnauld to Leibniz, 28 August 1687*

. . . [1] 3. I have more to say about these indivisible and indestructible *substantial forms which you think we must recognize in all animals and perhaps even in plants, because otherwise matter (which you take to be composed neither of atoms nor of mathematical points, but to be divisible to infinity) would not be *unum per se but only *aggregatum per accidens.

[2] (i) I replied that it is perhaps essential to matter, which is the most imperfect of all beings, to have no true unity of its own—as St *Augustine thought—and to be always a number of things, and not properly one thing. I said that it would be no more incomprehensible than the divisibility of matter to infinity, which you accept.

[3] Your response is that it cannot be, because there cannot be many things where there are no single things.

[4] But how can you use that argument, which M. *Cordemoy might have thought sound but which according to you must necessarily fail? Because apart from animated bodies, which do not make up a hundred thousand thousandth part of them, all the others, which according to you have no substantial forms, must necessarily be many things and not really one thing. It is therefore not impossible that there should be many things, when there are no single things.

[5] (ii) I do not see that your substantial forms could resolve this difficulty. For the attribute of the thing which is called 'one', taken as you take it in metaphysical rigour, must be essential and intrinsic to what is called 'one thing'. So if a parcel of matter is not one thing but many things, I do not see how a substantial form, which is really distinct from it and so could give it nothing but an extrinsic denomination, could make it cease to be many things, and become one thing by an intrinsic denomination. I can see that it could give us a reason for *calling* it 'one thing', if we do not take it in a strict metaphysical sense; but we have no need of substantial forms in order to *call* an infinite number of inanimate bodies 'one'. Is it not quite correct to say that the sun is 'one', that the earth on which we live is 'one', and so on? So I cannot see that there is any need to accept these substantial forms, in order to give a true unity to things which otherwise would not have it. . . .

[6] (iv) I have no clear idea of these substantial forms, or souls, of animals. You must regard them as substances, since you call them substantial, and you say that only substances are truly real beings, among which you include principally these substantial forms. Now, I know of only two sorts of substances, bodies and minds, and it is up to those who claim that there are others to show them to us . . . I assume, therefore, that these substantial forms are either bodies or minds. If they are bodies, they must be extended, and therefore divisible, and divisible to infinity—from which it follows that they are not one thing but many things, just as much as the bodies which they animate, and so will be far from being able to give them any true unity. But if they are minds, their essence will be to think— because that is what I understand by the word 'mind'. But I find it hard to believe that an oyster thinks, or a worm thinks. And, moreover, since you acknowledge in this letter that you are not sure that plants do not have a soul, or life, or a substantial form, it follows that you are not sure whether or not plants think, since as their substantial form, if they have one, is not a body (because then it would be extended), it would have to be a mind, which is to say a substance which thinks.

[7] (v) The indestructibility of these substantial forms or souls of animals seems to me even more untenable. I asked you what became of these animals' souls when they die, or when they are killed—for example, when caterpillars are burned, what becomes of their souls? You reply that in the body of each caterpillar the soul remains in a little part which is still alive, and which will always be as small as it needs to be in order to be safe from the action of the fire which pulls apart, or breaks up, the caterpillars' bodies [T2. 9 §8]. . . . I cannot imagine a more subtle way of resolving this difficulty. But take note, sir, of what I am going to say about it. When a silk moth produces its eggs, each of those eggs according to you has a silk-worm soul, as a result of which it comes about that five or six months later out come little silkworms. So if you had burned a hundred silkworms there would according to you be a hundred silkworm souls in as many little particles of the ashes. But, on the one hand, I don't know who you will find who will be persuaded that after being burned every silkworm remains the same animal, which has kept the same soul joined to a little particle of ash which used to be a part of its body; and, on the other hand, if that were so, why aren't silkworms born from these particles of ash, just as they are born from eggs?

[8] (vi) But this problem is all the greater in the case of animals which we know more certainly to be born only from a joining of the two sexes. I ask, for example, what became of the soul of the ram which Abraham

sacrificed instead of Isaac, and which he later burned. . . . Instead you will reply that it remained in a little particle of the body of the ram which was reduced to ashes, and therefore it was only a 'transformation of the same animal', which 'always kept the same soul'. That could be said with some plausibility in your theory of the substantial form of a caterpillar which becomes a butterfly, because the butterfly is an organized body, as is the caterpillar, and therefore it is an animal which can be taken to be the same as the caterpillar because it retains many of the parts of the caterpillar unchanged, and others changed only in shape. But this part of the ram which is reduced to ashes and into which the soul of the ram has withdrawn, because it is not organized, cannot be taken to be an animal, and so when the soul of the ram is joined to it it will not make up an animal, still less a ram, as the soul of a ram must do. So what will the soul of this ram do in the ashes? . . . And it would be the same with an infinity of other souls which would not make up animals because they are joined to parts of matter which are not organized, and which we cannot imagine could be so in accordance with the established laws of nature. . . .

2.11. *Leibniz to Arnauld, 9 October 1687*

. . . [1] I now come to the question of these Forms or Souls which I hold to be indivisible and indestructible. I am not the first to hold this opinion. *Parmenides (of whom *Plato speaks with veneration), as well as *Melissus, maintained that generation and corruption were only apparent, according to *Aristotle in chapter 2 of book 3 of *De Caelo*. . . . It seems to me that St *Thomas takes animal souls to be indivisible. And our *Cartesians go much further, because they maintain that every soul or true substantial form must be indestructible and ingenerable. That is why they deny souls to animals—although M. *Descartes in a letter to M. *More makes clear that he does not want to say for certain that they do not have them. Since no one takes offence at those who bring in permanently subsisting atoms, why should it be found strange that anyone should say the same of souls? Indivisibility belongs to souls by their nature, so that by combining the opinion of the Cartesians about substance and the soul with that of the whole world about the souls of animals, it follows by necessity. It would be very difficult to uproot from the human species the opinion which is accepted at all times and everywhere—a universal opinion if there ever was one—that animals have feeling. . . .

[2] But to come to your doubts about this indestructibility:

[3] (i) I had claimed that we have to allow that there is in bodies something which is truly a single being, since matter or extended mass in itself is

only ever *plura entia*, as St *Augustine, following *Plato, rightly pointed out. Now, I argue that there cannot be a plurality of beings where there is not one being, and that all multiplicity presupposes a unity. To this you reply in several ways . . . First you say you are astonished, sir, that I can use that argument, which might have been obvious for M. *Cordemoy, who has everything made up out of atoms, but which must necessarily fail according to me (in your opinion), 'because apart from animated bodies, which do not make up a hundred thousand thousandth part of [the rest], all the others . . . must necessarily be many things', and so the problem returns [T2. 10 §4]. But this is what shows me, sir, that I have not yet explained myself sufficiently well for you to take on my theory. Because not only do I not remember having said that there are no substantial forms other than souls, but I am in fact very far from the opinion that animated bodies are only a small part of the rest. Rather, I think that everything is full of animated bodies, and according to me there are incomparably more souls than there are atoms according to M. Cordemoy. He has only a finite number of atoms, whereas I hold that the number of souls, or at least of forms, is quite infinite. Since matter is endlessly divisible we could never say that there is any part of it which is so small that it does not contain animated bodies, or at least bodies which are endowed with a primitive *entelechy . . .

[4] (ii) Now for another objection that you raise, sir, namely that when the soul is joined to matter it does not make it into a being which is truly one, because matter is not truly one being in itself, and the soul, as you see it, gives it only an extrinsic denomination [T2. 10 §5]. I reply that it is the animated substance to which the matter belongs that is truly one being, and the matter taken as a mass in itself is only a pure phenomenon or well-founded appearance, as also are space and time. It does not even have the fixed and precise qualities which could make it pass as a determinate being, as I have already suggested in my previous letter. For shape itself, which is the essence of a bounded extended mass, is never exact and strictly determinate in nature, because of the actual division to infinity of the parts of matter. There is never a sphere without irregularities, no straight line without curves mixed in with it, no curve of any finite nature which is not combined with a different one. . . . I could say the same thing of size and of motion, namely that they are qualities or predicates which partake of the phenomenal, as do colours and sounds; although they contain more that is distinctly knowable, they too cannot sustain a final analysis, and therefore since extended mass considered without entelechies consists only of these qualities, it is not a corporeal substance, but a pure phenomenon, just like

the rainbow. . . . I accept, of course, that we can give the name 'one' to a collection of inanimate bodies even if no substantial form connects them, just as I can say 'there is *a* rainbow', 'there is *a* flock'; but that is a phenomenal unity or a unity of thought, which is not enough to constitute what is real in phenomena. But if we take for the matter of corporeal substances not a formless mass, but secondary matter,[7] which is the multitude of substances the mass of which is that of the body as a whole, we can say that those substances are parts of that matter, in the way that those which make up our bodies form parts of it. For just as our body is the matter and our souls are the form of our substance, so it is with other corporeal substances. I see no more difficulty with that than with the case of man, which we all accept. . . .

[5] To assert that every substance which is not divisible (which according to me means every substance in general) is a mind, and must think, seems to me to be beyond comparison more rash and more unfounded than to believe in the conservation of forms. We know of only five senses and a certain number of metals; should we conclude from that that there are no others in the world? It seems much more likely that nature, which loves variety, has produced other forms than those which can think. . . . [I]t seems to me that we can conceive that divisible phenomena, or phenomena of many beings, can be expressed or represented in a single indivisible being; and that is enough for us to conceive a perception, without its being necessary for us to attach thought or reflection to that representation. I would like to be able to explain the differences and different degrees of other forms of immaterial expression which do not have thought, in order to distinguish corporeal or living substances from animals, in so far as they can be distinguished. But I have not thought enough about it, and have not examined nature well enough to be able to estimate forms on the basis of a comparison of their organs and operations. M. *Malpighi, on the basis of very considerable anatomical analogies, has a great inclination to think that plants can be included in the same category as animals, and are in fact imperfect animals.

[6] (v) It remains for me now only to satisfy you with regard to the minor difficulties which you raise, sir, against the indestructibility of substantial forms. First, I am amazed that you find it strange and untenable, because according to your own position anyone who allows animals to have a soul and feelings must maintain their indestructibility. . . . People who think that there is a virtually infinite number of animals in the small-

---

[7] For the notion of 'secondary matter', see also T5. 7.

est drop of water, as M. *Leeuwenhoek's experiments have shown there are, and who do not find it strange that matter should be filled throughout with animated substances, will not find it any more strange that there should be something animated even in ashes, and that fire can only transform an animal and reduce it to something very small, rather than destroying it altogether. . . .

[7] It is only in appearance and according to the imagination that the problem is any greater with regard to larger animals which we can see are born only from a joining of two sexes [T2. 10 §8] (which it would appear is no less true for the smallest insect). I learned some time ago that M. Leeuwenhoek has opinions quite like my own, in that he holds that even the largest animals are born by a kind of transformation. . . . It is true that I am not aware that they have taken their view to the extent of saying that corruption and death itself is also a transformation with regard to living things devoid of rational souls, which is what I believe; but I think that if they had been aware of the idea they would not have found it absurd. There is nothing more natural than to think that what does not begin does not come to an end either. If we accept that all generation is only an augmentation and development of an already formed animal, we can easily persuade ourselves that corruption or death is nothing but a diminution and encapsulation of an animal which nevertheless still subsists and remains living and organized. . . . [S]leep, which is an image of death, and ecstasies; the enshrouding of a silkworm in its shell, which can be taken for death; the resuscitation of drowned flies brought about by covering them with some dry powder (whereas they remain completely dead if they are left unaided), and that of swallows which make their winter quarters in reeds and which are discovered with no semblance of life; experiments with people killed by cold, drowned, or strangled, and who are then brought back to life . . . all these things confirm my opinion that these different states differ only in degree . . . We ought not therefore to stick to notions of death and of life which the uneducated may have when there are analogies, and moreover solid arguments, to prove the opposite. For I believe I have shown that there must be entelechies if there are corporeal substances; and if we accept these entelechies or these souls, we have to recognize their ingenerability and their indestructibility. . . . Whether the animal made by the contraction of the body of the ram which Abraham burned instead of Isaac should be called a ram is only a question of the name, rather as would be the question whether a moth can be called a silkworm. The difficulty which you find, sir, with regard to this ram which is reduced to ashes, derives only from the fact that I had not explained myself

well enough. You suppose that there remains no organized body in the ashes . . . But I believe that naturally there is no soul without an animated body, and no animated body without organs; and neither ashes nor other masses seem to me incapable of containing organized bodies.

[8] As regards minds, substances which think, that is, and which are capable of knowing God and of discovering eternal truths, I maintain that God governs them in accordance with laws which are different from those in accordance with which he governs all these other substances. For while all forms of substance express the whole universe, we can say that animal substances express the world more than God, but that minds express God more than the world. God governs animal substances in accordance with the material laws of force, or of the communication of motion; but minds he governs in accordance with the spiritual laws of justice, which do not apply to the others . . . he takes on a different role in respect of minds. That role is one which makes us conceive of him clothed in will and moral qualities; for he is himself a mind, and as it were one of us, even to the extent of entering into relation with us in a society of which he is the head. It is that society, or general republic of minds under the sovereign monarch, which is the noblest part of the universe, made up of so many lesser gods under the great God. For we can say that created minds differ from God only as between greater and less, between finite and infinite. And we can truly claim that the whole universe is made only to contribute to the ornament and the happiness of this city of God. That is why everything is disposed in such a way that the laws of force or purely material laws operate in the whole universe in such a way as to carry out the laws of justice or of love; nothing can ever harm souls which are in the hand of God, and everything must work out for the greatest good of those who love him. That is why since minds must keep their personality and their moral qualities in order that the City of God should not lose anyone, they must in particular retain a kind of memory or consciousness, or the power to know what they are. All their morality, sufferings, and punishments depend on this, and as a result they must be exempt from the revolutions of the universe which would otherwise make them unrecognizable to themselves, and would make them morally speaking into a different person. For animal substances, on the other hand, it is enough that they remain the same individual only in metaphysical rigour, even though they are subject to all imaginable changes, since they also have no consciousness or reflection. . . .

[9] Finally, to gather up my thoughts into a few words, I hold that every substance contains within its present state all its past states and all those to

come, and indeed it expresses the whole universe according to its point of view. Nothing is so far away from anything else that it has no connection with it, in particular through its relation to the parts of its body, which it expresses more immediately. As a result, nothing can ever come to it except from its own resources and in virtue of its own laws, provided only that we add to that the concourse of God. But each substance is aware of other things, because it expresses them naturally, having been created from the first in such a way that it would do so later on, and would accommodate itself to them as necessary; and it is in this obligation imposed on it from the beginning that what we call the action of one substance on another consists. As for corporeal substances, I hold that mass, considering only what is divisible in it, is a pure phenomenon; that every substance has a true unity in metaphysical rigour, and that it is indivisible, ingenerable, and incorruptible. All matter must be filled with substances which are animated, or at least alive; generation and corruption are only transformations from small to large or vice versa, and there is no parcel of matter in which there is not a world made up of an infinity of created things, organized as well as collected together. Above all, the works of God are infinitely greater, more splendid, more numerous, and better ordered than we usually think; mechanism, or organization, order, that is, is as it were essential right down to their smallest parts. Thus there is no theory which shows us the wisdom of God better than this one, according to which there are substances which show his perfection everywhere, and which are all equally but in different ways mirrors of the beauty of the universe; nothing is empty, sterile, undeveloped, or without perception. . . .

2.12. *Leibniz to Arnauld, 4/14 January 1688*

. . . Turning to other things, I hope with all my heart that you will have the time to spend half an hour thinking about my objection to the *Cartesians . . . Your intelligence and your honesty convince me that I shall get the point across to you, and that you will recognize in good faith what is involved. The discussion is not long, and the matter is of some importance, not only for mechanics, but also for metaphysics, because motion in itself separated from force is only a relative thing, and its subject can never be determined. But force is something real and absolute, and since the calculation of force is different from that of motion, as I show clearly, we should not be surprised that nature retains the same quantity of force and not the same quantity of motion. However, it follows that in nature there is something other than extension and motion, unless we refuse all force and all power to things, which would be to change them from the substances they are into modes. That is what *Spinoza does; he thinks that only God is a substance, and that all other things are only modifications. Spinoza is full of fantasies, and his so-called demonstrations in 'Of God' don't even look like proofs. However, I claim that a created substance does not in metaphysical rigour act on another, that is, it does not have a real influence. We could never explain distinctly what such an influence consisted in, except in the case of God, whose operation is a continual creation, the source of which is the essential dependence of created things. But in order to talk like other people, who have good reason to say that one substance acts on another, I have to give another notion of what is called action. But that would take too long to work out here, and besides, I refer you to my last letter, which was fairly lengthy.

2.13. *Leibniz to Arnauld, 23 March 1690*

... [1] A body is an aggregation of substances, and not strictly speaking a substance. It must therefore be that there are substances in bodies everywhere, substances which are indivisible, ingenerable, and incorruptible, and which have something of the nature of souls. That all these substances have always been and will always be united to organic bodies which are transformable in various ways. That each one of these substances contains in its nature the law of the continuation of the series of its operations, and everything that has ever happened to it or will happen. That all its actions come from its own depths, except for its dependence on God. That every substance expresses the whole of the universe, but some more distinctly than others, each one more particularly with regard to certain things, and according to its own point of view. That the union of the soul and the body, and also the operation of one substance on another, consists only in the perfect mutual accord, specifically established by the order of the first creation, in virtue of which every substance fits in with what the others need in accordance with its own laws, so that the operations of the one follow or accompany the operation or change of the other. That intelligences, or souls capable of reflection, and of knowledge of eternal truths and of God, have many privileges which exempt them from the revolutions of bodies. That for them moral laws have to be combined with physical ones. That everything is done primarily for these intelligences. That together they make up the republic of the universe, of which God is the ruler. That there is a perfect justice and polity observed in this City of God, and there is no wrong action without punishment, and no good action without its appropriate reward. That the more we knew about things, the more we would see that they are excellent, and in accordance with what a wise person would want. That we should always be content with the events of the past, because they are in conformity with God's absolute will, which we discover only in the event; but that we should try to make the future, in so far as it depends on us, conform to God's *pre-sumptive will, or to his commandments. We should seek to grace this Sparta of ours,[8] and work to do good, but without upsetting ourselves, when we do not succeed, in the firm belief that God will know how to find more suitable occasions to change things for the better. That people who are not content with the order of things cannot claim to love God as they should. That justice is nothing but the charity of the wise. That charity is universal good will, the execution of which the wise person performs in conformity with the measure of reason, in order to obtain the greatest good. And that wisdom is the science of happiness, or of the means of arriving at lasting contentment, which consists in a continual journey towards greater perfection, or at least in a variation of the same level of perfection.

[2] With regard to physics, we have to understand the nature of force, which is quite different from motion, which is something more relative. That we must measure that force by the quantity of its effect. That there is an absolute force, a directive force, and a relative force. That each of these forces is conserved at the same level in the universe, and in each machine which is not in communication with the others, and that the two latter forces taken together make up the first, or absolute force. But that the same quantity of motion is not conserved, since I have shown that other-wise perpetual motion would be achieved, and the effect would be more powerful than the cause.

APPENDIX

Here, having recognized that it is the divisibility of extended matter that accounts for Leibniz's rejecting it as substantial, Arnauld, alluding to the Cartesian philoso-pher *Cordemoy, sees this as a possible reason for suggesting that, after all, matter is not divisible forever, but consists, in the end, of unified indivisible material atoms. As Arnauld suspected, Leibniz (T2. 7 §7) does not share this view. He applauds Cordemoy for having recognized the need for substantial material unities, but insists that these cannot be found in purely material atoms.

---

[8] A reference to the saying 'Sparta is your inheritance; add glory to it' (see Cicero, *Ad Atticum*, 4. 6. 2).

2. Correspondence with Arnauld

His own solution to the requirement for genuine substantial unities out of which material bodies such as human corpses, or marble tiles, can be aggregated can be seen as a combination of Cordemoy's purely material atoms with his own hylomorphic account of living corporeal substances, such as humans and animals. Extended matter for Descartes is continuous, homogeneous, potentially infinitely divisible, and has no ultimate parts; for Cordemoy, by contrast, it is actually divided into small, extended but indivisible atoms, ultimate material parts. Leibniz's view of it aligns him with Cordemoy: matter is actually divided into unitary parts. Yet it also aligns him with Descartes: matter is not divisible into ultimate parts. Moreover, in agreement with neither Descartes nor Cordemoy, he holds that the non-ultimate parts of mere non-substantial matter are not themselves non-substantial. All matter, whether marble tiles or human bodies, is divided into or aggregated out of small, animated, living material substances (see Introduction, Sect. 2).

3

REFLECTIONS ON THE ADVANCEMENT OF TRUE METAPHYSICS AND PARTICULARLY ON THE NATURE OF SUBSTANCE EXPLAINED BY FORCE (1694)

Summary of the Text

This text is an enlarged version of an article, 'On the Correction of Metaphysics and the Concept of Substance', which Leibniz had already published in a learned journal (Acta Eruditorum, *March 1694). He sent it to his correspondent Jacques-Bénigne Bossuet in July 1694.*

It aims to highlight the general importance of metaphysics as a 'first or primary science', and, in particular, within that science, the importance of the notion of substance (see Introduction, Sects. 1–2)—a rich notion from which there follow truths about God, the soul, and the nature of body (cf. T1. 12), and something about which *Descartes went wrong.

In order to give a flavour of his notion of it Leibniz says something (Sect. 4) about his notions of primary active force, which is an element of all substance, and of secondary active force or moving force which is derived from this. (For more of the relations between these, see T4 and Introduction, Sect. 3.)

Primary active force is explained as involving some positive tendency or striving—or 'conatus' or *'entelechy' (as of a bent bow to unbend); as such it is different from an inactive capacity—what the *Scholastics called a 'faculty' (as of a piece of bent wire to be made straight). As for derived active force, Leibniz states (without giving the argument of TT1. 7; 4. 26–31 for the point), that it is to be measured in terms of its effects and not, as with the *Cartesians, to be identified with quantity of motion (or 'impetus'). (See Introduction, Sect. 3.)

According to Leibniz, the important connection between force and substance was missed by the Cartesians, who saw corporeal substance as consisting of no more than extension. This mistake led also (Sect. 2) to their inability to explain the

From the French at UL vi. 532–8. For a fuller translation, see WF 31–5.

relation between body and mind. By contrast, Leibniz's insight into this matter (Sect. 5) will, he says, throw light onto that relation and also onto causal relations between substances in general.

THE TEXT

[1] I notice that most people who take pleasure in the science of mathematics have no taste for metaphysical meditations; they find enlightenment in the one, and darkness in the other. The main cause of this seems to be that general notions, which are thought to be the best known, have become ambiguous and obscure because of people's negligence and the inconsistent way in which they explain themselves. And ordinary definitions, far from explaining the nature of things, do not even explain the meanings of words. This problem has spread to other disciplines, which are subordinate in various ways to this first and architectonic science; thus, instead of clear definitions, we have been given petty distinctions, and instead of universal axioms, we have only local rules, which meet with almost as many exceptions as they have instances. Yet at the same time people are obliged to use metaphysical terms all the time, and they convince themselves that they understand words that they have grown used to using. People are always talking about substance, accident, cause, action, relation or ratio, and numerous other terms, whose true meanings have, however, not yet been made clear; for those true meanings are rich in excellent truths, whereas those we have given to them are barren. That is why we should not be surprised that this primary science, which is called 'first philosophy', and which *Aristotle called the 'sought after', is still to be found.[1]

[2] *Plato is often concerned, in his dialogues, to investigate the richness of these notions; and Aristotle does the same thing in the so-called metaphysical books; but they do not seem to have made much progress in it. The later *Platonists spoke in a mysterious way, which they carried to absurdity; and the *scholastic *Aristotelians were more interested in raising questions than in answering them. They should have had a Gellius, the Roman magistrate whom *Cicero reports as having offered his services to the philosophers of Athens, where he held office, in the belief that

---

[1] 'First philosophy' was what *Aristotle called the subject which came to be known as 'Metaphysics' (see *Metaphysics*, 983^{a}21, 995^{a}24, 996^{b}3).

their arguments could be settled like lawsuits. In our own day, several excellent men have extended their interests into metaphysics, but their success has so far not been very great. It must be admitted, though, that M. *Descartes did something of importance here: he revived Plato's efforts to free the mind from its enslavement to the senses, and he made good use of the doubts of the *Academicians. But having been too hasty in his assertions, and not having distinguished certainty from uncertainty sufficiently well, he didn't achieve his aim. He had a mistaken idea of the nature of body, which he saw, without proof, as being pure extension, and he couldn't see any way of explaining the union of the soul with the body. This was through not understanding the nature of substance in general; he made a kind of leap into examining difficult questions without having explained their component parts. The dubious nature of his *Meditations* couldn't be seen more clearly than it is in a little work in which he tried, at the request of Father *Mersenne, to condense them into the form of demonstrations. The work is included among his *Replies to Objections.*[2]

[3] There have been other able men who have had some profound thoughts; but they have lacked clarity, which is, however, more necessary here even than in mathematics. In mathematics truths carry their proofs along with them, and it is the fact that we can always examine those proofs that has made them so certain. This is why metaphysics, lacking such proofs, needs a new way of treating things which will take the place of calculation; it will serve as a thread in the labyrinth, and yet will retain an accessibility comparable to that which is found in the most popular speech.

[4] The importance of these investigations will be seen in what we have to say about the notion of substance. The idea I have of it is so rich, that there follow from it most of the most important truths about God, the soul, and the nature of body, which are generally either unknown or unproved. To give some flavour of it, I will say here that the consideration of *force*, to which I have assigned a special science which might be called 'Dynamics', is of great help in understanding the nature of substance. This active force is different from a 'faculty' of the *Schools, in that a faculty is only a proximate possibility of action, which in itself is dead, so to speak, and inactive unless it is excited by something from outside. But active force involves an *'entelechy', or an activity; it is half-way between a faculty and an action, and contains in itself a certain effort, or *conatus*. It is led by itself to action without any need of assistance, provided nothing prevents it. All

---

[2] *Replies to Objections to the Meditations*; see CSMK ii. 92, 113 ff.

this can be clarified by the example of a hanging heavy body, or a bent bow; for although it is true that weight and elastic force must be explained mechanically by the movement of ethereal[3] matter, it is nevertheless also true that the ultimate reason for the movement of matter is the force given at creation, which is there in every body, but which is as it were constrained by the mutual interactions of bodies. I hold that this power of action is there in every substance, and that in fact it always produces some actual activity, and that body itself could never be perfectly at rest—which is quite contrary to the idea of those who see body solely as extension.[4] It will also be seen from these meditations that a substance never receives its force from another created substance; what comes from there is only the constraint or determination which gives rise to secondary force, or what is called *moving force*, which must not be confused with what some authors call *impetus*, which they measure by the quantity of movement, and make proportional to speed, when bodies are equal. By contrast, moving force, which is absolute and vital, that is, that which is always conserved, is proportional to the possible effects which can arise from it. [See TT1. 17; 5. 25–6.] This is where the *Cartesians went wrong, in thinking that the same quantity of movement is conserved in meetings between bodies. And I see that M. *Huygens is of my opinion in this, according to what he gave us, some time ago, in the *Histoire des ouvrages des savants*, where he said that the same elevating force is always conserved.

[5] Finally, a most important point which will be clarified by these meditations is communication between substances, and the union of the soul with the body. I hope that this great problem will be thereby resolved in such a clear manner that that in itself will serve as a proof to show that we have found the key to part of these matters. I do not think there is any way of giving an alternative explanation without reference to an extraordinary concourse of the first cause in the ordinary workings of secondary causes. But I will talk more of this another time, if the public does not reject this, which is meant only to test the water. . . .

---

[3] Light, attenuated. Cf. T5. 50.
[4] i.e. *Descartes (see Introduction, Sect. 2).

NEW SYSTEM OF THE NATURE OF SUBSTANCES AND THEIR COMMUNICATION, AND OF THE UNION WHICH EXISTS BETWEEN THE SOUL AND THE BODY (1695)

Summary of the Text

This article, which Leibniz published anonymously in 1695 in the Journal des savants, *takes up ideas he discussed ten years earlier in T1 and T2. As he had hoped, it provoked much discussion, both public and private—in particular, with Simon Foucher (TT6–8) and Pierre Bayle (TT10–12, 14–17).*

As its title indicates, the article falls naturally into two parts. The first twelve paragraphs give an account of the nature of substance, while the remaining six deal with the question of causality between substances, in particular between body and mind.

*On the first of these matters Leibniz explains (Sects. 1–2) how, though he was in favour of giving detailed mechanical explanations of physical phenomena rather than explanations in terms of substantial forms (see Introduction, Sect. 2), he nevertheless saw that to give a proper metaphysical foundation for the principles of mechanics the *Cartesian account of material substance as merely extended was insufficient. It needed replacing by an account which (Sects. 3–4) had its basis in the notion of force (as in T3. 4), and which recognized substances as individual active unities—in short, an account which reintroduced *substantial forms.*

Sections 5–11 contain elements of Leibniz's philosophy of mind. Though the Cartesians were wrong to suppose that non-human animals do not have minds, such minds are different from ours. Unlike theirs, ours are rational, and have a moral identity and a close relationship with God (see also T1. 34–5, T18. 14–15, T19. 82–3; and Introduction, Sects. 6, 7).

From the French of *Journal des savants* (Paris edn.), no. 23 (27 June 1695), 294–300, no. 24 (4 July 1695) 301–6. GP iv. 477–87 prints a later unpublished version, some of the revisions of which are noted here in angle brackets.

These sections also briefly express ideas which Leibniz dwelt on at some length in his correspondence with *Arnauld (T2): the relation of souls (both animal and human) to an organic body, the way souls provide substantial unity, the nature of that organic body, and the nature of birth and death.

Leibniz then turns to the question of the relationship between the body and the mind. *Occasionalism has something to be said for it (Sects. 12–13), but it is not quite right. Realizing this led him, Leibniz says (Sect. 14), to his theory of *agreements. It is their 'representational agreement' which constitutes the union between mind and body. This theory shows, he says (Sects. 17–18), something about causality and the relation of physics and metaphysics.

THE TEXT

[1] I thought of this system several years ago and communicated some of it to various learned men, and in particular to one of the greatest theologians and philosophers of our time, who, having heard about them from a person of the highest rank, had found some of my opinions quite paradoxical. But after receiving my explanations, he withdrew what he had said in the most generous and admirable way possible; and, having accepted some of my points, he withdrew his censure of the others with which he did not yet agree.[1] Since then I have continued my meditations whenever I have had the opportunity, so as to give the public only well-considered opinions; and I have also tried to answer objections raised against my essays on dynamics, which have some connection with this. And now, because some notable people wanted to see my views clarified, I have ventured to offer these meditations, although they are by no means popular in style, nor such as can be appreciated by all types of mind. I am doing this mainly in order to benefit from the judgements of people who are enlightened in these matters, for it would be too troublesome to seek out and consult individually all those who might be willing to give me advice— which I shall always be glad to receive, provided it shows a love of the truth, rather than a passion for preconceived opinions.

[2] Although I am one of those people who have done a lot of work on mathematics,[2] ever since my youth I have continued to meditate upon phi-

---

[1] The reference is to the 'Discourse on Metaphysics' (T1) and the subsequent correspondence with *Arnauld (T2).

[2] For an account of Leibniz's mathematical work, which notably included the discovery of

losophy, for it always seemed to me that there was a way of establishing something solid in it by clear demonstrations. I had gone far into the country of the *Scholastics, when mathematics and modern authors drew me out again, while I was still quite young. Their beautiful way of explaining nature mechanically charmed me, and I rightly scorned the method of those who make use only of [*substantial] forms and faculties, from which we learn nothing. But afterwards, having tried to go more deeply into the principles of mechanics themselves in order to explain the laws of nature which are known through experience, I realized that the consideration of mere *extended mass* is insufficient, and that use must also be made of the notion of *force*, which is perfectly intelligible, though it belongs to the sphere of metaphysics. I realized also that the opinion of those [*Descartes] who transform or demote animals into mere machines, although it seems possible, is implausible, and indeed contrary to the order of things.

[3] At first, when I had freed myself from the yoke of *Aristotle, I was in favour of *atoms and the void, because this view best satisfies the imagination. But thinking again about this, after much meditation I saw that it is impossible to find *the principles of a real unity* in matter alone, or in what is only passive, since this is nothing but a collection or aggregation of parts *ad infinitum*. Now a multiplicity can derive its reality only from *true unities* which come from elsewhere, and which are quite different from ⟨mathematical⟩ points, ⟨which are only the extremities of extended things, and mere modifications,⟩ from which it is obvious that something continuous cannot be composed. So, in order to get to these *real unities* I had to have recourse to a formal atom ⟨what might be called a *real and animated point*, or to an atom of substance, which must contain some kind of form or activity in order to make a complete being⟩, since a material thing cannot simultaneously be material and perfectly indivisible, or possessed of a genuine unity. So it was necessary to recall and, as it were, to rehabilitate *substantial forms*, which are so much decried these days—but in a way which would make them intelligible, and which would separate the use which should be made of them from their previous misuse. I found, then, that the nature of substantial forms consists in force, and that from this there follows something analogous to feeling and desire; and that they must therefore be understood along the lines of our notion of *souls*. But just as the soul ought not to be used to explain in detail the workings of an

the differential and the integral calculus, see Aiton (1985: 48–53, 57–9, 125–7, 202–8), MacDonald Ross (1984b, ch. 2).

animal's body, I decided that similarly these forms must not be used to solve particular problems of nature, although they are necessary for grounding true general principles. *Aristotle calls them *first* *entelechies*. I call them, perhaps more intelligibly, *primary forces*, which contain not only *actuality*, or the mere fulfilment of a possibility, but also an originating *activity*.

[4] I saw that these forms and souls had to be indivisible, like our minds, and indeed I remembered that this was the opinion of St *Thomas about the souls of animals. But this truth reintroduced all the great difficulties about the origin and duration of souls and forms. For, since every ⟨simple⟩ *substance* which has a genuine unity can begin or end only by a miracle, it follows that they can come into being only by creation and end only by annihilation. So I had to recognize that (with the exception of souls which God still intends to create specially) the constitutive forms of substances must have been created with the world and must always continue to exist. Thus the Scholastics, such as *Albertus Magnus and John *Bacon, had glimpsed part of the truth about the origin of these forms. And this idea should not seem extraordinary, for we are only attributing to forms the duration which the *Gassendists accord to their atoms.

[5] Nevertheless, I held that we must not mix up with these ⟨or confuse with other forms or souls⟩ the *mind*, or rational soul, which is of a superior order and has incomparably more perfection than those forms which are sunk in matter ⟨, which in my view are to be found everywhere⟩. In comparison with those, minds or rational souls are like little gods, made in the image of God, and having within them a ray of the divine light. That is why God governs minds as a prince governs his subjects, or as a father looks after his children; whereas he deals with other substances as an engineer handles his machines. Thus minds have special laws which raise them above the mechanical operations of matter, ⟨which it carries out in accordance with the order God has imposed on it,⟩ and we might say that everything else is made only for them, for even those mechanical operations are arranged for the happiness of the good and the punishment of the wicked.

[6] To return to ordinary forms or *material* ⟨primitive⟩ *souls*, however, the duration which must now be attributed to them, rather than to atoms, as before, might give rise to the idea that they pass from body to body; this would be *metempsychosis*, rather like the transmission of motion and of species as certain philosophers have maintained it [*Scholastics]. But this fancy is very far from how things are: there is no such passing. And here the *transformations* noted by MM. *Swammerdam, *Malpighi, and

*Leeuwenhoek, who are among the best observers of our day, have helped me, and have led me to accept more readily that no animal or other organized substance begins when we think it does, and that its apparent generation is only a development, or a kind of augmentation. And I have noticed that the author of *The *Search after Truth*, M. *Regis, M. *Hartsoeker, and other able men have not been far from this opinion.

[7] But there still remained the even bigger question as to what becomes of these souls or forms on the death of the animal or the destruction of the individual organized substance.[3] This question is all the more difficult, because it seems hardly reasonable that souls should remain, useless, in a chaos of confused matter. This led me to decide in the end that there is only one view that can reasonably be taken, which is that not only is the soul conserved, but so also is the animal itself and its organic mechanism; although the destruction of its cruder parts has made it so small as to be as little perceptible to our senses as it was before its birth. And indeed, no one can exactly tell the true time of death, which for a long time may be taken for a mere suspension of observable actions and which ultimately is nothing more than that in the case of simple animals: witness the *resuscitation* of flies which have been drowned and then buried in powdered chalk, and several similar instances which show clearly that there would be many more resuscitations, even in more extreme cases, if men were in a position to repair the mechanism. It seems it was of something of this kind that the great *Democritus spoke, complete atomist though he was, even though *Pliny laughs at what he said. It is natural, then, that an animal, since it has always been living and organized (as some people of great insight are beginning to recognize), should always remain so. And so, since there is therefore no first birth or entirely new generation of an animal, it follows that it will have no final extinction or complete death in the strict metaphysical sense; and that consequently, instead of the transmigration of souls, there is nothing but a transformation of one and the same animal, according as its organs are differently packed up, and more or less developed.

[8] Meanwhile rational souls follow much higher laws, and are exempt from everything which could make them lose their status as citizens of the society of minds; God has provided for them so well that no changes in matter can ever make them lose the moral qualities of their personality. And we can say that everything tends to the perfection, not only of the

---

[3] Aristotle's *De Anima* (411[b]) stimulated discussion about what happens to its soul when an insect is divided.

universe in general, but also of these created beings in particular; for they are destined for such a degree of happiness that the universe becomes involved in it, in virtue of the divine goodness, which is communicated to each one to the extent that the sovereign wisdom can allow.

[9] As for the ordinary run of animals and other corporeal substances, which up until now have been thought to suffer total extinction and whose changes depend on mechanical rules rather than on moral laws, I was pleased to see that the ancient author of the book *Diet* (which is attributed to *Hippocrates) had glimpsed something of the truth, when he expressly said that animals are not born and do not die, and that the things which we suppose to come into being and to perish merely appear and disappear. This was also the opinion of *Parmenides and of *Melissus according to *Aristotle. (For these ancients are sounder than we think.)

[10] I am as ready as anyone to do justice to the moderns; nevertheless I think they have carried reform too far, among other things in conflating natural things with artificial ones, through not having sufficiently grand ideas of the majesty of nature. They take the difference between nature's machines and ours to be only that between great and small. This recently led a very able man, the author of *Conversations on the Plurality of Worlds*, to say that on close inspection nature appears less wonderful than we had thought, it being only something like a craftsman's window display. I think that this gives an inappropriate and unworthy idea of nature, and that it is only my system which shows the true and immense distance there is between the least productions and mechanisms of divine wisdom and the greatest masterpieces produced by the skill of a limited mind—a difference which is not merely one of degree, but one of kind. It needs to be recognized, then, that nature's machines have a truly infinite number of organic parts, and are so well provided for and proof against all accidents that it is not possible to destroy them. A natural machine is still a machine even in its smallest parts; and, what is more, it always remains the same machine it was, being merely transformed by being packed up in different ways; sometimes extended, sometimes contracted and as it were concentrated, when we think that it is destroyed.

[11] Furthermore, by means of the soul or form, there is in us a true unity which corresponds to what we call 'I'; this can have no place in artificial machines or in a simple mass of matter, however organized it may be. Such masses can only be thought of as like an army or a flock, or like a pond full of fish, or like a watch composed of springs and wheels. Yet if there were no true substantial unities there would be nothing substantial or real in such a collection. It was this that forced M. *Cordemoy to

abandon *Descartes and adopt Democritus' doctrine of atoms in order to find a true unity. But *atoms of matter* are contrary to reason, quite apart from being still composed of parts, since the invincible attachment of one part to another (even if it could rationally be understood or imagined) would certainly not take away the difference between them. It is only *atoms of substance*, that is to say real unities absolutely devoid of parts, that can be the sources of actions, and the absolute first principles of the composition of things, and as it were the ultimate elements in the analysis of substances ⟨substantial things⟩. They might be called *metaphysical points*; they have *something of the nature of life* and a kind of *perception*, and *mathematical points* are their *point of view* for expressing the universe. But when a corporeal substance is contracted, all its organs together make what to us is only a *physical point*. Thus the indivisibility of physical points is only apparent. Mathematical points really are indivisible, but they are only modalities. It is only metaphysical or substantial points (constituted by forms or souls) which are both indivisible and real, and without them there would be nothing real, since without true unities there would be no multiplicity.

[12] Having decided these things, I thought I had reached port, but when I set myself to think about the union of the soul with the body I was as it were carried back into the open sea. For I could find no way of explaining how the body can make something pass over into the soul or vice versa, or how one created substance can communicate with another. As far as we can see from his writings, M. Descartes gave up the game at this point, but his disciples, seeing that the popular opinion is incomprehensible, said that we are aware of the properties of bodies because God produces thoughts in the soul on the occasion of the motions of matter; and when in its turn our soul wishes to move the body, they said that it is God who moves the body for it. And as the communication of motion also seemed incomprehensible to them, they held that God gives motion to one body on the occasion of the motion of another. This is what they call the *System of *Occasional Causes*, which has been made very fashionable by the excellent reflections of the author of the *The Search after Truth*.[4]

[13] It must be admitted that they have gone a long way with this problem in telling us what cannot happen; but their account of what actually does happen does not appear to have solved it. It is quite true that in the strict metaphysical sense, one created substance has no real influence

---

[4] For an account of Leibniz's rejection of the *Scholastic influx theory of causation (both as regards bodies, and bodies and minds) and the theory of *occasionalism, see Introduction, Sects. 4, 5.

upon another, and that all things, with all their reality, are continually produced by the power of God. But to solve problems it is not enough to make use of a general cause and to introduce what is called a *deus ex machina*. For to do this, without giving any other explanation in terms of the order of secondary causes, is really to have recourse to a miracle. In philosophy we must try to show the way in which things are carried out by the divine wisdom by explaining them in accordance with the notion of the subject we are dealing with.

[14] Being thus obliged to admit that it is impossible that the soul or any other true substance should receive anything from outside, except through divine omnipotence, I was led gradually to an idea which surprised me, but which seems inevitable, and which in fact has very great advantages and very considerable attractions. This is that we should say that God first created the soul, or any other real unity, in such a way that everything in it arises from its own nature, with a perfect *spontaneity* as regards itself, and yet with a perfect *conformity* to things outside it. And thus, since our inner sensations (that is, those which are in the soul itself and not in the brain or in the subtle parts of the body) are only a sequence of phenomena relating to external things, or are really appearances or systematic dreams, as it were, these internal perceptions in the soul itself must arise from its own original constitution, that is to say from its representational nature (its ability to express external things which are in relation with its organs), which it has had since its creation, and which constitutes its individual character. And this means that since each of these substances accurately represents the whole universe in its own way and from a particular point of view, and since its perceptions or expressions of external things occur in the soul at just the right time in virtue of its own laws, as in a world apart, as if there existed nothing but God and that soul (to use the expression of a certain lofty-minded person [*Teresa], famous for her sanctity), there will be a perfect agreement between all these substances, which produces the same effect as would be observed if they communicated with one another by means of a transmission of species or qualities, such as most ordinary philosophers [*Scholastics] suppose. Furthermore, the organized mass in which the point of view of the soul lies is more immediately expressed by it, and is in turn ready, just when the soul desires it, to act of itself according to the laws of the bodily mechanism, without either one interfering with the laws of the other, the animal spirits and the blood having exactly at the right moment the motions which correspond to the passions and perceptions of the soul. It is this mutual relationship, arranged in advance in each substance in the uni-

verse, which produces what we call their communication, and which alone constitutes *the union of soul and body*. And in this way we can understand how the soul has its seat in the body by an immediate presence, which is as close as could be, since the soul is in the body in the way in which unity is in that resultant of unities which is multiplicity.

[15] This hypothesis is certainly possible. For why could not God give to a substance at the outset a nature or internal force which could produce in it in an orderly way (as in a *spiritual or formal automaton; but a free one*, in the case of a substance which is endowed with a share of reason) everything that is going to happen to it, that is to say, all the appearances or expressions it is going to have, and all without the help of any created thing? This is the more likely since the nature of a substance necessarily requires and essentially involves some progress or change, without which it would have no force to act. And as the nature of the soul is to represent the universe in a very exact way (though with more or less distinctness), the succession of representations which the soul produces for itself will naturally correspond to the succession of changes in the universe itself: just as on the other hand the body has also been adapted to the soul for the occasions when we think of the soul as acting externally. What is all the more reasonable about this is that bodies are made only for minds which are capable of entering into association with God, and of celebrating his glory. Thus as soon as we see that this *Theory of *Agreements* is possible, we see also that it is the most reasonable, and that it gives a wonderful sense of the harmony of the universe and the perfection of the works of God.

[16] It also has the great advantage that instead of saying that we are free only in appearance and in a way which is sufficient for practical purposes, as several clever people have held, we must rather say that we are determined only in appearance, and that, in strict metaphysical language, we are perfectly independent of the influence of all other created things. This again puts into a marvellous light the immortality of our soul and the perfectly unbroken conservation of our individuality, which is perfectly well-regulated by its own nature and sheltered from all external accidents, however it may appear to the contrary. Never has any system made our elevated position more clear. Every mind is like a world apart, sufficient to itself, independent of every other created thing, involves the infinite, and expresses the universe, and so it is as lasting, as continuous in its existence, and as absolute as the universe of created things itself. Thus we should conclude that each mind should always play its part in the way most fitted to contribute to the perfection of the society of all minds which constitutes their moral union in the City of God. There is also here a new and

surprisingly clear proof of the existence of God. For this perfect agreement of so many substances which have no communication with one
another could come only from their common cause.

[17] Besides all these advantages which this theory has in its favour, we
may say that it is something more than a theory, since it hardly seems possible to explain things in any other intelligible way, and because several
serious difficulties which have perplexed men's minds up until now seem
to disappear of themselves when we fully understand it. Our ordinary
ways of speaking may also be easily preserved. For we may say that the
substance whose state explains a change in an intelligible way (so that we
may conclude that it is this substance to which the others have in this
respect been adapted from the beginning, in accordance with the order of
the decrees of God) is the one which, so far as this change goes, we should
therefore think of as *acting* upon the others. So the action of one substance
upon another is not an emission or a transplantation of an entity as is commonly thought, and it can be reasonably understood only in the way I have
just described. It is true that we can easily understand in connection with
matter both the emission and the receiving of parts, by means of which we
quite properly explain all the phenomena of physics mechanically. But a
material mass is not a substance, and so it is clear that action as regards an
actual substance can only be as I have described.

[18] These considerations, however metaphysical they may seem, are
nevertheless marvellously useful in physics for grounding the laws of
motion, as my dynamics will be able to show. For we can say that when
bodies collide, each one is affected only by its own elasticity, caused by the
motion which is already in it.[5] And as for absolute motion, nothing can
determine it mathematically, since everything ends in relations: the result
being that there is always a perfect equivalence of theories, as in astronomy; so that, whatever number of bodies we take, we may arbitrarily
assign either rest or some degree of velocity to whichever we like, without
it being possible for us to be refuted by the phenomena of motion,
whether in a straight line, a circle, or composite.[6] It is still reasonable,
however, in conformity with the notion of activity which we have established here, to attribute genuine motions to bodies in accordance with
what explains the phenomena in the most intelligible way.

[5] See also TT4. 18; 5. 49, and end of Introduction, Sect. 4.
[6] Leibniz discusses all of this at greater length at T5. 37–8.

5

SPECIMEN DYNAMICUM: AN ESSAY IN DYNAMICS, SHOWING THE WONDERFUL LAWS OF NATURE CONCERNING BODILY FORCES AND THEIR INTERACTIONS, AND TRACING THEM TO THEIR CAUSES (1695)

Summary of the Text

Only the first of the two parts of this 'Essay in Dynamics' was published. The essay as a whole is an important, detailed working-out and application of Leibniz's notion of force, a notion which, as other works (such as T3) at any rate hint, lies at the heart of his dynamics. It has as its foundation the view (already familiar from TT1, 2, 3) that the Cartesian conception of corporeal substance as mere extension is unsatisfactory because of its omission of the idea of force. It is force that 'constitutes the inmost nature of bodies' (Sect. 2), and it is force that is the underlying reality of motion. In short, underlying the world of extended matter in motion (the world as conceived by the new mechanical philosophy) is force. Many other Leibnizian texts say this much, but this one is important for saying rather more. It expounds many of the ideas explained in the Introduction (Sect. 3).

Thus, for example, two important distinctions are made (Sects. 6, 7), between active *and* passive force, *and (in both these cases) between* primitive *and* derivative force. *Primitive active force corresponds to substantial form or soul. It appeared, though not by this rather technical name, in TT1. 15, 16, 18; 3. 4; 4. 2, 3. It is something which is crucial to a correct metaphysics of substances but, unlike derivative active force, of no concern for detailed physical explanations of phenomena. (See also TT1. 8; 4. 3, 13; 13. 7–8; and Introduction, Sects. 2, 3.1,*

From the Latin of 'Specimen Dynamicum . . .', Acta Eruditorum (Apr. 1695), 145–57, as printed at GM vi. 235–54.

3.3.) Derivative active force is 'as it were the limitation of primitive force brought about by the collision of bodies with each other' (T5. 6; see also T13. 11).

As explained in the Introduction (Sect. 3.2), passive force (Sect. 7) has to do with various other properties of matter, such as impenetrability, which, Leibniz thinks, Descartes ignored. At the metaphysical level it relates to the imperfection of created things (T19. 42).

Leibniz's concern in this 'Essay' is with derivative force, 'the force by which [moving] bodies actually act and are acted upon by each other' in collisions (Sect. 9). It is in terms of motion and the dynamical force associated with it that Leibniz, as a proponent of the 'mechanical philosophy', believes 'all other material phenomena are explicable' (Sect. 9), e.g. solidity (Sect. 52).

By considering it (Sects. 41–8), Leibniz demonstrates a law of continuity in physical phenomena. This highlights absurdities in Descartes's collision rules, and shows that all bodies are elastic and rules out indivisible atoms.

THE TEXT

[1] Part 1. Since the time I first mentioned the founding of a new *science of dynamics*, a number of distinguished people in various places have asked for a fuller explanation of the idea. As I have not yet had time to compose a book, therefore, I will give here something which may throw some light on the subject; and perhaps that light will be returned with interest, if I can get the opinions of people who can combine power of thought with elegance of style. Their judgement would be very welcome and I hope useful in advancing the project. [2] I have suggested elsewhere that corporeal things contain something other than extension, indeed something prior to extension, namely the force of nature implanted in all things by the Creator. This force does not consist of a mere faculty, of the kind with which the Schools seem to content themselves, but instead is endowed with a conatus or effort (*nisus*), such that it will attain its full effect unless it is impeded by some contrary striving. This effort often makes itself felt by the senses, but in my view reason shows that it is everywhere in matter, even when it is not apparent to the senses. Now, as we should not attribute this force (*vis*) to God's miraculous action, it is clear that he must have placed it in bodies themselves—indeed, that it constitutes the inmost nature of bodies. For to act is the mark of a substance, and extension alone, far from itself constituting substance, is no more than the continua-

154

tion or diffusion of a given effort-exerting and counter-straining (that is, resisting) substance. [3] I recognize that all corporeal action arises from motion, and that motion itself comes only from other motion, either already in the body or impressed from outside. But when we analyse it, motion, like time, does not really exist: for a whole never exists if it does not have coexistent parts. Thus there is nothing real in motion but the momentary state which a force endowed with an effort for change must produce. Therefore, whatever there is in corporeal nature besides the object of geometry, or extension, reduces to this. [4] This theory finally does justice both to the truth and to the teaching of the ancients. Just as our age has already rescued from scorn *Democritus' atoms, *Plato's ideas, and the *Stoics' tranquillity about the best possible arrangement of things, so we can now make intelligible the *Peripatetic doctrine of forms or entelechies, which for very good reason struck people as puzzling, and was hardly understood even by its own inventors. For it seems to me that this philosophy, which has been accepted for so many centuries, should not be rejected, but should be explained in such a way as to make it consistent with itself wherever possible, and should be extended and illustrated with new discoveries.

[5] This approach to inquiry seems to me both sensible for the teacher and useful for the student. We must be careful not to be more eager to destroy than to build, and not to be continually tossed about in uncertainty between the different theories of bold new thinkers. Instead, by restraining the urge to form sects (which the glory accorded to pointless novelties encourages), mankind will be able to establish secure principles, and to advance by steady steps towards greater heights, in philosophy just as in mathematics. For if we leave aside the harsh things they say about each other, the writings of distinguished men, both ancient and modern, usually contain a great deal that is true and good, and which deserves to be taken out and displayed in the treasury of public knowledge. If only people would prefer to do this rather than wasting time on criticisms which only serve to satisfy their own vanity! I do not know why, but although I have myself been lucky enough to discover certain new ideas—so that my friends often tell me that I should think about nothing else—I nevertheless can appreciate even hostile opinions, and judge them on their own differing merits. Perhaps it is because by doing a lot of things you learn to despise none of them. But let us return to the matter in hand.

[6] *Active force* (*vis*) (which some not unreasonably call *power* (*virtus*)) is of two kinds. There is *primitive active force*, which is inherent in all

corporeal substance as such, since it is contrary to the nature of things that there should be any body which is wholly at rest; and there is *derivative active force*, which is as it were the limitation of primitive force brought about by the collision of bodies with each other, and which is operative in various ways. Primitive force—which is none other than the first entelechy—corresponds to the *soul* or *substantial form*; but for that very reason it relates only to general causes, which are not enough to explain phenomena. I therefore agree with those who say that we should not appeal to forms in explaining the particular individual causes of things we experience. It is important to point this out since, although I am trying to give back to forms as it were their lost right to be counted among the ultimate causes of things, I do not want to appear to be also trying to return to the verbal disputes of the Scholastics. But some knowledge of forms is necessary for correct philosophizing: no one can claim to have properly understood the nature of body unless he has thought about such things, and has understood the imperfection, not to say the falsity, of the crude notion of corporeal substance. It is derived entirely from sensory imagination, and was wrongly introduced into the corpuscular philosophy—which in itself is most excellent and true—some years ago, through carelessness. This is shown by the fact that it cannot rule out matter's being completely inactive or at rest, and cannot explain the laws of nature which govern derivative force. [7] Passive force is similarly of two kinds, primitive and derivative. The *primitive force* of *being acted upon* or of *resistance* constitutes what, if properly understood, the Scholastics call *primary matter*. It is what explains why bodies cannot interpenetrate, but present an obstacle to one another, and also why they possess a certain laziness, as it were, or repugnance to motion, and will not allow themselves to be put into motion without lessening to some extent the force of any body which is acting on them. The *derivative force* of *being acted upon* therefore shows itself in various ways in *secondary matter*.[1] [8] Having set out these basic, general points, and shown that all bodies always act by virtue of their form, and are always acted upon and resist because of their matter, we must now move on to deal with the theory of *derivative powers* and *resistances*, showing how bodies act on and resist each other to differing extents in virtue of their different levels of effort. The laws of action which deal with these things must not only be understood rationally, but must also be confirmed by experience of the phenomena.

---

[1] See also T2. 11 §4 for the notion of secondary matter.

5. Specimen Dynamicum

[9][2] By derivative force, then, the force by which bodies actually act and are acted upon by each other, I mean here nothing other than that which is associated with motion (local motion, that is), and which in turn tends to produce further local motion. For I accept that all other material phenomena are explicable in terms of local motion. Motion is the continuous change of place, and so requires time. But as a movable thing which is in motion moves through time, so at any given moment it has a *velocity*, which is the greater as it covers more space with less expenditure of time. Velocity taken together with direction is called *conatus*, while *impetus* is the product of the mass (*moles*) of a body and its velocity. This is the quantity which the *Cartesians usually call the quantity of motion, that is, the quantity of motion at a moment—though, to speak more accurately, the quantity of motion actually exists over time, and is the sum of the products of the different impetuses existing in the moving thing at different times and the corresponding time intervals. [10] In discussing with the Cartesians we have, however, followed their way of speaking. But just as we can distinguish (and this is very convenient for technical language) between an increase which is now occurring and one which has occurred, or which is going to occur, and we can speak of it as an increment or element of the increase; and just as we can distinguish the present falling of a body from the fall which has already taken place, and which is increasing, so we can also distinguish the present or instaneous element of motion from the motion itself taken as extended over time. If we call this element instantaneous motion, then what is usually called quantity of motion could be called the quantity of instantaneous motion. (We can be flexible in our use of words once we have given them a precise meaning, but until then we must be careful so as not to be led astray by ambiguities.)

[11][3] Just as the value of a motion taken as extended over time is derived from an infinite number of impetuses, so in turn the impetus itself, even though it is momentary, is derived from an infinite series of increments imparted to the moving body. Therefore impetus too contains an element which can only arise from an infinite repetition. Consider a tube *AC* rotating in the horizontal plane of this page (Figure 5.1) with uniform speed about the fixed centre *C*. Consider, too, a ball *B* inside the tube, released

---

[2] See App. A.

[3] In this section, 'urge' (*solicitatio*) is, or produces (so long as it is allowed to), by way of acceleration (i.e. increase in Leibnizian 'velocity'), an increase of impetus. It (or its effect) is equal to mass multiplied by the differential of that velocity over time, i.e. to mass times acceleration.

5. Specimen Dynamicum

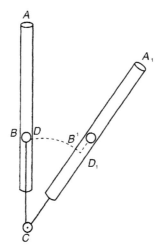

FIG. 5.1.

from any tie or restraint, and beginning to move by centrifugal force. It is clear that, at the start, the ball's striving to move away from the centre (that is, that in virtue of which it tends towards the end of the tube A) is infinitely small as compared with the impetus it already has from the rotation (that is, the impetus by which ball B, while remaining at the same distance from the centre C, has a tendency to move from D to D_1 along with the tube itself). But if the centrifugal impulse deriving from the rotation is continued for some time, then because of its motion there must arise in the ball the full centrifugal impetus D_1B_1, proportional to the rotational impetus DD_1. It is obvious from this that the effort is twofold—an elementary or infinitely small one, which I also call *an urge* (*solicitatio*), and another one—the *impetus* itself—which is formed by the continuation or repetition of the elementary ones. I am not therefore claiming that these mathematical entities as such are actually to be met with in nature, but only that they are useful as mental abstractions for making accurate calculations.

[12][4] *Force*, therefore, is also of two kinds. One is elementary, and I call it *dead force*, since there is no motion in it as yet, but only an urge (*solicitatio*) to motion, like that in the ball in the tube, or in a stone in a sling before the string is released. The other is in fact ordinary force, which is accompanied by actual motion. This I call *living force*. Centrifugal force, then, is an

---

[4] See App. B.

158

example of dead force, as is the force of gravity or centripetal force, and the force by which a stretched elastic body tries to spring back into shape. But in the case of an impact which arises from a heavy body which has been falling for some time, or from a bow which has been springing back into shape for some time, or from some similar cause, the force is living force, and it arises from an infinite number of continued impulses of dead force. This is what Galileo meant when he said rather enigmatically that the force of impact is infinite as compared with the mere effort of gravitational force. However, even though impetus is always accompanied by living force, I shall show below that the two are nevertheless different.

[13][5] *Living force* in an aggregate of bodies can also be understood in two ways—as *total* or as *partial*. In its turn *partial force* is either respective or directive—that is, it relates either to the individual parts, or to the aggregate as a whole. *Respective* or *individual force* is that by which the bodies which make up an aggregate can act on each other; *directive* or *common force* is that by which the aggregate itself can also act on something else. I call it directive because in this kind of partial force the whole force of the overall direction of the aggregate is conserved. If we imagine that the aggregate suddenly fused together, and its parts stopped moving relative to each other, this is the only force that would be left. Therefore, *total absolute force* consists of respective and directive force taken together. But this will be clearer from the rules presented below.

[14] As far as we can tell, the ancients only had a science of dead force. This is what is commonly called mechanics: it deals with levers, pulleys, inclined planes (which include both wedges and screws), the equilibrium of liquids, and similar matters. It considers only the primary conatus of individual bodies in themselves, prior to their acquiring impetus through action. Although there is a way in which the laws of dead force can be applied to living force, we have to be very careful in doing so not to be misled, like the people who realized that dead force is proportional to the product of mass and velocity, and so confused that with force in general. [15] As I once pointed out, there is a particular reason why that relation holds in that case: for example, when bodies of different weights are falling, then at the very beginning of the fall, when the descent itself, or the quantity of space covered in the descent, is infinitely small or elementary, then at that point the descent is proportional to the speed or conatus of descent. But when some progress has been made, and a living force has developed, the acquired speeds are no longer proportional to the distances

---

[5] See App. C.

fallen (which is, however, as I have shown before and will show again in more detail later, how the force should be measured) but to the elements of those distances.[6] [16] *Galileo began the treatment of living force (though he used a different name and, indeed, a different concept), and was the first to explain how motion arises from the acceleration of falling bodies. *Descartes correctly distinguished between velocity and direction, and also saw that the outcome of a collision between bodies is the state which is least different from the prior state. But he did not calculate that least change correctly, because he changed either only the direction or only the velocity, when the change should be determined by both at the same time. But he could not see how this could be done; because he was concerned with modalities rather than realities, he could not see how two such heterogeneous things could be compared and considered at the same time (not to mention his other errors on this matter).

[17] Honoratus *Fabri, Marcus *Marci, Giovanni Alfonso *Borelli, Ignace Baptista *Pardies, Claude *Déchales, and other very clever men have done a lot that is of value in the theory of motion, but they have been unable to avoid these fatal errors. As far as I know, *Huygens, who has enlightened our age with his brilliant discoveries, was the first to arrive at the pure and simple truth on this question, and to purge the subject of fallacies by means of the laws he published some time ago. *Wren, *Wallis, and *Mariotte, all distinguished men in this field in their own ways, have arrived at almost the same laws; but there is no agreement as to the causes, so that even these men, who are so outstanding in the area, do not always come to the same conclusions. It is clear, therefore, that the true basis of this science has not yet been discovered. Even the proposition, which to me seems quite certain, that rebound or reflection arises only from elastic force (that is, from resistance due to internal motion) is not accepted by everyone. And no one before me has explained the notion of force itself. This has always been a problem for the Cartesians and others, who could not understand that the sum total of motion or impetus—which they took to be quantity of force—could be different after a collision from what it

---

[6] In this paragraph Leibniz seems to suppose that at the very beginning of its fall a body moves uniformly, not yet accelerating—at which time the distance fallen will be proportional to that uniform speed.

However, as in the last sentence of the paragraph, it accelerates under gravity as it continues to fall. Its increased speed will be proportional (as *Galileo showed) to the square root of the distance fallen. As Leibniz argued in T2. 17, the living force of the body will be proportional to the distance it has fallen (in fact, that is, to the square of its speed).

was before, because they thought that would mean that the quantity of force would be different as well.[7]

[18] In my youth I agreed with Democritus (and also with *Gassendi and Descartes, who in this respect are his followers) that the nature of body consists only in an inert mass, and I put out a small book, called *A Physical Hypothesis*, in which I presented a theory of both abstract and concrete motion. Some distinguished men seem to have liked this book rather more than its mediocrity deserved. In it I showed that given this conception of body, an impacting body will give its conatus to whatever body it collides with, or whatever presents an obstacle to it. For at the moment of collision it strives to continue its motion, and so strives to carry the other body along with it, and (since at the time I believed that bodies are indifferent to motion and rest) this conatus must have its full effect on the body collided with, unless it is prevented by an opposing conatus. But even if it is opposed the same will be true, because the different conatuses will then have to be combined. This therefore showed that there could be no reason why the impacting body should not achieve the effect it was tending towards, or why the body collided with should not receive the full conatus of the impacting body, so that the motion of the body collided with would be the combination of its own original conatus and the new external conatus it had received. [19] From this I also showed that if body is understood as containing only the mathematical notions of size, shape, position, and their changes, and as containing a striving for change only at the moment of impact; if there is no explanation by means of metaphysical notions, such as active power in the form, and sluggishness or resistance to motion in matter; if, therefore, the outcome of a collision has to be determined purely by the geometrical composition of conatuses as just explained, then it would follow that since the whole conatus of the impacting body, however small it was, would be passed on to the body collided with, however large it was, then the largest body at rest would be carried away by the smallest body colliding with it, with no diminution in its speed—for on this account of matter it has no resistance to motion, but is wholly indifferent to it. This would mean that it would be no more difficult to move a large body than a small one, and therefore that there would be action without reaction, and there would be no way of measuring capacity for action (*potentia*), since anything could overcome anything. Because of this, and of many other things of the same kind which go against the order

---

[7] For an example of such a collision, see the third paragraph of Introduction, Sect. 3.5.

of things and conflict with the principles of true metaphysics, I therefore came to the conclusion (quite correctly) that in creating the system of things the all-wise Creator had been careful to avoid the consequences which otherwise would have followed by pure geometry from the laws of motion alone.

[20] When I later looked at all of this more thoroughly, however, I came to see what a systematic explanation of things would consist in, and I realized that my earlier theory as to the nature of body was incomplete. By means of this and other arguments I was able to establish that something other than size and impenetrability must be taken to be in bodies, something which gives rise to considerations of force. When the metaphysical laws which relate to this are added to the laws of extension there arise what I call systematic laws of motion—that all change is gradual; that every action also has a reaction; that no new force is produced without reducing an earlier one, so that any body which carries away another body will be slowed down by it; and that there is neither more nor less capacity for action (*potentia*) in an effect than in its cause. Since this law is not derivable from the concept of mass, it must follow from something else which is in bodies, namely from force itself, of which the same quantity is always maintained, even if it is carried by different bodies. I therefore concluded that in addition to what falls under pure mathematics and the imagination, we must accept something metaphysical which is perceptible only to the mind, and that some kind of superior, so to speak formal principle must be added to material mass. For not all truths about corporeal things can be derived from logical and geometrical axioms alone, that is, from those pertaining to great and small, whole and part, and shape and position; in order to give a satisfactory explanation of the order of things we have to bring in others, concerned with cause and effect, and activity and passivity. It does not matter whether we call this principle form, or *entelechy, or force, provided we remember that it can be intelligibly explained only through the concept of force.

[21] I cannot, however, agree with those distinguished men of the present day who, on seeing this very fact—that the usual concept of matter is not adequate—introduce God *ex machina* and deny that things have any force for action (a kind of Mosaic Philosophy, as *Fludd called it). I accept that they have clearly shown that if we examine the matter in strict metaphysical rigour there can be no real influx from one created substance into another, and I willingly admit that all things arise from God's continual creation. However, I hold that there is no natural truth about things for which the immediate explanation is to be sought in the activity or will of

God, but that God has always endowed the things themselves with something through which all their predicates can be explained. God has created not only bodies but also souls, to which there correspond primitive entelechies. But I shall show all this elsewhere when I give a more thorough account of the matter.

[22] Meanwhile, although I hold that there exists everywhere in bodies an active or, as we might say, vital principle which stands above all material concepts, I do not agree with Henry *More and other men of outstanding piety and intelligence who appeal to some kind of unheard of *archeus* or hylarchic principle in explaining the phenomena—as if not everything in nature can be explained mechanically, and as if those who attempt to give such an explanation were to be suspected of impiety for trying to deny incorporeal things; or as if we ought to assign intelligences that were required to rotate the spheres, as *Aristotle did, and say that the rising and falling of the elements is due to their forms—a theory which covers a great deal, but which tells us nothing. [23] I do not, as I say, agree with these theories, and philosophy of this kind is no more attractive to me than the theology of people who believed so firmly that it is Jupiter that causes thunder and snow, that they accused anyone who tried to find more specific causes of such things of atheism. In my opinion it is best to take a middle path, which satisfies both religion and science: I accept that all corporeal phenomena can be traced back to mechanical efficient causes, but those mechanical laws as a whole must be understood as themselves deriving from higher reasons. Higher efficient causes are therefore appealed to only in establishing those remote and general explanations, and once they have been established, entelechies or souls have no place in discussions of the immediate and specific efficient causes of natural things, any more than do useless faculties and inexplicable sympathies. The first and most universal efficient cause should not be considered in the discussion of specific problems, except when, in order that we should miss no opportunity for praising him and singing lovely hymns, we contemplate the purposes which God in his wisdom had in ordering things in that way.

[24][8] In fact (as I have shown by a quite remarkable example of a principle in optics, which the famous *Molyneux greatly approved of in his *Dioptrics*), final causes can sometimes also be introduced to great effect in particular problems in physics—not only so that we can better admire the most beautiful works of the supreme Creator, but also sometimes in order to find out things which by consideration only of efficient causes would be

[8] See also T1. 22; Introduction, Sect. 7.

less obvious, or only hypothetical. Philosophers have perhaps not yet really seen how useful such an appeal to final causes can be. I would maintain in general that everything can be explained in two ways: in terms of the *Kingdom of Power*, or *efficient causes*, and in terms of the *Kingdom of Wisdom*, or *final causes*. God governs bodies in the way that a designer governs machines, in accordance with *laws of size or of mathematics*; but he does so for the benefit of souls. And souls, which are capable of wisdom, he governs for his greater glory as citizens, or fellow members of society, in the manner of a prince, or indeed of a father, in accordance with *laws of goodness or of morality*. Though these two kingdoms thoroughly interpenetrate each other, their laws are never confused or disturbed, so that there arises both the greatest in the Kingdom of Power and the best in the Kingdom of Wisdom. But our task here is to establish general rules for operative forces, which we can then use to explain particular efficient causes.

[25] I have also worked out how to measure forces accurately, and in two very different ways. One way is a priori, simply from the consideration of space, time, and action; I shall explain this elsewhere. The other is a posteriori and measures force by the effects it produces when it is used up. By 'effect' here I mean not any effect, but one in which the force is expended or used up—one which may therefore be called *violent*. (The effect which a heavy body has in moving along a perfectly horizontal plane is not of this kind, for here the same force is retained, however long the effect may be produced; and although such effects, which might be called *harmless*, can be measured in the same way, we will ignore them here.) And the particular kind of violent force I have chosen is the one that is most homogeneous, or capable of being divided into similar and equal parts—such as that which is found in the upward motion of a heavy body. [26] For the ascent of a heavy body to two or three feet is exactly two or three times that of the same body to one foot, and the ascent of one body of double size to one foot is exactly twice that of a single-sized body to one foot. Therefore, the ascent of one double-sized body to three feet is exactly six times that of a single-sized body to one foot (assuming for the sake of exposition that heavy bodies weigh the same whatever height they are at— which in fact is not true, but the error is imperceptible). (Elastic bodies do not so easily lend themselves to considerations of homogeneity.) [27] Thus, to compare bodies with different sizes and different speeds, I easily saw that if body *A* is single and body *B* is double in size, but they have the same speed, then the one would have one unit of force and the other two units—because the second must have exactly twice what there is in the

first, since the only difference between B and A is that B is twice the size. But if bodies A and C are the same size, but the speed of A is single and that of C is double, then I saw that C would not have exactly twice what A has— since, although the speed of C is twice that of A, its size is not doubled. I therefore saw that a mistake had been made here by people who think that force is doubled merely by this kind of doubling of a modality. [28] I have already, some time ago, pointed this out, and warned that the true art of calculating (which, despite all the books that have been written on the 'elements of universal mathematics', has not yet been explained) consists ultimately in getting down to something homogeneous; that is, to an accurate and complete duplication, both in things and in their modalities. There is no better or more noteworthy example of this technique than that given by this very proof.

[29][9] In order to obtain a measure of force, then, I asked whether these two bodies A and C, which are equal in size but different in speed, could produce any effects which were equal in power to their causes and themselves homogeneous. In this way things which cannot easily be compared directly could still be accurately compared by means of their effects. I assumed that an effect must be equal to its cause if the whole power of the cause is expended or used up in producing it, irrespective of how much time it takes for the effect to be produced. Let us suppose therefore that A and C are heavy bodies, and that their forces are converted into a change of height—as would happen if, when they are moving with their speeds of one unit for A and two units for C, they are taken as being at the ends of the vertical pendulums PA_1 and EC_1 (as in Figure 5.2).

[30] Now it is clear from the demonstrations of Galileo and others that if body A, with its one unit of speed, rises at its highest above the horizontal HR by one foot (A_2H), then body C, with its two units of speed, will rise to a height of four feet (C_2R). It follows that a heavy body with two units of speed has four times the capacity for action (*potentia*) of one with one unit of speed, because when it expends all its power (*virtus*) it can do four times as much—because raising one pound (that is, itself) by four feet is just raising one pound by one foot four times. And in the same way we can conclude generally that the forces of equal bodies are proportional to the squares of their speeds and that, in general, a body's force is proportional to the product of its size and the square of its speed.

---

[9] The argument here is essentially that at T1. 17. But the terminology of 'living force' is new, as is its measure explicitly in terms of speed² rather than of height (see end of Introduction, Sect. 3.4).

5. Specimen Dynamicum

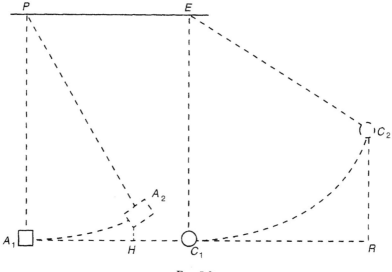

FIG. 5.2.

[31] I have confirmed this conclusion by reducing to absurdity (to perpetual motion, in fact) the opposite opinion, which is the usual one, especially among the Cartesians—that a body's force should be taken as being
proportional to the product of its size and speed. Using the same method I
give an a posteriori definition of *inequality of force*, and at the same time
provide a clear distinction between a larger force and a smaller one. If the
substitution of one force for another gives rise to perpetual mechanical
motion, or an effect which is greater than its cause, then the two are clearly
unequal; and the one which was substituted for the other must be the
more powerful, since it produced something greater. I take it to be certain
that nature never substitutes unequal forces for each other, and that the
complete effect is always equal to the total cause. Therefore, we in our calculations can always substitute equal forces one for another with complete
freedom, just as if we were actually substituting them in reality, and
without fear that perpetual mechanical motion will result. [32] If it were
true, therefore, as most people have persuaded themselves it is, that a
heavy body A, two units in size, let us say, and with one unit of speed, is
equal in power to a heavy body C, one unit in size and with two units of
speed, then we could safely substitute the one for the other. But this is not
so. For suppose that A, of two units in size, has acquired one unit of speed
by descending from A_2 to A_1, a height of one foot (A_2H). Now when it is at
A_1 on the horizontal, let us substitute for it weight C, of one unit in size and

two units of speed, which they claim is of equal power. It rises to C_2, a height of four feet. Thus, simply by the falling of the two-pound weight A from the height A_2H of one foot, and the substitution of something supposedly of equal power, we have brought about the raising of one pound to four feet, something which is twice what we had before. In this way we would have gained that amount of force, and achieved perpetual mechanical motion—which is absurd. [33] It does not matter whether because of the laws of motion we can actually make this substitution because we can always substitute for each other in the mind things which are of equal power. Even so, I have worked out various ways in which we can actually carry out, as nearly as we could wish, the transfer of A's whole force to C, so that A is brought to rest, and C, which was previously at rest, is now the only one in motion. So it could actually happen that, if they were equal in power, a two-pound weight with one unit of speed could be replaced by a one-pound weight with two units of speed; from which, as I have shown, an absurdity would result. [34] These considerations are not worthless, and they are not mere verbal quibbles; they are very useful in comparing machines and comparing motions. Suppose you had enough force—from water, animals, or some other source—to keep a heavy body of one hundred pounds in constant motion, so that it completed a horizontal circle thirty feet in diameter in a time of a quarter of a minute. If someone showed that something twice as heavy could complete half the circle in the same time and at less expense, and suggested that would be a benefit to you, you should realize that it would be a mistake, and that you would be being deprived of half your force. But now that we have disposed of the mistakes, let us set out a little more clearly the true and wonderful laws of nature in the second part of this study.

[35] Part 2. The fact that the nature of body, and indeed of substance in general, is not sufficiently well understood has meant, as I have already mentioned, that some distinguished philosophers of our time have located the notion of body in mere extension, and as a result have been driven to fall back on God in order to explain the union between the soul and the body, and even interactions between bodies themselves. Now, it must be admitted that it is impossible that pure extension, which contains only geometrical notions, should ever be capable of activity and passivity. There seemed, therefore, to be only one thing left: that when a person thinks and tries to move his arm, God, by a kind of prior agreement, moves it for him; and conversely, when there is a motion in the blood and animal spirits, God produces a perception in the soul. But that very fact, because it is so far from good philosophical reasoning, should have

indicated to these writers that they were starting from a false principle, and had set up a mistaken notion of body, from which such consequences followed. [36] I will show, therefore, that in all substances there is a force of acting, and that in all created substances there is also a force of being passive. I will show too that the notion of extension is not in itself complete, but is a relation to something which is extended, something whose diffusion or continuous repetition it implies; it presupposes bodily substance, which involves the capacity for action (*potentia*) and of resistance and which exists everywhere as corporeal mass, the diffusion of which is contained in extension. I shall one day use this to throw new light on the union of the soul and the body. For the present, though, what I have to show is how it gives rise to wonderful and extremely useful practical theorems in dynamics, which is the science which deals specifically with the laws governing forces in bodies.

[37] The first thing we must recognize is that force is something fully real, even in created substances, whereas space, time, and motion have something of the nature of beings of reason: they are not true or real in themselves, but only in so far as they involve the divine attributes of immensity, eternity, and activity, or the force of created substances. It follows immediately from this that there is no vacuum in space or in time, and also that motion considered apart from force (that is, considered as involving only the geometric notions of size and shape, and changes in them) is really nothing more than change of place. Therefore *motion, in so far as we experience it (quoad phaenomena) is nothing but a relationship*—as *Descartes also recognized, when he defined it as the removal of something from the neighbourhood of one body to that of another. [38] But in working out the consequences he forgot his definition, and he set up his laws of motion as if it were something real and absolute. What we must say, therefore, is that given a number of bodies in motion, there is no way of determining from the phenomena which ones are in absolute determinate motion or at rest. Any one of them you choose may be taken as being at rest, and yet the phenomena will be the same. It follows from this (what *Descartes did not notice) that *the equivalence of hypotheses still holds when there are collisions between bodies*; consequently, we must work out laws of motion which preserve the relative nature of motion: that is, there will be no way of determining from the phenomena after a collision which bodies before it had been at rest and which had been in absolute determinate motion. [39] *Descartes's law according to which a body at rest can never be displaced by a smaller body therefore will not do; and neither will his

other laws of the same kind, than which nothing could be further from the truth.[10] Another consequence of the relative nature of motion is that *the action or impact of bodies on each other will be the same, provided that the speed with which they come together is the same.* That is to say, if the appearances of the phenomena in question are the same, then whatever in the end may turn out to be the true hypothesis, that is, whichever bodies might in the end turn out to be truly in motion or at rest, the outcome in terms of the phenomena in question or the phenomena which result will be the same, even when we are dealing with bodies acting on each other. And this is exactly what we find: we would feel the same pain if our hand knocked against a stationary stone hanging from a thread, for example, as when a stone hits our stationary hand with the same speed. In practice what we say is whatever the situation requires, in order to give the simplest and most suitable explanation of the phenomena. [40] This is why we can make use of the motion of a first mover in studying the heavenly spheres, while in planetary theory we should use the *Copernican hypothesis. (So immediately those arguments which have been pursued so vigorously, and in which even theologians have become involved, completely disappear.) For while force is something real and absolute, motion belongs to the class of relative phenomena; and truth is to be found not in the phenomena but in their causes.

[41] Something further which follows from our notions of body and forces is that *everything that happens in substances can be understood as happening spontaneously and in an orderly way.* Connected to this is the idea that *no change takes place by leaps and bounds.* Given this, it also follows that *there can be no atoms.* [42] To see the force of this argument, let us assume that bodies *A* and *B* collide, as in Figure 5.3. *A* moves from A_1 to A_2, *B* moves from B_1 to B_2, and after colliding at $A_2 B_2$ they rebound from A_2 to A_3 and

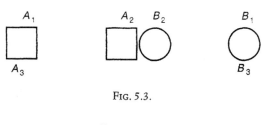

FIG. 5.3.

[10] See App. D.

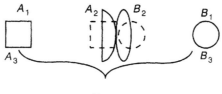

FIG. 5.4.

from B_2 to B_3. If we assume that there are atoms—that is, bodies of maximal hardness and inflexibility—then it is clear that change would be taking place in a leap, or instantaneously. For the forward motion changes to backward at the very moment of collision—unless we assume that the bodies become stationary for an instant immediately after the collision, that is, that they lose all their force. But, besides being absurd in other ways, this again would be a change taking place in a single leap, an instantaneous change from motion to rest, without any intermediate stages. [43] We must therefore recognize (as in Figure 5.4) that when bodies A and B collide by moving from A_1 and B_1 to the point of collision at A_2B_2, at that point they are gradually compressed, like two inflated balls. And as they approach each other more and more, the pressure continues to increase, and for that very reason the motion decreases as the force of conatus is taken up by the elasticity of the bodies, until they come to a complete standstill. Then, as the elasticity of the bodies eventually begins to restore them, they rebound from each other in the opposite direction; their motion begins from rest and gradually increases until they finally reach the same speed they had when they came together but in the opposite direction, moving away from each other until, assuming the bodies are of equal size and had equal velocity, they return to A_3 and B_3, which coincide with A_1 and B_1. [44] From this we see that none of these changes takes place in a single leap, but the forward motion decreases gradually to rest, after which the backward motion finally begins. In just the same way, one shape cannot be made into another (a circle into an oval, for example) except by passing through all the countless intermediate shapes, and nothing gets from one place to another, or from one time to another, except by passing through all the intermediate places and times. Therefore, rest can never arise from motion (and even less can motion in the opposite direction) without passing all the intermediate levels of motion. I am amazed that, in view of how important this is in nature, it has been so little noticed. [45] There also follows from it something which Descartes rejected in his letters, and which some great men are even now unwilling to admit—that *all reflection arises from elasticity.* This explains many excellent experiments which show, as Mariotte has beautifully demonstrated, that *bodies are deformed before they are propelled.* There also follows, finally, that most wonderful conclusion that there is no body so small that it does not have elasticity, and so is not permeated by an even more subtle fluid. This means that *there are no elements of bodies,* there is no perfectly fluid matter, and there are no solid spheres of some supposed second element, of fixed and unchanging shape: on the contrary, analysis continues to infinity.

[46] It is also in agreement with the *law of continuity,* which rules out changes taking place by leaps and bounds, that rest can be considered as a special case of motion—that is, as vanishingly small or minimal motion—and that equality can be considered as a case of vanishingly small inequality. It follows from this that the laws of motion must be formulated in such a way that there is no need of special laws for bodies which are equal or for bodies at rest, but that such laws arise simply from the laws of unequal and moving bodies. Alternatively, if we do want to give special laws for rest and equality, we must be careful that they are not inconsistent with the theory which takes rest as the limit of motion and equality as the smallest inequality; otherwise we will impugn the harmony of things, and our laws will not be compatible with one another. [47] I first published this new technique for testing laws, both my own and those of other people, in the *Nouvelles de la république des lettres* for July 1687, article 8. I called it a general principle of order which arises from the notions of infinity and continuity, and leads to the axiom that the order of what is sought for is the same as that of what is given. I put the point generally as follows: when instances (or what is given) approach each other continually and eventually disappear into one another, the consequences or outcomes (or what is sought for) must do so also. Thus in geometry the case of the ellipse continuously approaches that of the parabola; if we assume that one focus is fixed and the other is moved further and further away, then when it reaches infinity, the ellipse finally turns into a parabola. Consequently, all the laws of the ellipse must necessarily hold for the parabola, understood as an ellipse whose second focus is infinitely distant. We can therefore consider parallel rays striking a parabola as either coming from or going to the other focus. Therefore, in the same way, the case in which body *A* collides with the moving body *B* can be continuously varied so that, with the motion of *A* taken as constant, the motion of *B* can be made smaller and smaller until it eventually vanishes into rest, and then turns into increasing motion in the opposite direction. I hold that when *A* and *B* are both in motion, the result (whether for *A* or for *B*) of the collision between them continuously

approaches the result of that when B is at rest, and eventually vanishes into it. So the case of rest, both in the givens and in the outcomes or results, is the limit of cases of motion along a line, or the common limit of continuous linear motion, and so a special case of it. [48] When I examined the Cartesian laws of motion by means of this touchstone, which I have converted from geometry to physics, it brought out an amazing gap or leap, which is quite contrary to the nature of things. If we draw lines to represent the quantities involved, with B's motion before the collision taken as given and shown on the abscissa, and its motion after the collision taken as unknown and shown on the ordinate, then if we draw a line through all the ordinate values in accordance with Descartes's laws it turns out not to be continuous, but to have amazing gaps, and to somersault about in an absurd and incomprehensible way.[11] I also noted on that occasion that the laws proposed by the Reverend Father *Malebranche did not entirely pass this test either. The distinguished gentleman reconsidered the matter, and with his usual honesty he admitted that this had given him occasion to change his laws, which he published in a small book.[12] It must be said, however, that he has yet not fully mastered this new technique, for there are still some things in his theory which do not quite work.

[49] A further remarkable consequence of what I have said is that *every passive state of a body is spontaneous, or arises from an internal force, even if occasioned by something external.* I mean here the passive state which belongs to the body itself, which results from the impact and which is unchanged whatever theory we eventually adopt, that is, whichever body we eventually regard as being absolutely at rest or in motion. For since the impact is the same whichever body the motion truly fits with in the end, it follows that the effect of the impact is equally distributed between them. Consequently, *in a collision, both bodies are equally active,* and half of the effect results from the action of one, and half from the action of the other. And since half of the resulting effect, or the passive state, is in one body, and half in the other, the passive state of either one of them can be derived from its own action, so that there is no need for any influx from one into the other, even though the action of the one provides the occasion for the other to produce a change within itself. [50] When A and B collide, the resistance of the bodies, together with their elasticity, causes them to be

---

[11] See App. D.
[12] See the fifth paragraph of Introduction, Sect. 3.5.

compressed by the collision, and the compression is the same in each of them, whatever theory we adopt. And this is what we find in experience. Imagine two inflated balls which collide. Whether both are in motion or one is at rest, or if the one at rest is hanging from a string, so that it can easily swing back; nevertheless, if the relative speed of approach is the same in each case, then the amount of compression or elastic tension will be the same, and will be equal in both. Similarly, when balls A and B restore themselves by the force of the elasticity or compression they contain, and each one drives the other away from itself so that they shoot out as if from a bow, each one is driving itself away from the other by force, so that each one recedes from the other through its own force, not through the force of the other. What is true of these inflated balls must be understood as applying to all passive states of bodies in impact: their repercussion or flying apart arises from their own elasticity—that is, from the motion of the ethereal fluid matter by which they are permeated—and so from a force existing within them, or internally to them. As I have said, I have in mind here the *individual motion* of bodies, as opposed to their *common motion*, which we can ascribe to their common centre of gravity. This individual motion can be thought of for the purposes of theory as if the bodies concerned were being carried on a ship, whose motion is that of their common centre of gravity, while they themselves are moving around on the ship. The phenomena can be saved from the composite of the common motion of the ship or of their common centre of gravity, and their own individual motion. From what I have said we can also see that *there is no action of bodies without a reaction, and that they are equal and in opposite directions*.

[51] Since only force and its resultant effort exist at any moment (for, as explained above, motion never really exists), and since every effort tends in a straight line, it follows that *all motion is rectilinear or composed of rectilinear motions*. It follows from this not only that *anything which moves along a curve strives always to go off along the straight tangent*, but also—what one would least expect—there follows *the true notion of solidity (firmitatis)*. In fact nothing is absolutely solid or fluid, and everything has a certain degree of both solidity and fluidity: which term we apply depends on the overall appearance which the thing presents to our senses. However, if we consider something which we call solid rotating about its centre, its parts will be striving to fly off along the tangent; indeed they will actually begin to do so. But as each one's moving away from the others interferes with the motion of the bodies around it, they are repelled and pushed back

together again, as if there were a magnetic force at the centre which was attracting them, or as if the parts themselves contained a centripetal force. Consequently, the rotation is composed of the rectilinear effort (*nisus*) of the parts along the tangent, together with their centripetal striving among themselves. Thus we see that all curvilinear motion arises from the composition of rectilinear and centripetal efforts, and at the same time that all solidity is caused by this pushing together by surrounding bodies—otherwise it could not be the case that all curvilinear motion is composed only from rectilinear motions. This also gives us another—and no less unexpected—argument against atoms. [52] For nothing more contrary to nature can be imagined than to think that solidity derives from rest, because *there is never any true rest in bodies*, and nothing but rest can come from rest. Suppose that *A* and *B* are at rest with respect to each other—if not truly at rest, then at least at rest relative to each other. (Though strictly speaking this never happens, because *no body ever keeps exactly the same distance from another for even the shortest time.*) Suppose further that a thing at rest will remain at rest unless some new cause comes along to put it into motion. It does not follow from this that because *B* resists being moved when another body strikes it, it will also resist being separated from *A*, so that once *B*'s resistance is overcome and *B* is set in motion, *A* will immediately follow. Yet if there were some real *attraction* (which is not found in nature), something to be explained by primitive solidity, or by rest or somesuch, this certainly would follow. Solidity should be explained, therefore, only in terms of this pushing together by surrounding bodies. Pressure alone is not enough to explain it, as if *B* were just prevented from moving away from *A*; we have to understand that they do in fact separate from each other, but that they are then driven back towards each other by the surrounding bodies. It is therefore from the combination of two motions that the conservation of their togetherness derives. [53] Some people explain the solidity of hard, perceptible bodies by thinking in terms of there being imperceptible slabs or layers in bodies—like two slabs of polished marble which fit perfectly together—which the resistance of surrounding bodies makes it difficult to separate. Although much of what they say is true, because it assumes that the plates are themselves solid it cannot provide the ultimate explanation of solidity. [54] All of this shows why I cannot agree with some of the philosophical opinions of certain important mathematicians, who not only accept that there is empty space and seem to have no objections to attraction, but also maintain that motion is something absolute, and claim to prove this through rotation and the centrifugal force which arises from it. However, if rotation too arises only from a combination of rectilinear motions, then it follows that since in the case of rectilinear motion the equivalence of hypotheses is maintained whichever object we take as actually moving, then the same will be true in the case of curvilinear motions.

[55] From what we have said we can also see that *motion which is common to a number of bodies does not change their actions on one another*, because the speed with which they approach one another—and therefore also the force of impact by which they act on one another—does not change. This is what lies behind those fine experiments on motion imparted by something which is itself being carried, which Gassendi reported in his letters as a reply to those who thought they could infer from the motion of projectiles that the earth is stationary. Consider people who are travelling in a big ship—one which is enclosed, let us say, or at least set up in such a way that the passengers cannot see anything outside of it. Clearly, however fast the ship was moving, provided it was moving smoothly and uniformly they would have no criterion for deciding, on the basis only of what was happening on the ship, whether it was moving or not—even if they play ball, and move around in all sorts of ways. [56] This must be noted in support of those who misunderstand the Copernican theory, and think it means that things that are thrown up into the air from the earth are carried along by the air, which is rotating with the earth, so that they follow the motion of the earth and fall back down as if it were not moving. They rightly see that this is not acceptable. However, the most learned users of the Copernican theory believe rather that whatever is on the surface of the earth is moved along with it, so that a thing which is shot up from a bow or catapult will carry with it the impetus it has received from the motion of the earth, as well as that which it was given when it was projected. Therefore, since it has two motions, one in common with the earth and one belonging to the projection, it is not surprising that the common motion doesn't make any difference. At the same time, it must not be denied that if something could be thrown up far enough, or if we imagine the ship as being so large and so fast that, before the body fell back down, the earth or the ship had traced out enough of an arc for it to be noticeably different from a straight line, then we would be able to tell the difference, because then the circular motion of the earth or of the boat would not remain in common with the rectilinear motion given to the projectile by the rotation of the earth or the ship. [57] The effort of heavy bodies to move towards a centre also brings in an external influence which can produce a further difference in the phenomena, as would be the case if there were a compass in the enclosed ship which, by pointing to the pole,

could indicate changes in the ship's direction. But when we are concerned with the equivalence of hypotheses, everything which plays a part in the phenomena must be taken into account. These things also show us that the composition of motions and the resolution of one motion into two or any number more can safely be applied—even though according to Wallis one clever man has expressed reasonable doubts. For the matter certainly needs to be proved, and cannot simply be taken as self-evident, as many have done.

APPENDICES

A

Four important notions in this paragraph are 'motion' (*motus*), 'velocity' (*velocitas*), 'conatus' (or 'striving'), and 'impetus' (*impetus*). 'Motion' is something which takes place *over a period of time*, as when a body moves from one place to another; 'velocity' is what a body which has motion has *at an instant of time*. (Motion, or *motus*, at an instant of time—what Leibniz here calls 'velocity'—is called in the next paragraph *motio*, which we have translated as 'instantaneous motion'.)

In more recent times 'velocity' has come to mean not, as here, the 'instaneous motion', or speed, of a body, but rather its speed *in a certain direction* (so that a body moving with a constant speed but in a circle is changing its velocity). Leibniz's 'conatus' is velocity in this sense.

Leibniz's 'impetus' is the mass (*moles*) of a body multiplied by its Leibnizian 'velocity'. This is the same thing as the *Cartesians' 'quantity of motion' (see Introduction, Sect. 3.4). It is different from what Leibniz calls 'directed force' (TT8. 7; 19. 80), which we would call 'momentum'—mass multiplied by 'conatus' (i.e. multiplied by velocity with direction taken into account).

Leibniz's description, at the end of this section, of 'quantity of motion . . . over [a period, say t_1 to t_2 of] time' effectively amounts to $\int_{t_1}^{t_2}$ (mass $\times$ velocity)dt, which, when velocity is a constant, will be $mv(t_1 - t_2)$.

B

The 'dead force' of this section is the urge or *solicitatio* of the previous section, which, as it continuously has its effect, produces a continuous acceleration or continuing increase in velocity. Living force is a function (mv^2, Leibniz holds) of that increasing velocity—as Leibniz says, living force 'arises from an infinite number of continued impulses of dead force', i.e. from the velocity which develops as acceleration acts over time.

C

Within a collection of moving bodies, each body has its own 'respective' or 'individual' living force—due to its own mass and its motion within the system as a whole. The system as a whole has 'directive' or 'common' living force—due to its whole mass and its motion as considered from a point outside of it. Both these forces are 'partial'.

'Total' or 'absolute' living force is the 'common, directive' living force of the whole added to the arithmetical sum of the 'respective' living forces of the individual bodies. (It is equivalent to the arithmetical sum of the living force of each individual body when their individual motions are considered, not relative to each other (as with 'respective' individual force), but to some point outside the system.)

D

Some of what Leibniz has in mind here can be seen by considering Descartes's first and third collision laws. According to the third, when A and B, two equally sized bodies, collide when travelling in opposite directions with B the more rapid, the direction of A will be reversed and they will travel together with a speed equal to half the sum of their original speeds. Suppose, accordingly, a series of collisions in which the original speed of B is gradually decreased (4, . . . 3, . . . 2, . . .) so as to approach the original speed of A (which, let us suppose, is one unit, from right to left) (see Figure 5.A1(a)). The result when B's original speed is the same as A's cannot be given by this rule (which governs only cases where B's original speed is greater than A's), but the graph suggests that in this case B would continue on its way with undiminished speed, reversing, but not increasing, A's original speed.

The result is actually governed by Descartes's first rule, for equally sized bodies colliding from opposite directions with the same speed. According to it, A and B on collision will each simply reverse direction, and travel backwards with their original speeds. That is, B will travel from right to left with unit speed—as at $\times$ on Figure 5.A1(a)—and not, as the continuation of (a) would indicate, from left to right with unit speed. So at the limit of this series of collisions Descartes's rules give us, as Leibniz says, 'an amazing gap'.

In fact, while his first rule is correct, Descartes's third rule is not. As explained in the third paragraph of Introduction, Sect. 3.5, the *direction* of the speeds of A and B need to be taken into account and the graph, for A moving with unit speed, should be as in Figure 5.A1(b). That is to say, when A and B, two equally sized

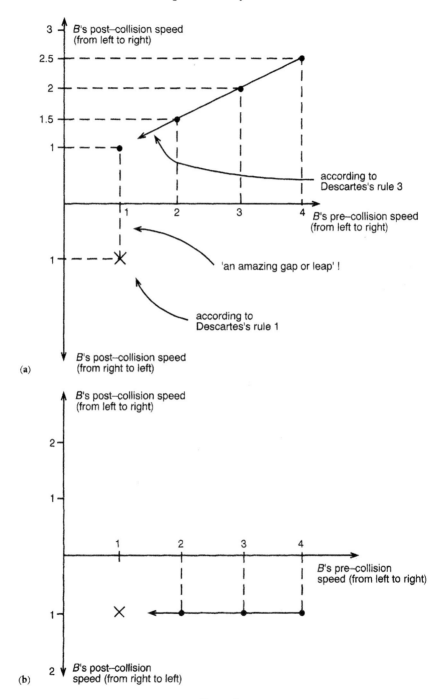

FIG. 5.A1.

bodies, collide when travelling in opposite directions, their directions will be reversed and each will take over the other's pre-collision speed. There is no 'leap' here when the first rule takes over at ✕, the point where B's speed is equal to A's.

6

REPLY OF M. S. F. TO M. DE L. B. Z. ON HIS NEW SYSTEM OF THE COMMUNICATION BETWEEN SUBSTANCES (1695)

Summary of the Text

Leibniz's 'New System of the Nature of Substances' (T4) provoked much discussion. Simon Foucher's (1644–96) reply to it was the first to appear in print.

*Foucher had met Leibniz in Paris in the 1670s. He devoted his intellectual activities to reviving *Academic scepticism. In argument he aimed to uncover the underlying principles on which his opponent's position rested, and then to point out that they are mere assumptions. His main work was A Critique of [Malebranche's] Search after Truth (1675).*

*In Sections 1–3 Foucher gives a good account of the first part of T4. He recognizes that Leibniz introduces *substantial forms partly because of the need for a basis for extension, and partly as something which unifies and which is a source of activity. He then (Sects. 4–5) turns to Leibniz's hypothesis of *concomitance about the relationship between body and soul. He agrees that the idea of a body acting completely by itself is perfectly possible, but argues that on Leibniz's account bodies really are perfectly useless and needless.*

———————

THE TEXT

... [2] The first part is intended only to show that in all substances there are unities which constitute their reality, and which, since they distinguish them from others, form (to speak in *Scholastic terms) their *individuation*.[1]

From the French of *Journal des savants* (Paris edn.) no. 36 (12 Sept. 1695), 422–6 (see also GP i. 424–7, iv. 487–90). The section numbers are as in the fuller translation in WF 41–4. The superscripts [A], [B], [C], [D] refer to the comments (as in T7) Leibniz made on this 'Reply'.

[1] The question of the 'principle of individuation'—the question of what constitutes the indi-

That is your first point on the subject of matter and extension. I agree with you that it is right to look for unities which underlie the structure and reality of extension. Otherwise, as you quite rightly say, an infinitely divisible extension is only an imaginary composite, the foundations of which do not exist, since without unities there is no genuine multiplicity. However, I am amazed that you do not go any further, because the essential foundations of extension could never really exist.[A] In reality, points without parts could not exist in the universe, and two points joined together do not produce extension. It is impossible that there should exist any length without breadth, or any surface without depth. And it is useless to bring in physical points, because such points are extended, and involve all the difficulties we wanted to avoid. . . .

[3] You also bring in unities of a different kind, which are strictly speaking unities of composition or of relation, and which concern the perfecting or the completing of a whole which, being organic, performs certain functions. For example, a clock is one, an animal is one; and you want to give the name *substantial forms* to these natural unities of animals and of plants, so that it will be these unities which constitute their individuation, by distinguishing them from every other composite. It seems to me that you are right to give animals a principle of individuation different from that which they are usually given, which relates only to their external accidents. This principle must indeed be internal, as regards both the soul and the body; but however the organs of the animal may be arranged, the animal will not thereby be made sentient, for, after all, all this concerns only the organic mechanical structure, and I do not see that it gives you any reason for introducing a principle of consciousness into animals, substantially different from that in man.[B] After all, it is not without reason that the *Cartesians hold that if we allow a principle of consciousness in animals, capable of distinguishing between good and bad, it will then be necessary also to allow them reason, discernment, and judgement. And so, if I may say so, sir, this does not resolve the difficulty either.

[4] Coming now to your *concomitance*, which is the second and most important part of your system. I can agree that God, the great constructor of the universe, can assemble the organic parts of the body of a man so

viduality of (for example) one man as distinct from another—was much debated among Scholastic philosophers. *Aquinas held that the foundation of individuality lay in 'designated matter'—the difference between me and you is that I am this material object and you are that one. John Duns Scotus (1265–1308) later took the opposite view, that a thing's individuality resides in the formal property of 'haecceity' ('thisness') which is directly apprehended by the intellect.

well that they would be capable of producing all the movements which the soul joined to that body might want to produce in the course of its life-time, without the soul's having the power to change those movements or to modify them in any way; and that correspondingly God can so structure the soul (whether or not this will be a new kind of machine) that all the thoughts and modifications which correspond to those movements come successively into being, just when the body performs its actions. And I will also agree that this is no more impossible than it would be to make two clocks which are so well synchronized, and which operate so uniformly, that just when clock A strikes midday, clock B does the same, so that one would think that the two clocks were driven by the same weight, or the same spring. But after all, what could be the point of this great contrivance with substances, if not to make us believe that they act on one another, even though this is not so? In fact, it seems to me that this system is hardly any better than that of the Cartesians. We reject theirs because it point-lessly supposes that God, having regard to the movements which he himself produces in the body, also produces in the soul the thoughts which correspond to them—as if it were not more worthy of him to produce the thoughts and modifications of the soul straight away, without there being any bodies to guide him,^{C} and so to speak to tell him what to do. If we are right in that, then is it not reasonable to ask you why God is not content to produce all the thoughts and modifications of the soul (whether he does it immediately or by means of some contrivance, as you wish) without there being any useless bodies which the mind can never either move or know? After all, even if there were no movement in these bodies, the soul might still think that there was; just as those who are asleep think they are moving their limbs, and walking, when all the time their limbs are at rest, and not moving at all. In the same way, even while awake, souls would be convinced that their bodies moved according to their wills, even though in reality these vain useless lumps were inactive, and remained in continual torpor. [5] In truth, sir, is it not clear that these opinions are concocted spe-cially for the purpose, and that all these systems are only invented after the event, to defend certain preconceived principles? Thus the Cartesians, having assumed that there was nothing in common between spiritual and corporeal substances, cannot explain how the one operates on the other, and so are reduced to saying what they say. But you, sir, who could have disentangled yourself from that in various ways, astonish me by burden-ing yourself with their problems. For who does not understand that when an extra weight is added to one side of a balance which is in equilibrium and at rest, there is an immediate movement, and one side makes the other

182

go up, in spite of its efforts to go down? You realize that material beings are capable of effort and of movement, and it follows very naturally that the greater effort must overcome the weaker. But then, you also recognize that spiritual beings can make efforts;[D] and since there is no effort which does not presuppose some resistance, this resistance must turn out to be either stronger or weaker. If it is stronger, it overcomes; if weaker, it gives way. Now, it is not impossible that when the mind tries to move the body, it finds that the body makes an opposing effort which resists it sometimes more and sometimes less—in which latter case the body would give in to it. . . .

7

REMARKS ON M. FOUCHER'S
OBJECTIONS (1695)

Summary of the Text

On the way towards making a formal response to Foucher's 'Reply' (T6) to the
'New System' (T4) Leibniz recorded some remarks on his objections. These focus
on two or three points which, in Leibniz's view, rest on a misunderstanding: in
particular, Foucher's claim that on Leibniz's account of the relation between them
and the soul, material bodies are quite needless.

THE TEXT

[A] 'it is right . . . never really exist': It appears that the author of the objection has not understood my opinion very well. Extension or space, and the
surfaces, lines, and points which can be conceived of within it, are only
systems of relations, or relations of coexistence, as regards both the actual
existent and the possible existent which could be put in the place of what
there is. So they have no constitutive principle at all, any more than
number has. A divided number, for example $\frac{1}{2}$, can be divided again, into
two quarters or four eighths, etc., and so on to infinity; we cannot arrive
at the smallest fraction, and think of the number as a totality formed by
putting together such ultimate elements. And it is the same with a line,
which can be divided just like that number. Thus, properly speaking, the
number $\frac{1}{2}$ in the abstract is a simple relation, in no way formed by a composition of other fractions, even though among numbered things there is
equality between two quarters and one half. And the same can be said of
an *abstract* line; for there is composition only in *concrete* things, or *masses*,
the relations between which are marked by such abstract lines. And this
is also the way that mathematical points come about; they too are mere

From the French at GP iv. 490–3. For the complete set of Leibniz's remarks, see WF 45–7.

184

modalities, that is, extremities. And as everything about an abstract line is indefinite, they have regard only to what is possible, as do the fractions of a number; we are not concerned with divisions which are actually made, and which mark out these points in a different way. But in actual substantial things, the whole is a result, or assembly, of simple substances, or indeed of a multiplicity of real unities. It is this confusion of the ideal and the actual which has quite obscured, and made a labyrinth of, 'the composition of the continuum'.[1] Those for whom lines are made up out of points have quite mistakenly looked for primary elements in ideal things, or in relations; and those who realized that relations like number, or space (which comprises the system or relations of possible coexistent things), could never be formed by the putting together of points, have for the most part then gone wrong by saying that substantial realities have no basic elements, as if they had no primary unities, and there are no simple substances. However, number and line are not *imaginary* things, even though they are indeed not made up in that way, because they are relations which involve eternal truths, in accordance with which the phenomena of nature are structured. In this way we can say that $\frac{1}{2}$ and $\frac{1}{4}$, taken in the abstract, are independent of one another, or rather, the complete relation $\frac{1}{2}$ is prior (in nature, as the *Scholastics say) to the partial relation $\frac{1}{4}$, since as regards the order of ideas it is by subdivision of a half that we arrive at a quarter; and similarly with the line, where the whole is prior to the part, because the part is only possible, or ideal. But in real things, where we are concerned only with divisions which are actually made, the whole is only a result, or assemblage, like a flock of sheep. In fact, the number of simple substances which make up a mass, however small that mass may be, is infinite, since in addition to the soul which constitutes the real unity of an animal, the body of a sheep (for example) is actually subdivided: that is to say, it too is an assemblage of invisible animals or plants, which themselves are also compounded, in addition to also having that which makes up their own real unity. And even though this goes on to infinity, it is obvious that, all in all, everything comes down to these unities, all the rest, or the resultants, being only well-founded phenomena.

[B] 'I do not see . . . from that in man': I do this because we do not consider animals to engage in the kind of reflection which constitutes reason, and which, by providing knowledge of necessary truths or of science, makes the soul capable of being a self. Animals can distinguish good from

---

[1] There is an allusion here to a book, *Labyrinthus, sive de Compositione Continui* (1631), by Liber Fromond (1587–1653), a Belgian philosopher and theologian, who raised some problems for *Descartes's account of matter as infinitely divisible extension.

bad, since they have perception; but they are certainly not capable of moral good and bad, which presuppose reason and consciousness.

[C] 'as if it were not . . . to guide him': God produced straight away not all thoughts (for thoughts need to succeed one another), but a nature which produces them in sequence. And that is exactly my point: all the body does is to act in conformity with them. But bodies were necessary to produce not only our unities or souls, but also those of the other corporeal substances, animals and plants, which are in our bodies and in those which surround us.

[D] 'material beings are capable . . . can make efforts': You want to conclude from this that they can act on one another. But their efforts are contained within themselves, and do not pass from one into another, because they are only tendencies to change in accordance with the particular laws of each one.

8

[FIRST] EXPLANATION OF THE NEW SYSTEM OF THE COMMUNICATION BETWEEN SUBSTANCES, IN REPLY TO WHAT WAS SAID OF IT IN THE *JOURNAL* FOR 12 SEPTEMBER 1695 (1696)

Summary of the Text

Following on from the informal notes (T7) he had made on Foucher's objections (T6) to his 'New System' (T4), Leibniz published a reply, which has come to be known as the 'First Explanation of the New System'. It appeared in April 1696, the very month Foucher died.

Section 2 relates to Foucher's T6. 3; Sections 3–4 to T6. 4; and Section 5 to T6. 5.

THE TEXT

... [2] I wanted to explain here, not the foundations of extension, but those of what is actually extended, of corporeal mass; and these foundations, according to me, are real unities, that is to say, substances with a genuine unity. In my view the unity of a clock, which you mention, is completely different from that of an animal; for an animal may be a substance with a genuine unity, like what we call 'I' in ourselves, while a clock is nothing but an aggregate. I do not locate the principle of the animal's consciousness in the arrangement of its organs, which I quite agree concerns only the corporeal mass. I mention these things so as to avoid misunderstandings, and to show that what you say about them is not at all contrary

From the French of *Journal des savants* (Paris edn.), no. 14 (2 Apr. 1696), 166–8, no. 15 (9 Apr. 1696), 169–71 (repr. at GP iv. 493–8). The section numbers used here are as in the fuller translation in WF 47–52.

to what I have maintained. It also seems that you do not disagree with me when I demand genuine unities, and so am led to rehabilitate *substantial forms. But when you seem to say that the soul of animals must be rational, if we give it feeling, you draw a conclusion for which I see no grounds.

[3] With admirable candour you acknowledge that my theory of harmony or concomitance is possible, but you are still rather unhappy with it. No doubt that is because you think it is purely arbitrary, through not having realized that it follows from my views about unities; but everything is connected to that. Thus you ask, sir, what could be the point of all this contrivance which I attribute to the author of nature. As if we could attribute too much contrivance to him, and as if this exact correspondence between substances, through their own laws that each received at the beginning, were not something wonderfully beautiful in itself, and worthy of its author. You also ask what advantage I find in it. I could refer to what I have already said about this; however, I reply, first, that when something cannot not be, there is no need to ask what the point of it is, before we accept it. What is the point of the incommensurability of the side with the diagonal? I reply in the second place that the point of this correspondence is to explain the communication between substances, and the union of the soul with the body, through laws of nature laid down in advance, and so without recourse either to a *transmission* of species, which is unintelligible, or to a further *intervention* by God, which seems inappropriate. For we must realize that as there are natural laws in matter, so there are also natural laws *in souls or forms*. And the operation of those laws is as I have just described.

[4] Again, I am asked why God does not think it enough to produce all the thoughts and 'modifications of the soul', without these 'useless' bodies, which the soul, it is said, could neither 'move nor know'. The answer is easy. It is that God wanted there to be more substances rather than fewer, and he thought it best that these 'modifications of the soul' should correspond to something outside. No substance is 'useless'; they all co-operate in fulfilment of God's plans. I am also far from willing to admit that the soul 'does not know' bodies, even though this knowledge arises without any influence of the one on the other. I am even willing to say that the soul 'moves' the body: just as, provided we understand them properly, a *Copernican speaks truly of the rising of the sun, a *Platonist of the reality of matter, and a *Cartesian of the reality of sensible qualities, so I hold that it is quite true to say that substances act on each other—provided we understand that one is the cause of changes in the other in consequence of the laws of harmony. The objection about the 'torpor' of

bodies, which could be at rest while the soul believed them to be in motion, cannot hold, because of this same unfailing correspondence which the divine wisdom has established. I have no knowledge of these 'vain, useless, and inactive lumps' which you mention. There is activity everywhere; I have established this more firmly than the received philosophy, for I hold there is no body without motion, no substance without effort.

[5] I do not understand the objection that is contained in these words: 'In truth, sir, is it not clear that these opinions are concocted specially for the purpose, and that all these systems are only invented after the event, to defend certain preconceived principles.' All theories are 'concocted for the purpose', and all systems are invented 'after the event', in order to save the phenomena or appearances.[1] But I do not see what the preconceived principles are that I am supposed to want to defend. If the idea is that I am led to my theory by a priori reasons, or by certain principles, as is indeed the case, then this is a commendation of the theory rather than an objection to it. It is usually enough that a theory should be proved a posteriori by its fitting the phenomena; but when there are also other reasons for it, and these are a priori, then so much the better. But perhaps the idea is that, having fashioned for myself a new opinion, I was glad to make use of it, more to pride myself on being original than because I had found it useful. I do not think, sir, that you have such a bad opinion of me as to attribute these thoughts to me. For you know I love truth, and that, if I were so fond of novelties, I would be keener to put them forward than I am, even those whose soundness is recognized. [6] But in order that those who know me less should not give your words a meaning which we wouldn't want, it is enough to say, that in my view it is impossible to give any other explanation of 'emanating activity'[2] which conforms with natural laws, and that I thought that the usefulness of my theory would be obvious in view of the difficulty which some of the wisest philosophers of our time have found in the communication between minds and bodies, and even between corporeal substances themselves: and I do not know but that you yourself haven't found some difficulty in it. It is true that, according to me, there is effort in all substances; but this force is, strictly, only in the substance itself,

---

[1] The phrase 'saving the appearances' derives from an ancient tradition according to which *Plato set the mathematicians in his Academy the problem of finding some regular rule or hypothesis which would generate or explain what appeared from Earth as the irregular movements of the planets (the 'wandering stars' as they were called).

[2] MP 129 and Lt 326 translate 'l'action emanente' as 'transeunt activity', which MP 255 explains as 'activity which passes from the agent to some other; distinct from "immanent activity"'.

and what follows from it in other substances is only in virtue of a 'pre-established harmony' (if I may use the expression), and not by a real influence or by the transmission of some species or quality. As I have explained what activity and passivity are, the nature of *effort* and of *resistance* can also easily be inferred. . . . [7] I will add a further reflection, which seems to me helpful in making the true nature and use of my system better understood.[3] You know that M. *Descartes believed in the conservation of the same quantity of motion in bodies. It has been shown that he was wrong about this; but I have made clear that it is still true that there is conservation of the same moving force, which he mistook for the quantity of motion. However, the changes which take place in the body as a consequence of modifications of the soul caused him some difficulty, because they seemed to break this law. He therefore thought he had found a solution, which is certainly ingenious, by saying that we must distinguish between motion and direction; and that the soul can neither increase nor decrease the *moving force*, but does change *the direction or determination* of the course of the *animal spirits: and this is how voluntary motions take place. Even so, he made no attempt to explain *how* the soul changes the course of bodies, which seems just as incomprehensible as its giving motion to bodies—at least so long as we do not have recourse to my pre-established harmony. But what we have to realize is that there is *another law of nature*, which I have discovered and demonstrated, and which M. Descartes did not know: *there is conservation* not only of the same quantity of moving force, but also *of the same quantity of direction towards whichever side one chooses*. That is to say, draw any straight line you please, and take whichever and however many bodies you like; you will find, considering all these bodies together, and without omitting any of those which act upon any one of those you have taken, that there will always be the same quantity of progress in a given direction in all lines parallel to your straight line. Note that the total amount of progress is to be calculated by subtracting the amount of progress of the bodies which go in the opposite direction from the amount of progress of those which go in the chosen direction. Since this law is as excellent and as general as the other, it as little deserves to be broken; and this is what my system achieves, for it conserves both force and direction. In a word, it preserves all the natural laws of bodies, despite the changes which take place in body as a consequence of changes in the soul.

---

[3] For an explanation of the ideas of this section, see Introduction, Sect. 5.

9

EXTRACT FROM A LETTER WRITTEN BY MONSIEUR LEIBNIZ ABOUT HIS PHILOSOPHICAL HYPOTHESIS (1696) ('THIRD EXPLANATION OF THE NEW SYSTEM')

Summary of the Text

Shortly after the appearance of the 'New System' (T4) Leibniz outlined some of its main ideas in a letter of which Henri Basnage de Beauval, editor of Histoire des ouvrages des savants, *published a shorter version. This was followed in November 1696 by the publication in the* Journal des savants *of some of what Basnage had edited out, together with some further material.*

This latter article came to be known as the 'Third Explanation of the New System'. For the most part its focus is sharply on Leibniz's account of the union of body and mind. Referring to this account for the first time in public as the 'way of pre-established harmony', Leibniz uses the now well-known analogy of two clocks to make a contrast with the 'way of influence' (the *Scholastics) and the *occasionalists' 'way of assistance'.

THE TEXT

[1] Some learned and acute friends of mine, who have considered my new theory on the great question of *the union of soul and body* and have found it to be of value, have asked me to provide explanations of some of the difficulties which have been found with it, and which arise from its not having been properly understood. I think the matter might be made intelligible to all types of mind by the following illustration.

From the French of *Journal des savants* (Paris edn.), no. 38 (19 Nov. 1696), 451–5 (repr. at GP iv. 500–3).

[2] Imagine two clocks, or two watches, which always tell exactly the same time. This can be done *in three ways*. The first is by the mutual influence of one clock on the other; the second, by the attentions of a man who looks after them; the third, by their own accuracy. *The first way*, that of influence, was discovered experimentally to his great surprise by the late M. *Huygens. He had two large pendulums attached to the same piece of wood, and the continual swinging of these pendulums imparted corresponding vibrations to the particles of wood. But these different vibrations could continue as they were and not interfere with one another only if the pendulums kept time together, and so it happened, by a kind of marvel, that even when their swinging was deliberately interfered with, they still came back to swinging together, almost like two strings vibrating in unison.

[3] *The second way* of making two clocks (even poor ones) always tell the same time would be to have them constantly looked after by a skilled workman, who adjusts them from moment to moment. I call this the way of assistance.

[4] Finally, *the third way* would be to make these two clocks, from the beginning, with such skill and accuracy that we could be sure that they would always afterwards keep time together. And this is the way of pre-established agreement.

[5] Now put the soul and the body in the place of these two clocks. Their agreement or sympathy can also come about in one of these three ways. *The way of influence* is that of the commonly accepted philosophy; but as we cannot conceive either material particles or species or immaterial qualities which can pass from one of these substances into the other, we are obliged to reject this view. *The way of assistance* is that of the system of occasional causes; but I maintain that this is to bring a *deus ex machina* into natural and everyday things, where reason says that God should intervene only in the way in which he concurs with all other natural things. Thus there remains only my theory, *the way of pre-established harmony*, set up by a contrivance of divine foreknowledge, which formed each of these substances from the outset in so perfect, so regular, and so exact a manner, that merely by following out its own laws, which were given to it when it was brought into being, each substance is nevertheless in harmony with the other, just as if there were a mutual influence between them, or as if in addition to his general concurrence God were continually operating upon them.

[6] Beyond that I do not think I have need of any further proof, unless I need to prove that God is adequate to produce a contrivance of such fore-

sight, of which in fact we have instances even among men, where they have the skill. Assuming that God is capable of this, it is quite evident that this is the most admirable way, and the one most worthy of him. In fact I do have other proofs, but they are deeper, and it is unnecessary to present them here. . . .

[7] Let me say a word about the dispute between two very clever people, the author of the recently published *Principles of Physics* and the author of the *Objections* (which appeared in the journal of August 13 and others), because my theory helps to settle it. I do not understand how matter can be conceived as extended and yet without either actual or ideal parts; if it can, I do not know what it is for something to be extended. In fact, I hold that *matter* is essentially *an aggregate*, and consequently that it always has actual parts. Thus it is by reason, and not only by the senses, that we see that it is divided, or rather that it is ultimately nothing but a multiplicity. I hold it true that matter (and indeed every part of matter) is divided into a greater number of parts than it is possible to imagine. This is why I often say that each body, however small, is a world of infinitely many creatures. Thus I do not believe there are atoms, that is to say parts of matter which are perfectly hard or of unbreakable solidity; nor, on the other hand, do I believe that there is perfectly fluid matter: my opinion is that each body is *fluid* as compared with more solid bodies, and *solid* as compared with more fluid ones. I am amazed that people still say that there is conservation of the same *quantity of motion*, in the *Cartesian sense; for I have proved the opposite, and some excellent mathematicians have already admitted as much. Nevertheless, I do not regard the solidity or cohesion of bodies as a primary quality, but as a consequence of motion. [See T5. 51–2.] . . .

10

NOTE H TO BAYLE'S *DICTIONARY* ARTICLE 'RORARIUS' (1697)

Summary of the Text

Pierre Bayle (1647–1706), professor of history and philosophy at Rotterdam, founded the learned journal Nouvelles de la république des lettres. *His extensive* Dictionnaire historique et critique, *his masterpiece, had great influence on eighteenth-century thought.*

*In its first edition (1697) he made comments on Leibniz's 'New System' (T4) in a lengthy footnote to the article on Jerome Rorarius (1485–1566), who had written a booklet, 'That Animals use Reason Better than Man', published in 1654, as a contribution to the debate over *Descartes's view of animals as unthinking machines (see Introduction, Sect. 6). In the article Bayle holds that the common view, that animals are capable of reason, has the disadvantage that it obscures the distinction between humans and animals, and so makes it very hard to show that the human soul is immortal. He says that both Descartes (successfully) and the *Aristotelians (unsuccessfully) try to maintain the distinction, but that neither account can make sense of cases of animal cleverness such as those which Rorarius presented. Leibniz is introduced into the picture as '[a] great mind in Germany, who has understood these problems, [and who] has provided some insights which are worth developing'.*

Bayle's note is a reaction to his reading of Leibniz's 'New System' (T4), of Foucher's objections (T6) to it, and of a further explanation of his ideas which he published in the Histoire des ouvrages des savants *in February 1696 (a text closely related to T9).*

Bayle begins his discussion (Sects. 1–3) by noting some of the things which Leibniz holds (as T4. 4, 5, 6, 8) about animals and their souls. Then, turning to the doctrine of pre-established harmony between bodies and souls (Sects. 5–7), he questions the comprehensibility of Leibniz's view that thoughts or perceptions are

From the French in Pierre Bayle, *Dictionnaire historique et critique* (Amsterdam, 1696–7), i. 966–7. The section numbers used here are as in the fuller translation in WF 72–5. The superscripts [A], [B], [C], etc. refer to the comments (as in T11) Leibniz made on this piece. The lower-case superscripts [a], [b] are cues for Bayle's own notes, which are given here at the end of the text.

produced quite spontaneously from within a soul, and quite independently of whatever else is going on in the universe. It is understandable (Bayle thinks) that a dog should pass from pleasure to pain when hit with a stick, but not understandable that it should pass from pleasure to pain independently of being hit. Why should a soul spontaneously give itself any unpleasant feeling? Leibniz's T11. E, F and T12. 6 provide some clarification of this.

Is it true, furthermore (Sect. 7), that the alternative *occasionalist account (the 'way of assistance' of T9. 5) of the relation between soul and body involves God's acting miraculously? After all, it does not have God acting otherwise than according to general laws (see T11. E).

Moreover (Sect. 7), the way of assistance is really the only plausible theory. We do not always know what perceptions we are later to have and so the course of our perceptions must be guided, not by some internal principle (as Leibniz holds), but from outside.

Bayle asks, finally, how souls, which are said to be simple, can act like complex clocks and do different things at different times. A simple thing, left to itself, will always do the same thing. Where, in a unitary substance, would one find the cause of any change in activity?

THE TEXT

[1] He [Leibniz] agrees [T4. 6] with the opinion of some of the moderns, that animals are already organized in the seed, and he also thinks [T4. 3] that matter alone cannot constitute a true unity, and therefore that animals are unified by a form, which is a simple, indivisible being, truly unique. In addition, he holds [T4. 4] that this form never leaves its subject, which means that properly speaking there is neither death nor generation in nature. He makes the soul of man an exception to all this [T4. 5, 8]; he sets it apart, etc.ᴬ [2] This theory frees us from one part of the problem; we no longer need to reply to the crippling objections that are made against the *Scholastics. The soul of an animal, it is said against them, is a substance distinct from the body; it must therefore be produced by creation, and destroyed by *annihilation*; it would therefore be necessary for heatᵃ to have the power to create souls, and to destroy them,ᵇ and what could be more absurd than that? The *Peripatetics' replies to this objection are not worth reporting, or worth bringing out of the darkness of the classroom where they are expounded to young students; they serve only to convince us that

as far as they are concerned, the objection is unanswerable. They are no better at avoiding the precipice towards which they are driven when they are required to find some sense and some shadow of reason in this continual production of an almost infinite number of substances, which are totally destroyed a few days later, even though they are much more noble and much more excellent than matter, which always remains in existence. [3] M. Leibniz's theory parries all these blows, for it would have us believe (i) that at the beginning of the world God created the forms of all bodies, and hence all the souls of the lower animals; (ii) that these souls continue in existence for ever from that time on, inseparably united with the first organized body in which God lodged them.[B] That rescues us from *metempsychosis,[C] which would otherwise have been an asylum to which we would have had to run. . . . [5] There are some problematic things in M. Leibniz's theory, even though they show the breadth and power of his genius. For example, he holds that the soul of a dog operates independently of its body: 'that everything in it arises from its own nature, with a perfect *spontaneity* as regards itself, and yet with a perfect conformity to things outside it. And . . . thus its internal perceptions must arise from its own original constitution, that is from its representational nature (its ability to express external things which are in relation with its organs), which it has had since its creation, and which constitutes its individual character' [T4. 14]. From this it follows that the dog's soul would feel hunger and thirst at certain times, even if there were no bodies in the universe; even if 'there existed nothing but God and that soul' [T4. 14].[D] He has explained [as in T9] his thinking by the example of two clocks which are perfectly synchronized: that is, he suggests that because of the particular laws which control its operation, the soul will feel hunger at a certain time, and because of the particular laws which govern the movement of matter, the body which is united to that soul will be modified at the same time, in the way it is modified when the soul feels hunger. [6] I shall wait until the clever author of this system has improved it before preferring it to that of occasional causes: I cannot understand the series of spontaneous internal actions which could make a dog's soul feel pain immediately after having felt pleasure, even if it were all alone in the universe. I can understand why a dog passes immediately from pleasure to pain when, whilst it is very hungry and eating some bread, it is suddenly hit with a stick; but that its soul should be constructed in such a way that it would have felt pain at the moment that it was hit, even if it had not been hit, and even if it had continued to eat the bread without being disturbed or prevented, that is what I cannot understand.[E] [7] I also find the *spontaneity* of this soul wholly incompatible with its feelings of pain, and in general with all feelings it finds unpleasant.[F] Moreover, the reason why this clever man finds the *Cartesian system not to his taste seems to me to be based on a false supposition; it cannot be said that the system of *occasional causes, with its reciprocal dependence of body and soul, makes the actions of God into the miraculous interventions of a *deus ex machina*.[1] For since God intervenes between them only according to general laws, in doing so he never acts extraordinarily. Does the internal active power which M. Leibniz thinks is communicated to the forms of bodies know what succession of actions it has to produce? Surely not; for we know from experience that we do not know what perceptions we will have in an hour's time. It would therefore be necessary for the forms to be directed by some external principle in the production of their actions. Would that not be a *deus ex machina*, just the same as in the system of occasional causes? [8] Finally, as he supposes, with very good reason, that all souls are simple and indivisible, it is impossible to see how they can be compared to clocks; how, that is, their original constitution can enable them to do different things, as a result of the spontaneous activity they received from their creator. It is obvious that a simple being will always do the same thing, if no outside cause interferes with it; but if it were made up of several parts, like a machine, it could do different things, because at any moment the particular activity of one part could interfere with that of the others. But in a unitary substance, where would you find the cause of any change of activity?

[BAYLE'S NOTES]

a. Chickens are hatched by putting eggs in a slightly warmed oven. This is the practice in Egypt.
b. Various kinds of animal can be killed by putting them in an over-heated oven.

---

[1] It should be noted that, as made at T9. 5, Leibniz's objection that the *occasionalists' 'way of assistance' introduces a *deus ex machina* does not describe this divine intervention as 'miraculous'. But the closely associated text to which Bayle is responding (an article in *Histoire des ouvrages des savants* for Feb. 1696) does, and, as the discussion develops, it becomes clear that for Leibniz God's intervention is, *as such*, miraculous. (See Introduction, Sect. 4.) (For a discussion of Leibniz on miracles, see G. Brown (1995), Rutherford (1993), McRae (1985).)

11

LEIBNIZ'S COMMENTS ON NOTE H TO BAYLE'S *DICTIONARY* ARTICLE 'RORARIUS' (1705?)

Summary of the Text

After its appearance in the second edition of Bayle's Dictionary (1702) Leibniz wrote down these comments on note H (T11). Of particular interest are his further explanations (E, F) of the system of pre-established harmony, in response to Bayle's puzzlement as to how and why an animal should pass from pleasure to pain without external cause. (See Introduction, Sect. 5.)

THE TEXT

[A] [See T10. 1.] [Leibniz comments:] Because these rational substances have a double status or position: one physical, like all animals, as a consequence of their bodily mechanism, and the other moral, as a result of which they are in society with God, as citizens of the City of God. This means that they conserve not only their substance, but also their personality and the knowledge of who they are.

[B] [See T10. 3.] It is not that a certain mass always remains inseparable from the animal or the soul, but rather that certain organs always remain, at least by the substitution of an equivalent, as happens when a river remains the same, although matter of the same kind is always entering and leaving it.

[C] [See T10. 3.] According to which the soul passes all at once into another body, quite differently organized.

From the French at GP iv. 528–33. For a fuller and differently labelled set of these comments, see WF 75–8. The comments belong with T15, and their date of composition must be no earlier than 1705 (see WF 71 n. 19).

[D] [See T10. 5.] I meant this only as a fiction, which is not compatible with the order of things but which might help make my thought more intelligible. For God so made the soul that it must correspond to everything external to it, and indeed represent it, in accordance with the impressions that things make on its organic body, which constitute its point of view. If there were other motions in the body than those which usually accompany the feeling of hunger or thirst, the soul would not have that feeling. It is true that if God were to decide to destroy everything external to the soul, but to keep the soul in isolation, with its affections and modifications, they would bring it, through its own dispositions, to have the same sensations as before, just as if bodies were still there, although this would then be nothing but a kind of dream. But since this is contrary to the designs of God, who wanted there to be agreement between the soul and things external to it, it is clear that this pre-established harmony removes such a fiction: it is metaphysically possible, but it doesn't accord with the facts and their explanations.

[E] [See T10. 6.] That is also what I do not say, if it is understood correctly. The pre-established harmony means that pain comes into a dog's soul when its body is hit. And if the dog were not going to be hit at this moment, God would not at the outset have given its soul a constitution which would produce that pain in it at this moment, and that representation or perception which corresponds to the blow of the stick. But if (though this is impossible) God had changed his mind and had changed the history of the material world in such a way that the blow never fell, without changing the nature of the soul and the natural course of its modifications, the soul would feel what corresponds to the blow, even though its body never received it. But, says M. Bayle, I understand the reasons through which the dog's body is hit by the stick, but I don't understand how the dog's soul, which experiences pleasure while the dog is eating hungrily, suddenly passes to pain without the stick's being the cause (in the manner of the schools), and without God's particular action (as with the *'occasionalists'). But neither does M. Bayle understand how the stick can have an influx into the soul, nor how the miraculous operation takes place by means of which God gets the body and the soul continually to agree. I, however, have explained how this agreement happens naturally, by supposing that each soul is a living mirror representing the universe from its point of view, and above all with respect to its body. Thus the causes which move the stick (that is, the man stationed behind the dog, getting ready to hit it while it eats, and everything in the history of the material world which contributes to his being in that position) are also represented in the dog's soul from the outset, exactly and truly, but feebly, by small confused perceptions and without apperception, that is, without the dog's knowing it—because the dog's body also is affected by them only imperceptibly. And just as in the history of the material world these dispositions eventually produce the blow firmly on the dog's body, so similarly the representations of these dispositions in the dog's soul eventually produce the representation of the blow of the stick; and since that representation is prominent and strong (which the representations of the predispositions were not, since the predispositions affected the dog's body only feebly), the dog apperceives it very distinctly, and this is what constitutes its pain. So we don't have to imagine that in this encounter the dog's soul passes from pleasure to pain arbitrarily, and without any internal reason.

[F] [See T10. 7.] The crux of M. Bayle's objection here is that we have no spontaneous inclination towards what we find unpleasant. I make a distinction: I admit this when we know that something will displease us, but in this case the dog does not know. We must also distinguish between the spontaneous and the voluntary. The principle of change is in the dog, the disposition of its soul moves imperceptibly towards giving it pain: but this is without its knowing, and without its wanting it. The representation of the present state of the universe in the dog's soul produces in it the representation of the subsequent state of the same universe, just as in the things represented the preceding state actually produces the subsequent state of the world. *In a soul, the representations of causes are the causes of the representations of effects.* And since this subsequent state of the world includes the blow on the dog's body, the representation of that subsequent state in its soul includes the pain which corresponds to that blow.

12

A LETTER FROM M. LEIBNIZ TO THE EDITOR, CONTAINING AN EXPLANATION OF THE DIFFICULTIES WHICH M. BAYLE FOUND WITH THE NEW SYSTEM OF THE UNION OF THE SOUL AND BODY (1698)

Summary of the Text

Having read with evident interest and care what Bayle had to say about the 'New System' in his note H (T10), Leibniz wrote, and published in the Histoire des ouvrages des savants, *'A Letter . . . Containing an Explanation of the Difficulties which M. Bayle Found with the New System'. In it Leibniz tries to answer some of the difficulties Bayle found with the system of pre-established harmony.*

In answer to T10. 5–7 he explains (Sects. 2–5) just what is involved in his idea that thoughts and perceptions arise in the soul quite independently of whatever else is going on in the universe, and he explains that the spontaneous *production of pain (which Bayle found puzzling) is not the same as its* voluntary *production.*

As against T10. 7 he argues (Sect. 7) that it matters not to his objection to it that the occasionalists' 'way of assistance' has it that God's intervention between body and mind is in accordance with general laws (e.g. that God does not produce pain arbitrarily but rather as a general correlate of bodily injury). Occasionalism involves miracles, he says, because it involves the production of changes in the body and soul by God's action *rather than by the natural activity of the body or soul themselves. That these changes are regular does not of itself mean that they are not miraculous.*

He addresses himself (Sects. 8–9) to Bayle's suggestion (T10. 7) that since we can't always foresee them, changes in the soul cannot be natural consequences of earlier states, but must be guided by some external principle. We can foresee the

From the French of *Histoire des ouvrages des savants* (July 1698), 329–42 (repr. at GP iv. 517–24). A complete translation is given at WF 79–86.

changes in our soul (though as a matter of confused sensation, rather than of distinct knowledge).

Finally (Sects. 10–12), by means of a distinction between two senses of 'do the same thing', Leibniz answers Bayle's claim (T10. 8) that simple souls, unlike complex clocks, must always 'do the same thing'.

In his concluding paragraph (Sect. 13) Leibniz comments on another article in Bayle's Dictionary, and makes some remarks about extension, and about the force and power involved in motion (see Introduction, Sect. 3.3).

The end of that paragraph provides a good illustration of Leibniz's philosophical catholicity and his desire to take the best from and reconcile different philosophical perspectives. It also provides a very succinct distillation of his metaphysical scheme.

THE TEXT

[1] I am taking the liberty, sir, of sending you this explanation with regard to the difficulties which M. Bayle found with the theory I proposed to explain the union of the soul and body. . . . He doesn't deny what I have said about the conservation of souls and even of animals, but he doesn't yet seem satisfied with the way I tried to explain the union and commerce between the soul and the body, in the *Journal des savants* of 27 June and 4 July 1695 [i.e. T4], and in the *Histoire des ouvrages des savants*, February 1696.

[2] Here are his words, which seem to indicate what he found difficulty with: 'I cannot understand', he says, 'the series of spontaneous internal actions which could make a dog's soul feel pain immediately after having felt pleasure, even if it were all alone in the universe' [T10. 6]. My reply to this is that when I said that the soul would still feel all that it feels now even if there were only it and God in the world, I was only employing a fiction. In order to show that the feelings of the soul are only a consequence of what is already within it, I was imagining something which could never happen naturally. I do not know whether M. Bayle's argument for the incomprehensibility which he finds in this series of actions is to be found in what he says lower down, or whether it is meant already to be there in the example of the spontaneous transition from pleasure to pain. Perhaps he is suggesting that such a transition contradicts the axiom that a thing will always remain in the same state if nothing occurs to make it change, and

therefore that an animal which once experiences pleasure will have it for ever if it is all alone, or if nothing external makes it move on to pain. In any case, I agree with the axiom, and indeed I claim that it supports me, for it is in fact one of my basic principles. [3] Do we not take this axiom to mean not only that a body which is at rest will always remain at rest, but also that a moving body will always retain its motion or progression, that is to say the same speed and the same direction, if nothing occurs to prevent it? Thus not only will a thing left to itself remain in the state it is in, but also, when that state is one of change, it will continue to change, still in accordance with that same law. Now, according to me it is the nature of a created substance to change continually in accordance with a certain order, which conducts it *spontaneously* (if one may use the word) through all its states, in such a way that someone who saw everything would see in its present state all its past and future states. And this law of order, which constitutes the individuality of each particular substance, exactly corresponds to what happens in every other substance, and in the universe as a whole. I hope it is not too much to claim that I can demonstrate all of this; but for the moment all that matters is to show the possibility of the theory, and its ability to explain the phenomena. So in this way the law of the changes in the substance of an animal takes it from pleasure to pain just when there is a break in the continuity of its body, because the law of this animal's indivisible substance is to represent what happens in its body, just as we know from our own cases, and indeed to represent in some fashion, through its relation to the body, everything that happens in the world. Substantial unities are nothing other than different concentrations of the universe, which is represented in them in accordance with the different points of view which distinguish them.

[4] M. Bayle goes on: 'I can understand why a dog passes immediately from pleasure to pain when, whilst it is very hungry and eating some bread, it is suddenly hit with a stick' [T10. 6]. I am not sure that we do understand this so well. No one knows better than M. Bayle himself that this is what the great difficulty consists in: how to explain why what happens in the body makes a change in the soul. This is what forced the defenders of occasional causes to have recourse to God's continually taking care to represent in the soul changes which take place in the body. Whereas I believe that it is its own God-given nature to represent to itself, in accordance with its own laws, what happens in its organs. He goes on:

[5] 'But that its soul should be constructed in such a way that it would have felt pain at the moment that it was hit, even if it had not been hit, and

even if it had continued to eat the bread without being disturbed or prevented, that is what I cannot understand' [T10. 6]. And I don't remember
having said it either. One can speak in this way only by a metaphysical
fiction, as when one imagines God as annihilating a certain body to
produce a vacuum: the one is as much against the order of things as the
other. For since the soul's nature was made from the outset in such a way
that it would represent in succession the changes in matter, the case imagined here could never occur in the natural order. God could have given
each substance its own phenomena, independent of all others; but in so
doing he would have made as many unconnected worlds, so to speak, as
there are substances—rather as we say that when dreaming one is in a
world of one's own, and one enters the common world on awakening.
(Though dreams themselves are related to the organs, and to the rest of
the body, but in a less distinct manner.) Let us continue with M. Bayle:

[6] 'I also find', he says, 'the spontaneity of this soul wholly incompatible with its feelings of pain, and in general with all feelings it finds unpleasant' [T10. 7]. There certainly would be an incompatibility if spontaneity
and voluntariness were the same thing. Everything voluntary is spontaneous, but there are spontaneous actions which are not chosen, and which
consequently are not voluntary. The soul is not able always to give itself
pleasant feelings, since the feelings it has are dependent on those it has had.
M. Bayle continues: 'Moreover, the reason why this clever man finds the
*Cartesian system not to his taste seems to me to be based on a false sup-
position; it cannot be said that the system of occasional causes, with its reciprocal dependence of body and soul, makes the actions of God into the
miraculous interventions of a *deus ex machina*. For since God intervenes
only according to general laws, in doing so he never acts extraordinarily'
[see T10. 7].

[7] This is not the only reason why the Cartesian system is not to my
taste; and a little consideration of my own system will clearly show that
the reasons why I adopt it are contained within itself. After all, even if the
hypothesis of occasional causes did not involve miracles, it seems to me
that mine would still have other advantages. I have said that we can think of
three systems for explaining the intercommunication we find between
soul and body: (1) the system of influence understood literally as a flow
from one into the other. This is the system of the *Schools, which I consider impossible, as do the Cartesians. (2) The system of the perpetual
caretaker, who represents in the one what happens in the other, rather like
a man who is employed constantly to synchronize two inferior clocks
which cannot keep the same time by themselves. This is the system of

occasional causes. And (3) that in which two substances naturally agree, as would two perfectly accurate clocks. I find this as possible as that of the caretaker, and more worthy of the creator of these substances, clocks or machines. Let us see, however, whether the system of occasional causes really doesn't involve a perpetual miracle. Here it is said that it does not, because the system holds that God acts only according to general laws. I agree that he does, but in my view that isn't enough to remove miracles. Even if God produced them all the time, they would still be miracles, if the word is understood not in the popular sense, as a rare and marvellous thing, but philosophically, as something which exceeds the power of created things. It isn't sufficient to say that God has made a general law, for in addition to the decree there has also to be a natural way of carrying it out. It is necessary, that is, that what happens should be explicable in terms of the God-given nature of things. Natural laws are not as arbitrary and groundless as many think. If, for example, God decreed that all bodies had a tendency to move in circles with radii proportional to their size, we would have to say that there was some way of bringing this about by simpler laws; otherwise we would have to admit that God brings it about miraculously, or at least by angels expressly charged with it, rather like those that used to be assigned to the celestial spheres.[1] It would be the same if someone said that God has given natural and primitive gravities to bodies, by which they each tend to the centre of their globe without being pushed by other bodies. For in my view this system too would need a perpetual miracle, or angelic help at least.

[8] 'Does the internal active power which is communicated to the forms of bodies know what sucession of actions it has to produce? Surely not; for we know from experience that we do not know what perceptions we will have in an hour's time' [T12. 7]. I reply, that this power or, better, this soul or form doesn't know them distinctly, but senses them confusedly. In each substance there are traces of everything that has happened to it, and of everything that is going to happen. But this infinite multitude of perceptions prevents us from distinguishing them, just as I cannot distinguish one voice from another when I hear the loud and confused noise of a crowd.

[9] 'It would therefore be necessary for the forms to be directed by some external principle in the production of their actions. Would that not be a *deus ex machina*, just the same as in the system of occasional causes?' [T10. 7]. The preceding reply blocks this inference. On the contrary, the present

---

[1] Cf. Aquinas, *Summa Theologiae*, 1a. 70. 3.

state of each substance is a natural consequence of its preceding state, but it is only an infinite intelligence which can see that consequence, because it embraces the whole universe, souls as well as every portion of matter.

[10] M. Bayle concludes with these words: 'Finally, as he supposes, with very good reason, that all souls are simple and indivisible, it is impossible to see how they can be compared to clocks; how, that is, their original constitution can enable them to do different things, as a result of the spontaneous activity they received from their creator. It is obvious that a simple being will always do the same thing, if no outside cause interferes with it; but if it were made up of several parts, like a machine, it could do different things, because at any moment the particular activity of one part could interfere with that of the others. But in a unitary substance, where would you find the cause of any change of activity?' [T10. 8]. I find that this objection is worthy of M. Bayle, and it is one of those most deserving of clarification. But I also think that if I had not allowed for it from the outset, my system would not be worth examining. I compared the soul with a clock only in respect of the ordered precision of its changes, which is imperfect even in the best clocks, but which is perfect in the works of God. In fact, one can say that the soul is a very exact immaterial automaton. [11] When it is said that a simple being will always do the same thing, a certain distinction must be made: if 'doing the same thing' means perpetually following the same law of order or of continuation, as in the case of a certain series or sequence of numbers, I admit that all simple beings, and even all composite beings, do the same thing; but if 'same' means acting in the same way, I don't agree at all. Here is an example which explains the difference between these two senses: a parabolic motion is uniform in the first sense, but not in the second, for the segments of a parabola are not the same as each other, as are those of a straight line. . . . [12] We must also bear in mind that the soul, even though simple, always has feelings composed of several simultaneous perceptions; which for our purposes has the same effect as if it were composed of parts, like a machine. For, in conformity with a law of order which exists in perceptions as much as in motions, each preceding perception influences succeeding ones. Moreover, for several centuries most philosophers have attributed thoughts to souls and to angels which they believe are completely incorporeal (not to mention the intelligences of *Aristotle), and have also admitted spontaneous change in simple beings. I will add that the perceptions which are simultaneously together in the same soul involve a truly infinite multitude of small indistinguishable feelings that will be developed in what follows, so one should not be astonished at the infinite

variety of what emerges over time. All of this is only a consequence of the representational nature of the soul which must express what happens, and indeed what will happen, in its body, and, because of the connection or correspondence of all the parts of the world, it must also express in some way what happens in all the others. It might perhaps have been enough to say simply that God, having made corporeal machines, could also easily have made immaterial ones which represent them; but I thought it would be good to explain things a little more fully.

[13] As for the rest, I read with pleasure what M. Bayle says in the article on *Zeno. He will perhaps appreciate that what comes out of it fits in with my system better than with any other; for what is real in extension and in motion consists only in the foundation of the order and regular sequence of phenomena and perceptions. Also, the *Academics and the *Sceptics, as well as those who have sought to reply to them, seem to have got into serious difficulties only because they looked for more reality in external sensible things than that of regular phenomena. In conceiving of *extension* we are conceiving of an order among coexistences; but we should not think of it, any more than space, as though it were a substance. It is like *time*, which presents to the mind only an order of changes. And as for *motion*, what is real in it is *force* or power; that is to say, what there is in the present state which carries with it a change in the future. The rest is only phenomena and relations. Consideration of this system shows us also that when we get to the bottom of things, we find in most philosophical sects more good sense than we had realized. The *Sceptics' lack of substantial reality in sensible things; the *Pythagoreans' and *Platonists' reduction of everything to harmonies and numbers, ideas and perceptions; the one and the whole of *Parmenides and *Plotinus (though not of *Spinoza); the *Stoic connectedness, compatible with the spontaneity maintained by others; the vitalistic philosophy of the *Cabbalists and the Hermetics, who attributed feeling to everything; the forms and entelechies of Aristotle and the Scholastics; and meanwhile also the mechanical explanations, by *Democritus and the moderns, of all particular phenomena, and so on— all these are reunited as in a common centre of perspective from which the object (confused when looked at from anywhere else) reveals its regularity and the congruence of its parts. Our biggest fault has been sectarianism, limiting ourselves by the rejection of others. The formalists criticize the materialists or the corpuscularians, and vice versa. We wrongly set limits to the division and subtlety of nature, as well as to its richness and beauty, when we posit *atoms and the void, and suppose certain first elements (as even the Cartesians do) in place of true unities; and also when we do

not recognize the infinite in everything, and the exact expression of the greatest in the smallest, or the tendency of each thing to develop in a perfect order which is the most admirable and most beautiful effect of a Sovereign Principle, the wisdom and goodness of which leave nothing more to be desired by those who understand its economy.

13

NATURE ITSELF; OR, THE INHERENT FORCE AND ACTIVITY OF CREATED THINGS—CONFIRMING AND ILLUSTRATING THE AUTHOR'S DYNAMICS (1698)

Summary of the Text

This important article, published in September 1698 in the Leipzig journal Acta Eruditorum, *contributes to a debate which began with Robert *Boyle's* Free Inquiry into the Vulgarly Received Notion of Nature *(1682) (and his* On Nature Itself, *1688).* Boyle's argument that nature should be understood in purely mechanical terms was defended, in his* Idol of Nature *(1692), by J. C. *Sturm, who (along with Boyle) was attacked by G. C. *Schelhammer in his* Vindication of Nature *(1697). Sturm's 'Defence', to which Leibniz refers in his opening sentence, was in volume 2 of his* Elective Physics *(1698).*

Leibniz firmly rejects the idea that the natural world, as studied in physics, contains anything non-mechanical such as Henry *More's hylarchic principles (Sect. 2). But he argues that mechanics itself involves dynamical forces which themselves require a metaphysical grounding in created substances.

This article is interesting not merely as a defence and elaboration of Leibniz's own metaphysics, but also as a sustained and detailed exploration and criticism of the Cartesian-based metaphysics of the *occasionalists.

THE TEXT

1. I have recently received from the famous John Christopher *Sturm—a man of outstanding merit in mathematics and physics—the 'Defence', published in Altdorf, of his treatise on *The Idol of Nature*, which was

From the Latin at GP iv. 504–16.

attacked by the eminent and accomplished doctor of Kiel Günther Christopher *Schelhammer, in his book on *Nature*. I too once gave some thought to this question, and there followed a discussion in letters between myself and the excellent author of this treatise; he recently spoke kindly of me in his *Elective Physics* (vol. 1, bk. 1, sect. 1, ch. 3, Epilogue para. 5, pp. 119–20), where he reported some of what passed between us. I was therefore all the more willing to think carefully about what is an inherently important topic, and I thought I should set out more clearly my opinion, and the whole issue, in the light of the principles which I have already presented on several occasions. The writing of the 'Defence' would seem to offer a good opportunity for attempting this, since in it the author has obviously set out the most important points briefly and in summary form. But I shall not otherwise enter into the argument between these two excellent men.

2. I want to ask two questions. Firstly, what makes up the nature which we normally attribute to things, the attributes of which as generally understood are considered by the famous Sturm to be redolent of paganism? Secondly, whether there is any *energeia* in created things, which he seems to deny. As to the first question, concerning *nature itself*: if we may consider what it is not, as well as what it is, I certainly agree that there is no world soul; and I would also admit that those everyday things with regard to which we rightly say that the work of nature is a work of intelligence should not be ascribed to created intelligences with appropriate levels of wisdom and of power. Rather the whole of nature is, so to speak, the *ingenious handiwork of God*, so much so that every natural machine (and this is the true but rarely recognized *distinction between nature and art*) is made up of an infinite number of other organisms,[1] and therefore requires infinite wisdom and power on the part of its creator and ruler. I therefore hold that *Hippocrates' omniscient heat, *Avicenna's soul-giving *cholcodea*, *Scaliger and others' all-wise plastic virtue, and Henry *More's hylarchic principles are all partly impossible, and partly unnecessary. I say that it is enough for the machine of things to have been constructed with such wisdom that these wonders come about through its own workings, and in particular, I believe, through organic beings which unfold themselves in accordance with some kind of pre-arranged plan. I therefore agree with the illustrious author in rejecting these supposed wise created natures which produce and govern the mechanisms of bodies. But I do not think it

---

[1] This translation of *organis* diverges from the 'organs' of other translators.

follows from that, and I do not think it is reasonable, that we should deny that there is any active created force inherent in things.

3. I have said what it is not; let us now examine more closely what this nature is which *Aristotle has appropriately called the *principle of motion and rest*—though it seems to me that the philosopher takes this more broadly, and understands by it not merely local motion and staying in place, but rather *change* and stasis, or persistence, in general. Consequently, I may note in passing, the definition he gives of motion, though more obscure than it should be, is nevertheless not so silly as it seems to those who take him to be defining only local motion. But, to return to the matter in hand, Robert Boyle, a distinguished man experienced in the careful observation of nature, wrote a little book *On Nature Itself*, the point of which, if I remember rightly, came down to this: that we must take nature as being just the mechanism of bodies. In broad terms we can agree with this; but on a closer look we must distinguish between the principles of this mechanism and what is derived from them. For example, in explaining a clock it is not enough to say that it is driven by mechanical means, without saying whether it is done by a weight or by a spring. I have already more than once expressed the view (which I think should be useful in preventing mechanical explanations of material things from being carried too far, and to the detriment of piety—as if matter could stand by itself and mechanism needed no intelligence or spiritual substance) that mechanism itself has its origin not merely in a material principle or in mathematical reasons, but in some higher and, so to speak, metaphysical source.

4. Important evidence for this is provided by, among other things, the *foundation of the laws of nature*. This foundation is not to be found, as has usually been thought, in the conservation of the same quantity of motion, but rather in the fact that *the same quantity of active power* must be conserved, and indeed also (and I have found that this happens for a most wonderful reason) *the same quantity of motive action*—a quantity which is quite different from the *Cartesians' quantity of motion. When two clearly first-class mathematicians argued with me about this, partly in private letters and partly publicly, one of them came completely over to my side, and the other, after long and careful thought, got as far as abandoning all his objections and openly confessing that he could not yet think of an answer to my argument. I was therefore very surprised that when this distinguished man explains the laws of motion in the published part of his *Elective Physics*, he takes the common view of them for granted, as if there could be no doubt

about it (though he does acknowledge that it has not been proved, and only has a certain plausibility—something which he repeats in this latest discussion, ch. 3, sect. 2). Perhaps he was writing before my work appeared, and then did not have the time to change what he had written, or did not think of it, especially as he believed that the laws of motion are arbitrary—a view which seems to me to be not entirely coherent. For I believe that God considered principles of wisdom and reasons of order when he established the laws which are observed in nature. And I think that this makes it clear (as I once pointed out when discussing the laws of optics, and which the famous *Molyneux later accepted in his *Dioptrics*) that consideration of final causes is useful not only to virtue and piety—in ethics and natural theology—but also for discovering and detecting hidden truths in physics itself. So I wish that when, during his discussion of final causes in his *Elective Physics*, the famous Sturm gave my view as one of various theories, he had also examined it at sufficient length in his discussion, because then he would surely have taken the opportunity to say a lot of excellent things about the argument, with regard to both its fruitfulness and its usefulness for piety.

5. But we must now examine what he himself says about the idea of nature in this article which he has written in his defence, and what seems still to be lacking in what he says. He admits (in ch. 4, sects. 2 and 3, and often) that the motions which take place now come about as the result of an *eternal law* which God has set up, a law which he then calls a volition and a *command*; and also that no new command or volition is then necessary, far less a new effort or laborious process (sect. 3). And he rejects the view, which he says is wrongly attributed to him by his opponent, that God moves things in the way that a woodcutter moves an axe, or a miller controls his mill by holding back the water and then letting it run onto the wheel. But this explanation really does not seem to me to be good enough. For, I ask, has this volition or command, or, if you prefer, this earlier-laid-down divine law, bestowed on things merely an *external denomination*? Or has it really produced some permanent impression in things themselves, an 'inherent law' (as M. Schelhammer, who is as distinguished in his judgement as he is in his experiments, nicely puts it) from which their actions and passions follow—even if it is one which is not always known to the created things in which it inheres? The first appears to be the doctrine of the authors of the system of *occasional causes, particularly of the most intelligent Father Malebranche. The latter is the usual view and, I believe, the true one.

6. For since this earlier command does not now exist, it cannot now do

anything unless it left behind some continuing effect which still endures and operates. Anyone who thinks otherwise, if I am right, gives up all clear explanation of things: for if what is distant in time and place could operate here and now without an intermediary, then anything could be said to follow from anything else equally well. It therefore is not enough to say that when in the beginning God created things he willed that their progression should be in accordance with a certain law, if his will is supposed to have been so ineffective that things were not affected by it, and it had no lasting effect on them. And in any case it contradicts the notion of pure and absolute power or will to suppose that God could will, and nevertheless produce or change nothing through his willing, and that although he always acts he never achieves anything, and leaves no work or accomplishment behind. If the divine words 'let the earth be fruitful and the animals multiply'[2] made no impression on created things, if after the command things were just the same as if there had been no command, then surely it follows (since there must be some connection, whether direct or through some intermediary, between cause and effect) either that nothing now obeys that command, or that it was effective only at the time of its making, and had always to be renewed in the future—which the learned author rightly rejects. But if, on the other hand, the law God decreed has in fact left some trace of itself impressed upon things—if things have been formed by the command in such a way that they are capable of fulfilling the meaning of the command—then it must be admitted that things have been given a certain ability, a form or force (such as we usually call a 'nature'), from which the series of phenomena follows in accordance with the dictates of the original command.

7. This inherent force can certainly be distinctly understood, but it cannot be explained through the imagination; and it should not be explained in that way, any more than should the nature of the soul. For force is one of those things which are grasped, not by the imagination, but by the understanding. So when this learned gentleman (in ch. 4, sect. 6, of his 'Defence') asks for an 'imaginable' explanation of how an inherent law works in bodies which are ignorant of that law, I take him to be wanting it explained intelligibly—for he certainly would not ask us to picture sounds, or to hear colours. And, moreover, if difficulty in explaining things were sufficient grounds for rejecting them, then he would be involved in something he complains is unfairly attributed to him (ch. 1, sect. 2), namely, preferring to hold that nothing is moved except by divine agency rather than

---

[2] See Gen. 1: 22: 'God blessed them, saying "Be fruitful, and multiply".'

accept something called a nature, the nature of which he does not know. Indeed this way of thinking can equally well support Hobbes and others, who make everything corporeal because they have convinced themselves that nothing but body can be explained distinctly through the imagination. But they are thoroughly refuted by the fact that there is a power of action in things, which is not derived from anything that can be imagined. And simply to trace this back to a command by God, issued once and for all at some point in the past, and not affecting things in any way or leaving behind any effect, is so far from making the matter more explicable that it is more like abandoning the role of the philosopher, and cutting the Gordian knot with a sword. A more distinct and more accurate explanation of active force than has so far been given may be drawn from my *dynamics*, which gives an account of the laws of nature and of motion which is true and in accordance with the facts.

8. But if some defender of the new philosophy, which maintains the inertness and inactivity of things, were to go so far as to deprive God's commands of any lasting effect or efficacy in the future, and if he did not mind forever requiring new labours on the part of God (something which M. Sturm wisely says is not what he wants), then it would be for him to decide how worthy of God he thinks that is. But he would still need to explain why things themselves can endure through time while their attributes (what we call their 'nature') cannot. For it is reasonable that just as the words 'let there be' leave something behind them, namely the persisting thing itself, so the no less wonderful word 'blessing' should leave something behind it, namely a fruitfulness in things, an impulse to produce actions and to have effects, from which consequences follow if nothing prevents it. To this we can add a point I have made elsewhere, even if perhaps it is not yet perfectly clear to everyone, that the very substance of things consists in the force for acting and being acted on. It follows from this that no enduring thing can be produced if the divine power cannot impress on it some force which lasts through time. If that were so, then no created substance, no soul, would remain the same thing, and nothing would be conserved by God. Everything would reduce to just transitory, evanescent modifications or phantasms, so to speak, of one permanent divine substance. Or, what comes to the same thing, nature itself, or the substance of all things, would be God—a doctrine of very ill repute which an irreligious, though admittedly clever, author has recently introduced to the world (or at least revived).[3] If corporeal things contained nothing but

---

[3] Spinoza, *Ethics*, pt. 1, prop. 14: 'Besides God no substance can be granted or conceived'.

matter, it would indeed be true to say they are in flux and have nothing substantial, as the Platonists once correctly recognized.

9. The *second question* is whether created things can properly and truly be said to act. Once we understand that their internal nature is no different from the force of acting and being acted on, this question reduces to the first. For there cannot be action without a force for acting, and, conversely, a power which can never be exercised is empty. But since action and power are nevertheless different things (the one momentary, the other lasting) let us consider action. Here I confess I find some difficulty in explaining the thought of the famous Sturm. For he denies that created things can really act of themselves, but then goes on to admit that they do, in that in some way he denies the comparison between created things and an axe moved by a woodcutter. I don't know what to conclude from this; he seems to have explained very clearly neither the extent to which he departs from received opinions, nor what precise idea of action he has in mind (for, as is clear from the debates of the metaphysicians, that is something which is far from obvious and easy). For my part, in so far as I have made the concept of action clear to myself, I believe that the widely received philosophical doctrine that actions belong to subjects[4] follows from it, and is grounded in it. And I hold this to be so true that it holds reciprocally: not only is everything that acts an individual substance, but also every individual substance acts continuously, even body itself, in which there is never absolute rest.

10. But let us now consider a little more closely the view of those who deny true and proper activity to created things—as Robert *Fludd, author of *The Mosaic Philosophy*, did long ago, and as nowadays do some Cartesians, who believe that it is not things which act, but God who acts in them, in accordance with what is appropriate to them. They believe that things are occasions and not causes, and that they receive, but never effect, or produce. Although *Cordemoy, *La Forge, and other Cartesians had already proposed this doctrine, *Malebranche in particular, with his characteristic acumen, presented it very persuasively; but, so far as I know, no one has given any good reason for it. Indeed, nothing could be further from reason than this view, if it is extended so far as to deny even the *immanent actions* of substances (something which Sturm, in his *Elective Physics*, bk. 1, ch. 4, Epilogue, sect. 11 shows his considerable caution by rejecting). For who would doubt that the mind thinks and wills, that many of our

---

[4] In some translations 'subjects' (*suppositorum*) is rendered, more specifically, as 'substances'. See also T1. 8.

thoughts and volitions are produced by us, and that we possess a certain spontaneity? To do so would not only mean denying human freedom and pushing the cause of evil back to God, but it would also contradict the evidence of our inmost experience or consciousness, which makes us feel that the things which these opponents have, without any semblance of reason, transferred to God are in fact ours. But if we attribute to our mind an inherent force for producing immmanent actions, or (in other words) of acting immanently, then there is nothing to prevent the same force from being in other souls or forms, or, if you prefer, in the natures of substances. Indeed this would be only reasonable—otherwise one would have to say that in the nature of things as we know it, only our minds are active, and that all power of acting immanently, and so to speak *vitally*, is coupled with an intellect. Such claims have no justification in reason, and cannot be defended without distorting the truth. What we should say about the *transeunt actions of created things* can be explained better elsewhere. In fact part of it I have explained: the *interaction* between *substances* or monads does not arise from an influx, but from an agreement produced by divine pre-formation, which means that while each one is adjusted to the others they each follow the internal force and laws of their own natures; and this is what the *union of the soul and body* consists in.

11. However, it is indeed true that bodies in themselves are inert, provided that this is correctly understood, as meaning that what is in some respect at rest cannot set itself in motion in that respect, or allow itself without resistance to be set in motion by another; just as it can never of itself change its degree of velocity or its direction, or easily and without resistance allow some other body to change them for it. And so it must be admitted that extension, or what is geometrical in bodies, if taken by itself contains nothing which can give rise to action and motion. Indeed on the contrary, we must admit that matter resists being moved by a certain *natural inertia* (as Kepler nicely calls it), so that it is not indifferent to motion and rest (as is commonly thought), but requires for its motion an active force proportional to its size. It is therefore this passive force of resistance (which involves impenetrability and something more) that according to me the notion of *primary matter* or mass (which is the same in all bodies and proportional to their size) consists in. And from this I show that there follow very different laws of motion than would obtain if body and matter itself consisted only of impenetrability and extension. Moreover, just as matter has a natural *inertia* which is opposed to *motion*, so in a body itself, and indeed in every substance, there is a natural *constancy* which is opposed to *change*. But this view does not support—in fact it opposes—

those who deny that things act. For, just as it is certain that matter cannot of itself begin a motion, so (as well-known experiments on the communication of motion by moving bodies also show) it is equally certain that a body considered in itself retains any impetus imparted to it, and that it remains *constant* in its mobility—that is, it has a tendency to persevere in whatever sequence of changes it has begun. Now, since these activities and entelechies certainly cannot be modifications of primary matter or mass, which is something essentially passive, we can conclude (as the judicious Sturm himself clearly recognizes—as we shall see in the next paragraph), that a *first *entelechy* or first subject of activity must be recognized in corporeal substance; that is, a primitive motive force, additional to extension (or what is purely geometrical) and mass (or what is purely material), which indeed always acts but which in interactions between bodies is modified in various ways through conatus and impetus. And it is this substantial principle which is called the *soul* in living things, and a *substantial form* in others, and in so far as together with matter it makes up a substance which is truly one, or one *per se*, it forms what I call a *monad.*[5] For without these true and real unities there would only be beings through aggregation; indeed it would follow that there would be no real beings in bodies. For even though there are atoms of substance, namely my monads, which have no parts, there are no atoms of mass, or smallest extensions, or ultimate elements; because a continuum is not composed of points. In the same way there is no such thing as the greatest mass, or the infinitely extended, even though for each thing there is always something bigger; there is only the greatest in intensity of perfection, or the infinitely powerful.

12. I see, however, that in his 'Defence' (ch. 4, sect. 7 and following) the famous Sturm has put forward certain arguments to attack this motive force inherent in bodies. 'I shall clearly show here', he says, 'that corporeal substance is not capable of any *active* motive power'—though I do not understand what a non-active motive power might be. He says that he will use two parallel arguments, one from the nature of matter and body, the other from the nature of motion. The first comes down to this: in its nature and essentially matter is a passive substance, so it is no more possible for it to be given an active force than it is for God to will that a stone, while remaining a stone, should be alive and rational—that is, should be not a stone. Furthermore, whatever things we may suppose in body can only be modifications of matter; but (and this I accept is well put) a modi-

---

[5] This is Leibniz's first published use of this now-famous term.

fication of something essentially passive cannot render it active. But it is easy to reply to this, following either the traditional or the true philosophy, that matter must be understood as either secondary or primary. [See also T5.5.] Secondary matter is indeed a complete substance, but it is not merely passive, whereas primary substance is merely passive, but is not a complete substance—there needs to be added to it a soul, or form analogous to a soul; a first *entelechy*, that is a striving or primitive active force which is itself an inherent law imprinted by divine decree. I do not think the famous and ingenious man who recently defended the view that body is composed of matter and spirit will deny this. But a 'spirit' is not to be understood here, as it usually is, as an intelligent being, but as a soul, or a form analogous to a soul; nor is it to be understood as a mere modification, but as something constitutive, substantial, and enduring—what I usually call a *monad*, which has something like perception and desire. This received doctrine, therefore, which is consistent with the doctrine (when properly explained) of the *Schoolmen, must first be refuted if the argument of this illustrious man is to have any force. It is similarly clear from this that his assumption that whatever is in corporeal substance is only a modification of matter cannot be conceded. For, as is well known, the bodies of living beings, according to the traditional philosophy, have in them souls, which are certainly not modifications of matter. For although it seems that this illustrious man holds the opposite opinion, and denies all real sensation and real souls to brute animals, he cannot assume this as a basis for his argument before it itself has been proved. I believe on the contrary that it is not consistent either with the order, or the beauty, or the intelligibility of things that there should be something vital or internally active only in such a small part of matter, when there would be greater perfection if it were the same in all of it. And there is nothing to prevent souls, or things analogous to souls, from being everywhere, even though dominant and hence intelligent souls like ours cannot.

13. The second argument, which the distinguished gentleman draws from the nature of motion, seems to me no more compelling than the first. He says that motion is merely the successive existence of a thing in different places. Let us grant this for the moment (even though it is not entirely satisfactory, and captures the result of motion rather than its formal definition); but even then, a moving force is still not ruled out. For at any moment of its motion, not only is a body in a specific place, but it also has a tendency or strives to change that place, so that its next state follows of itself from its present one, by the force of nature. If this were not so then at the present moment (and therefore at any moment) a

moving body *A* would in no way be different from a body at rest *B*; and it would follow from this distinguished man's view, if he holds the opposite position, that there would be no way at all to distinguish between bodies, since in a plenum of masses which are uniform in themselves there is no way of distinguishing except by motion. This view would also mean that there would be absolutely no change in bodies, and everything would always remain the same. For if there is no difference between one portion of matter and another equal and congruent to it (which this distinguished man must admit, since he has rejected active forces, impetuses, and all other qualities and modifications, except for existing in this place and successively existing in some other place), and if, furthermore, the state of the corporeal world at one moment does not differ from that at another except by the transposition of equal and congruent portions of matter which are exactly similar, it obviously follows that no momentary state of the corporeal world can be distinguished in any way from any other by this perpetual substitution of indistinguishables. For it would be by a merely *extrinsic denomination* that one portion of matter would be distinguished from another: namely, by what will happen to it—that it will later be in one place rather than another. In the present there would in fact be no difference; indeed we could not derive a well-grounded difference even from the future, because even in the future we would never arrive at any true distinction for the present, since there would be no mark by which one place could be distinguished from another, nor (on the assumption of perfect uniformity in matter itself) one portion of matter from another in the same place. It is also useless to turn to *shape* in addition to motion. For in a plenum of perfectly homogeneous and undifferentiated mass no shape, no boundary or distinction between its various parts can arise, except through motion itself. So if motion provides no distinguishing mark then it cannot provide one for shape. And since everything which replaced something else would be exactly equivalent to it, no observer, not even an omniscient one, would see even the slightest indication of change. So everything would be just as if there were no change or differentiation in bodies, and we could never explain the varied appearances we perceive. It would be the same as if we imagine two perfect concentric spheres, perfectly similar both overall and in their parts, one inside the other, without even the smallest gap between them. Now assume that the inner sphere is either revolving or at rest: not even an angel (to say no more than that) could detect any difference between their states at different times, or have any way of deciding whether the inner sphere is at rest or is revolving, and according to what law of motion. Indeed, just as the motion cannot be decided because of the lack of any *difference*, we could not even establish a boundary between the two spheres, because we have neither a *gap* nor a *difference*. Therefore, we should take it as certain (even if those who have not gone sufficiently deeply into these matters may not have recognized it) that such things are foreign to the nature and order of things, and that *nowhere* (and this is one of my important new axioms) *is there perfect similarity*. It also follows from this that there are in nature no perfectly hard corpuscles, no perfectly thin fluids, no universally diffused subtle matter. and no ultimate elements of the kind some call 'primary' or 'secondary'. It is, I think, because *Aristotle (who in my view is more profound than many think) had understood something of this that he saw the necessity for alteration over and above change in place, and also that matter cannot be everywhere the same, or it would never change. And in fact this dissimilarity, or diversity of qualities, and the *alloiosis* or alteration which Aristotle did not properly explain, result from the different degrees and directions of impulses, and so from the modifications of the indwelling monads. We can therefore see from this that bodies must necessarily involve something more than uniform mass, and its motion from place to place, which could not change anything. Of course, those who maintain there are *atoms* and a *vacuum* do think that matter varies to an extent, in that they think some is divisible, some indivisible, some places are full, some have gaps. But long ago I overcame my youthful prejudices, and realized that atoms and the void must be rejected. The celebrated gentleman adds that the existence of matter through different moments of time should be attributed to God's will. So why not, he asks, also attribute to the same thing its existence here and now? I reply that this, like everything else that involves perfection, is undoubtedly to be attributed to God. But just as this first and universal cause which conserves all things does not take away but actually produces the natural subsistence of a thing coming to exist, or its perseverance in existence once it does exist, in the same way that cause does not take away but actually supports the natural efficacy of a thing in motion, or its perseverance in action once it has begun.

14. There are many other things in the 'Defence' which are problematic, such as what is said in chapter 4, section 11 to the effect that when motion is transferred from one ball through several intermediaries to another, that last ball is moved by the *same force* as the first. It seems to me that it is moved by an equivalent force, but not by the same force. For, surprising as this may be, as each one is pushed by the next one's colliding with it, it is put into motion by *its own force*, or elasticity. (I am not discussing here the cause of this elasticity, and am not denying that it must be

explained mechanically, by the motion of an internal fluid which flows within bodies.) Similarly, what he says in section 12—namely, that something which cannot cause itself to move cannot keep itself in motion—should strike us as very surprising. For, on the contrary, it is clear that just as force is needed to produce motion, so once an impetus is given, a new force is needed, not to continue the motion, but rather to stop it. The necessity of a universal cause which conserves things is not at issue here; as I have said already, if it took away the efficacy of things, it would also take away their existence.

15. This again shows that the doctrine of occasional causes which some defend can lead to dangerous consequences (unless in explaining it we make certain modifications, some of which the distinguished Sturm makes, some of which he seems almost to make); though these conquences are doubtless not intended by its very learned defenders. Far from increasing the glory of God by removing the idol of nature, this doctrine seems, with *Spinoza, to make God into the very nature itself of things, and to reduce created things to mere modifications of a single divine substance. For that which does not act, which has no active force, which is robbed of any distinguishing characteristic, and finally of all reason and ground of permanence, can in no way be a substance. I am firmly convinced that the distinguished M. Sturm, a man notable for piety and learning, is very far from such monstrosities. So doubtless either he will show how his doctrine allows there to be some substance, and even some change, in things, or he will surrender to the truth.

16. Actually there are many things which make me suspect more and more that I have failed to understand his views properly, and he mine. Somewhere he admitted to me that a certain *portion of the divine power* (meaning, I suppose, an expression, resemblance, or immediate effect of the divine power—since that power certainly cannot be divided into parts) can, and even in a way must, be understood as belonging to and attributed to things. (See his letters to me, repeated in the passage from the *Elective Physics* cited at the beginning of this essay.) If, as would appear from what he says, this is to be understood in the sense in which we say that the soul is part of the divine breath, then there is no longer any disagreement between us. But I am not confident that this is what he means since he says hardly anything like it, or that seems to follow from it, anywhere else. On the contrary, I note that things he says elsewhere are hardly consistent with this view, and also that the 'Defence' leads to quite different conclusions. It is true that, after he had raised, in a letter, some objections to my views on inherent force which were first published in the *Acta Eruditorum* of Leipzig

in March 1694 (and further explained in my '*Specimen Dynamicum*' [T5], same journal, April 1695), he magnanimously agreed in response to my reply that there were only verbal differences between us. But when, having noted this, I went on to raise some other points, he changed his position, and pointed to many differences between us, differences which I acknowledge. Quite recently, however, he put these on one side and wrote again that there were only verbal differences between us—something that would be most pleasing to me. So I have tried, on the occasion of this latest 'Defence', finally to explain things in such a way that both of our views, and the truth of them, can the more easily be ascertained. For this distinguished man has great insight and clarity of exposition; so it is to be hoped that his work will throw no small light on this issue, and that therefore my own endeavours will perhaps not prove useless if they give him an opportunity to consider, and, with his usual industriousness and strength of judgement, to throw light upon important things in the present discussion which have so far been missed by other authors. If I am not mistaken, I have supplemented these things by new, more profound, and more general principles, from which there may sometime arise a restored and corrected system of philosophy, midway between the formal and the material, and combining and preserving them both.

NOTE L TO BAYLE'S *DICTIONARY* ARTICLE 'RORARIUS' (1702)

Summary of the Text

One of the changes to the 1702 second edition of Bayle's Dictionary *article on 'Rorarius' was the addition of note L, which replied to what Leibniz had said (T12) about Bayle's original, first edition, note H (T10). As in note H, the main focus is on Leibniz's system of pre-established harmony between body and mind.*

Bayle is unmoved by Leibniz's insistence (T12. 7) that the occasionalist account of the relation between body and mind involves miracles simply by virtue of its involving God's activity rather than the activity of created bodies or minds. But he agrees to set this matter aside and, in effect, to concede that, whatever the case with *occasionalism, Leibniz's system of pre-established harmony (a system he describes as being an important 'breakthrough') does not involve miracles. He also agrees to set aside other things (e.g. human freedom) which are no less problematic for occasionalism than they are for Leibniz's pre-established harmony.

Sections 3–6 question the cogency of what Leibniz maintains about the body in its pre-established harmony with the soul or mind. (They, and Sections 7–11, merely develop thoughts on which, as Bayle concedes (Sect. 11), Leibniz has already commented.) The mechanism which this theory attributes to the body is of just unbelievable complexity; and why is its harmony with the mind never upset by interference from surrounding bodies, or by those supposedly spontaneous bodies which make it up?

In Sections 7–9 Bayle considers the harmony from the point of view of the soul. In general terms his concern here is with the compatibility of the supposed simplicity of the soul and its spontaneous production of a series of thoughts. He develops at greater length the objection he originally made at T10. 8 to the effect that the supposed simplicity, indivisibility, and autonomy of the soul is incompatible with its ever having different states. Taking up the reply Leibniz had already

From the French in Pierre Bayle, *Dictionnaire historique et critique* (2nd edn. Rotterdam, 1702), iii. 2610–13. For a complete translation, see WF 86–96. The superscripts [A], [B], [C], etc. refer to some comments (as in T15) on it which Leibniz wrote. The lower-case superscript cues [a], [b], [c] are to Bayle's own notes, which are given here at the end of the text.

made (T12. 2, 11), Bayle suggests that though the thought that the soul's state is precisely one of change will go some way with the difficulty, there are some changes it cannot explain satisfactorily. Why should a soul spontaneously and without external influence change from a feeling of pleasure to one of pain—the change which, on our ordinary way of looking at it, happens non-spontaneously when a suckling child is pricked with a pin? The possible solution that the soul is not one simple substance but a collection is of no avail (Sect. 10).

From Section 12 onwards Bayle, rather than developing his original objections, replies to Leibniz's replies in T12 to those objections. Remarking that in its appeal to God (as the instigator of the pre-established harmony) Leibniz's system has some similarity to occasionalism, Bayle is clear that Leibniz holds that what happens to the soul (even a change from pleasure to pain) happens as a matter of its own internal development (though in representation of changes in the body). But he still cannot see how this can happen. Experience shows that our souls have no knowledge of their future states—unlike a singer presented with a musical score to follow. Though it honestly addresses a crucial and quite central difficulty, Leibniz's suggestion (T12. 8) that we sense our future perceptions confusedly needs further development.

THE TEXT

[1] I begin by saying that I am very pleased with the small difficulties I raised against this great philosopher's system, for they have given rise to replies which have further explained the matter to me, and have made me see more distinctly how marvellous it is. I now consider this new system to be an important breakthrough, which advances the frontiers of philosophy. We used to have only two theories: the *Schools' and that of the *Cartesians; the one was a *way of influence* of the body on the soul and the soul on the body, the other was a *way of assistance*, or of occasional causality. But here we have a new acquisition; . . . the *way of pre-established harmony*. [2] We are indebted to M. Leibniz for it, for nothing can be imagined which gives so exalted an idea of the power and intelligence of the author of all things. Together with the advantage that it avoids any implication of miraculous conduct, that fact would incline me to prefer this new system to that of the Cartesians, if only I could see the way of *pre-established harmony* as being at all possible. It must be stressed that when I say that this way avoids any implication of miraculous conduct, I am not

retracting what I said before to the effect that the system of occasional causes does not involve God's intervening miraculously. I am still as convinced as ever that for an action to be miraculous it must be produced by God as an exception to general laws, and that anything he does immediately according to such laws is not, properly speaking, a miracle. But as I want to cut out of this discussion as many points as I can, I will accept the suggestion that the best way to get rid of any idea of miracles is to suppose that created substances are active, immediate causes of natural effects. So I will not say what I could in response to this part of M. Leibniz's replies. I am also leaving out all those objections which can be made against the views of other philosophers just as much as against his, so I will not raise all the difficulties which confront the idea that God can give created things the power of self-movement. Those difficulties are severe,[1] and almost insurmountable; but M. Leibniz's system is no more open to them than is that of the *Peripatetics, and I do not know that even the Cartesians would dare to say that God couldn't give our soul the ability to act. If they do say that he couldn't, how can they claim that Adam sinned? And if they daren't say so, they weaken the reasons they give for saying that matter is incapable of any kind of action. I do not see either that it would be any more difficult for M. Leibniz than for the Cartesians, or other philosophers, to defend himself against the objection of a mechanical fate, that is, the destruction of human freedom. So let us leave all that, and consider only what is particular to the system of *pre-established harmony*.

[3] 1. My first point is that it raises the power and intelligence of divine art far beyond anything that we can understand. Imagine a ship which, without having any senses or any knowledge, and without being steered by any being, either created or uncreated, has the ability to manœuvre itself so perfectly that it always has a favourable wind, avoids currents and rocks, anchors where need be, and goes into harbour exactly when necessary. Suppose that such a ship sails like that for several years, always altering course and manœuvring as required by changes of wind and differing circumstances of land and sea. You will agree that even the infinity of God is not too much for giving such a power to a ship; and you will also say that a ship is not the sort of thing which could be given such a faculty by God. M. Leibniz, however, supposes that the mechanism of the human body is more admirable and more astonishing than all this. Let us apply his system of the union of soul and body to Caesar.

---

[1] In a note Bayle refers here to Sturm's *Elective Physics* and Leibniz's discussion of it (as in T13).

[4] 2. According to this system we have to say that Julius Caesar's body exercised its power of movement in such a way that from birth to death it followed out a continual sequence of changes which corresponded in the smallest detail to the incessant changes in a certain soul, of which it had no knowledge, and which had no effect on it.[A] We have to say that even if it had pleased God to annihilate Caesar's soul the day after it was created, the principle, according to which this faculty of Caesar's body had to produce its acts, was such that the body would have gone to the Senate on a certain day at a certain time, and would have uttered such and such words, etc. We have to say that this power of movement produced its changes and modifications punctually to correspond to the volubility of the thoughts of this ambitious mind, and that it moved into some particular state rather than any other, because Caesar's soul moved on from one thought to another. Can a blind force modify itself so appropriately as a consequence of an impression communicated to it thirty or forty years before, when it has not been renewed since, when it is left all by itself, and without ever having had any knowledge of its instructions? Isn't that much more incomprehensible than the voyage I spoke of in the preceding paragraph?[B]

[5] 3. What adds to the difficulty is that the human mechanism has an almost infinite number of organic parts, and[a] is continually exposed to the impact of surrounding bodies, which by an innumerable variety of disturbances will stimulate in it a thousand kinds of modification. How can we make sense of the fact that this *pre-established harmony* is never upset, and always stays on course through even the longest life of a man, despite the infinite variety of actions of all these parts one on another, surrounded on all sides by an infinity of corpuscles, sometimes cold, sometimes hot, sometimes dry, sometimes wet, always active, always pricking at the nerves, in this way or that? I think that this multiplicity of parts and of external agents is essential for the almost infinite variety of changes in the human body. But could this variety be as perfectly ordered as this system requires? Will it never disturb the correspondence between these changes and those of the soul? This is what seems to be quite impossible.

[6] 4. It is useless to hide behind God's power, and to maintain that animals are only automata; it is useless to claim that God was able to make machines which are so cleverly put together that a man's voice, the light reflected from an object, etc., strikes them exactly as is necessary to make them move in such or such a manner. Everyone except some of the Cartesians rejects that idea; and no Cartesian at all would be prepared to accept it, if we were to extend it to man, that is, if we were to say that God had been able to make bodies which did mechanically everything that we

see other men do.^C In denying this possibility we are not claiming to set limits to God's power and knowledge; the intention is only to convey that the nature of things means that the faculties which can be given to a created thing must have certain limitations. It is absolutely necessary that the activity of created things be appropriate to what they essentially are, and that it be carried out in accordance with the character of all machines, for according to the philosophers' axiom, whatever is received is commensurate with the capacity of the receiver. So we can reject M. Leibniz's theory as impossible, since it involves more serious difficulties even than that of automata: it suggests a continuous harmony between two substances which do not act on each other. But even if servants were machines and punctually did this or that every time their master ordered, the master would still be having a real effect on them: he would utter words, he would make gestures, and these would set up a real disturbance in these servants' organs.^D

[7] 5. Let us now consider Caesar's soul: we will find even more impossibilities. This soul was in the world without being exposed to the influence of any body or any mind. The power God had given it was the sole source of the particular actions it produced at each moment, and if these actions were of different kinds, that was not because some were produced by the operation of agencies which did not contribute to the production of the others, for man's soul is simple, indivisible, and immaterial. M. Leibniz admits this. And indeed, if he did not admit it, and instead were to suppose with the common run of philosophers and with several of the best metaphysicians of this century that something consisting of several suitably arranged material parts is capable of thought,[2] I would regard his theory as absolutely impossible, and there would be many other ways to refute it, which are of no relevance here, since he recognizes the immateriality of our soul and takes it as a starting-point. [8] Returning to Julius Caesar's soul, let us call it an immaterial automaton [cf. T12. 10], and let us compare it with an *Epicurean atom—I mean an atom surrounded by a void on all sides, and which never comes into contact with any other atom. The comparison is very close; for on the one side this atom has a natural power of self-movement which it exercises without being helped in any way, and without being hindered or crossed by any thing; and on the other side Caesar's soul is a mind which has been given the ability to produce its thoughts, and exercises it without the influence of any other mind, or of

---

[2] In a note Bayle gives *Locke as an example (see *Essay concerning Human Understanding*, 4. 3. 6).

any body. Nothing assists it, nothing crosses it. According to common notions and ideas of order this atom will never stop, and having been moving a moment ago, it will be moving now and in all following moments, and the manner of its movement will always be the same. This follows from an axiom accepted by M. Leibniz [T12. 2], 'that a thing will always remain in the same state if nothing occurs to make it change'. 'We conclude', he says, 'not only that a body which is at rest will always remain at rest, but also that a moving body will always retain its movement or progression, that is to say the same speed and the same direction, if nothing occurs to prevent it' [T12. 3]. It is clear to everyone that this atom (whether it moves itself by an innate power, as *Democritus and Epicurus hold, or by a power given by the Creator) will keep on moving forward uniformly and regularly along the same straight line, without ever turning to the right or to the left, or reversing direction. Epicurus was derided for inventing the motion of declination; he introduces it gratuitously only in order to try to escape the labyrinth of everything's being necessitated by fate, and he could give no explanation for this addition to his theory. It conflicts with our most obvious ideas, for we can see clearly that if an atom which has moved in a straight line for two days is to turn aside at the beginning of the third day, it has either to meet some obstacle, or to form some desire to depart from its course, or to incorporate in it some device which comes into play at that moment. The first of these is ruled out in an empty space. The second is impossible, because an atom has no power of thought. The third is similarly impossible in an absolutely unitary corpuscle.^E Let us now apply all of this.

[9] 6. Caesar's soul is a being which possesses unity in the strictest sense. The ability to give itself^b thoughts belongs to its nature: it received from God both the possession and the use of it. If the first thought it gives itself is a feeling of pleasure,^F it is hard to see why the second should not also be a feeling of pleasure; for when the total cause of an effect remains the same, the effect cannot change. Now, in the second moment of its existence, this soul does not acquire a new ability to think, but only keeps the ability it had in the first moment; and it is as independent of the effects of any other cause in the second moment as it was in the first. So it ought to reproduce in the second moment the same thought it had produced before. If you object against me that the soul must be in a state of change, and that in the situation I describe it would not, I reply that its change will be like the atom's change: for an atom which keeps on moving along the same line is in a new situation at each moment, but one which is the same as the previous situation. Therefore, for a soul to persist in its state of

change, it is enough for it to give itself another thought which is the same as the previous one.^{G} But let us not take it so narrowly: let us allow that its thoughts might be different; but it would at least still be necessary that the change from one thought to another involved some affinity which connects them. Suppose that at one moment Caesar's soul sees a tree with flowers and leaves; I can^c understand that it might suddenly want to see one which has only leaves, and then one which has only flowers, and in this way how it might make for itself several successive images which arise one out of another. But we could never make sense of the possibility of bizarre changes from black to white or from yes to no, or those wild leaps from earth to heaven which are quite common in human thought. We could never understand how God might have been able to put into Julius Caesar's soul the principle of a change such as the following: no doubt more than once whilst he was suckling he was pricked by a pin; according to the theory we are examining here, the soul would have had to modify itself with a feeling of pain immediately after the pleasant sensations of the sweetness of milk which it had been having for two or three minutes together. By what means was it determined to interrupt its pleasures and suddenly give itself a feeling of pain, without anything's having alerted it to prepare it for the change, and without anything new happening in its substance? If you review the life of this first Roman emperor, you will at each stage find material for an objection even stronger than this one.^{H}

[10] 7. We could make some sense of this if we supposed that a man's soul is not a mind but rather a host of minds, each of which has its functions which come into play exactly as required by the changes which take place in the human body. We would then have to say that something analogous to a great apparatus of wheels and springs, or of fermenting material, arranged in accordance with the vicissitudes of our bodily mechanism, arouses or deadens for such and such a time the action of each of these minds. But then man's soul would no longer be a substance; it would, just like a material being, be an *ens per aggregationem, a mass or collection of substances. What we are looking for here is a single being which experiences now joy, now sadness, etc.; we are not looking for several beings, one of which produces hope, another despair, etc.^{I}

[11] The observations you have just read only develop those that M. Leibniz has done me the honour of examining. I am now going to comment on his replies.

[12] 8. He says that 'the law of the changes in the substance of an animal takes it from pleasure to pain just when there is a break in the con-

tinuity of its body, because the law of this animal's indivisible substance is to represent what happens in its body, just as we know from our own cases, and indeed to represent in some fashion, through its relation to the body, everything that happens in the world' [T12. 3]. These words give a very good account of the fundamentals of this system: they are, so to speak, its denouement and its key. But at the same time they are the point which provides the perspective from which we can most clearly see the objections of those who think that this new theory is impossible. The law that is spoken of here supposes a decree of God, and shows in what respects this system is similar to that of occasional causes.^J These two systems agree on the following point: that there are laws according to which a man's soul must *represent what happens in his body, just as we know from our own cases* [T12. 3]. They differ about the way in which these laws are implemented. According to the Cartesians, God implements them: M. Leibniz says that the soul implements them itself. This is what seems impossible to me, for the soul does not have the equipment it would need for this kind of implementation. However infinite God's knowledge and power might be, he couldn't do with a machine which was lacking a certain part something for which that part was necessary. He would have to make up for that lack, and then it would be he, and not the machine, which produced the effect. Let us try to show that the soul lacks the equipment necessary for implementing the divine law in question by means of a comparison.

[13] Let us imagine, at random, an animal created by God, and designed to sing incessantly. It will sing all the time, that is obvious; but if God intended it to follow a certain score, it is absolutely necessary that he either puts it in front of its eyes, or imprints it in its memory, or arranges the animal's muscles in such a way that by the laws of mechanics one note is made to follow another exactly according to the score. Otherwise it is inconceivable that this animal should ever be able to follow the complete series of notes which God has written.^K [14] Let us consider a man's soul in the same way. M. Leibniz holds that it has been given not only the power of continually giving itself thoughts, but also that of always following a certain sequence in its thoughts, corresponding to the continual changes in the bodily machine. This sequence of thoughts is like the score set down for the musical animal described above. Would it not then be necessary, if the soul is to change its perceptions or modifications at each moment according to that score of thoughts, for it to know the sequence of notes, and to think of it at the time? But experience shows us that it knows nothing of it.^L In the absence of such knowledge, is it not necessary that at least there should be in the soul a set of specific devices, each of which is a

necessary cause of such and such a thought? Is it not necessary that they should be precisely arranged so that just this one operates after that, according to the 'pre-established' correspondence between the changes in the bodily machine and the thoughts in the soul? But it is quite certain that an immaterial, simple, indivisible substance cannot be composed of this innumerable multitude of specific devices arranged one in front of another according to the order of the score in question. It is therefore not possible for the human soul to implement this law.

[15] M. Leibniz supposes that the soul has no distinct knowledge of its future perceptions, 'but senses them confusedly', and that 'in each substance there are[d] traces of everything that has happened to it, and of everything that is going to happen.[M] But this infinite multitude of perceptions prevents us from distinguishing them [T12. 8] . . . the present state of each substance *is a natural consequence of its preceding state* . . . the soul, even though simple, always has feelings composed of several simultaneous perceptions; which for our purposes has the same effect as if it were composed of parts, like a machine. For, in conformity with a law of order which exists in perceptions as much as in movements, each preceding perception influences succeeding ones [T12. 12]. . . . the perceptions which are simultaneously together in the same soul involve a truly infinite multitude of small indistinguishable feelings that will be developed in what follows, so one should not be astonished at the infinite variety of what emerges over time. All of this is only a consequence of the representational nature of the soul which must express what happens, and indeed what will happen, in its body, and, because of the connection or correspondence of all the parts of the world, it must also express in some way what happens in all the others' [T12. 8, 9, 12]. [16] I don't have much to say about that: I say only that this suggestion, if it were fully developed, would be the real means of resolving all the difficulties. By the penetration of his great genius, M. Leibniz has perfectly appreciated the full extent and force of the objection, and where the solution to the main difficulty is to be found. I am sure that he will iron out what might otherwise have been most worrying about his system, and that he will be able to teach us some wonderful things about the nature of minds. . . .

[17] It does not matter that, whereas the Cartesians suppose that there is only one general law for the union of all minds with bodies, he holds that God gives a particular law to each mind, which seems[e] to entail that the primitive constitution of one mind is specifically different from that of another. Don't the *Thomists say that in the realm of angels there are as many species as there are individuals?[N]

231

14. *Bayle's Note L to 'Rorarius'*

a. Note that according to M. Leibniz that which is active in each substance is something which is reducible to a true unity. So since each man's body is composed of several substances, each of these substances must have a source of action really distinct from that of each of the others. He wants the action of each such source to be spontaneous. But their effects will necessarily be disturbed; and will vary in an infinite number of ways, because neighbouring bodies will to some extent constrain the natural spontaneity of each one.°

b. This is said from the point of view of M. Leibniz's system.

c. In saying this I am making a concession; that is to say, I am not insisting on the reasons which make it impossible for us to understand how a created spirit could give itself ideas.

d. This is what is incomprehensible in an indivisible, simple, immaterial substance.

e. Two men never have the same thoughts, not merely for a whole month, but even for two minutes. So the principle of thought in each one must have its own rule and its own nature.

15

LEIBNIZ'S COMMENTS ON NOTE L
TO BAYLE'S *DICTIONARY* ARTICLE
'RORARIUS' (1705?)

Summary of the Text

Some time after its first appearance in the second edition of Bayle's Dictionary
*(1702) Leibniz wrote these detailed comments on particular points in note L (T14).
They all answer, correct, or adjust various of Bayle's puzzles about, or misunderstandings of, the pre-established harmony between body and mind.*

Comment C is of particular interest. Here Leibniz gives a clear and very pleasing summary of both the similarities and the differences between his account of the mind and the body and those of his predecessors.

His account essentially consists of three points. (1) That every state of the body is caused by previous states of the body, never by states of the mind; (2) that every mental state is caused by earlier mental states, never by bodily states. The materialists accept (1)—though, since they deny minds, they can hardly accept (2). The *Platonists and the *Peripatetics reject both (1) and (2), holding that some (though not all) states of the body are caused by mental states and that some (though not all) mental states are caused by states of the body. The *occasionalists accept (1) so far as non-human animals go—except that the causation is mediated by God. But they agree with the Platonists about human beings—except that (along with Leibniz) they deny that the causation between mind and body can be a matter of direct and immediate influence.

A third element in Leibniz's view is (3) that, though there is no causal interaction (whether direct or indirect) between mind and body, (a) every bodily state has and is represented by a corresponding mental state; (b) every mental state has and is represented by a corresponding bodily state. But (as in Sect. H) this representation of the body by the mind is often a matter of confused unconscious perception (see also Sects. G, J, L, M). All these notes help us (though not Bayle, who did not

From the French at GP iv. 533–54. A complete set of Leibniz's comments is given at WF 96 107. The comments belong with those of T11, and their date of composition must be no earlier than 1705 (see WF 71 n. 19).

see them!) with what Bayle said was the most important question: what Leibniz meant in talking about confused perception.

Apart from the doctrine of pre-established harmony, one point of particular interest is in Section E where Leibniz outlines a difference between true substances and non-substantial matter. Unlike substances or complete beings '[m]atter remembers only what happened in the previous moment'.

<hr>

THE TEXT

[A] [See T14. 4.] Bodies do not know what happens in the soul, and the soul makes no physical impression on the body. M. Bayle is right about that; but God makes up for this—not by himself giving the body new impressions from time to time, so as to make it obey the soul, but by constructing this automaton from the outset in such a way that, at the right time and place, it will do just what the soul requires.

[B] [See T14. 4.] It emerges more and more that M. Bayle has not fully grasped my thought, which is that the body modifies itself as necessary not by some kind of received impression or power, but by its structure, which is designed for that purpose. We can again use the automaton which acts as a servant to resolve the whole problem. The structure it has been given is sufficient for all its functions, even though it is left to itself, even though its first impressions are not renewed, and even though it has no knowledge of what it is to do, or of the instructions it was given. And the difference between Caesar's body and this automaton is only one of degree.

[C] [See T14. 6.] The *Cartesian would not deny that such an automaton is possible for God; but he would not accept that other people are in fact inanimate automata of this sort. He would rightly say that they are like him. According to me, however, they are all automata, human as well as animal bodies; but they are all animated, animal as well as human bodies. So pure materialists, like the *Democriteans, and also formalists, like the *Platonists and the *Peripatetics, are partly right and partly wrong. The Democriteans had the perfectly justified belief that human as well as animal bodies are automata and do everything completely mechanically; but they were wrong to believe that these machines are not associated with an immaterial substance or form, and also that matter could think. The Platonists and the Peripatetics believed that the bodies of animals and men are animated, but they were wrong to think that souls change the rules of bodily movement; in this way they took away the automatic side of animal and human bodies. The Cartesians were right to reject that influence, but went wrong in taking away the automatic side of man and the thinking side of animals. I think we should keep both sides for both things: we should be Democritean and make all actions of bodies mechanical and independent of souls, and we should also be more than Platonic and hold that all the actions of souls are immaterial and independent of mechanism.

[D] [See T14. 6.] But there are servants so well primed that they need no signs. They anticipate them. Chiming watches, for example, and alarm clocks are servants of this kind. Far from waiting for signs, they give them to us. The artificial servant I described above, who imitates or mimics a real one, does not even need to be wound up or set by us as do watches and alarm clocks; its maker has set it for us. Our body is a servant of this kind.

[E] [See T14. 8.] It is as well to take note, before going further, of a big difference between matter and the soul. Matter is an incomplete being; it lacks the source of action. And when some impression is produced in it, it registers precisely only that, and what is in it in that moment. This is why matter is not even capable of keeping itself in circular motion, for this movement is not simple enough for it to remember, so to speak. Matter remembers only what happened in the previous moment . . . It remembers, that is to say, the direction of the tangent, but has no ability to remember the rule it would need to be given for diverging from that tangent and staying on the circumference. That is why, without something making it do so, a body can't keep moving in a circle, even when it has begun in one. That is why an atom can only learn to go in a simple straight line: it is so stupid and imperfect. It is completely different with a soul or a mind. Because this is a true substance, or a complete being, and the source of its own actions, it, so to speak, remembers (confusedly, of course) all its preceding states, and is affected by them. It retains not only its direction, as does the atom, but also the law of changes of direction, or the law of curvature, which the atom cannot do. And whereas in the atom there is only one change, there is an infinity of changes in the modifications of a soul, each of which has its law; for the *Epicurean atom, although it has parts, has a uniform interior, whereas the soul, even though it has no parts, has within it, because of the multitude of representations of external things, or rather because of the representation of the universe lodged within it by the Creator, a great number, or rather an infinite number, of variations.

M. Bayle would not bring against me the comparison between an Epicurean atom and the human soul, as he does here, if he had considered this difference between the *conatuses* of bodies and those of souls. . . .

[F] [See T14. 9.] I do not think of the soul as 'giving itself' its first feelings. It received them with its existence from God at the moment of creation, for it has had feelings from the outset; and in its first ones it received potentially all the others.

[G] [See T14. 9.] I have already explained above the great difference which exists between the laws of change of a body such as an atom and those of the soul; and it is also shown by the difference between the thought of a soul and the movement of an atom. Spontaneous movement consists in the tendency to move in a straight line; there is nothing so uniform. But thought involves an actual external material object, the human body; and this is a composite object which contains a very large number of modifications, through which it is connected with surrounding bodies and, by means of them, step by step with all others. And the soul's tendencies towards new thoughts correspond to the body's tendency towards new shapes and new movements. And as these new movements can make the object pass from order to disorder, their representation in the soul can also make the soul pass from pleasure to displeasure.

[H] [See T14. 9.] Let us review what is said here. It is certainly necessary that the change from one thought to another 'involves some affinity which connects them'; this has been shown. If Caesar's soul had only distinct thoughts, and produced them all voluntarily, the change from one thought to another could be as M. Bayle suggests, for example from the thought of one tree to that of another. But besides the perceptions which the soul remembers, there is a mass which is made up of an infinite number of confused perceptions which it does not disentangle. It is through these that it represents outside bodies, and comes to have distinct thoughts which are unlike the preceding ones, because the bodies which the soul represents have suddenly changed to something which strongly affects its own. So the soul sometimes passes from white to black or from yes to no, without knowing how, or at least involuntarily, for what its confused thoughts and its feelings produce in it we attribute to the body. So we should not be surprised if a man who is stung by some insect when eating jam should, despite himself, pass immediately from pleasure to pain. For, in approaching the man's body before stinging it, this insect was already affecting it, and the representation of this was, albeit unconsciously, already affecting his soul. However, in the soul as in the body, little by little the insensible becomes the sensible. That is how the soul changes itself even against its will, for it is enslaved by the feelings and confused thoughts which occur according to the states of its body, and of other bodies through their relation to it. These, then, are the means through which pleasures are sometimes interrupted and followed by pains, without the soul's always being alerted or prepared for it; as for example when the insect which stings approaches without making a noise, or, if it is a wasp for example, when some distraction prevents our noticing the approaching wasp's buzz. Thus we must not say that nothing new happens in the substance of the soul which makes it feel the sting; for what happens is confused presentiments or, better, insensible dispositions of the soul, which represent the dispositions of the body with regard to the sting.

[I] [See T14. 10.] M. Bayle is right to deny any such composition to the soul, which would make it destructible and dissipatable, for it would then be a mass. But we have no need for the soul's substance to be composite; it is enough that its thoughts are composite, and involve a large number of objects and modifications distinctly or confusedly understood, as experience in fact shows us. For even though the soul is a simple and single substance, it never has simple and single perceptions. It always has, all at the same time, several distinct perceptions which it can remember, and, associated with them, an infinite number of confused ones which it cannot distinguish. Since this composition of thoughts has only to produce other composite thoughts, it has no need of such a host of minds. Each partial modification of the preceding state of the soul contributes to the next total modification of the same soul, and gives it a new variation.

[J] [See T14. 12.] I think of the law of succession of a soul's modifications not as a simple decree of God, but as an effect of an enduring decree within the soul's nature, like a law inscribed in its substance. When God puts a certain law or programme of future action into an automaton, he is not content merely to impose an order on it as a decree; at the same time he provides the means for its implementation—that is, he inscribes a law in its nature or constitution. He gives it a structure in virtue of which the actions which he wants or allows the animal to do are produced naturally and in order. My notion of the soul is the same: I think of it as an immaterial automaton whose internal constitution contains in concentrated form, or represents, a material automaton, and produces in the soul representations of its actions.

[K] [See T14. 13.] All we need do is picture a chorister or opera singer hired to sing at certain times, who finds, at the church or the opera, a book of music in which are written the pieces of music or scores to be sung, and on what days and at what times. This singer sings by sight-reading: his eyes are guided by the book, and his tongue and throat are guided by his eyes; but his soul sings, so to speak, from memory, or something equivalent to memory. For since the music book, the eyes, and the ears can have no influx into the soul, it has to find for itself, though with no trouble or effort, and without searching for it, what its brain and its organs find with the help of the book. This is because the whole score in the book or series of books that are followed in singing is imprinted potentially in his soul from the beginning of its existence; just as the score was in some way imprinted in its material causes before the pieces were put together and made into a book. But the soul is not conscious of all this, for it is encapsulated in its confused perceptions, which express all the detail of the universe; it perceives it distinctly only when its organs are noticeably struck by the notes in the score.

[L] [See T14. 14.] I have already shown more than once that the soul does many things without knowing how it does them—when it does them by means of confused perceptions and unconscious inclinations or appetitions, of which there are always an extremely large number, so that it is impossible for the soul to be conscious of them, or to distinguish them clearly. Our perceptions are never perfectly uniform, as a straight line is; they are always clothed in something sensible, which involves something confused, even though it is itself clear. It is in this way that notions of colours are clear, and are easily noticed. But they are confused, for their composition is not manifest in the sensation we have of them. They involve in themselves something of the light source which generates them, of the object from which they come, and of the medium through which they pass. And they are bound to be affected by all that, and as a consequence by an infinity of things which have an effect on the medium they pass through, just as water is always affected a little by its channel. I have shown elsewhere that the confused perception of pleasantness or unpleasantness which we find in consonances or dissonances consists in an occult arithmetic. The soul counts the beats of the vibrating object which makes the sound, and when these beats regularly coincide at short intervals, it finds them pleasant. Thus it counts without knowing it. And it is also in this way that it performs an infinity of other small operations which are very precise, although they are not at all voluntary, and are known only by the noticeable effect in which they eventually culminate. They give us a feeling which is clear but confused, because its sources are not perceived. Reasoning has to come to our aid—as in music, where the proportions which produce an agreeable sound have been discovered.

[M] [See T14. 15.] What is meant here by traces are marks (which can be immaterial) such as relations, expressions, representations—that is, the effects by means of which some past cause can be known, or the causes by which some future effect can be known. And since there is the greatest amount of diversity within the present state of the soul, which knows many things at once and still senses infinitely more, and since this present diversity is an effect of that of a preceding state and a cause of that of a future state, I thought they could be called 'traces', in which a sufficiently penetrating mind would be able to recognize the past and the future; but our own penetration could never reach so far.

[N] . . . In the end my system comes down to this: each monad is the universe in concentrated form, and each mind is an imitation of the divinity. In God the universe is not only concentrated, but perfectly expressed; but in each created monad there is distinctly expressed only one part, which is larger or smaller according as the soul is more or less excellent, and all the infinite remainder is expressed only confusedly. But in God there is not only this concentration of the universe, but also its source. He is the originating centre from which all else emanates, and if something emanates out from us, it does not do so without mediation, but only because from the outset God wanted to accommodate things to our desires. In fact when we say that each monad, soul, or mind has received a specific law, we must add that this is only a variation of the general law which orders the universe; it is like the way in which the same town appears different from the different points of view from which it is seen. So human souls do not have to be of different species from each other. The contrary is nearer the truth; for it is certain that two leaves, two eggs, two bodies, although of the same species, are never perfectly alike, and all these infinite variations, which we could never comprehend under one notion, make up different individuals, but not different species.[1] The marvel is that the sovereign wisdom has found in representing substances a way to vary the same world at the same time to an infinite degree, for since the world already contains in itself an infinite variety, and has that variety diversely expressed by an infinity of different representations, it possesses an infinity of infinities, and could not be more appropriate to the nature and intentions of its inexpressible author, who exceeds in perfection everything that can be thought.

---

[1] See also TT1. 9, 2. 4 §11 for the principle of the identity of indiscernibles. For discussion of the principle, see Chernoff (1981), Clatterbaugh (1971), Frankel (1981), Khamara (1988), McCullough (1977), B. Russell (1900, 1937, ch. 5, sects. 23–6), Vinci (1974), N. L. Wilson (1973).

[O] [See T14. 5 note a.] I agree that this will vary in an infinite number of ways the effects of the sources or true unities, but not that it will 'disturb' these unities or souls themselves, or conflict with their spontaneity. The impact of bodies causes changes in mere masses, but not in souls or monads, which spontaneously follow out their courses, adjusted to and representing everything that happens in masses.

REPLY TO THE COMMENTS IN THE SECOND EDITION OF M. BAYLE'S *CRITICAL DICTIONARY*, IN THE ARTICLE 'RORARIUS', CONCERNING THE SYSTEM OF PRE-ESTABLISHED HARMONY (1702; PUBLISHED 1716)

Summary of the Text

An early reaction to Bayle's new note L (T14) to the 'Rorarius' article was the reply Leibniz sent him in August 1702. A couple of months later Bayle wrote back that he had read the manuscript (in which 'you were good enough to consider my small objections'), and that he hoped that Leibniz would publish it. Indeed he did so— but not until 1716, some years after Bayle's death.

In common with the text to which it replies (i.e. T14), the focus here is on the system of pre-established harmony between body and soul. It is a feature of that system that states of the body are never caused by mental states but (as Descartes held of non-human animals) always by other bodily states.

In Sections 1–8 Leibniz addresses himself to Bayle's worry (T14. 3–6) that the required mechanism is quite incredible. The difference between an automaton capable of walking around a town for a while (something we could produce) and a machine which completely simulated the bodily activities of a human being is only one of degree; and the production of the latter would not be beyond God. Of course, on Leibniz's account of them, human beings are not just complex automata, for they embody souls. But though these represent everything that goes on in the body (and though nothing goes on in souls which has no correspondence in the body (Sect. 7)) the body is causally completely independent of them.

As at T15. C, Leibniz gives a good account of the various points of similarity and difference between the details of the soul–body relation as

From the French of *Histoire critique de la république des lettres*, 11 (1716), art. 4, 78–114 (repr. with some differences of which some are noted here in angle brackets, at GP iv. 554–71). The section numbers are from the complete translation in WF 107–26.

described in his pre-established harmony and as maintained by various of his predecessors.

Leibniz then turns to the problems Bayle feels that the system of pre-established harmony produces for the human soul. From Sects. 9–14 he addresses Bayle's worries about how a supposedly simple and indivisible soul can produce out of itself a complex and varied series of perceptions and sensations. As Leibniz notes to himself at T15. E, the soul, though simple and indivisible, is not like an Epicurean atom (Sect. 10). Unlike the atom, the soul has a 'compound tendency' (Sect. 10); as he says elsewhere, in it 'there are traces of everything that has happened to it, and of everything that is going to happen' (T12. 8). This compound tendency has to do with the fact that our thoughts are complex—a point which Bayle (T14. 15) saw as possibly 'the real means of resolving all the difficulties' (T14. 16). Leibniz develops this thought, his theory of small unconscious perceptions, in T12. 8.

Section 22 broaches the fresh question of why there should be evil in a world created by a good God. (See Introduction, Sect. 7, note 9.) Finally, Sections 23 and 24 deal with Leibniz's views about the ideality of space, time, and of mathematical entities such as points. For some discussion of this see Fox (1970), Hartz and Cover (1988), Ishiguro (1972b), Winterbourne (1982). Other aspects of Leibniz's views on space and time—his rejection of the Newtonian absolute theory—are discussed in Arthur (1985), Ballard (1960), Broad (1946), Cook (1979), Cox (1975), Khamara (1988), Parkinson (1969), Vinci (1974), N. L. Wilson (1973).

THE TEXT

[1] I published in the Paris *Journal des savants* (June and July 1695) some essays on a new system, which seemed to me to give a good explanation of the union between body and soul [i.e. T4]. In them, instead of the way of *influence* of the *Schools, or the way of *assistance* of the *Cartesians, I adopted the way of *pre-established harmony*. M. Bayle, who can give to the most abstract thoughts the charm they need if they are to capture the attention of the reader, and yet who goes deeply into them at the same time as bringing them into public view, was kind enough to take the trouble to develop this system in his comments in the article on 'Rorarius' in his *Dictionary*. But as at the same time he also raised some problems which he thought needed to be cleared up, I attempted to do so in the *Histoire des ouvrages des savants* for July 1698 [i.e. T12]. M. Bayle has now replied to this in the second edition of his *Dictionary* in the same article on

'Rorarius' [i.e. T14]. [2] He is good enough to say that my replies have developed the subject further, and that if it were certain that the theory of harmony is a possibility, he would have no hesitation in preferring it to the Cartesian theory, since it gives an exalted idea of the author of things, and avoids any implication of miraculous guidance of the ordinary course of nature. But at present he finds it hard to understand how such a pre-established harmony is possible, and to show why he begins with something which in his view is easier, and yet which we would agree is hardly feasible. He compares my theory with the supposition of a ship, which, without being steered by anyone, manages to get itself to its intended port. He says that it will be agreed that even the infinity of God is not too much for giving this kind of ability to a ship: he does not definitely say that it is impossible, but he thinks that others will say it is; for 'you will also say', he adds, 'that a ship is not the sort of thing which could be given such a faculty by God' [T14. 3]. [3] Perhaps he thought that according to the theory in question we would have to think of God as giving the ship a *Scholastic-style faculty for achieving this effect, like that which the Schools attribute to heavy bodies for steering them towards the centre. If this is what he means, I would be the first to reject such a supposition. But if he means a faculty of the ship which is explicable by mechanical rules, through a combination of internal agencies and external circumstances, and yet he still rejects the supposition as impossible, then I would ask him to give some reason for doing so. For although, as I shall show below, I have no need of the possibility of anything quite like the ship as M. Bayle appears to understand it, nevertheless I think that if we consider the thing thoroughly, far from there being any difficulty here with regard to God, it would appear that even a finite mind might be clever enough to bring it about. There is no doubt that a man could make a machine which was capable of walking around a town for a time, and of turning precisely at the corners of certain streets. And an incomparably more perfect, although still limited, mind could foresee and avoid an incomparably greater number of obstacles. And this being so, if this world were, as some[1] think it is, only a combination of a finite number of atoms which interact in accordance with mechanical laws, it is certain that a finite mind could be sufficiently exalted as to understand and predict with certainty everything that will happen in a given period. This mind could then not only make a ship capable of getting itself to a certain port, by first giving it the route, the direction, and the requisite equipment, but it could also

---

[1] *Epicurus and his followers.

build a body capable of simulating a man. The difference, after all, is only one of degree, which is no difference at all in the realm of possibilities; and however large the multitude of a machine's operations, the power and the skill of the workman could increase in proportion, so that to be unable to see the possibility of the thing is just a matter of not considering the intervening stages sufficiently well. [4] In fact the world is not composed of a finite number of atoms; rather, it is a machine, each part of which is composed of a truly infinite number of devices. But it is also true that the one who made it, and governs it, is of a yet more infinite perfection, since he encompasses an infinity of possible worlds, from which he selected the one that pleased him. To return to limited minds, however: we can see from the odd isolated cases which we sometimes come across how far others, which we don't know about, could go. For example, there are people who can do large arithmetical calculations very quickly in their heads. . . . And what is a man, however excellent he may be, in comparison with all the many possible and even actual creatures?—creatures such as angels and geniuses, who in all sorts of understanding and reasoning might surpass us incomparably further than these marvellous possessors of natural arithmetical ability surpass us in the matter of numbers. I realize that ordinary people have no time for these things: they are bemused by considerations where it is necessary to think about what is out of the ordinary, or even completely unheard of. But when we think about the size and the complexity of the universe, we see things quite differently. M. Bayle above all cannot fail to see the validity of these conclusions. In point of fact, my theory doesn't depend on them, as I shall show presently; but even if it did, and even if it were right to say that it is more surprising than the above-mentioned theory of automata (and I shall show later on that in fact it is only an extension of its good parts, or of what is solid and reliable in it), I should not be at all worried by that, given that there is no other way of explaining things in conformity with the laws of nature. For we must not be ruled by popular notions in these matters, to the prejudice of conclusions which are certain. Moreover, it is not because of its strangeness that a philosopher should object to the theory of automata, but because of its lack of a foundation, since there must be *entelechies everywhere. It is to have a very impoverished idea of the author of nature (who multiplies, as far as he can, his *little worlds*, or *indivisible active mirrors*) to accord them only to human bodies: it is in fact impossible that they are not everywhere.

[5] So far we have only talked of what a limited substance can do; but in the case of God, it is quite another matter, and far from its being the case

that what at first seemed impossible actually is impossible, we must in fact say that it is impossible that God should act otherwise, since he is infinitely powerful and wise, and maintains order and harmony in everything as far as is possible. But what is more, that which seems so strange when considered in the abstract is a necessary consequence of the constitution of things; and so the universal marvel dispels and, so to say, absorbs the particular marvel, by explaining it. For everything is regulated and bound together in such a way that these natural mechanisms which never go wrong, that we can compare to ships which steer themselves to port despite all the course changes and all the storms, should not be thought any stranger than a rocket which runs along a rope, or a liquid which flows along a channel. Moreover, since bodies are not *atoms*, but are divisible—and indeed actually divided—to infinity, and since everything is filled with them, it follows that the smallest little body is individually affected by the smallest of changes in any of the others, however distant and however small it may be, and so must be an exact mirror of the universe. This means that a sufficiently penetrating mind would, in proportion to its penetration, be able to see and foresee in each corpuscle what is happening and what will happen both in the corpuscle and outside it. So nothing happens to it, not even as a result of the impact of surrounding bodies, which does not follow from what is already internal to it, or which disturbs its internal order. This is even more obvious in the case of simple substances, or the active principles themselves, which, following *Aristotle, I call primitive *entelechies*, and which according to me nothing can disturb. [6] This answers one of M. Bayle's marginal notes [T14 note a] where he objects to me that since an organic body is composed of several substances, each of these substances must have a source of action really distinct from that of each of the others, and since the action of each such source is spontaneous, their effects will vary in an infinite number of ways, because neighbouring bodies will to some extent constrain the natural spontaneity of each one. But we must bear in mind that for all time each one has been accommodated to every other, and adapts itself to suit what the others will demand of it. There is therefore no constraint in substances except in external appearances. And this being so, any point you take in the world develops along a predetermined line, which that point has adopted once and for all, and which nothing can make it abandon. I think this point can be shown very clearly and precisely to the geometrical mind, even though there are infinitely more lines of this kind than a finite mind can comprehend. In fact the line would be straight if the point were all alone in the world; as things are, it owes its shape, in virtue of mechanical laws, to the collaboration of all other bodies, and it is by just that collaboration that it is *pre-established*. So I claim that there is no real spontaneity in a mass (unless we consider the universe as a whole, which encounters no resistance); for if this point could be isolated from everything else, it would continue not in the pre-established line, but in the straight tangent. So, strictly speaking, what is spontaneous is the *entelechy* (of which this point is the point of view); and whereas the point, because it has no memory, so to speak, nor prescience, can have of itself only the tendency along the touching straight line, the entelechy expresses the pre-established curve itself, so that in this sense, no change is violent[2] with regard to it. [7] This shows us that in fact there is no longer any difficulty in all those marvels such as the ship which gets itself to port, or the machine without intelligence which performs all the actions of a man, and I don't know how many other fictions that might still be raised against me, and which make our suppositions appear unbelievable when considered in the abstract. And it also shows how everything that had seemed strange disappears completely, when we understand that things are determined to do what they have to do. Everything that ambition or whatever other passion produces in Caesar's soul is also represented in his body; and all the movements involved in these passions come from impressions of objects connected to internal movements. And the body is so constructed that the soul never makes decisions to which bodily movements don't correspond, even the most abstract reasonings having their place there, through the symbols which represent them to the imagination. [8] In a word, everything happens in the body with regard to the details of phenomena as if the wicked doctrine of those who, following *Epicurus and *Hobbes, believe that the soul is material were true; or as if man himself were only body, or an automaton. Thus they extended to man what the Cartesians maintain with regard to all other animals, since they have in effect shown that man, with all his reason, does nothing which is not a set of images, passions, and movements in the body. We have prostituted ourselves in trying to prove the opposite, and have only prepared the way for the triumph of the mistake by approaching it in that way. The Cartesians came off very badly (rather like Epicurus with his *declination of the atoms*, which *Cicero made such fun of), when they tried saying that the soul, though unable to give motion to the body, could nevertheless change its direction.[3] But it is neither possible nor necessary for it to do either; and since

---

[2] For Aristotle's distinction between 'natural' and 'violent motion', see Introduction, Sect. 3.3.

[3] See Introduction, Sect. 5.

the materialists have no need to resort to any such thing, nothing which happens on the outside of a man is capable of refuting their doctrine—which suffices to establish one part of my theory. Those who point out to the Cartesians that the way they prove that animals are only *automata* could be taken as justifying someone who said that all other men, except himself, are simple automata, have said exactly and precisely what I need for this half of my theory, which concerns the body. But as well as the metaphysical principles which establish the *monads*, of which composites are only resultants, internal experience—the consciousness we have of the 'I' which perceives what passes in the body—refutes the Epicurean doctrine. And perception, since it cannot be explained by shapes and movements, establishes the other part of my theory: we are obliged to admit an *indivisible substance* in ourselves, which must itself be the source of its phenomena. So according to this second half of my theory, everything happens in the soul as if there were no body, just as according to the first half, everything happens in the body as if there were no soul. Besides which, I have often shown that, even in bodies, although in detail phenomena are explicable mechanically, the ultimate analysis of mechnical laws and the nature of substances in the end oblige us to appeal to active indivisible principles; and I have also shown that the admirable order which we find in them shows that there is a universal principle whose intelligence as well as whose power is supreme. And just as we can see from what is good and sound in the false and wicked doctrine of Epicurus, namely that there is no need to say that the soul changes the tendencies of the body, so it is also easy to see that it is not necessary either for the material mass to send thoughts to the soul by the influence of I know not what chimerical Scholastic species, or for God always to act as interpreter of the body to the soul, any more than he needs to interpret the soul's wishes to the body, as the Cartesians would have it: the *pre-established harmony* is a good mediator between both sides. All this shows us that what is of value in the theories of Epicurus and of *Plato, of the greatest materialists and the greatest idealists, is united here; and there is no longer anything surprising in it, except the sole pre-eminent perfection of the sovereign principle, now displayed in his work far above anything that had been thought before. So why is it any wonder that it all goes well and smoothly, when all things co-operate and lead each other by the hand, once we suppose them all to be perfectly planned? On the contrary, what would be the greatest of wonders, or rather the strangest of absurdities, would be if the ship which was destined to find port, or the machine whose path was mapped out from all time, were to fail despite the measures which God had taken. *As regards corporeal* *masses, therefore, we should not compare our theory with a ship which steers itself to port*—but rather with those ferries, fixed to a rope, that run across a river. Just as with stage-machines and fireworks, whose perfect operation we no longer find strange when we know how it is all done, we transfer our admiration from the invention to the inventor—just as we do nowadays when we see that the planets have no need of intelligences to guide them.

[9] As yet we have spoken of almost nothing except those objections which concern the body or matter, and no difficulty has been raised other than that of the marvellousness (but beautiful, regular, and universal) which there will have to be in bodies if they are to agree with each other and with souls. And in my view this should be taken as a proof, rather than as an objection, by people who correctly assess 'the power and intelligence of divine art' [T14. 3]—to quote M. Bayle, who has also said that 'nothing can be imagined which gives so exalted an idea of the power and intelligence of the author of all things' [T14. 2]. We must now turn to the *soul*, where M. Bayle has found further difficulties after what I said in resolution of his initial ones. He begins [T14. 8] by comparing a soul which is completely isolated and taken by itself, receiving nothing from outside, with an Epicurean *atom*, surrounded by a void; and indeed I do consider souls, or rather *monads*, as *atoms of substance*, for in my view there are no *material atoms* in nature, since even the smallest piece of matter still has parts. [10] Now, since the atom, as imagined by Epicurus, has a moving force, which gives it a certain direction, it will, assuming that it doesn't meet any other atom, execute that motion without hindrance, and uniformly. In the same way the soul, placed in the same circumstances, where nothing from outside affects it, if it has once received a feeling of pleasure, it seems (according to M. Bayle [T14. 9]) that it must always retain that feeling—for when the total cause remains the same, the effect must always remain the same. If I object that the soul should be considered to be in a state of change, and that therefore the total cause does not remain the same, M. Bayle replies that this change must be like that of an *atom* which is moving continually along the same (straight) line and at a uniform speed. And even if it were allowed (he says) that its thoughts might be different, it would at least still be necessary that the change that I am alleging from one thought to the other should involve some rationale or affinity which connects them. I quite accept the principles underlying these objections, and I use them myself to explain my system. The state of a *soul*, like that of the *atom*, is a state of change, a tendency: the atom tends towards a change of place, the soul towards a change of thought; each of them changes of itself in the simplest and most uniform way that its state allows. So how does it

come about (I will be asked [T14. 9–10]) that there is such simplicity in the changes of an *atom*, and such variety in those of the *soul*? It is because the atom (as we are imagining it, for there is no such thing in nature), even though it has parts, has nothing to cause any variety in its tendency, because we are supposing that these parts do not change their relations; on the other hand, the soul, though completely indivisible, involves a compound tendency, that is to say a multitude of present thoughts, each of which tends towards a particular change, depending on what is involved in it, and which are all in it at the same time, in virtue of its essential relatedness to all the other things in the world. [11] It is in fact the lack of this relatedness which rules Epicurean atoms out of nature. For there is no individual thing which must not express all the others, in such a way that the soul, because of the variety of its *modifications*, should be compared not with a *material atom*, but rather with the *universe* which it represents from its own *point of view*, and in a way even with God, whose *infinity* it represents *finitely* (because of its confused and imperfect perception of the infinite). And the reason for a change in the soul's thoughts is the same as for the change in things in the *universe* which it represents. For mechanical causes, which work themselves out in the body, are brought together, and, so to speak, concentrated in souls or *entelechies*, and indeed originate there. In fact, not all entelechies are, like our soul, *images of God*; for they are not all intended to be members of a society or a state of which he is the head. But they are all still *images of the universe*. They are in their own way scaled-down *worlds*: fertile *simplicities*; *unities* of *substance*, though, because of the multitude of their modifications, *virtually infinite*; centres, which express an *infinite circumference*. [12] And it is necessary that they should be like this, as I have explained previously in correspondence with M. Arnauld [T2. 4 §15]. And their enduring should cause no one any difficulty, any more than the enduring of the *Gassendists' atoms. As for the rest, as Socrates in Plato's *Phaedo* remarked of a man who scratches himself, often it is only a step from pleasure to pain: 'mirth may end in sorrow'.[4] So we need not be surprised by this change; it sometimes seems that pleasure is only a complex of small perceptions, each of which, if it were large, would be a pain.

[13] M. Bayle has already recognized that I have done my best to reply to a good part of his objections. He also observes that in the system of occasional causes God has to implement his own laws, whereas in mine the soul does it; but he objects that the soul has no tools for doing so. I reply

---

[4] The reference is to Plato's *Phaedo*, 60ʙ, but the quotation is directly from Prov. 14: 13.

as I have replied, that it has: it has its present thoughts, from which the subsequent ones are born; and one can say that in the soul, as everywhere else, *the present is big with the future.*

[14] I think M. Bayle will accept, and all other philosophers with him, that our thoughts are never simple, and that in the case of some thoughts the soul can of itself pass from one to the other, as it goes from premises to a conclusion, or from the end to the means. Even the Reverend Father Malebranche agrees that the soul has internal voluntary actions. Why shouldn't this be the case with all thoughts? Perhaps because it has been thought that confused thoughts are completely different in kind from distinct thoughts, whereas they are only less well distinguished and less developed because of their multiplicity. This has meant that certain movements, which are rightly called involuntary, have been attributed to the body to such an extent that they have been believed to have nothing corresponding to them in the soul: and conversely it has been thought that certain abstract thoughts were not represented in the body. But both of these are mistaken, as often happens with this sort of distinction, for we have taken note only of what is most obvious. [15] The most abstract thoughts need some imagination: and when we consider what confused thoughts (which invariably accompany the most distinct that we can have) are ⟨such as those of colour, odours, tastes, of heat, of cold, etc.⟩ we realize that they always involve the infinite, and not only what happens in our body but also, by means of it, what happens elsewhere. Confused thoughts thus serve our purpose as the tool which seemed necessary for the functions I attribute to the soul much better than the legion of substances of which M. Bayle speaks. It is true that the soul does have these legions in its service, but not in its interior. ⟨For there is no soul or entelechy which is not dominant over an infinity of others which enter into the parts of its body, and the soul is never without some organized body appropriate to its present state.⟩ It is, then, present perceptions, with an orderly tendency to change, that make up the musical score which tells the soul what to do. [16] But (says M. Bayle) 'would it then not be necessary that it know (distinctly) the sequence of notes, and be thinking (distinctly) about them?' [T14. 14]. I reply that this is not so: it is enough that the notes are contained in its confused thoughts; otherwise, every *entelechy* would be God. For God distinctly and perfectly expresses everything at once, the possible and the actual, past, present, and future. He is the universal source of everything, and created *monads* imitate him as far as created things can: he has made them the sources of their phenomena, which contain relations to everything, more or less distinct according to the degree of perfec-

tion of each substance. What is impossible about that? I want to see some positive argument which leads me to some contradiction, or the denial of some established truth. It would be no objection just to say that it is surprising. Far from it: everyone who accepts immaterial indivisible substances attributes to them a simultaneous multitude of perceptions, and a *spontaneity* in their reasonings and their voluntary acts. I am therefore only extending that *spontaneity* to their confused and involuntary thoughts, and showing that their nature is to contain relations with everything that is external. [17] Can it be proved that that cannot be, or that everything which is in us must be distinctly understood? Isn't it true that we can't always remember even things that we know, and which can immediately be brought back by some little reminder? Then how many other kinds of thing might there not be in the soul, which we cannot get at so easily? Otherwise the soul would be a God, when it is enough for it to be a little world, that is as *imperturbable* as the big one, once we realize that there is just as much spontaneity in the confused, as in the distinct. In another sense, however, it is reasonable to call those things which consist in confused thoughts, and in which there is involuntariness and incomprehension, 'perturbations' (as the ancients did) or 'passions'. And this is what in ordinary speech we not unreasonably attribute to the conflict of the body with the mind, since our confused thoughts represent the body or the flesh, and constitute our imperfection.

[18] When I gave substantially this response before, that confused perceptions implicitly contain everything that is external, and involve infinite relations, M. Bayle recorded it, but did not refute it; instead, he said 'that this suggestion, if it were fully developed, would be the real means of resolving all the difficulties' [T14. 16]; and he does me the honour of saying that he expects that I will completely resolve his own. Even if he said this only out of politeness, I would not have failed to try to resolve his difficulties. I believe I have not missed any out; and if I have left something out without trying to resolve it, it must have been because I didn't understand exactly what objection was being put to me—something which sometimes makes it most difficult for me to reply. I would have liked to see why it is thought that there could not be the multitude of perceptions that I suppose there to be in an *indivisible substance*; for I believe that even if experience and common sense did not force us to recognize a large variety in our soul, it would still be possible to suppose it. It is no proof of the impossibility of something merely to say that one cannot conceive this or that, when one doesn't make clear where it conflicts with reason, and when the difficulty is only one of imagination, and not of understanding.

... [20] M. Bayle was kind enough to make a point of sparing me those objections which apply equally to other systems, and I am obliged to him for that, too. With regard to the force given to created things, I shall say only that I believe I have replied [about this] in the journal of Leipzig for September 1698 [i.e. T13; see T14 n. 1] ... which M. Bayle cites ... and indeed I have demonstrated that without an *active* force in bodies there would be no variety in phenomena, which would be the same as if there were nothing at all. ...

[22] Turning now to [some other] articles of M. Bayle ... whose subject is very relevant here, it seems that the reason why evil is permitted has to do with the eternal *possibilities* according to which a universe such as this, which allows evil and yet which has been allowed into actual existence, turns out to be overall the most perfect of all the possibilities. But it is a mistake to try to show in detail, as the *Stoics did, what St *Augustine perfectly understood in general: how useful evil is for drawing attention to the good, and, so to speak, for helping us step back in order to jump forward the further. For how can we grasp all the infinite particularities of the *universal harmony*? However, if I had to make a rational choice between the two, I would be in favour of the *Origenist, and never of the *Manichaean. Neither does it seem to me that we have to deny action or power to created things on the grounds that if they produced modifications they would be creators.[5] For it is God who conserves and continually creates their power, that is to say, the *source* of *modifications* within a created thing, or a state of that thing from which it can be seen that there will be a change of modifications. Otherwise, it seems to me (as I have said above that I have shown elsewhere) that God would have produced nothing, and there would be no substances other than God—which would bring back all the absurdities of the God of *Spinoza. And indeed it seems that the error of that author comes only from his having worked out the consequences of the doctrine which takes away the power and action of created things.

[23] I hold that time, extension, motion, and in general all forms of continuity as dealt with in mathematics, are only ideal things; that is to say that, just like numbers, they express possibilities. In the same way, Hobbes defined space as *phantasma existentis*.[6] But, to speak more accurately, extension is the order of *possible coexistences*, just as time is the order of *inconsistent* but nevertheless connected *possibilities*, such that these orders

---

[5] Perhaps a reference to Mal. 1674–5, 3. 2. 3.
[6] 'Space is the phantasm of a thing existing without the mind simply' (*De Corpore*, 2. 7. 2).

relate not only to what is actual, but also to what could be put in its place, just as numbers are indifferent to whatever may be being counted. Yet in nature there are no perfectly uniform changes such as are required by the idea of movement which mathematics gives us, any more than there are actual shapes which exactly correspond to those which geometry tells us about. Nevertheless, the actual phenomena of nature are ordered, and must be so, in such a way that nothing ever happens in which the law of continuity (which I introduced . . . [see T5. 46–7]) . . . or any of the other most exact mathematical rules, is ever broken. Far from it: for things could only ever be made intelligible by these rules, which alone are capable—along with those of *harmony* or of perfection, which the true metaphysics provides—of giving us insight into the reasons and intentions of the author of things. In fact the unmanageable multitude of infinite combinations means that when we try to apply metaphysical rules, in the end we get lost and have to stop, just as when we apply mathematical rules to physics. And yet these applications never mislead us, and if there is any mistake after a careful calculation, it is because we can never examine the facts sufficiently closely, so that there is some imperfection in the assumptions. And we are the more capable of carrying this application further, the better we are able to deal with the infinite, as our latest methods have shown. [24] So the utility of mathematical meditations is not in any way diminished by their being ideal, because actual things could never go against their rules; and in fact we can say that this is what the reality of phenomena consists in, and what distinguishes them from dreams. However, mathematicians have no need at all of metaphysical discussions, or to puzzle over the real existence of *points, indivisibles,* the *infinitely small,* or *strict infinities.* . . .

[25] . . . M. Bayle is right to say, with the ancients, that God is a geometer, and that mathematics is a part of the intellectual world, and more suitable than anything else for gaining entry to it. But for myself I believe that within it there is something more. I have suggested elsewhere that there is a calculus more important than those of arithmetic and geometry, and which depends on the *analysis of ideas.* This would be a universal characteristic, whose construction seems to me to be one of the most important things that could be attempted.[7]

---

[7] See Aiton (1985: 91–2), Rescher (1979: 124–5), C. Wilson (1989, ch. 1), for discussion of Leibniz's universal characteristic or 'alphabet of human thought'—a rational language which would enable reasoning to be carried out mechanically like arithmetical calculation.

DRAFT LETTERS FROM LEIBNIZ TO BAYLE (DECEMBER 1702)

Summary of the Text

Bayle's reponse to Leibniz's reply (T16) to note L (T14) was a letter he sent him in October 1702. It must have disappointed Leibniz for it contained little to further their discussion other than these two sentences: 'It seems to me that we cannot really deny the feasibility of your theory as long as we do not clearly understand the substantial basis of the soul and the way in which it can modify itself from one thought to another. Perhaps if we understood that really clearly we would see that nothing is more probable than what you maintain.'

This problem about how the soul can move on from one thought to another is one which Bayle has had throughout (TT10. 5–8; 14. 7–10, 12–16). Leibniz tried again to explain it in two versions of a reply to Bayle which he drafted.

The third of the extracted passages printed here is from a draft later than the first two. It arose out of a conversation Leibniz had with the English philosopher John *Toland, and is of interest as an expression of Leibniz's anti-materialism, and for the light it throws on the spiritual side of his pre-established harmony.

THE TEXT

[A] If your difficulty, sir, now concerns principally only the spontaneous progression of thoughts, I shall not give up hope that it might one day disappear, since everything that is active is in a state of transition, or succession, and I know of nothing in nature which is not so. Otherwise where would change come from? If someone were to say, with some recent philosophers,[1] that only God is active, they must say that God at least is in

---

From the French at GP iii. 66, 68–9, 71–2. For a complete translation of these draft letters, see WF 126–32.

[1] A reference to *Malebranche (see Introduction, Sect. 4).

a spontaneous progression from action to action on the things he created. So such a spontaneous progression is a possibility, and it would then be necessary to prove that it is possible only in God. But why couldn't souls be imitations of God in this? And to tell the truth, if we take away their activity, and therefore the consequences of their activity, or the transition to other actions, I do not see what they have left. But if it *were* said that only God is active, it would be enough for our purposes that the soul or other substance has in it a progression which is spontaneous in all other respects, that is to say that in that instance this spontaneous progression would then come only from God and from itself. And leaving aside that general concurrence of God's, and speaking only of relations between created things, there must be some tendency, or a spontaneous progression, in all substances. It is that force or tendency which I can call by no better name than an *'entelechy', which has been so little regarded. Yet amongst fundamentals there is almost nothing which is more significant or of greater importance, although *Aristotle seems not to have sufficiently well understood, or at least explained, what he called by that name. And so since it seems to me that the soul is allowed to have such spontaneity on some occasions, the theory that it also has it on others is all the more plausible. But in the end it is something more than a theory, as is the maxim which I put in what I wrote, that 'the present is always big with the future', or that 'every substance must express in the present all its future states'.

[B] *Dicaearchus, according to *Cicero, denied that the soul was something substantial, and reduced it to a temperature or modification of matter or of extended mass, rather as did one of the interlocutors in *Plato's *Phaedo*,[2] who said that the soul was a harmony. It seems to me that *Epicurus, *Hobbes, and *Spinoza are of the same opinion. Epicurus allows only the interplay of small bodies. Hobbes reduces everything to body, and explains feeling by reaction, like that of an inflated balloon. And *Spinoza claims that the soul is the idea of the body, so that it becomes like what the shape or the mathematical body is to the physical body. It is in some such way that the *Cartesians think of the souls of animals. But they rightly do not allow them any perception: they see them purely as machines. Our learned Englishman[3] seems also to claim that matter can become able to think, as it can become round, and thus that a certain organization, or a certain shape, can produce thought, and that when that organization is destroyed, thought will cease. But I took the liberty of telling him that thought seems to be of a completely different kind. Even if we

---

[2] *Phaedo*, 85B–86D.   [3] John Toland.

had eyes as penetrating as you like, so as to see the smallest parts of the structure of bodies, I do not see that we would thereby be any further forward. We would find the origin of perception there as little as we find it now in a watch, where the constituent parts of the machine are all visible, or in a mill, where one can even walk around among the wheels. [See also T19. 17.] For the difference between a mill and a more refined machine is only a matter of greater and less. We can understand that a machine could produce the most wonderful things in the world, but never that it might perceive them. Among visible things there is nothing which gets nearer to thought than does an image in a mirror (and brain traces could be no more accurate than that is), but the accuracy of that image doesn't produce any perception in the thing it is in. We do not even come close to it, whatever mechanical theory we make up; we remain infinitely far away from it, as must happen with things which are absolutely heterogeneous, just as a surface, when folded up on itself as often as you like, can never become a body. We can also see that since thought is an action of one thing on itself, it has no place among shapes and motions, which could never provide the basis of a truly internal action. Moreover, there must be simple beings, otherwise there would be no compound beings, or beings by aggregation, which are phenomena rather than substances, and exist (to use the language of *Democritus) by *nomos* [convention] rather than by *phūsis* [nature], that is, notionally, or conceptually, rather than physically. And if there was no change in simple things, there would be none in compound things either, for all their reality consists only in that of their simple things. Now, internal changes in simple things are of the same kind as that which we understand to be in thought, and we can say in general that perception is *the expression of a multitude in a unity*. You have no need, sir, of this clarification of the immateriality of thought, of which you have talked admirably in many places. However, putting these considerations together with my specific theory, it seems to me that the one helps to throw some light on the other.

[C] Before finishing, I will say something with regard to your letter, where you say, sir, that the plausibility of my theory cannot be assessed unless we understand clearly the substantial basis of the soul, and how it can modify itself. I do not know if it is possible to explain the constitution of the soul any better than by saying (1) that it is a simple substance, or what I call a true unity; (2) that this unity nevertheless expresses a multitude, that is, bodies, and that it does so as well as is possible according to its point of view, or its relations; (3) and that therefore it expresses phenomena according to the metaphysico-mathematical laws of nature, according, that is, to the order most befitting to intelligence or reason. From which it follows, finally, (4) that the soul is an imitation of God as far as is possible for a created thing, for like him it is simple and yet also infinite, in that it contains everything implicitly through confused perceptions—though with respect to clear perceptions it is limited, whereas everything is clear to the sovereign substance, from which everything emanates, which is the cause of existence and of order, and is in a word the ultimate reason for things. God contains the universe eminently, and the soul or unity contains it actually, being a central mirror, though active and vital, so to speak. Indeed, we can say that each soul is a world apart, but that all these worlds agree, and represent a different relation to the same phenomena. And this is the most perfect way of multiplying beings as far as possible, and in the best way possible.

18

PRINCIPLES OF NATURE AND GRACE, BASED ON REASON (1714)

Summary of the Text

The 'Principles of Nature and Grace' was written at the same time as the 'Monadology' (T19). It appears to have been meant as a popular introductory and overall account of Leibniz's philosophy of nature and metaphysics. Condensed into its few short paragraphs are references to, and brief accounts of, most of the central features and principles of the philosophy which he had developed over the years since the 'Discourse on Metaphysics' (T1). To begin with, Leibniz speaks at what he calls the 'physical level'. Thus he describes simple substances with their multiplicity of perceptions and their harmony with (Sect. 3) their organic bodies, which are constituted from other substances and with which the whole of nature is full (Sects. 1–4). He outlines the difference between animal and human minds (Sects. 4–5), and the metamorphoses of life and death (Sect. 6). Then, moving from nature up to metaphysics he introduces the principle of sufficient reason (Sect. 7), and (given the application of that principle to the existence of the world (Sect. 8)) God, the 'first reason for things'. The supreme perfection of God has resulted in the world's being the best possible (Sects. 9–10), and in certain laws of motion (Sect. 11). It has also resulted in the mirroring of the whole world by each substance in it (Sect. 12), and in order and harmony amongst the perceptions of all substances (Sect. 13). In the concluding sections (Sects. 14–18) Leibniz discusses the moral relationship of community there is between rational souls such as ourselves and God, and our love for him and the nature of his for us.

THE TEXT

1. A *substance* is a being which is capable of action. It is either simple or composite. A *simple substance* is one which has no parts. A *composite sub-*

From the French at GP vi. 598–606.

stance is a collection of simple substances, or *monads*. *Monas* is a Greek word which means unity, or that which is one. Composites, or bodies, are multiplicities, but simple substances—lives, souls, minds—are unities. And there must be simple substances everywhere, because without simples there would be no composites; and therefore the whole of nature is full of life.

2. Monads, because they have no parts, could never be either made or unmade. They cannot naturally either begin or end, and therefore they last as long as the universe, which will change, but will never be destroyed. They cannot have shapes, because then they would have parts; and therefore one monad in itself, and at a moment, cannot be distinguished from another except by its internal qualities and actions; which can only be its *perceptions* (that is, the representations of the composite, or of what is external, in the simple), or its *appetitions* (its tending to move from one perception to another, that is), which are the principles of change. For the simplicity of a substance does not in any way rule out a multiplicity in the modifications which must exist together in one simple substance; and those modifications must consist in the variety of its relationships to things outside it—like the way in which in a *centre*, or a *point*, although it is completely simple, there are an infinity of angles formed by the lines which meet in it.

3. In nature, everything is full. There are simple substances everywhere, genuinely separated one from another by their own actions, which continually change their relationships. Every simple substance, or individual monad, which forms the centre of a composite substance (an animal, for example) and the principle of its unity, is surrounded by a *mass* made up of an infinity of other monads which constitute the body of that central monad; and in accordance with the ways in which that body is affected, the central monad represents, as in a kind of *centre*, things which are outside it. This *body* is *organic*, when it forms a kind of natural automaton or machine, which is a machine not only in its entirety, but also in its smallest noticeable parts. Because of the plenitude of the world everything is linked, and every body acts to a greater or lesser extent on every other body in proportion to distance, and is affected by it in return. It therefore follows that every monad is a living mirror, or a mirror endowed with internal activity, representing the universe in accordance with its own point of view, and as orderly as the universe itself. The perceptions of monads arise one out of another by the laws of appetite, or of the *final causes of good and evil* (which are prominent perceptions, orderly or disorderly), just as changes in bodies or in external phenomena arise one from

another by the laws of *efficient causes*, of motions, that is. Thus there is perfect *harmony* between the perceptions of the monad and the motions of bodies, pre-established from the outset, between the system of efficient causes and that of final causes. And it is in that harmony that the agreement or physical union between the soul and body consists, without either of them being able to change the laws of the other.

4. Each monad, together with its own body, makes up a living substance. Thus not only is there life everywhere, together with limbs or organs, but there are infinite levels of life among monads, some of which are dominant over others to greater or lesser extents. But when the organs of a monad are set up in such a way that by means of them the impressions which they receive, and consequently the perceptions which represent them, stand out more clearly and are more distinct (as, for example, when rays of light are focused by means of the shape of the humours of the eye, and so operate with more force), this can amount to a *feeling*, which is to say a perception accompanied by a *memory*—that is, of which a certain echo remains for a long time and makes itself heard in appropriate circumstances. A living thing of this kind is called an *animal*, since its monad is called a *soul*. And when that soul is at the level of *reason*, it is something more sublime, and we count it as a mind, as will be explained shortly. But sometimes animals are at the level of simple living things, and their souls at the level of simple monads. This is when their perceptions are not sufficiently distinct to be remembered, as happens during a profound dreamless sleep, or during a black-out. But when perceptions in animals have become entirely confused they will necessarily redevelop, for reasons that I shall give shortly (paragraph 12). Thus it is important to make a distinction between *perception*, which is the internal state of a monad which represents external things, and *apperception*, which is *consciousness*, or the reflective knowledge of that internal state. Apperception is not given to all souls, and is not given to particular souls all the time. It was for the lack of this distinction that the *Cartesians went wrong, by regarding perceptions which are not perceived as nothing, just as people regard imperceptible bodies as nothing. And this is also what made those same Cartesians think that only minds are monads, that there are no souls of animals, and still less any other *principles of life*. The Cartesians offended too much against people's ordinary beliefs by refusing all feeling to animals; but at the same time they agreed too much with popular prejudices by confusing a *long stupor* arising from a great confusion of perceptions with *death in the strict sense*, in which all perception would cease. This confirmed the ill-founded opinion of the destruction of certain souls, and also the mistaken opinion

of certain so-called free-thinkers who have denied the immortality of our own.

5. There is a connectedness between the perceptions of animals which has some resemblance to reason. But it is grounded only in the memory of *facts* or effects, and not at all in the knowledge of *causes*. That is what happens when a dog runs away from the stick with which it was beaten, because memory represents to it the pain it was caused. In fact human beings, to the extent that they are empirical—which is to say in three quarters of what they do—act just like animals. For example, we expect it will be daylight tomorrow, because we have always experienced it that way; only an astronomer foresees it rationally. And even his prediction will one day prove wrong, when the cause of daylight, which is not eternal, ceases. But *true reasoning* depends on necessary or eternal truths like those of logic, numbers, and geometry, which make indubitable connections between ideas, and conclusions which are inevitable. Animals in which such conclusions are never perceived are called *brutes*; but those which recognize such necessary truths are what are rightly called *rational animals*, and their souls are called *minds*. These souls are capable of acts of reflection, and of considering what we call myself, substance, soul, or mind: in a word, things and truths which are immaterial. And this is what renders us capable of science, or of demonstrable knowledge.

6. The researches of the moderns have shown, and reason confirms, that the living things the organs of which we know, that is to say plants and animals, do not come from putrefaction or from chaos, as the ancients believed, but from *pre-formed* seeds, and therefore from the transformation of pre-existing living beings. There are little animals in the seeds of big ones, and through the process of conception they take on a new casing which becomes their own, and which gives them the means to feed and to grow, so as to pass onto a larger stage, and so propagate the larger animal. The souls of human spermatic animals are not rational, and do not become so until conception determines a human nature for such animals. And just as animals in general do not entirely originate with their conception or *generation*, so they do not entirely come to an end in what we call their *death*; for it is only reasonable that what does not begin naturally should have no end in the order of nature either. And so, throwing off their cloak or tattered coating, they merely return to a more subtle stage on which nevertheless they can be just as perceptible and orderly as they were on the larger one. And what we have just said about large animals applies also to the generation and death of those spermatic animals themselves; that is to say, they have grown up out of other spermatic animals smaller

still, in relation to which they would count as large. For in nature, everything goes on to infinity. Thus not only souls, but even animals, are ingenerable and imperishable; they are only unfolded and refolded, recovered and stripped bare, transformed. Souls never leave behind their whole body, and never pass from one body to another which is entirely new to them. There is therefore no *metempsychosis,* but there is *metamorphosis.* Animals change, merely taking on and leaving off parts. In the process of nutrition this happens little by little, by tiny, imperceptible steps, but continually. It happens all at once, very obviously, but also very rarely, in conception or in death, when they gain or lose a great deal all at once.

7. So far we have spoken only at the level of *physical* inquiry; now we must move up to the *metaphysical,* by making use of the *great principle,* not very widely used, which says that *nothing comes about without a sufficient reason;* that is, that nothing happens without its being possible for someone who understands things well enough to provide a reason sufficient to determine why it is as it is and not otherwise. Given that principle, the first question we are entitled to ask will be *why is there something rather than nothing?* After all, a nothing is simpler and easier than a something. And moreover, even if we assume that things have to exist, we must be able to give a reason *why they have to exist as they are,* and not otherwise.

8. Now, the sufficient reason for the existence of the universe can never be found in the series of contingent things, in bodies and their representations in souls, that is; because matter in itself is indifferent to motion or rest, and to this motion or that. Therefore we could never find in matter a reason for motion, and still less that for any particular motion. And since any motion which is in matter at present comes from a previous motion, and that too from a previous one, we are no further forward if we go on and on as far as we like: the same question will still remain. Therefore the sufficient reason, which has no need of any further reason, must lie outside that series of contingent things, and must be found in a substance which is the cause of the series: it must be a necessary being, which carries the reason for its existence within itself, otherwise we still would not have a sufficient reason at which we can stop. And that final reason for things is what we call God.

9. This simple, primal substance must contain eminently the perfections which are contained in the derivative substances which are its effects. Thus, it will have perfect power, knowledge, and will; in other words, it will have omnipotence, omniscience, and supreme goodness. And as *justice,* taken quite generally, is nothing other than goodness in conformity

with reason, clearly God must possess supreme justice. The Reason which made things exist through itself also makes them depend on itself for their existence and operation, and whatever perfection they possess they continually receive from it; but the imperfections which they retain derive from the essential and inherent limitation of a created thing.

10. It follows from the supreme perfection of God that in producing the universe he chose the best possible design, in which there was the greatest variety, together with the greatest order. Ground, location, and time were used to the greatest advantage: the maximum effect was produced by the simplest possible methods. Created things were given the highest levels of power, knowledge, happiness, and goodness which the universe would allow. For in the understanding of God all possible things put forward their claims to existence in proportion to their perfections; therefore the outcome of all those claims must be an actual world which is the most perfect possible. If this were not so, it would not be possible to give any reason why things have gone as they have, rather than otherwise.

11. The supreme goodness of God made him choose in particular the *laws of motion* which were the most appropriate, and which fitted best with abstract or metaphysical reasoning. They conserve the same quantity of total or absolute force, or of action, the same quantity of relative force, or of reaction, and finally the same quantity of directive force. And what is more, action is always equal to reaction, and the complete effect is always equivalent to the total cause. And what is striking is that these laws of motion which have been discovered in our own time—and some of them discovered by myself—cannot be explained by the mere consideration of *efficient causes*, or of matter. For I have found that we have to bring in *final causes*, and that these laws do not depend on the *principle of necessity*, as logical, arithmetical, and geometrical truths do, but on the *principle of compatibility*, the choices of wisdom, that is. For anyone who looks deeply into things, this is one of the most successful and most evident proofs of the existence of God.

12. It follows from the perfection of the Supreme Maker not only that the order of the entire universe is the most perfect that could be, but also that every living mirror which represents the universe according to its own point of view, that is to say every monad, every substantial centre, must have its perceptions and its appetites ordered in the best way that remains compatible with all the rest. And from that it follows also that souls, that is to say the most dominant monads—or rather the animals themselves—cannot fail to wake up from that state of stupor into which death, or some other accident, might put them.

13. For everything in things is ordered once and for all with as much regularity and interconnection as possible, because the Supreme Wisdom and Goodness cannot work except perfectly harmoniously. The present is therefore big with the future, the future could be read in the past, the distant is expressed in the close at hand. The beauty of the universe could be seen in each individual soul, if we could only unfold all that is enfolded in it, and which will become perceptible only as it develops over time. But just as each of the soul's distinct perceptions involves an infinity of confused perceptions which encapsulate the entire universe, so the soul itself doesn't know the things of which it has a perception except in so far as it has a perception which is distinct and revealed. And the soul is perfect to the extent that it possesses distinct perceptions. Every soul knows infinity, knows everything, but confusedly. Just as when I walk beside the sea and I hear the great noise that it makes I hear, though without distinguishing them, the individual sound of every wave out of which that total sound is made up, so in the same way our confused perceptions are the outcome of the impressions which the whole universe makes on us. It is the same with each monad. Only God has a distinct knowledge of everything, because he is its origin. It has been very well said that it is as if God is centred everywhere; but God's circumference is nowhere, because to him everything is immediately present, at no distance from that centre.

14. As far as the rational soul or the *mind* is concerned, there is something more than there is in monads, or in simple souls. The rational soul is not only a mirror of the universe or created things, but also an image of the divinity. The mind not only has a perception of the works of God, but it is even capable of producing something which resembles them, although on a smaller scale. For our soul (to say nothing of the wonders of dreams, in which we invent without difficulty—but also involuntarily—things which we would have to think about for a long time before we could come up with them while awake) is also architectonic in its voluntary actions, and in discovering the sciences in accordance with which God has ordered things (by *weight, measure, number*, etc.). The soul imitates in its own sphere, and in the little world in which it is permitted to operate, what God does in the world at large.

15. That is why all minds, whether of men or of spirits, because by virtue of reason and of eternal truths they enter into a kind of community with God, are members of the City of God; that is to say, they are members of the most perfect state, formed and governed by the greatest and best of monarchs, in which there is no crime without punishment, no good act without its appropriate reward, and all in all the highest level of

virtue and goodness possible. And all of this is achieved, not by a disturbance of nature, as if what God had laid down for souls might interfere
with the laws of bodies, but through the very order of natural things itself,
in virtue of the harmony which has been pre-established from all time
between the kingdoms of nature and of grace, between God as architect
and God as monarch, in such a way that nature itself leads on to grace, and
grace perfects nature while at the same time making use of it.

16. Thus, although reason cannot tell us in detail about the great future
that awaits us—a task that is reserved for revelation—that same reason can
assure us that things have been done in a way which is better than we could
wish. Since God is the most perfect and the happiest, and therefore the
most lovable, of substances, and since *true pure love* consists in being in a
state which enables one to take pleasure in the perfections and the happiness of the person one loves, it follows that when God is its object love
must give us the greatest pleasure of which we are capable.

17. And it is easy to love God as we should, if we know him in the way I
have said. Because although God is certainly not perceptible to our external senses, that does not prevent him from being very lovable, and from
giving very great pleasure. We know what pleasure honours give to
people, even though they do not consist in qualities detectable by our
external senses. Martyrs, and fanatics (although in this latter case their
emotion is uncontrolled), show what the pleasures of the mind can do.
And moreover, the pleasures of the senses themselves come down in the
end to intellectual pleasures which are known in a confused way. Music
can charm us, even though its beauty consists only in the interrelations
between numbers, and in the count, which we are not aware of but which
the soul nevertheless makes, of the beats or vibrations of the sounding
body, which coincide at certain intervals. The pleasures which sight
derives from proportion are of the same kind; and those which the other
senses produce will come down to something similar, even though we
cannot explain them so clearly.

18. In fact we can say that God's love already permits us to enjoy a fore-
taste of our future happiness. And although that love is disinterested, it
provides in itself our greatest good and our greatest benefit, even if we do
not look for it, and think only of the pleasure we receive, without regard to
the advantages it provides. For it gives us perfect confidence in the goodness of our creator and lord, and that provides us with genuine tranquillity
of mind; we are committed to patience not by force, as with the Stoics, but
by present contentment, which itself assures us of a happy future. And
quite apart from our present pleasure, nothing could be more useful to us

for the future, for here too the love of God satisfies all our hopes. It leads us in the path of supreme happiness, because in virtue of the perfect order established in the universe everything is made the best possible, both for the general good and for the greatest particular good of those who are aware of it and who are content with the government of God. In reality supreme happiness, whatever *beatific vision* or knowledge of God it may be accompanied by, can never be complete, because God is infinite and so can never be known entirely. Thus our happiness will never consist, and should not consist, in a full enjoyment in which there is nothing left to desire and which stupefies our minds, but instead in a perpetual progression towards new pleasures and new perfections.

19

MONADOLOGY (1714)

Summary of the Text

The 'Monadology' was written when Leibniz was nearing 70, at about the same time as the similarly synoptic 'Principles of Nature and Grace' (T18). It is, though, perhaps less popular, less easily accessible than it. When he first encountered it, it struck Bertrand Russell as a 'fantastic fairy tale, coherent perhaps, but wholly arbitrary' (B. Russell 1900/1937, p. xiii). But, as he came to recognize, it loses some of this appearance when approached with some prior appreciation and understanding of Leibniz's case from a reading of the 'Discourse on Metaphysics' (T1) and Leibniz's correspondence with Arnauld (T2). The truth is, it stands as a very elegant, aesthetically pleasing, and systematic summary of the central tenets of Leibniz's metaphysics as they were at the end of his life.

Leibniz begins by characterizing what are now at the centre of his metaphysics—'monads' (see the mental substance theory (b), in Introduction, Sect. 2), non-extended, simple, 'atoms of nature', or souls. They are indivisible (Sect. 3), 'windowless' (and so with changes that arise from an internal principle (Sects. 7–11, 18; see Introduction, Sects. 2, 4)), and they are of various kinds, according as how heightened and distinct their perceptions are (Sects. 19–30; see Introduction, Sect. 2) and whether, like ours, they are capable of reflective acts. Our minds or souls are capable of reasoning too (Sect. 30), and Leibniz gives an account of its principles (of contradiction and of sufficient reason), and of the distinction between necessary and contingent truths (Sects. 31–7). Leibniz then turns to God. This necessary substance is the ultimate reason of things, a perfect being from which all else derives its very existence and perfections (Sects. 38–48). The interconnected harmonious world he created is the best possible (Sects. 53–60). Each part of it dense with created life (Sects. 61–70), the whole is reflected by each individual monad (Sect. 77), and birth and death are merely growth and diminution (Sects. 71–8).

Leibniz concludes by speaking of two harmonies: one between body and soul, or

From the French at GP vi. 608–23. The numbers in parentheses which follow some of the sections are references Leibniz made to various sections of his *Theodicy* (1710). Leibniz's manuscript was headed 'The Principles of Philosophy'; the title 'Monadology' is that of an 18th-century editor.

mind (Sects. 78–81; see Introduction, Sect. 5); the other between the physical Kingdom of Nature (the world as studied by natural philosophy), and the moral Kingdom of Grace (Sects. 82–90; see Introduction, Sect. 6). This latter consists of God as monarch, and minds or rational souls, which mirror not only the natural world, but also, and to an extent, its creator. To him they are related as subjects, or even as children to a father.

THE TEXT

1. The *monad*, of which we will be speaking here, is nothing but a simple substance, which enters into composites; *simple*, meaning without parts. (10)

2. And there must be simple substances, because there are composites; for the composite is nothing but a collection, or **aggregatum*, of simples.

3. Now, in that which has no parts, neither extension, nor shape, nor divisibility is possible. And so monads are the true atoms of nature; in a word, the elements of things.

4. There is also no dissolution to be afraid of, and no conceivable way in which a simple substance could come to an end naturally. (89)

5. For the same reason, there is no way in which a simple substance could begin naturally, since it could never be formed by composition.

6. Thus we can say that monads can only ever begin or end all at once: that is, they can only ever begin by creation, and end by annihilation; whereas what is composite can begin and end bit by bit.

7. There is also no way in which it could make sense for a monad to be altered or changed internally by any other created thing. Because there is nothing to rearrange within a monad, and there is no conceivable internal motion in it which could be excited, directed, increased, or diminished, in the way that it can in a composite, where there is change among the parts. Monads have no windows, through which anything could come in or go out. And accidents cannot detach themselves and stroll about outside of substances, as the *Scholastics' sensible species used to; so neither substance nor accident can come into a monad from outside.

8. Nevertheless, monads must have some qualities, otherwise they would not even be beings. Moreover, if simple substances did not differ in their qualities, there would be no way of detecting any change in things. Because what is in the composite can only come from its simple ingredi-

ents, and if monads had no qualities they would be indistinguishable one from another, given that they also do not differ in quantity. Therefore, assuming a plenum, each place could only ever receive through motion the equivalent of what it had had previously, and so one state of things would be indistinguishable from another. (Pref.)

9. Indeed, every monad must be different from every other. Because in nature there are never two beings that are perfectly alike, and between which it is not possible to discover some difference which is internal, or founded on an intrinsic denomination.

10. I also take it for granted that every created thing is subject to change, and therefore the created monad as well; and indeed that such change is continual in every one.

11. It follows from what we have just said that natural changes in a monad come from an *internal principle*, since no external causes could ever have an influence into its interior. (396, 400)

12. But we must also accept that in addition to this principle of change *there is a detailed specification of the changes*, which as it were determines a simple substance's species and variety.

13. This detailed specification must amount to a multiplicity within a unity, or within what is simple. Because since every natural change happens by degrees, something changes, and something else stays the same; therefore although there are no parts in a simple substance, there must be a plurality of states, or of relationships.

14. The transitory state which incorporates and represents a multitude within a unity or within a simple substance is nothing but what we call *perception*—which must be carefully distinguished from apperception or consciousness, as will become clear in what follows. That is where the *Cartesians went badly wrong, because they regarded perceptions which are not apperceived as nothing. That also made them think that only minds were monads, and that there were no souls of animals or other *entelechies; and like uneducated people they confused a long stupor with death in the strict sense, which also led them into the *Scholastic error of believing in souls which are entirely detached, as well as confirming misguided minds in a belief in the mortality of souls.

15. The action of the internal principle which brings about change, or the passage from one perception to another, can be called *appetition*. In fact appetite cannot always attain in its entirety the whole of the perception towards which it tends, but it always obtains some part of it, and attains new perceptions.

16. We ourselves experience multiplicity in a simple substance when

we find that the smallest perception we can apperceive incorporates some variety in its object. Thus everyone who accepts that the soul is a simple substance should accept this multiplicity in the monad, and M. Bayle should not have found any difficulty in it, as he did in the article 'Rorarius' in his *Dictionary* [see TT10. 8; 16. 7–10].

17. Moreover, everyone must admit that *perception*, and everything that depends on it, is *inexplicable by mechanical principles*, by shapes and motions, that is. Imagine there were a machine which by its structure produced thought, feeling, and perception; we can imagine it as being enlarged while maintaining the same relative proportions, to the point where we could go inside it, as we would go into a mill. But if that were so, when we went in we would find nothing but pieces which push one against another, and never anything to account for a perception. Therefore, we must look for it in the simple substance, and not in the composite, or in a machine. And that is all we can find within a simple substance, namely perceptions and their changes; and that is all that the *internal actions* of simple substances can consist in. (Pref.)

18. We could give the name *entelechy* to all simple substances or created monads, because they have within them a certain perfection; there is a kind of self-sufficiency which makes them sources of their own internal actions, or incorporeal automata, as it were. (87)

19. If we want to call anything that has *perceptions* and *appetites* in the general sense that I have just explained a *soul*, then all simple substances or created monads could be called *souls*. But as feeling is something more than a simple perception, I think that the general name of *monad* or *entelechy* is adequate for simple substances which have that and nothing more, and that we should call *souls* only those which have perceptions which are more distinct and accompanied by memory.

20. For we experience within ourselves a state in which we can remember nothing and have no distinct perception, such as when we fall into a faint, or when we are overtaken by a deep sleep with no dreams. In that state the soul is not discernibly different from a simple monad; but as that state is not lasting, and it recovers from it, the soul is something more. (64)

21. But it does not at all follow that a simple substance therefore has no perception at all. Indeed that could not be so, for reasons given above. Because it cannot come to an end, it also cannot continue to exist without being in some state; and that is nothing else but its perception. But when there is a great multiplicity of small perceptions, in which there is nothing distinct, we are overcome; as, for instance, when you turn round continu-

ally in the same direction several times together, which produces a dizziness which can cause you to faint and prevents you from distinguishing anything. Death can put animals into that state for a time.

22. And since every present state of a simple substance is a natural consequence of its previous one, so that the present is big with the future (360) . . .

23. . . . then since as soon as you recover from the faint you *apperceive* your perceptions, it clearly follows that you were having perceptions immediately before, even though you did not apperceive them. Because a perception can only arise naturally from another perception, much as a motion can only arise naturally from another motion. (401–3)

24. We can see from this that if we had nothing distinct in our perceptions, nothing heightened, or of a stronger flavour, so to speak, we would be in a permanent stupor. And that is the condition of the completely naked monad.

25. And we can see that nature has given heightened perceptions to animals by the care it has taken to provide them with organs which bring together a number of rays of light or of undulations in the air, thus making them more effective by combining them. There is something approaching this in the case of scent, taste, and touch, and perhaps in numerous other senses which we are not aware of. I shall explain shortly how what happens in the soul represents what goes on in the organs.

26. Memory provides souls with a kind of *sequencing* which mimics reason, but which must be distinguished from it. Thus we see that through the representations of their memory animals which are struck by the perception of something of which they have had a similar perception before are led to expect whatever was connected to that previous perception, and are therefore taken with feelings similar to those which they had on the previous occasion. For example, when you show a stick to a dog, it remembers the pain it was caused by it, and it whines, or runs away. (Prelim. Disc. 65)

27. The powerful imagination, which strikes them and moves them in this way, comes from either the size or the multiplicity of the preceding perceptions. Often a powerful impression achieves all at once the same effect as a long *habituation*, or the repetition of a large number of lesser perceptions.

28. Human beings operate in the same way as animals to the extent that the sequencing of their perceptions is brought about only by the principle of memory, like the Empirical physicians, who have mere technique without theory. And we are all merely empirical in three quarters of what

we do. For example, when we expect there will be daylight tomorrow on the grounds that it has always been like that up to now, we act like the Empirics. Only the astronomer believes it on the basis of reason.

29. But the knowledge of necessary and eternal truths is what distinguishes us from mere animals and gives us *reason* and science, raising us to the knowledge of ourselves and of God. And that is what in us is called a *rational soul*, or a *mind*.

30. And it is by the knowledge of necessary truths, and by the abstractions they involve, that we are raised to *acts of reflection*, which make us aware of what we call *myself*, and make us think of this or that thing as in *ourselves*. And in this way, by thinking of ourselves, we think of being, of substance, of simples and composites, of the immaterial—and, by realizing that what is limited in us is limitless in him, of God himself. And so these *acts of reflection* provide the principal objects of our reasonings. (Pref.)

31. Our reasonings are founded on two great *principles: the principle of contradiction*, in virtue of which we judge to be false anything that involves contradiction, and as true whatever is opposed or contradictory to what is false. (44, 169)

32. And that *of sufficient reason*, in virtue of which we hold that no fact could ever be true or existent, no statement correct, unless there were a sufficient reason why it was thus and not otherwise—even though those reasons will usually not be knowable by us. (44, 196)

33. There are also two kinds of *truth*: those of *reasoning*, and those of *fact*. Truths of reasoning are necessary, and their opposite is impossible; those of fact are contingent, and their opposite is possible. When a truth is necessary, the reason for it can be found by analysis, by resolving it into simpler ideas and truths until we arrive at the basic ones. (170, 174, 189, 280–2, 367, Summary, obj. 3)

34. Thus mathematicians use analysis to reduce speculative *theorems* and practical *canons* to *definitions, axioms*, and *postulates*.

35. And finally there are the simple ideas, which cannot be given a definition; and there are axioms and postulates—in a word, *basic principles*, which can never be proved, but which also have no need of proof: these are *identical propositions*, the opposite of which contains an explicit contradiction.

36. But a *sufficient reason* must also be found for *contingent truths*, or *truths of fact*—for the series of things which fills the universe of created things, that is. Here the resolution into particular reasons could be continued endlessly, because of the immense variety of things in nature, and

because of the infinite divisibility of bodies. There are an infinite number of shapes and of motions, present and past, which play a part in the efficient cause of my present writing; and there are an infinite number of tiny inclinations and dispositions of my soul, present and past, which play a part in its final cause. (36, 37, 44, 45, 49, 52, 121, 122, 337, 340, 344)

37. But since all this detail only involves other prior and more detailed contingencies, each one of which also stands in need of a similar analysis in order to give an explanation of it, we are no further forward: the sufficient or final reason must lie outside the succession or *series* in this detailed specification of contingencies, however infinite it may be.

38. And that is why the final reason for things must be in a necessary substance, in which the detailed specification of changes is contained only eminently, as in their source; and that is what we call God. (7)

39. Now, since this substance is a sufficient reason for all this detail, which is interconnected throughout, *there is only one God, and that God is enough*.

40. We can also see that this supreme substance, which is unique, universal, and necessary (because there is nothing outside it which is independent of it, and it is a straightforward consequence of possible being), must be incapable of limits, and must contain fully as much reality as is possible.

41. From which it follows that God is absolutely perfect, since *perfection* is nothing but the total amount of positive reality taken in the precise sense, leaving aside the limitations or boundaries of things that have them. And there, in something which has no boundaries—in God, that is—perfection is absolutely infinite. (Pref. 22)

42. It also follows that created things have their perfections from the influence of God, but that they have their imperfections from their own natures, which are necessarily bounded. For that is what distinguishes them from God. (20, 27–31, 153, 167, 377) This original imperfection of created things is shown by the natural inertia of bodies. (30, 380; Summary, obj. 5)

43. And what is more, God is the source not only of existences, but also of essences, in so far as they are real; he is the source of what reality there is among possibilities. This is because God's understanding is the realm of eternal truths, or of the ideas on which they depend, and without God there would be no reality among possibilities: not only would nothing exist, but nothing would even be possible. (20)

44. Because it is clear that if there is any reality among essences or possibilities, or among eternal truths, that reality must be grounded in something actually existent; therefore it must be grounded in the existence of

nec̄: if poss → necc

the necessary being, in whom essence includes existence, that is, for whom being possible is sufficient for being actual. (184, 189, 335)

45. Thus only God, or the necessary being, has this privilege: that he must exist if he is possible. And as nothing can prevent the possibility of something which contains no boundaries, no negation and therefore no contradiction, that in itself is enough for us to perceive the existence of God a priori. We have also proved his existence by means of the reality of eternal truths, and we have now also proved it a posteriori, because contingent things exist, and their final or sufficient reason could only be found in the necessary being, which has the reason for its existence within itself.

46. However, we should not, as some have done, imagine that because eternal truths are dependent on God they must be arbitrary and dependent on his will—as *Descartes seems to have thought, and after him M. *Poiret. That is true only of contingent truths, the principle of which is *suitability*, or the choice of what is *best*; by contrast, necessary truths depend solely on God's understanding, of which they are the internal object. (180, 184, 185, 335, 351, 380)

47. Thus God alone is the primary unity, or the original simple substance, of which all created or derivative monads are products. They are generated by the continual flashes of divinity, so to speak, which pour out from moment to moment, and they are bounded by the receptivity of the created thing, to which limitation is essential. (382–91, 395, 398)

48. In God there is *power*, which is the source of everything; there is *knowledge*, which contains all ideas; and finally there is *will*, which produces changes or developments in accordance with the principle of what is best. And these are what correspond to what in created monads constitute the subject, or base, the faculty of perception, and the appetitive faculty. But in God these attributes are absolutely infinite or perfect, whereas in created monads or *entelechies* (or *perfection-havers*, as Ermolao *Barbaro translated the word) they are only limitations, proportional to the perfection they possess. (7, 87, 149, 150)

49. A created thing is said to be *active* externally in so far as it has perfection, and to be *passive* towards another in so far as it is imperfect. Thus we attribute *activity* to a monad in so far as it has distinct perceptions, and *passivity* in so far as it has confused ones. (32, 66, 386)

50. And one created thing is more perfect than another to the extent that we find within it what serves to explain a priori what happens in the other; and that is what makes us say that it acted on the other.

51. But in simple substances this influence of one monad over another

is only *ideal*, and it can have its effect only through the intervention of God; in the sense that in God's ideas one monad requires of God, and with reason, that he take account of it when he organizes the others at the very beginning of things. Because, as one created monad could never have a physical influence over the interior of another, this is the only way in which one monad can depend on another. (9, 54, 65, 66, 201, Summary, obj. 3)

52. And this is the way in which there is mutual action and passivity between created things. God, in comparing two simple substances, finds in each of them reasons which oblige him to adapt the other one to it, and as a result the one which is active in certain respects is passive with regard to a different point of comparison. It is *active* in so far as what can be clearly understood in it serves to explain what happens in the other; and it is *passive* in so far as the explanation for what happens in it is to be found in what is known distinctly in the other. (66)

53. Now, since there are an infinite number of possible universes in the ideas of God, but only one can exist, there must be a sufficient reason for the choice God makes, which determines him to choose one of them rather than another. (8, 10, 44, 173, 196f., 225, 414–16)

54. And that reason can only be found in the *suitability*, or the degrees of perfection, that these worlds contain; each possible world being entitled to claim existence in proportion to the perfection it embodies. (74, 130, 167, 201, 345f., 350, 352, 354)

55. And that is the reason for the existence of the best, which God's wisdom brings him to know, his goodness brings him to choose, and his power brings him to produce. (8, 78, 80, 84, 119, 204, 206, 208, Summary, objs. 1, 8)

56. Now, this *interconnection*, or this adapting of all created things to each one, and of each one to all the others, means that each simple substance has relationships which express all the others, and that it is therefore a perpetual living mirror of the universe. (130, 360)

57. And just as the same town when seen from different sides will seem quite different, and is as it were multiplied *perspectivally*, the same thing happens here: because of the infinite multitude of simple substances it is as if there were as many different universes; but they are all perspectives on the same one, according to the different *point of view* of each monad. (147)

58. And that is the way to obtain the greatest possible variety, but with all the order there could be; i.e. it is the way to obtain as much perfection as could be. (120, 124, 241f., 214, 243, 275)

59. It is, moreover, only this theory (which I venture to say has now been demonstrated) which shows up the greatness of God in an appropriate way. This is what M. Bayle recognized when he raised objections in his *Dictionary* (the article on Rorarius), where he was even tempted to say that I had accorded too much to God, in fact more than is possible [T14. 3]. But he was unable to bring forward any reason why this universal harmony, which means that every substance exactly expresses every other through the relationships it has with them, was impossible.

60. And what is more we can see from the account I have just given the a priori reasons why things could not have gone otherwise. Because, in organizing the whole, God has regard to every part, and specifically to every monad; and since a monad is representative in its nature, nothing could restrict it to representing only a part of things. But it is of course true that this representation of the details of the whole universe is confused, and can only be distinct with respect to a small part of things, namely those which are either closest or largest in relation to each monad. Otherwise every monad would be divine. It is not in the object of their knowledge, but in its modification, that monads are bounded. They all reach confusedly to infinity, to everything; but they are limited and differentiated by their level of distinct perception.

61. And in this respect composites are analogous to simples. Everything is full, which means that all matter is interlinked. In such a plenum, any movement must have an effect on distant bodies in proportion to their distance. Each body is affected by the bodies which are in contact with it, and in some way or other it feels the effects of everything that happens to them; but in addition, by means of those bodies with which it is in direct contact, it also feels the effects of all the bodies which they are in contact with, so that such communication extends indefinitely. As a result, every body feels the effects of everything that happens in the universe, so that he who sees everything could read off from each one what is happening everywhere; and indeed, because he could see in its present state what is distant both in space and in time, he could read also what has happened and what will happen. 'All things conspire', as *Hippocrates said. But a soul can only read within itself what is represented in it distinctly; it could never develop all at once everything that it enfolds, because it goes on to infinity.

62. Thus, although each created monad represents the whole universe, it represents more distinctly the body which is particularly assigned to it, and of which it forms the entelechy. And as that body expresses the whole universe through the interconnection of all matter in the plenum, the soul

also represents the entire universe by representing the body which particularly belongs to it. (400)

63. The body belonging to a monad, which is either its entelechy or its soul, makes up together with an entelechy what we can call a *living thing*, and together with a soul what we call an *animal*. Now that body of a living thing or animal is always organic, because since every monad is a mirror of the universe in its own way, and since the universe is regulated in a perfectly orderly manner, there must also be order within that which represents it, i.e. in the perceptions of the soul. And therefore also in the body by means of which the universe is represented in the soul. (403)

64. Thus every organic body of a living being is a kind of divine machine or natural automaton, which infinitely surpasses any artificial automaton, because a man-made machine is not a machine in every one of its parts. For example, the tooth of a brass cog-wheel has parts or fragments which to us are no longer anything artificial, and which no longer have anything which relates them to the use for which the cog was intended, and thereby marks them out as parts of a machine. But nature's machines—living bodies, that is—are machines even in their smallest parts, right down to infinity. That is what makes the difference between nature and art, that is, between the divine art and our own. (134, 146, 194, 403)

65. And the creator of nature was able to carry out this divine and infinitely marvellous workmanship because every portion of matter is not only divisible to infinity, as the ancients realized, but is actually subdivided without end, every part into smaller parts, each one of which has its own motion. Without this it would be impossible for each portion of matter to express the whole universe. (Prelim. Disc. 70; 195)

66. And from this we can see that there is a world of creatures—of living things and animals, entelechies, and souls—in the smallest part of matter.

67. Every portion of matter can be thought of as a garden full of plants, or as a pond full of fish. But every branch of the plant, every part of the animal, and every drop of its vital fluids, is another such garden, or another such pond.

68. And although the earth and the air in between the plants in the garden, and the water in between the fish in the pond, are not themselves plants or fish, they do nevertheless contain others, though usually they are so tiny as to be imperceptible to us.

69. Thus there is no uncultivated ground in the universe; nothing barren, nothing dead. There is no chaos, and all confusion is merely

apparent: rather in the way that there might seem to be confusion in a pond seen from a distance, when you can only see some confused movement, a heaving, so to speak, of the fish, but can't make out the fish themselves. (Pref.)

70. We can see from this that every living body has a dominant entelechy, which in an animal is its soul; but the parts of that living body are full of other living things—plants, animals—each one of which also has its entelechy or dominant soul.

71. But it should not be thought—as some who have misunderstood my ideas have thought—that every soul has a mass or portion of matter which is its own and which is assigned to it for ever, and therefore that every soul has other living things which are inferior to it, destined always to be in its service. Because all bodies are in a perpetual state of flux, like rivers, and parts are constantly coming into them and going out.

72. Thus the soul changes its body only in stages, a little at a time, and it is never suddenly stripped of all its organs. There is therefore frequent metamorphosis among animals, but never *metempsychosis, or transmigration of souls. There are also no *souls* which are completely *detached* from matter, and no *spirits* without bodies. Only God is completely removed from matter. (90, 124)

73. And it is also because of this that there is never either complete generation or total death in the strict sense, which consists in the detaching of the soul. What we call *generation* is unfolding and growth; just as what we call *death* is enfolding and diminution.

74. Philosophers have had great difficulties over the origin of forms, entelechies, or souls. Recently, however, we have discovered through careful investigations carried out on plants, insects, and animals that nature's organic bodies are never produced from chaos or from putrefaction, but always from seeds, in which there is without doubt already some *pre-formation. As a result, we have come to see that not only was there an organic body already there before conception, but there was also a soul in that body: in a word, there was the animal itself. Through the process of conception that animal was merely committed to a great transformation so as to become an animal of a different kind. And indeed we see something similar to this in cases other than generation, such as when maggots turn into flies, or when caterpillars turn into butterflies. (Pref.; 86, 89, 90, 187, 188, 397, 403)

75. These *animals*, of which some come to be raised to the level of larger animals through the process of conception, we can call *spermatic*. But even those among them which remain within their own kind, i.e. the

majority of them, are born, reproduce themselves, and are destroyed, just like the larger animals. It is only a small number of the elect who move up onto a larger stage.

76. But that is only half the story. From this I realized that if the animal has no natural beginning, it can have no natural end either, and that not only can there be no generation, but also no complete destruction, or death in the strict sense. And this a posteriori reasoning drawn from observation fits in perfectly with the a priori principles I derived above. (90)

77. Thus we can say that not only is the soul—the mirror of an indestructible universe—indestructible, but so too is the animal itself; even though its machine may often come to an end in part, and throw off or take on organic coating.

78. These principles gave me a way of providing a natural explanation of the union, or the conformity, of the soul with the organic body. The soul follows out its own laws, just as the body too follows its own. They are in agreement in virtue of the fact that since they are all representations of the same universe, there is a *pre-established harmony* between all substances. (Pref.; 340, 352, 353, 358)

79. Souls act according to the laws of final causes, through appetition, ends, and means. Bodies act according to the laws of efficient causes, or of motions. And these two realms, that of efficient causes and that of final causes, are in mutual harmony.

80. Descartes recognized that souls can never give force to bodies, because there is always the same quantity of force in matter.[1] He believed, though, that the soul could change the directions of bodies. But that was because in his day the law of nature which maintains the conservation of the same total direction in matter was unknown. If he had seen it, he would have ended up with my system of pre-established harmony. (Pref.; 22, 59–61, 63, 66, 345, 346f., 354, 355)

81. This system maintains that bodies act as if (*per impossibile*) there were no souls; and souls act as if there were no bodies. And both act as if the one had some influence over the other.

82. As for minds, or rational souls: I hold, as I have just said, that at bottom there is the same thing in all living things and animals—namely, both the soul and the animal begin only when the world begins, and do not end any more than the world does. But in spite of that, there is something unique about rational souls, in that their little spermatic animals, to the extent that they are no more than that, possess only ordinary or sensitive

---

[1] See Introduction, Sect. 3.3.

souls; but as soon as those who are of the elect, so to speak, achieve through an act of conception the nature of a human being, their sensitive souls are raised to the level of reason, and to the prerogatives of minds. (91, 397)

83. In addition to the other differences which exist between ordinary souls and minds, some of which I have already pointed out, there is also the following: souls in general are living mirrors or images of the universe of created things, but minds are also images of the divinity itself, or of the very creator of nature. They are capable of knowing the system of the universe, and of imitating it in part through their own samples of architectonic endeavour, each soul being like a little divinity within its own sphere. (147)

84. This is what makes it possible for minds to enter into a kind of community with God, and it is what makes him with respect to them not only what an inventor is to his machine (which is what God is with regard to his other creations), but also what a prince is to his subjects, and indeed what a father is to his children.

85. And from this it clearly follows that the totality of all minds must make up the City of God—the most perfect possible state, under the most perfect of monarchs. (146; Summary, obj. 2)

86. This City of God, this truly universal monarchy, is a moral world within the natural world, and it is the most noble and the most divine of God's creations. And it is in this moral world that the glory of God truly consists, since there would be no such glory if God's greatness and goodness were not known and admired by minds. It is also with respect to that divine city that God strictly speaking has goodness, whereas his wisdom and his power can be seen in everything.

87. Just as we earlier established a perfect harmony between two natural realms, the one of efficient causes and the other of final causes, so we must also point out here another harmony, between the physical realm of nature, and the moral realm of grace; that is, between God considered as designer of the machine of the universe, and God considered as monarch of the divine city of minds. (62, 74, 112, 118, 130, 247, 248)

88. This harmony ensures that things lead towards grace through the paths of nature itself, so that this globe, for example, must be destroyed and restored by natural means at such times as is required by the government of minds in order to achieve the punishing of some and the rewarding of others. (18f., 110, 244, 245, 340)

89. We can also say that God the designer meets the requirements of God the legislator in every respect, and therefore that sins must bring

along with them their own punishment through the natural order, and in virtue of the mechanical structure of things themselves. And in the same way, good actions will attract their reward through mechanical means in relation to bodies, even though that reward cannot and should not always arrive right away.

90. Finally, under this perfect government there will be no good action which doesn't have its reward, and no bad one without its punishment, and everything must work out for the benefit of the good, that is of those in this great state who are not discontented, who trust in providence when they have done their duty, and who love and copy as they should the author of all good. They delight in the consideration of his perfections, in accordance with the nature of genuinely *pure love*, which leads them to take pleasure in the happiness of what is loved. That is what makes wise and virtuous persons work at everything which seems to conform to God's *presumptive or antecedent will, and what makes them content nevertheless with what God actually brings about through his secret will, which is consequent and decisive. They recognize that if we could understand the order of the universe well enough we would find that it surpasses all the hopes of the wisest people, and that it is impossible to make it better than it is, not only for everything in general, but also for our own selves in particular, as long as we are dedicated as we should be to the creator of everything; dedicated to him not only as to the designer, and the efficient cause of our being, but also as to our master, and to the final cause, which must be the entire goal of our wills, and who alone can produce our happiness. (Pref.; 134 end, 278)

PART 3

Notes, Bibliography, and Index

Notes

Academicians: members of *Plato's Academy, which, in its later years (around 270 BC) increasingly adopted a sceptical, anti-dogmatic approach.

aggregatum per accidens: a Latin Scholastic phrase meaning 'an accidental aggregate'; see *unum per accidens*.

agreements, theory of: Leibniz's earlier name for what he later called 'the way of pre-established harmony'.

Albertus Magnus: Albert the Great (*c*.1200–80). German Dominican and teacher of *Aquinas.

animal spirits: the physiological theory of the Greek physician Galen (AD 129–99), which was still influential in the seventeenth century, was based on three kinds of so-called 'spirits' or vaporous matter—'natural spirits' (to do with the liver), 'vital' (heart), and 'animal spirits' (to do with the brain and nerves).

Aquinas, Thomas (1225–74): Italian Dominican and the most influential medieval philosopher. He sought in his extensive philosophical work, such as his unfinished masterpiece *Summa Theologiae*, to effect a synthesis of Aristotle and Christian theology. TT2. 11 §1; 4. 4: see *Summa Theologiae*, 1a. 76. 8; TT1. 9; 14. 17: see *Summa Theologiae*, 1a. 50. 4.

archeus: the alchemist Theophrastus Paracelsus (1493–1541) and, later, Jean-Baptiste van Helmont (1577–1644) made use of *archei* or spiritual principles in giving physical explanations.

Aristotelians: followers of *Aristotle; sometimes, the *Peripatetics, the *Scholastics.

Aristotle (384–322 BC): T4. 3: perhaps the reference is to his denials of empty void space and of atoms (*De Caelo*, 303^{a}5 ff., 3. 3. 4; *De Generatione et Corruptione*, 1. 8); perhaps (as later in T4. 3) to the question of *substantial forms or *entelechies; T5. 22: see Aristotle, *Metaphysics*, 1073^{a}13–^{b}5; T12. 12: perhaps as at T5. 22; or a reference to 'the active intellect' (*De Anima*, 430^{a}17–18); T13. 3: see *Physics*, 192^{b}1–24; T13. 13: see *Physics*, 226^{a}22–3, *De Generatione et Corruptione*, 1. 4.

Arnauld, Antoine (1612–94): theologian and philosopher whom Leibniz met during his years in Paris. Though initially critical of *Descartes's philosophy, he later, as is evident during his lengthy correspondence with Leibniz (T2), had more sympathy with it.

atoms and void: moving atoms in an empty void were the basic elements of the mechanical world picture of *Democritus, *Epicurus, and some of the 'new philosophers' of the seventeenth century, such as *Gassendi. Along with Descartes, Leibniz (in the end) rejected them (see T4. 3).

Augustine, St, of Hippo (354–430): at first a Manichaean, he came to reject the idea of a positive principle of evil, and to see evil simply as a falling-away from God. He held that the soul was superior to the body (and, as a consequence, could not be acted on by it) (*On the Greatness of the Soul*, 23. 41, 25. 48).

Averroës (Ibn Rushd; 1126–98): Arab Aristotelian commentator who held that there is a world soul of which ours are just parts.

Averroists: see 'Averroës'.

Avicenna (Ibn Sīnā; 980–1037): Persian philosopher and physician. His metaphysical system contains an 'active (tenth) intellect'—the intellect of the terrestrial world, from which souls emanate.

Bacon, John: John of Baconthorpe (d. 1346), an English Carmelite philosopher and theologian.

Barbaro, Ermolao (1454–93): Italian philosopher and translator of Aristotle.

Bernier, François (1620–88): a noted traveller and anthropologist. He published a *Summary of the Philosophy of* *Gassendi (1678), and *M. Bernier's Doubts concerning Some of the Most Important Chapters of his Summary of the Philosophy of Gassendi* (1684).

Borelli, Giovanni Alfonso (1608–79): Italian astronomer, physicist, and mathematician, amongst whose works is *De Vi Percussionis* (1667).

Boyle, Robert (1627–91): known as the 'father of modern chemistry' and perhaps popularly best known for his work on the expansion of gases, his philosophical writings are less well known.

Buridan, Jean (*c*.1300–85): a member of the school of Paris Terminists who, with their impetus theory of motion, made contributions to the study of dynamics.

Cabbalists: members of a school of medieval Jewish thought.

Cartesians: followers of *Descartes; often, specifically, the *occasionalists. T8.4: see e.g., *Princs. Phil.* 4. 197–8.

Cicero, Marcus Tullius (104–43 BC): Roman lawyer, politician, and writer. T3. 2: see *De Legibus*, 1. 20; T17. B: see *Tusculan Disputations*, 1. 18. 42.

concomitance, system of: what Leibniz later called 'the way of pre-established harmony'.

Conversations on the Plurality of Worlds, author of. *Fontenelle.

Copernicus, Nicolas (1473–1543): astronomer whose *On the Revolution of the Celestial Orbs* (1543) presented an account of the planets according to which the earth revolves round the sun.

Cordemoy, Gerauld de (d. 1684): a French *occasionalist. Though a *Cartesian, he is deviantly so in that in his *Le Discernement de l'âme et du corps* (1666) he accepts indivisible material 'bodies' or atoms, which he distinguishes from 'matter', a divisible collection of such atoms.

Déchales, Claude François (1621–78): French mathematician and author of *Cursus seu Mundus Mathematicus* (1674).

Democritus (*c*.460–*c*.370 BC): held a strictly materialist and mechanistic theory according to which the whole world reduces to collisions between indivisible but differently sized atoms in their movement (a movement which, *Aristotle complains, is not causally explained) through the void. All else besides the atoms, he said, exists only 'by opinion, by convention'. T4. 7: see 'Pliny'.

Descartes, René (1596–1650): T1. 22: it is not known whether, in his work on the sine law of light refraction (CSMK i.156–64) Descartes knew of *Snell's discovery; T2. 4 §3 (also T19. 46): for Descartes's view on necessary truth and God, see Introduction, Sect. 7 n. 29; T2. 11 §1: see letter to *More, 5 Feb. 1649 (CSMK iii. 365); T3. 2: in his *Meditations* (1641) Descartes, using a method of doubt, makes a sharp distinction between the human soul and the body and shows how the former is better known than the latter; T4. 2: see Introduction, Sect. 6; T4. 11: it is not clear just what Leibniz has in mind here, since Descartes actually does not seem much troubled by this question (see Introduction, Sect. 5). In reply to Princess Elizabeth of Bohemia's question how a thinking substance, the soul, can affect bodily substance Descartes did offer some explanation (CSMK iii. 217–20); T5. 16: see *Princs. Phil.* 2. 41; T5. 37: see *Princs. Phil.* 2. 25; T5. 38: as a consequence, his collision rules (*Princs. Phil.* 2. 46–52) are flawed; T5. 39: see *Princs. Phil.* 2. 49; T19. 46: see CSMK ii. 291.

Dicaearchus: a pupil of *Aristotle. T17. B: as reported by Cicero (*Tusculan Disputations*, 1. 10), he viewed the soul materialistically and held that the power of sensation is due to the arrangement of the parts of the body.

ens per aggregationem: A Latin *Scholastic phrase meaning 'an aggregated being'; see '*aggregatum per accidens*', '*unum per accidens*'.

ens per se: a Latin *Scholastic phrase meaning 'a being through itself'—not dependent on anything else for its existence.

entelechy: according to Aristotle, the soul is the 'first entelechy' (or actuality) of the body (*De Anima*, 412ᵃ27–8). Leibniz tends to use the term interchangeably with *'substantial form', particularly when he is thinking in terms of 'force'. Thus, though an Aristotelian 'first entelechy' is a capacity or potential, Leibniz stresses that he is thinking of something more than that, of something which is not passive but which is *striving towards* the realization or exercise of that potential (striving towards what Aristotle called a 'second entelechy').

Epicurus (341–270 BC): adopted the earlier, completely materialistic atomic theory of *Democritus. In order to avoid its absolute deterministic implications and preserve free-will he added the doctrine of an arbitrary 'swerve' amongst atoms (and was mocked for it by *Cicero; *De Fato*, 10).

Fabri, Honoratus (1607–88): mathematician, friend of Leibniz, and author of various works of natural philosophy.

Fermat, Pierre de (1601–65): French mathematician who, by appeal to the assumption that nature works in the simplest way, gave a mathematical demonstration of the sine law of light refraction.

Fludd, Robert (1574–1637): according to his *Philosophica Mosaica* (1638), the true philosophy was revealed to Moses and can be got from the first five books of the Old Testament.

Fontenelle, Bernard de (1656–1756): French scientist and writer, Secretary to the Paris Academy of Sciences. His very successful *Conversations on the Plurality of Worlds* (1686) presented a popular but accurate account of contemporary astronomy, physics, and cosmology, together with a series of speculations on the possibility and implications of a plurality of inhabited worlds.

Galileo Galilei (1564–1643): Italian astronomer and physicist. His *Discourses concerning Two New Sciences* (1632), which dealt with the accelerated motion of falling bodies, proved the results to which Leibniz appeals at T1. 17.

Gassendi, Pierre (1592–1655): French priest and author of the fifth set of *Objections* to Descartes's *Meditations*. His posthumously published *Syntagma Philosophicum* (1658), an extensive commentary on *Epicurus, both revives classical Greek atomism and develops his own empiricist ideas. With Epicurus he holds that atoms are everlasting (though created by God; *Syntagma*, 2. 1. 3. 8). T5. 55: Gassendi's *De Motu Impresso a Motore Translato Epistolae Duae* (1642) reports his experiment of dropping weights from the mast of a moving ship to show that they fell at the foot of and not behind the mast.

Gassendists: followers of *Gassendi.

Hartsoeker, Nicolas (1656–1725): Dutch physicist who worked on optics. As implied at T4. 6, he was a pre-formationist.

Heliodorus of Larissa: Greek mathematician to whom is attributed a book on optics, which had an edition in 1657.

Hermetics: the Hermetic philosophy is derived from a series of texts supposedly written by the ancient Egyptian divinity Hermes Tristmegistus, but actually written between AD100 and 300.

Hippocrates of Cos (460–*c*.370 BC): the 'Father of Medicine'. He taught that disease is caused by imbalances and irregularities among the constituents of the body, and that nature uses an 'innate heat' to correct them. He also taught (according to Plato, *Phaedrus*, 270c) that the nature of the body cannot be understood independently of an understanding of the nature of the universe. The book entitled *Diet* is now not attributed to him.

Hobbes, Thomas (1588–1679): English philosopher and proponent of materialism.

Notes

Huygens, Christian (1629–95): Dutch mathematician, astronomer, physicist, under whom Leibniz studied during his years in Paris (1672–76). T3. 4: 'M. Huygens' Remarks . . .', *Histoire des ouvrages des savants* (June 1690), art. 2, pp. 449–52. Huygens was in effect agreeing with Leibniz (as at T1. 17) 'that a body falling from a certain height acquires enough force to rise back up again. . . . For example, a pendulum would raise itself back to exactly the height from which it had fallen'; T5. 17: Huygens published work on the laws governing the collisions of (perfectly elastic) bodies in 1669. This showed various things which, later, are insistent themes in Leibniz's thought—that Cartesian motion is not conserved in collisions, but that 'directive motion' and what Leibniz came to call 'living force' are (see Introduction, Sect. 3). The work was built upon the idea (as later in T6), that motion is essentially relative to a chosen environment; T9. 2: Huygens's account of the pendulum clock in his *Horologium* (1658) was followed by his *Horologium Oscillatorium* (1673), a more theoretical investigation of the questions it raises.

Kepler, Johannes (1571–1630): German astronomer who formulated laws of planetary motion in his important *New Astronomy, or Celestial Physics* (1609).

La Forge, Louis de: his *Traité de l'ésprit de l'homme . . . suivant les principes de René Descartes* (1666) argues for the *occasionalist account of the union of body and mind.

Leeuwenhoek, Anton van (1632–1723): Dutch microscopist and embryologist. His observation of spermatozoa led him to consider them as the source of the new organism.

Locke, John (1632–1704): English philosopher on whose masterpiece *An Essay concerning Human Understanding* (1690) Leibniz extensively commented in his *New Essays concerning Human Understanding* (1704; pub. 1765).

Malebranche, Nicolas (1638–1715): a *Cartesian and the best-known elaborator of *occasionalism (see *The Search after Truth* (1674–5), 6. 2. 3). T4. 6: in his *Search* (2. 1. 7. 3) he expresses *pre-formationism, saying of children that they are pre-formed 'even before the act by which they are conceived'.

Malpighi, Marcello (1628–94): Italian anatomist, embryologist, and early microscopist. He held a form of *pre-formationism.

Manichaeans: followers of Manes (3rd century AD), who taught the real existence of the two principles of good and evil.

Marci, Johannes Marcus (1595–1667): physicist and mathematician whose *De Proportione Motus* (1639) describes the properties of free fall.

Mariotte, Edmé (c.1620–84): French physicist priest whose *Treatise on Percussion or the Impact of Bodies* (1677) described a method for experimentally verifying the laws of collision worked out by *Huygens, *Wallis, and *Wren. It also discussed elasticity.

materialism: a doctrine, usually with overtones of atheism, held by *Democritus, *Epicurus, and *Hobbes, according to which all that exists is matter or is dependent on it, and which denies the existence of immaterial souls or minds.

Mathematical Principles of Natural Philosophy: the *Principles* of Isaac Newton (1642–1727) not only famously contains his theory of universal gravitation, but also provides a systematic development of what is now known as 'classical mechanics'.

Melissus of Samos (fl. *c.*441 BC): a disciple of *Parmenides. T4. 9: see Aristotle, *De Caelo* 298^{b}14.

Mersenne, Marin (1588–1648): he collected objections (including the second set, his own) to the *Meditations* of his friend *Descartes (see CSMK ii. 86–92).

metempsychosis: the doctrine that at death the soul is not destroyed but reincarnated, moving into another person or animal. It is traditionally associated with *Pythagoras.

Molyneux, William (1656–98): Irish scientist and writer on optics. The first volume of his *Dioptrica* was published in 1692.

More, Henry (1614–87): Cambridge Platonist philosopher who at first admired Cartesianism (see 'Descartes') and later strongly opposed it. T2. 11 §1: see letter to More, 5 Feb. 1649 (CSMK iii. 365); TT5. 22; 13. 2: the name given in *Enchiridion Metaphysicum* (1671) to a vitalistic principle or spirit of nature which directs the parts of matter and their motion.

occasionalism (system of occasional causes): a doctrine, held, for example, by *La Forge and *Malebranche, according to which there is no real causation or activity in the created world, God being the sole true cause of the motions of bodies and of the apparent action of the human mind on the body. Leibniz often calls occasionalism the doctrine of the *Cartesians, or the way of assistance (in contrast to the way of influx of the *Scholastics, or his own way of pre-established harmony).

Origenists: followers of Origen of Alexandria (*c.* AD 185–253) held that even fallen angels will ultimately be saved.

Pardies, Ignace (1636–73): physicist who gave an account of the laws of impact. Amongst his writings are *Discours du mouvement local* (1670), *and La Statique ou la science des forces mouvantes* (1673).

Parmenides of Elea (b. *c.*518 BC): he taught that reality is a single, undifferentiated, unchanging unity. T4. 9: see Aristotle, *De Caelo*, 298^{b}14. 3. 2.

Peripatetics: *Aristotelians; followers of *Aristotle, so-called because he walked around a covered way (a *peripatos*) as he taught.

per se **being:** a Latin Scholastic term meaning a being 'through itself', in its own right; see '*unum per se*'.

Philoponus, John (early 6th cent. AD): an Aristotelian commentator who anticipated the impetus theory of *Buridan.

Plato (*c.*427–347 BC): classical Greek philosopher whose many works are in dialogue form. For Plato the intelligible world of the unchangeable eternal 'forms' or 'ideas' is contrasted with the fluctuating sensible world.

Platonists: in most of his references to them Leibniz probably has in mind what are now called the Neoplatonists, such as *Plotinus.

Pliny (*c.* AD 23–79): T4. 7: he remarks in his *Natural History*, 7. 55: 'Similar also is the vanity about preserving men's bodies, and about Democritus's promise of our coming to life again—who did not come to life again himself' (*Pliny: Natural History*, trans. H. Rackham (London, 1942), ii. 635).

Plotinus (AD 205–70): originator of Neoplatonism. According to his *Enneads* the first principle or source of being was the One or Good. The material sensible world is (as with Plato) not a world of true and substantial being; and the identity of material things through time is a matter of stipulative definition.

Poiret, Pierre (1646–1719): a one-time *Cartesian.

pre-formationism: there are various forms of this theory. Ovism holds that an animal exist already pre-formed in miniature in an unfertilized egg; animalculism, that it is pre-formed in the sperm.

presumptive will: the distinction between presumptive, or antecedent, will and consequent will derives from Aquinas (see *Summa Theologiae*, 1a. 19. 6). There is a presumption, antecedent to the details of any particular case, that God will (for example) will of any man that he should be saved. But in the circumstances of a particular case, his consequent decision may be for damnation.

Pythagoras of Samos (b. *c.*575 BC): Greek philosopher who believed in the transmigration of souls, even between human and non-human animals. He discovered the numerical basis of musical harmonies, and perhaps believed (as his followers certainly did) that not only music but also the material world had a basis in number.

Regis, Pierre-Sylvain (1632–1707): author of *Cours entier de philosophie . . . d'après les principes de Descartes* (1691), who maintained a variety of *pre-formationism.

Regius, Henricus (Henri le Roy, 1598–1679): professor of medicine at the University of Utrecht where he became involved in a famous dispute over his advocacy of Cartesian principles.

Scaliger, Julius Caesar (1484–1558): Italian scientist and philosopher.

Sceptics: *Plato's *Academy went through various phases of scepticism (with its denial that truths about external reality could be inferred from the 'appearances' of sense-perceptions) under Arcesilaus (315–240 BC) and Carneades (214–129 BC), with a return under Antiochus (*c.*130–68 BC) to a more constructive Platonism.

Schelhammer, Günther: a physician from Kiel.

Scholastics: Scholasticism is the philosophy of the medieval 'schools' or universities, often with leanings towards *Aristotle (as, for example, in *Aquinas). Its doctrines and approaches were still prominent in the seventeenth century, when most of the 'moderns' (e.g. *Descartes) prided themselves on rejecting it. While Leibniz's rehabilitation of *substantial forms is a notable exception to this, his rejection of the Scholastic 'influence' or 'influx' theory of causation (which he contrasts with his own theory of pre-established harmony and the *occasionalist theory of the *Cartesians) is not. TT4. 6, 14; 19. 7: *Aquinas and later Scholastics explained sense-perception and knowledge in terms of the transmission to the mind of immaterial 'species' (both 'sensible' and 'intelligible') which represented material objects and their features. The idea was generally rejected by the 'moderns' of the seventeenth century (see e.g. Malebranche, *The Search after Truth* (1674–5), 3. 2. 2; Descartes, CSMK i. 153). For the question of the transfer of motion, see Introduction, Sect. 4; T19. 14: whilst, according to his hylomorphic theory (see Introduction, Sect. 2), the soul is the form of the body, Aquinas nevertheless held that after death it could, for a time, exist and exercise its higher functions in an unnatural state of separation.

Schools: See 'Scholastics'.

Search after Truth, The: *Malebranche's famous book (first pub. 1674–5), which was anonymous until the fifth edition of 1700.

Snell, Willebrord (1591?–1626): Dutch mathematician who, around 1620, discovered the sine law of light refraction by experimental means.

Socinians: followers of Fausto Socinus (1539–1604), who based religion on reason.

Spinoza, Benedict (1632–77): Dutch philosopher whose *Ethics* (1677) argued that there is no substance other than 'God or Nature'—all else being only its modifications. Often taken to uphold *materialism. Leibniz's disagreement with him was profound and he saw similarities between Spinozism and *occasionalism. T2. 12: see *Ethics*, 1. 11; T17. B: see *Ethics*, 2. 13.

Stoics: the Stoic school of philosophy was formed around 300 BC in Athens by Zeno of Citium. According to the Stoics, everything forms part of an organic, connected whole; and the virtuous life consists in adherence to its rational order. Chrysippus (*c.*280–207 BC), one of the most notable heads of the school, discussed at length the place of evil in this scheme.

Sturm, Johann Christopher: professor of mathematics in Altdorf.

substantial forms: an aspect of *Scholastic doctrine which, though standardly rejected by the 'new philosophers' of the seventeenth century, is taken over by Leibniz for his own purposes. (See Introduction, Sect. 2.)

Swammerdam, John (1637–80): Dutch microscopist observer of insect life who held a form of *pre-formationism according to which the parts of a fly are already there in the maggot, waiting to 'inflate' or 'expand'.

Teresa, Saint, of Avila (1515–82): in her *Life* (ch. 13) she urges us to 'remember that in the entire world there is only God and the soul'.

Thomas, St: see 'Aquinas'.

Thomists: followers of Thomas *Aquinas.

Toland, John (1670–1722): author of the deistic *Christianity not Mysterious* (1696).

unum per accidens: a Latin *Scholastic phrase meaning an 'accidental unity'—such as a flock of sheep or a block of marble. This, and an *ens per aggregationem and an *aggregatum per accidens are contrasted with a *unum per se (and a *per se* being, or being through itself). (See Introduction, Sect. 2.)

unum per se: A Latin *Scholastic phrase meaning 'a unity through itself', as are individual substances such as human beings—as contrasted with a *unum per accidens or accidental unity such as a flock of sheep. (See Introduction, Sect. 2.)

Wallis, John (1616–1703): English physicist who in 1668 presented to the Royal Society of London work on the laws of collision of inelastic bodies.

William of St Amour (*c*.1200–73): French philosopher and theologian.

Wren, Christopher (1632–1723): English mathematician and architect who in 1668 presented to the Royal Society of London work on the laws of collision of elastic bodies.

Zeno of Sidon (fl. *c*.100 BC), an Epicurean who wrote a (now lost) book against mathematics.

Bibliography and Further Reading

ABRAHAM, WILLIAM E. (1969), 'Complete Concepts and Leibniz's Distinction between Necessary and Contingent Propositions', *Studia Leibnitiana*, 1: 263–79.

ADAMS, R. M. (1972), 'Must God Create the Best?', *Philosophical Review*, 81: 317–32.

——(1977), 'Leibniz's Theories of Contingency', *Rice University Studies*, 63: 1–41 (also in Woolhouse 1994: i. 128–73).

——(1983), 'Phenomenalism and Corporeal Substance in Leibniz', *Midwest Studies in Philosophy*, 8: 217–57.

——(1994), *Leibniz: Determinist, Theist, Idealist* (New York).

AITON, E. J. (1985), *Leibniz: A Biography* (Bristol).

ALEXANDER, PETER (1985), *Ideas, Qualities, and Corpuscles: Locke and Boyle on the External World* (Cambridge).

ALLEN, DIOGENES (1984), 'From *vis viva* to Primary Force in Matter', *Studia Leibnitiana*, sonderheft 13: 55–61.

ALLES, ADAM (1933), 'Leibniz's Dual Conception of Human Reason', *The Personalist*, 14: 177–84 (also in Woolhouse 1994: iv. 60–6).

ARIEW, ROGER (1995), 'G. W. Leibniz: Life and Works', in Jolley 1995: 18–42.

ARTHUR, RICHARD T. W. (1985), 'Leibniz's Theory of Time', in Okruhlik and Brown 1985: 263–313.

BALLARD, K. E. (1960), 'Leibniz's Theory of Space and Time', *Journal of the History of Ideas*, 21: 49–65.

BARBER, W. H. (1955), *Leibniz in France from Arnauld to Voltaire: A Study in French Reactions to Leibnizianism* (Oxford).

BARTHA, PAUL (1993), 'Substantial Form and the Nature of Individual Substance', *Studia Leibnitiana*, 25: 43–54.

BAXTER, DONALD L. M. (1995), 'Corporeal Substances and True Unities', *Studia Leibnitiana*, 27: 157–84.

BERNSTEIN, HOWARD R. (1981), 'Passivity and Inertia in Leibniz's *Dynamics*', *Studia Leibnitiana*, 13: 97–113 (also in Woolhouse 1994: iii. 273–88).

——(1984), 'Leibniz and Huygens on the "Relativity" of Motion', *Studia Leibnitiana*, 13: 85–102.

BLUMENFELD, DAVID (1972), 'Leibniz's Modal Proof of the Possibility of God', *Studia Leibnitiana*, 4: 132–40.

——(1973), 'Leibniz's Theory of the Striving Possibles', *Studia Leibnitiana*, 5: 163–77 (also in Woolhouse 1981: 77–88; 1994: ii. 1–13).

——(1975), 'Is the Best Possible World Possible?', *Philosophical Review*, 84: 163–77.

——(1982), 'Superessentialism, Counterparts, and Freedom', in Hooker 1982: 103–23.

——(1984–5), 'Leibniz on Contingency and Infinite Analysis', *Philosophy and Phenomenological Research*, 45: 483–514.

——(1988–9), 'Freedom, Contingency, and Things Possible in Themselves', *Philosophy and Phenomenological Research*, 49: 81–101.

——(1995*a*), 'Leibniz's Ontological and Cosmological Arguments', in Jolley 1995: 353–81.

——(1995*b*), 'Perfection and Happiness in the Best Possible World', in Jolley 1995: 382–410.

BOAS, M. (1952), 'The Establishment of the Mechanical Philosophy', *Osiris*, 10: 412–541.

BORST, CLIVE (1992), 'Leibniz and the Compatibilist Account of Free Will', *Studia Leibnitiana*, 24: 49–58.

BRANDOM, R. B. (1981), 'Leibniz and Degrees of Perception', *Journal of the History of Philosophy*, 19: 447–79.

BROAD, C. D. (1946), 'Leibniz's Last Controversy with the Newtonians', *Theoria*, 12: 143–68 (also in Woolhouse 1981: 157–74).

——(1972), 'Leibniz's Predicate-in-Notion Principle and some of its Alleged Consequences', in Frankfurt 1972: 11–18.

——(1975), *Leibniz: An Introduction* (Cambridge).

BRODY, BARUCH (1977), 'Leibniz's Metaphysical Logic', *Rice University Studies*, 63: 43–55 (also in Woolhouse 1994: i. 82–96).

BROWN, GREGORY (1987*a*), 'Compossibility, Harmony, and Perfection in Leibniz', *Philosophical Review*, 96: 173–203 (also in Woolhouse 1994: ii. 261–87).

——(1987*b*), 'God's Phenomena and the Pre-established Harmony', *Studia Leibnitiana*, 19: 200–14 (also in Woolhouse 1994: iv. 187–206).

——(1988), 'Leibniz's *Theodicy* and the Confluence of Worldly Goods', *Journal of the History of Philosophy*, 26: 571–91.

——(1992), 'Is there a Pre-established Harmony of Aggregates in the Leibnizian Dynamics, or do Non-substantial Bodies Interact?', *Journal of the History of Philosophy*, 30: 53–75.

——(1995), 'Miracles in the Best of all Possible Worlds: Leibniz's Dilemma and Leibniz's Razor', *History of Philosophy Quarterly*, 12: 19–39.

BROWN, STUART (1984), *Leibniz* (Brighton).

——(1990), 'Malebranche's Occasionalism and Leibniz's Pre-established Harmony', *Studia Leibnitiana*, suppl. 27: 116–23 (also in Stuart Brown (ed.), *Nicolas Malebranche: His Philosophical Critics and Successors* (Assen 1991), 81–93).

BUCHDAHL, GERD (1969), *Metaphysics and the Philosophy of Science* (Oxford).

CARRIERO, JOHN (1993, 1995), 'Leibniz on Infinite Resolution and Intra-mundane Contingency', *Studia Leibnitiana*, 25: 1–26; 27: 1–30.

CHERNOFF, FRED (1981), 'Leibniz's Principle of the Identity of Indiscernibles', *Philosophical Quarterly*, 31: 126–38 (also in Woolhouse 1994: iii. 112–26).

CLATTERBAUGH, KENNETH C. (1971), 'Leibniz's Principle of the Identity of Indiscernibles', *Studia Leibnitiana*, 3: 241–52.

COOK, JOHN W. (1979), 'A Reappraisal of Leibniz's Views on Space, Time, and Motion', *Philosophical Investigations*, 2: 22–63 (also in Woolhouse 1994: iii. 20–61).

COUTURAT, LOUIS (1901), *La Logique de Leibniz* (Paris).

——(1972), 'On Leibniz's Metaphysics', in Frankfurt 1972: 19–45 (also in Woolhouse 1994: i. 1–19).

COVER, J. A. (1989), 'Relations and Reduction in Leibniz', *Pacific Philosophical Quarterly*, 70: 185–211.

——and HAWTHORNE, J. (1992), 'Leibnizian Essentialism, Transworld Identity, and Counterparts', *History of Philosophy Quarterly* 9: 425–44.

COX, CHIARA B. (1975), 'The Defence of Leibniz's Spatial Relativism', *Studies in History and Philosophy of Science*, 6: 87–111.

CURLEY, E. M. (1972), 'The Root of Contingency', in Frankfurt 1972: 69–97 (also in Woolhouse 1994: i. 187–207).

D'AGOSTINO, F. B. D. (1976), 'Leibniz on Compossibility and Relational Predicates', *Philosophical Quarterly*, 26: 125–38 (also in Woolhouse 1994: ii. 245–60).

DICKER, GEORGES (1982), 'Leibniz on Necessary and Contingent Propositions', *Studia Leibnitiana*, 14: 221–32.

DIJKSTERHUIS, E. J. (1961), *The Mechanization of the World Picture* (Oxford).

DUGAS, RENÉ (1955), *A History of Mechanics* (Neuchâtel).

EARMAN, JOHN (1977), 'Perceptions and Relations in the Monadology', *Studia Leibnitiana*, 9: 212–30.

FITCH, GREGORY W. (1979), 'Analyticity and Necessity in Leibniz', *Journal of the History of Philosophy*, 17: 29–42 (also in Woolhouse 1994: i. 290–307).

FLEMING, NOEL (1987), 'On Leibniz on Subject and Substance', *The Philosophical Review*, 96: 69–95 (also in Woolhouse 1994: ii. 105–27).

FOUKE, DANIEL C. (1991), 'Spontaneity and the Generation of Rational Beings in Leibniz's Theory of Biological Reproduction', *Journal of the History of Philosophy*, 29: 33–45.

FOX, MICHAEL (1970), 'Leibniz's Metaphysics of Space and Time', *Studia Leibnitiana*, 2: 29–55.

FRANKEL, LOIS (1981), 'Leibniz's Principle of Identity of Indiscernibles', *Studia Leibnitiana*, 13: 192–211 (also in Woolhouse 1994, ii. 112–26).

——(1984), 'Being Able to do Otherwise: Leibniz on Freedom and Contingency', *Studia Leibnitiana*, 15: 45–59 (also in Woolhouse 1994: iv. 284–302).

——(1986), 'From a Metaphysical Point of View: Leibniz and the Principle of Sufficient Reason', *Southern Journal of Philosophy*, 24: 321–33 (also in Woolhouse 1994: i. 58–73).

FRANKFURT, HARRY G. (ed.) (1972), *Leibniz: A Collection of Critical Essays* (New York).

—— (1977), 'Descartes on the Creation of the Eternal Truths', *Philosophical Review*, 86: 36–57.

FRIED, DENNIS (1978), 'Necessity and Contingency in Leibniz', *Philosophical Review*, 87: 575–84 (also in Woolhouse 1981: 55–63).

FURTH, MONTGOMERY (1967), 'Monadology', *Philosophical Review*, 76: 169–200 (also in Frankfurt 1972: 99–135; Woolhouse 1994: iv. 2–27).

GABBEY, ALAN (1971), 'Force and Inertia in Seventeenth-Century Dynamics', *Studies in History and Philosophy of Science*, 2: 1–67.

GALE, GEORGE (1970), 'The Physical Theory of Leibniz', *Studia Leibnitiana*, 2: 114–27 (also in Woolhouse 1994: iii. 227–39).

—— (1974), 'Did Leibniz have a Practical Philosophy of Science? Or does "Least-Work" Work?', *Studia Leibnitiana*, suppl. 13, no. 2, 151–60.

—— (1976), 'On what God Chose: Perfection and God's Freedom', *Studia Leibnitiana*, 8: 69–87.

—— (1984), 'Leibniz's Force: Where Physics and Metaphysics Collide', *Studia Leibnitiana*, sonderheft 13: 62–70.

—— (1988), 'The Concept of "Force" and its Role in the Genesis of Leibniz's Dynamical Viewpoint', *Journal of the History of Philosophy*, 26: 45–67 (also in Woolhouse 1994: iii. 250–72).

—— (1989), 'Physics, Metaphysics, and Natures: Leibniz's Later Aristotelianism', in N. Rescher (ed.), *Leibnizian Inquiries: A Group of Essays* (Lanham, Md.), 95–102.

GARBER, DANIEL (1983), 'Mind, Body and the Laws of Nature in Descartes and Leibniz', *Midwest Studies in Philosophy*, 8: 105–33.

—— (1985), 'Leibniz and the Foundations of Physics: The Middle Years', in Okruhlik and Brown 1985: 27–130.

—— (1994), 'Leibniz: Physics and Philosophy', in Jolley 1994: 270–352.

GOTTERBARN, DONALD (1976), 'Leibniz's Completion of Descartes's Proof', *Studia Leibnitiana*, 8: 105–12.

GRIMM, ROBERT (1970), 'Individual Concepts and Contingent Truths', *Studia Leibnitiana*, 2: 200–23 (also in Woolhouse 1994: i. 308–29).

HACKING, IAN (1975), 'The Identity of Indiscernibles', *Journal of Philosophy*, 72: 249–56.

—— (1982), 'A Leibnizian Theory of Truth', in Hooker 1982: 185–95.

HALL, MARIE BOAS (1960), 'The Machinery of Nature', in A. R. Hall (ed.), *The Making of Modern Science*, (Leicester), 31–8.

HANFLING, OSWALD (1981), 'Leibniz's Principle of Reason', *Studia Leibnitiana*, sonderheft 9: 67–73 (also in Woolhouse 1994: i. 74–81).

HART, ALAN (1987), 'Leibniz on God's "Vision"', *Studia Leibnitiana*, 19: 182–99.

HARTZ, GLENN A. (1992), 'Leibniz's Phenomenalisms', *Philosophical Review*, 101: 511–49.

HARTZ, GLENN A., and COVER, J. A. (1988), 'Space and Time in the Leibnizian Metaphysic', *Noûs* 22: 493–519.

HINTIKKA, JAAKKO (1972) 'Leibniz on Plenitude, Relations, and the "Reign of Law"' in Frankfurt 1972: 155–90 (also in Woolhouse 1994: ii. 187–212).

HIRSCHMANN, DAVID (1988), 'The Kingdom of Wisdom and the Kingdom of Power in Leibniz', *Proceedings of the Aristotelian Society*, 88: 147–59 (also in Woolhouse 1994: iii, 380–9).

HOOKER, MICHAEL (ed.), (1982), *Leibniz: Critical and Interpretive Essays* (Minneapolis).

HOSTLER, JOHN (1973), 'Some Remarks on *omne possibile exigit existere*', *Studia Leibnitiana*, 5: 281–5.

HOWE, LEROY T. (1971), 'Leibniz on Evil', *Sophia*, 10/3: 8–17.

HUNTER, GRAEME (1981), 'Leibniz and the "Super-essentialist" Misunderstanding', *Studia Leibnitiana*, 13: 123–32.

ILTIS, CAROLYN (1971), 'Leibniz and the *vis viva* Controversy', *Isis*, 62: 21–35.

——(1973a), 'The Decline of Cartesianism in Mechanics: The Leibnizian–Cartesian Debates', *Isis*, 64: 356–73.

——(1973b), 'The Leibnizian–Newtonian Debates: Natural Philosophy and Social Psychology', *British Journal for the History of Science*, 6: 343–77.

ISHIGURO, HIDÉ (1972a), *Leibniz's Philosophy of Logic and Language* (New York).

——(1972b), 'Leibniz's Theory of the Ideality of Relations', in Frankfurt 1972: 191–213.

——(1977), 'Pre-established Harmony versus Constant Conjunction: A Reconsideration of the Distinction between Rationalism and Empiricism', *Proceedings of the British Academy*, 63: 239–63 (also in Woolhouse 1994: iii. 399–420).

——(1979a), 'Contingent Truths and Possible Worlds', *Midwest Studies in Philosophy*, 4: 357–67 (also in Woolhouse 1981: 64–76).

——(1979b), 'Substances and Individual Notions', in E. Sosa (ed.), *The Philosophy of Nicholas Rescher* (Dordrecht), 125–37.

JARRETT, CHARLES E. (1978), 'Leibniz on Truth and Contingency', *Canadian Journal of Philosophy*, suppl. 4: 83–100 (also in Woolhouse 1994: i. 97–113).

JOHNSON, A. H. (1960), 'Leibniz's Method and the Basis of his Metaphysics', *Philosophy*, 35: 51–61 (also in Woolhouse 1994: i. 20–30).

JOHNSON, OLIVER A. (1954), 'Human Freedom in the Best of all Possible Worlds', *Philosophical Quarterly*, 4: 147–55.

JOLLEY, NICHOLAS (1978), 'Perception and Immateriality in the *Nouveaux Essais*', *Journal of the History of Philosophy*, 16: 181–94 (also in Woolhouse 1994: iv. 228–44).

——(1986), 'Leibniz and Phenomenalism', *Studia Leibnitiana*, 18: 38–51 (also in Woolhouse 1994: i. 150–67).

——(ed.) (1995), *The Cambridge Companion to Leibniz* (Cambridge).

KEMP SMITH, NORMAN (1952), *New Studies in the Philosophy of Descartes* (London).

KHAMARA, EDWARD J. (1988), 'Indiscernibles and the Absolute Theory of Space and Time', *Studia Leibnitiana*, 20: 140–59.

KULSTAD, MARK A. (1977), 'Leibniz's Conception of Expression', *Studia Leibnitiana*, 9: 55–76.

——(1980), 'A Closer Look at Leibniz's Alleged Reduction of Relations', *Southern Journal of Philosophy*, 18: 417–32 (also in Woolhouse 1994: ii. 213–30).

——(1981), 'Leibniz, Animals, and Apperception', *Studia Leibnitiana*, 13: 25–60.

——(1982), 'Some Difficulties in Leibniz's Definition of Perception', in Hooker 1982: 65–78.

——(1983), 'Leibniz on Consciousness and Reflection', *Southern Journal of Philosophy*, suppl. 21: 39–65 (also in Woolhouse 1994: iv. 28–59).

——(1991), *Leibniz on Apperception, Consciousness, and Reflection* (Munich).

——(1993), 'Two Interpretations of the Pre-established Harmony in the Philosophy of Leibniz', *Synthèse*, 96: 477–504.

LATZER, MICHAEL (1994), 'Leibniz's Conception of Metaphysical Evil', *Journal of the History of Ideas*, 55: 1–15.

LOMANSKY, LOREN E. (1970), 'Leibniz and the Modal Argument for God's Existence', *Monist*, 54: 250–69.

LOVEJOY, ARTHUR O. (1972), 'Plenitude and Sufficient Reason in Leibniz and Spinoza', in Frankfurt 1972: 281–334.

McCULLOUGH, LAURENCE B. (1977), 'Leibniz and the Identity of Indiscernibles', *Southwestern Journal of Philosophy*, 8.

MACDONALD ROSS, GEORGE (1981), 'Logic and Ontology in Leibniz', *Studia Leibnitiana*, sonderheft 9: 20–6.

——(1984*a*), 'Leibniz's Phenomenalism and the Construction of Matter', *Studia Leibnitiana*, sonderheft 13: 26–36 (also in Woolhouse 1994: iv. 173–86).

——(1984*b*), *Leibniz* (Oxford).

McGUIRE, J. E. (1976), '*Labyrinthus continui*: Leibniz on Substance, Activity, and Matter', in Machamer and Turnbull, 1976: 291–326.

MACHAMER, PETER K., and TURNBULL, ROBERT G. (eds.) (1976), *Motion and Time, Space and Matter* (Columbus, Ohio).

McLAUGHLIN, PETER (1993), 'Descartes on Mind-Body Interaction and the Conservation of Motion', *Philosophical Review*, 102: 155–82.

McRAE, ROBERT (1976), *Leibniz: Perception, Apperception, and Thought* (Toronto).

——(1985), 'Miracles and Laws', in Okruhlik and Brown 1985: 171–81.

MAHER, PATRICK (1980), 'Leibniz and Contingency', *Studia Leibnitiana*, 12: 236–42.

MANNS, JAMES (1987), 'The Nature of a Nature in Leibniz', *Studia Leibnitiana*, 19: 173–81 (also in Woolhouse 1994: ii. 164–75).

MATES, BENSON (1968), 'Leibniz on Possible Worlds', in *Logic, Methodology, and Philosophy of Science*, iii (Amsterdam), 507–29 (also in Frankfurt 1972: 335–64).

MEIJERING, THEO (1978), 'On Contingency in Leibniz's Philosophy', *Studia Leibnitiana*, 10: 22–59.

MILES, MURRAY (1994), 'Leibniz on Apperception and Animal Souls', *Dialogue*, 33: 701–24.

MILLER, RICHARD B. (1988), 'Leibniz on the Interaction of Bodies', *History of Philosophy Quarterly*, 5: 245–55.

MONDADORI, FABRIZIO (1973), 'Reference, Essentialism, and Modality in Leibniz's Metaphysics', *Studia Leibnitiana*, 5: 74–101 (also in Woolhouse 1994: i. 230–55).

——(1975), 'Leibniz and the Doctrine of Inter-world Identity', *Studia Leibnitiana*, 7: 21–57 (also in Woolhouse 1994: i. 256–89).

——(1985), 'Understanding Superessentialism', *Studia Leibnitiana*, 17: 162–90.

MUGNAI, MASSIMO (1981), 'Leibniz on the Structure of Relations', in M. L. Dalla Chiara (ed.), *Italian Studies in the Philosophy of Science* (Dordrecht), 389–409.

——(1988), 'On Leibniz's Theory of Relations', *Studia Leibnitiana*, sonderheft 15: 145–61.

MURRAY, MICHAEL J. (1995), 'Leibniz on Divine Foreknowledge of Future Contingents and Human Freedom', *Philosophy and Phenomenological Research*, 55: 75–108.

NADLER, STEVEN (ed.) (1993), *Causation in Early Modern Philosophy* (University Park, Penn.).

NASON, JOHN (1942), 'Leibniz and the Logical Argument for Individual Substances', *Mind*, 51: 201–2 (also in Woolhouse 1981: 11–29).

——(1946), 'Leibniz's Attack on the Cartesian Doctrine of Extension', *Journal of the History of Ideas*, 7: 447–83.

OKRUHLIK, KATHLEEN (1985), 'Ghosts in the World Machine: A Taxonomy of Leibnizian Forces', in J. C. Pitt (ed.), *Change and Progress in Modern Science* (Dordrecht), 85–105.

——and BROWN, JAMES R. (eds.) (1985), *The Natural Philosophy of Leibniz* (Dordrecht).

O'NEILL, EILEEN (1993), '*Influxus Physicus*', in Nadler 1993: 27–55.

PAPINEAU, DAVID (1977), 'The *vis viva* Controversy: Do Meanings Matter?', *Studies in History and Philosophy of Science*, 8: 111–42 (also in Woolhouse 1981: 139–56; 1994: iii. 198–216).

PARKINSON, G. H. R. (1965), *Logic and Reality in Leibniz's Metaphysics* (Oxford).

——(1969), 'Science and Metaphysics in the Leibniz–Newton Controversy', *Studia Leibnitiana*, suppl. 2: 79–112.

——(1970), 'Leibniz on Human Freedom', *Studia Leibnitiana*, sonderheft 2: 1–67.

——(1982), 'The "Intellectualization of Appearances": Aspects of Leibniz's Theory of Sensation and Thought', in Hooker 1982: 3–20 (also in Woolhouse 1994: iv. 67–86).

——(1995), 'Philosophy and Logic', in Jolley 1995: 199–223.

PHEMISTER, PAULINE (1991), 'Leibniz, Freedom of Will and Rationality', *Studia Leibnitiana*, 23: 25–39.

——(1996), 'Can Perceptions and Motions be Harmonised?', in R. S. Woolhouse (ed.), *Leibniz's 'New System'* (Florence), 141–68.

PYLE, ANDREW (1995), *Atomism, and its Critics* (Bristol).

REMNANT, PETER (1979), 'Descartes: Body and Soul', *Canadian Journal of Philosophy*, 9: 377–86.

RESCHER, NICHOLAS (1952), 'Contingence in the Philosophy of Leibniz', *Philosophical Review*, 61: 26–39 (also in Woolhouse 1994: iv. 174–86).

——(1955), 'Monads and Matter: A Note on Leibniz's Metaphysics', *The Modern Schoolman*, 32: 172–5 (also in Woolhouse 1994: iv. 168–72).

——(1969), 'Logical Difficulties in Leibniz's Metaphysics', *Essays in Philosophical Analysis* (Pittsburgh), 159–70 (also in Woolhouse 1994: ii. 176–86).

——(1979), *Leibniz: An Introduction to his Philosophy* (Oxford).

——(1981*a*), *Leibniz's Metaphysics of Nature: A Group of Essays* (Dordrecht).

——(1981*b*), 'Leibniz on Intermonadic Relations', *Studia Leibnitiana*, sonderheft 9: 1–19 (also in Rescher 1981*a*: 56–83).

——(1981*c*), 'Leibniz on Creation and the Evaluation of Possible Worlds', in Rescher 1981*a*: 1–9.

——(1981*d*), 'Leibniz on the Infinite Analysis of Contingent Truths', in Rescher 1981*a*: 42–55.

RESNIK, LAWRENCE (1973), 'God and the Best Possible World', *American Philosophical Quarterly*, 10: 313–17.

RUSSELL, BERTRAND (1900/1937), *A Critical Exposition of the Philosophy of Leibniz* (London).

——(1903), 'Recent Work on the Philosophy of Leibniz', *Mind*, 12: 177–201 (also in Frankfurt 1972: 365–400).

——(1959), *My Philosophical Development* (London).

——(1967), *The Autobiography of Bertrand Russell* (Boston).

RUSSELL, L. J. (1976), 'Leibniz's Philosophy of Science', *Studia Leibnitiana*, 8: 1–17.

RUTHERFORD, DONALD (1990*a*), 'Leibniz's "Analysis of Multitude and Phenomena into Unities and Reality"', *Journal of the History of Philosophy*, 28: 525–52.

——(1990*b*), 'Phenomenalism and the Reality of Body in Leibniz's Later Philosophy', *Studia Leibnitiana*, 22: 11–28.

——(1992), 'Leibniz's Principle of Intelligibility', *History of Philosophy Quarterly*, 9: 35–49.

——(1993), 'Natures, Laws and Miracles: The Roots of Leibniz's Critique of Occasionalism', in Nadler 1993: 135–58.

——(1994), 'Leibniz and the Problem of Monadic Aggregation', *Archiv für Geschichte der Philosophie*, 76: 65–90.

——(1995*a*), '[Leibniz's] Metaphysics: The Late Period', in Jolley : 1995: 124–75.

——(1995*b*), *Leibniz and the Rational Order of Nature* (Cambridge).

SABRA, A. I. (1967), *Theories of Light from Descartes to Newton* (London).

SEAGER, WILLIAM (1981), 'The Principle of Continuity and the Evaluation of Theories', *Dialogue: Canadian Philosophical Review*, 20: 485–95 (also in Woolhouse 1994: iii. 369–79).

SEAGER, WILLIAM (1991), 'The Worm in the Cheese: Leibniz, Consciousness and Matter', *Studia Leibnitiana*, 23: 79–91.

SEIDLER, MICHAEL J. (1985), 'Freedom and Moral Therapy in Leibniz', *Studia Leibnitiana*, 17: 15–35 (also in Woolhouse 1994: iv. 334–60).

SHIELDS, CHRISTOPHER (1986), 'Leibniz's Theory of the Striving Possibles', *Journal of the History of Philosophy*, 24: 343–57 (also in Woolhouse 1994: ii. 14–28).

SLEIGH, R. C. Jr. (1982), 'Truth and Sufficient Reason in the Philosophy of Leibniz', in Hooker 1982: 209–42.

——(1983), 'Leibniz on the Two Great Principles of all our Reasonings', *Midwest Studies in Philosophy*, 8: 193–215 (also in Woolhouse 1994: i. 31–57).

——(1990a), *Leibniz and Arnauld: A Commentary on their Correspondence* (New Haven).

——(1990b), 'Leibniz on Malebranche on Causality', in J. A. Cover and Mark Kulstad (eds.), *Central Themes in Early Modern Philosophy* (Indianapolis), 161–93.

SPECTOR, MARSHALL (1975), 'Leibniz vs. the Cartesians on Motion and Force', *Studia Leibnitiana* 7: 135–44 (also in Woolhouse 1994: iii. 217–26).

VAILATI, EZIO (1986), 'Leibniz on Necessary and Contingent Predication', *Studia Leibnitiana*, 18: 195–210 (also in Woolhouse 1994: i. 330–49).

VINCI, THOMAS C. (1974), 'What is the Ground for the Principle of the Identity of Indiscernibles in the Leibniz–Clarke Correspondence?', *Journal of the History of Philosophy*, 12: 95–101.

WESTFALL, RICHARD F. (1971), *Force in Newton's Physics: The Science of Dynamics in the Seventeenth Century* (New York).

WIGGINS, DAVID (1987), 'The Concept of the Subject Contains the Concept of the Predicate', in J. J. Thompson (ed.), *On Being and Saying: Essays for Richard Cartwright* (Cambridge, Mass.) 263–84 (also in Woolhouse 1994: ii. 141–63).

WILSON, CATHERINE (1982), 'Leibniz and Atomism', *Studies in the History and Philosophy of Science,* 13: 175–99 (also in Woolhouse 1994: iii. 342–68).

——(1983), 'Leibnizian Optimism', *Journal of Philosophy*, 80: 765–83 (also in Woolhouse 1994: iv. 435–52).

——(1987), '*De ipsa natura*: Sources of Leibniz's Doctrines of Force, Activity and Natural Law', *Studia Leibnitiana*, 19: 148–72.

——(1989), *Leibniz's Metaphysics: A Historical and Comparative Study* (Manchester).

——(1995), 'The Reception of Leibniz in the Eighteenth Century', in Jolley 1995: 442–74.

WILSON, MARGARET D. (1969), 'On Leibniz's Explication of "Necessary Truth"', *Studia Leibnitiana*, suppl. 3: 50–63 (also in Frankfurt 1972: 401–19; Woolhouse 1994: i. 114–27).

——(1974), 'Leibniz and Materialism', *Canadian Journal of Philosophy*, 3: 495–513 (also in Woolhouse 1994: iv. 207–27).

——(1976), 'Leibniz's Dynamics and Contingency in Nature', in Machamer and Turnbull 1976: 264–89 (also in Woolhouse 1994: iii. 321–41).

——(1978), *Descartes* (London).

——(1979), 'Possible Gods', *Review of Metaphysics*, 32: 717–33 (also in Woolhouse 1994: i. 350–65).

——(1987), 'The Phenomenalisms of Leibniz and Berkeley', in E. Sosa (ed.), *Essays on the Philosophy of George Berkeley* (Dordrecht), 3–22.

WILSON, N. L. (1973), 'Individual Identity, Space, and Time in the Leibniz–Clarke Correspondence', in I. Leclerc (ed.), *The Philosophy of Leibniz and the Modern World* (Nashville), 189–206.

WINTERBOURNE, A. T. (1982), 'On the Metaphysics of Leibnizian Space and Time', *Studies in the History and Philosophy of Science*, 13: 201–14 (also in Woolhouse 1994: iii. 62–75).

WONG, DAVID (1980), 'Leibniz's Theory of Relations', *Philosophical Review*, 89: 241–56 (also in Woolhouse 1994: ii. 231–44).

WOOLHOUSE, R. S. (ed.) (1981), *Leibniz: Metaphysics and Philosophy of Science* (Oxford).

——(1982), 'The Nature of an Individual Substance', in Hooker 1982: 45–64 (also in Woolhouse 1994: ii. 83–104).

——(1985), 'Pre-established Harmony Retuned: Ishiguro *versus* the Tradition', *Studia Leibnitiana*, 17: 204–19.

——(1988), 'Leibniz and Occasionalism', in R. S. Woolhouse (ed.), *Metaphysics and Philosophy of Science in the Seventeenth and Eighteenth Centuries: Essays in Honour of Gerd Buchdahl* (Dordrecht 1988), 165–83 (also in Woolhouse 1994: iv. 267–83).

——(1993), *Descartes, Spinoza, Leibniz: The Concept of Substance in Seventeenth-Century Metaphysics* (London).

——(ed.) (1994), *Gottfried Wilhelm Leibniz: Critical Assessments*, 4 vols. (London).

WRENN, THOMAS E. (1972), 'Leibniz's Theory of Essences', *Studia Leibnitiana*, 4: 181–95.

Index

Index

bodies, extended *see* extension
body:
  nature of 7, 162, 167–8, 172–3; *see also* collisions of moving matter
body and mind:
  causal relationship between 149–52
  union of 30–6, 188–9; *see also* union of body and soul
Boineburg, Baron von 46
Borelli, Giovanni Alfonso 160, 286
Boyle, Robert 209, 211, 286
British Empiricism 48
Broad, C. D. 12n, 16, 25n, 36n, 42n, 242
Brody, B. 42n, 91
Brown, G. 16n, 30n, 44n
Brown, S. 16n, 36n
Brunswick, Duke of 46
Bucephalus (Alexander's horse) 8, 13
Buchdahl, G. 25n, 75n
Buridan, Jean 21, 286

Cabbalists 207, 286
Caesar, Julius 64, 65, 225–6, 227–9, 234, 236, 246
Calvinists 82n
Candide (Voltaire) 47
Carriero, J. 43n
'Cartesian doctrine' *see* occasionalism
Cartesians 39, 49, 93, 130, 141–2, 204, 286
  and automata 234–5
  motion and force 160, 172, 211
  quantity of motion 211
catoptrics 75
causation 26–36, 149n
causes, final *see* final causes
changes in material bodies 31, 211, 216, 228–9, 236–7, 269–70
Châtelet, Gabrielle du 47
Chernoff, F. 239n
Cicero, Marcus Tullius 140, 246, 255, 286
City of God 45, 88, 89, 134, 151, 198, 280
Clagett, Marshall 21n
Clatterbaugh, K. C. 239n
clocks as analogy 192, 197, 204–5, 206, 235
collisions between bodies 19, 21, 22–3, 26, 32, 93, 161, 168–76
command, God's eternal law of 212–13
community of rational minds 44–5, 279–81
'complete notion' account of individual substances 59–62, 90, 92, 94, 109
conatus 141, 154, 157, 161, 176, 190, 217, 236
concepts 48, 79, 92

concomitance 33, 34–5, 60–1, 66–9, 94, 95, 96, 113, 114, 117, 286
  Foucher on 180, 181–3
  Leibniz's reply to Foucher 188
  see also pre-established harmony
Condillac, Étienne 47
consciousness 38; *see also* apperception
conservation of physical force 23–5, 69–71
constancy in bodies, natural 216–17
Continental Rationalism 47–8
contingency 46n, 272–3
continuity, law of 171–2, 252–3
continuum 62, 217
contradiction 272
Conversations on the Plurality of Worlds (Fontenelle) 148
Cook, J. W. 242
Copernicus, Nicolas/Copernicans 79, 169, 175, 188, 286
Cordemoy, Gerauld de 27, 119, 123, 128, 131, 148, 215, 286
corporeal bodies, nature of 69–75, 187–90
corpuscularianism 17, 114, 207
Couturat, L. 42n, 47, 90
Cover, J. A. 90, 92, 242
Cox, C. B. 242
creation *see* God, creation
Critical Exposition of the Philosophy of Leibniz (B. Russell) 47
Critique of Search after Truth (Foucher) 180
Curley, E. M. 90

D'Agostino, F. B. D. 90
De Anima (Aristotle) 79n, 147n
death 40–1, 126, 133, 147–8, 260–1, 271, 278–9
Déchales, Claude 160, 287
decrees, absolute 82, 83
Deleuze, Gilles 47
Democritus 17, 147, 149, 155, 161, 207, 234, 287
Descartes, René 7, 8, 287
  causal interaction of mind and body 35
  collision laws 177–9
  conservation of motion 32–3, 69–71, 190
  existence of God 42
  human and animal minds 38–41
  impetus theory of motion 21
  material substance 8–11, 18
  motion and force 20–5, 26, 168, 172, 190
  velocity and direction 160
  see also Cartesians
determinism 151

306

Index

Index

Kant, Immanuel 46, 48
Kemp Smith, N. 42n
Khamara, E. J. 239n, 242
Kingdom of Grace 44, 268
Kingdom of Heaven 89
Kingdom of Nature 44, 268
Kingdom of Power 164
Kingdom of Wisdom 164
knowledge, kinds of 76–9, 82
Kulstad, M. A. 90, 92

La Forge, Louis de 27, 31, 215, 289
Labyrinthus, sive de Compositione Continui
    (Fromond) 185
language acquisition 48
law, inherent *see* inherent law
'Laws concerning the Communication of
    Motion' (Malebranche) 24–5
Leeuwenhoek, A. van 133, 147, 289
Leibniz, Gottfried W.:
    early reception 47, 47n
    ideas and interests 5–7
    life and influences 46–9
    three classic 'landmark' works 5, 6
    two possible readings of 10–13
Leibniz's law 48
Locke, John 7, 289
Lomansky, L. E. 42n
Louis XIV, king of France 46
love of God *see* God, love of
Lovejoy, A. O. 44n

McCullough, L. B. 239n
MacDonald Ross, G. 16n, 46n, 145n
McGuire, J. E. 16n, 25n
machines *see* automata
Maher, P. 43n
Malebranche, Nicolas 24–5, 46, 212, 250, 289
    power of God and motion 26–8, 29–30, 31,
    172, 215
Malpighi, M. 131, 146, 289
Manicheans 252, 289
Manns, J. 92
Marci, Marcus 160, 389
Mariotte, Edmé 160, 389
mass *see* matter
materialists 39, 73, 207, 290
Mates, B. 90
mathematical points, indivisibility of 149
Mathematical Principles of Natural Philosophy
    (Newton) 21–2, 24, 290
mathematics 141, 144–5, 252–3, 272

matter:
    active properties of 19–22
    difference between the soul and 235–6
    divisibility of 193
    and form 13
    passive properties of 18–19, 217–18
    primary and secondary 19–20, 156, 216, 218
    unity of 134–5
    see also aggregation; extension
'matter in motion world' picture 17
Maupertuis, Pierre de 47
'Mechanical Philosophy' 17–18, 44, 74–6
mechanics 145, 209, 256
mechanism 34, 124, 211, 243–8
    difference between automaton and human
    being 243–8
Meditations (Descartes) 141
Meijering, T. 90
Melissus of Samos 130, 148, 290
memory 86, 112, 235, 260, 270, 271
mental states and states of the body 241
mental substance theory 10, 267
Mersenne, M. 141, 290
metamorphoses of life and death 258, 261–2
metaphysical points, indivisibility of 149
metaphysical terms 140
metaphysics:
    defence of Leibniz 209
    distillation of Leibniz's 203, 267
    morality and 87
    and notion of substance 139, 149
    origin of the term 7
metempsychosis 146, 262, 290
Miller, R. B. 30n
miller and water-wheel analogy 212
mind 9–11, 126, 272, 280
    difference between other substances and 86,
    280
    differences between animal and human
    260–1, 279–80
    different kinds of 38
    excellence of 87
    governed by God 134
    see also soul
miracles 28–9, 58–9, 68–9, 85, 107, 146, 197n,
    224–5, 243
mirroring of world by each substance in it 61,
    263
modal notions 48
Molina, Luis de 82n
Molyneux, William 163, 212, 290
momentum of a system of bodies 25

309

Index

'Monadology' (Leibniz) 5, 8, 11, 12, 15, 36,
    267–81
monads 11, 12, 15, 16, 216–18, 239–40, 247,
    259, 268–72
  changes arising from internal principle 8–16,
    26–30, 268–9
  indivisibility of 268
  perceptions 270–2
  see also soul
Mondadori, F. 92
More, Henry 130, 163, 209, 210, 290
Mosaic Philosophy, The (Fludd) 215
motion 19–22, 152, 173, 218–20, 252, 263
  conservation of directed 33
  conservation of quantity of 23–5, 32, 69–71,
    211
  distinction between force and quantity of
    71–2
  instantaneous 157
  measurement of 22–3
  as nothing but a relationship 168
  relative nature of 168–9
  and rest principle 211
  speed of 160, 175–6
  theory of 160
  see also force
motive force of moving matter 22–3, 93, 211,
    217
Mugnai, M. 90

Nason, J. 25n, 43, 90
natural philosophy and nature of corporeal
    bodies 69–75
nature 148, 210, 210–14
'Nature Itself' (Leibniz) 29, 209–22
necessity 48, 63–6, 94–5, 98–102
New Essays (Leibniz) 48
'New System of the Nature of Substances . . .'
    (Leibniz) 5, 8, 180
Newton, Isaac 21–2, 23n, 24, 47, 242
nomos (convention) 256
notion of substance *see* substances, individual
Nouvelles de la république des lettres publication
    171

occasionalism 27–30, 31, 33, 34, 49, 113, 192,
    197, 203, 205, 212, 221, 249, 290
Okruhlik, K. 25n
On Nature Itself (Boyle) 209, 211
'On the Ultimate Origination of Things'
    (Leibniz) 43n
O'Neill, E. 30n

optics 163–4
Origen, 252, 290

pain/pleasure and change 196, 198, 201, 202–3,
    229–30, 236–7, 249
Papineau, D. 23n, 25n
Paracelsus, Theophrastus 285
Pardies, Ignace Baptista 160, 290
Paris Academy of Sciences 46
Parkinson, G. H. R. 42n, 242
Parmenides 130, 148, 207, 290
Paul, Saint 84
perception:
  and animals 186, 261
  complexity of sensations and 242
  confused 85, 251
  God as the only immediate object of 79–80
  inexplicable by mechanical principles 270
  and memory 260
  nature of 256
  order and harmony 258, 263–4
  as principle of life 37, 150
  in the soul 206–7, 207, 231, 237–8, 247, 259
  see also thought
Peripatetics 71, 155, 225, 234, 290
Phaedo (Plato) 73, 249, 255
phantasma existentis 252
Phemister, P. 20n
phenomena 66–7, 72, 73, 150, 163, 168, 207,
    213
phenomenalism 15, 16
Philoponus, John 20, 291
philosophy, nature of natural 69–75
phūsis (nature) 256
Physical Hypothesis, A (Leibniz) 161
piety 84–5
plants 132, 277
Plato 8, 73, 78–9, 140, 155, 247, 291
Platonists 8, 63, 140, 207, 215, 234
Pliny 147
Plotinus 207, 291
Poiret, Pierre 274, 291
postulates 272
powers, derivative 156
pre-established harmony 33, 35, 39, 45, 49, 151,
    152, 190
  Bayle on 196–7, 224–31
  and clock analogy 192–3, 204–5, 206
  Leibniz reply to Bayle 199–200, 233–40,
    241–53
  spiritual side of 254, 279–81
  see also concomitance

310